North
Canada

Yukon • Northwest Territories • Nunavut

THE BRADT TRAVEL GUIDE

The Bradt Story

The first Bradt travel guide was written by Hilary and George Bradt in 1974 on a river barge floating down a tributary of the Amazon in Bolivia. From their base in Boston, Massachusetts, they went on to write and publish four other backpacking guides to the Americas and one to Africa.

In the 1980s Hilary continued to develop the Bradt list in England, and also established herself as a travel writer and tour leader. The company's publishing emphasis evolved towards broader-based guides to new destinations – usually the first to be published on those countries – complemented by hiking, rail and wildlife guides.

Since winning *The Sunday Times* Small Publisher of the Year Award in 1997, we have continued to fill the demand for detailed, well-written guides to unusual destinations, while maintaining the company's original ethos of low-impact travel.

Travel guides are by their nature continuously evolving. If you experience anything which you would like to share with us, or if you have any amendments to make to this guide, please write; all your letters are read and passed on to the author. Most importantly, do remember to travel with an open mind and to respect the customs of your hosts – it will add immeasurably to your enjoyment.

Happy travelling!

Hilary Bradt

Hilary Bradt

19 High Street, Chalfont St Peter, Bucks SL9 9QE, England
Tel: 01753 893444 Fax: 01753 892333
Email: info@bradt-travelguides.com
Web: www.bradt-travelguides.com

North
Canada

Yukon • Northwest Territories • Nunavut

THE BRADT TRAVEL GUIDE

Geoffrey Roy

Bradt Publications, UK
The Globe Pequot Press Inc, USA

First published in 2000 by Bradt Publications,
19 High Street, Chalfont St Peter, Bucks SL9 9QE, England
Published in the USA by The Globe Pequot Press Inc,
246 Goose Lane, PO Box 480, Guilford, Connecticut 06437-0480

British Library Cataloguing in Publication Data
A catalogue record for this book is available from the British Library
ISBN 1 84162 003 3

Library of Congress Cataloging-in-Publication Data is available

Photographs
Front cover Inuik hunter on dogsled, Igloolik, Northwest Territories
(Bryan and Cherry Alexander)
Text Geoffrey Roy (GR), Travel Manitoba (MT)
Illustrations Carole Vincer
Maps Alan Whitaker

Typeset from the author's disc by Donald Sommerville and Wakewing
Printed and bound in Spain by Grafo SA, Bilbao

Author

Geoffrey Roy is ex-Australian Army Special Forces and a Fellow of the Royal Geographical Society. In 1981 he went travelling across Asia, caught a truck in Kathmandu, and became hooked on the overlanding bug. Subsequently he led eight journeys across Africa and another four across Asia, including numerous shorter tours throughout India and East Africa. In 1992 he set up Kaa Photographics to provide a photographic service to adventure travel companies and partake in his favourite pastime – photojournalism with a travel twist. Nowadays, Geoffrey spends most of his time somewhere else, chasing that special adventure travel story for a number of UK magazines and national daily and Sunday newspapers.

Geoffrey's travel experiences have taken him to a wide variety of destinations including dog-sledging with the Inuit in Greenland and bear watching from horseback in the Yukon. In Nunavut he went searching for polar bears, walrus and muskox and he has motorcycled across America's southwest. He was the winner of the Best Consumer Travel Writer at the 1998 Canada Travel Awards for an article on the Yukon.

Contents

Introduction   XI

PART ONE   **BACKGROUND INFORMATION**   I

Chapter 1   **General Information**   3
Geography 3, Physical conditions 4, History of the
north 8

Chapter 2   **Natural History**   27
Large land mammals 28, Small land mammals 34,
Other smallish mammals 40, The little critters 42, Sea
mammals 43, Arctic birds 49, Northern plants 58

Chapter 3   **The People**   63
The First Nations 63, The Inuit 71, The coming of
Nunavut 75, The Europeans 78

PART TWO   **PRACTICAL INFORMATION**   81

Chapter 4   **Planning Your Trip**   83
Choosing what to do 83, When to go 87, Tourist
information 87, Red tape 88, Getting there 89, Getting
about 92, What to take 93, Money matters 94,
Accommodation 96, Food and drink 96, Shopping 96,
National holidays 97, Electric current 98, Media and
communications 98, Fishing and hunting 99, Arctic
photography 100

Chapter 5   **Health and Safety**   109
Health 109, Safety 115

Chapter 6   **Wilderness Survival**   117
Car travel 119, On the trail 119, Bears 124

Chapter 7   **The Gateway Cities**   137
Introduction 137, Vancouver 138, Edmonton 141,
Winnipeg 143, Ottawa 146, Montréal 149

PART THREE	THE GUIDE	153
Chapter 8	**The Yukon Territory**	155
	History 156, Whitehorse 161, Haines Junction 168, Kluane National Park 169, The route north to Alaska 171, South of Whitehorse 173, North of Whitehorse 176, The Silver Trail 185	
Chapter 9	**The Northwest Territories**	191
	History 193, Yellowknife 195, South of Yellowknife 199, The Deh Cho region 202, Mackenzie river valley 204, The far northern communities 208	
Chapter 10	**Nunavut**	211
	The communities 214, The Baffin Island communities 215, The mainland communities 222	
Chapter 11	**The Fringes**	231
	Alaska 231, Churchill, Manitoba 244	
Appendix 1	**Language**	249
Appendix 2	**Glossary**	252
Appendix 3	**Birds of Northern Canada**	254
Appendix 4	**Mammals of the Yukon**	262
Appendix 5	**Plants of the Yukon**	264
Appendix 6	**Further Reading**	269
Index		272

LIST OF MAPS

Alaska border area	232	Montréal centre	150
Baker Lake	224	North Canada &	
Cambridge Bay	228	Alaska	IFC, 2
Churchill	246	Northwest Territories	190
Dawson City	183	Nunavut	212–13
Dawson City area	182	Ottawa centre	147
Distribution of American		Rankin Inlet	223
subarctic cultures group	62	Skagway	239
Distribution of Northwest		Vancouver centre	139
Coast Indians Group	65	Whitehorse	163
Edmonton centre	142	Winnipeg centre	144
Inuvik	207	Yellowknife	197
Iqaluit	218	The Yukon Territory	154

Acknowledgements

A long time ago I was looking for ideas for stories for a magazine. I wanted to travel up the Amazon River in Brazil but had no idea how to go about it. By accident in a bookshop I came across a copy of a Bradt Travel Guide called *Backcountry Brazil* by Alex Bradbury. Whilst travelling around Europe on a bus full of young antipodeans I read the Amazon section. It was exactly what I wanted to read – how to travel up the Amazon on local boats with the Brazilians. I had already provided the photographs for the first edition of *Ethiopia: The Bradt Travel Guide* and before I knew it I was updating the Amazon section for the second edition of what is now called *Brazil: The Bradt Travel Guide*. Having thus been inspired by a Bradt guide to Brazil I have now written one to another wilderness zone of a completely different type, somewhere where it is cold for eight months of the year and the sun is fickle about whether it shines all day or not at all. I hope this book inspires someone out there to see northern Canada in the same way as that earlier guide inspired me to go to Brazil.

I was a late starter to Canada but it all came about when my editor at *Wanderlust* magazine, Lyn Hughes, said go to Canada and come back with something suitable. I fancied sea-kayaking with orcas in Johnson Strait off British Columbia; the Canadian Tourism Commission's press office here in London wanted me to go to the Yukon. On my first trip I got to do both. My editor very generously published both stories and the Yukon article won me the title of Best Consumer Travel Writer at the 1998 Canada Travel awards. I got lucky! My thanks go to Lyn for opening the door in such a big way.

Besides Lyn there are several people to whom I owe a great debt of gratitude in the writing of this book. They are not in order of importance as they are all important to me but someone has to come first and someone has to be mentioned at the end. My apologies if I upset anyone.

Firstly, there is Jim Kemshead. He is the marketing and media person with Tourism Yukon in Whitehorse. Besides setting me up for my first visit to the Yukon he was wonderful company on those quiet nights where a bar was the only entertainment. Although I may be his idea of a 'right royal pain', I do look forward to meeting up each time I visit the Yukon. The other thing he did was to introduce me to Chuck Hume. Chuck runs an outfitting operation out of Haines Junction, is a Champagne Aisihik First Nation elder, and the JP who married Jim and his wife. When in the Yukon my partner Debra and I spent a night in Chuck's cabin at Klukshu. There was no electric light and the toilet was a drop-pit out in the forest surrounded by the sounds of bears and wolves.

Cooking was done on a potbelly stove and poor Debra had to sleep on the floor in a sleeping bag. This may be heaven to some people including me but it could have been hell to Debra. Instead she was amazed and rather moved by the experience, and hasn't stopped talking about it since. Chuck is one of those people who are a delight to be with. I learnt more about the wilderness in a couple of days with him than most people would ordinarily find out in a lifetime.

In the Northwest Territories I want to thank my friend Cooper Langford. He is the editor of *UpHere* magazine in Yellowknife. I first contacted Cooper when I wrote the northern Canada section of another guidebook and needed help on a place I knew little about. When we eventually met in Yellowknife in some loud and raucous bar, we never stopped talking until the wee hours and I woke with one of the best hangovers I have ever had and enjoyed every minute of it. We are now planning a dog-sledging adventure to follow the route of the Lost Patrol with a modern day RCMP officer.

In Nunavut I want to thank all those who helped me on my way. Madeline Redfern-Alexander, Maureen Bundgaard and their staff at the Tourist Board in Iqualit; Dyan Gray in Rankin Inlet; Phil Burak in Cambridge Bay and David Western in Baker Lake. When I was photographing walrus Jimmy Stanley was my bodyguard and I have never felt safer in the presence of wild animals than I have with him. Thanks go to Lucassie Nakoolak and all the boys on the boat out of Coral Harbour who had their fun, but so did I. I would also like to extend a great many thanks to Brenda Jancke and her family in Cambridge Bay for their wonderful hospitality. Her husband Bob cooked the best muskoxen steaks I've ever had. The same debt of thanks goes to Ken Beardsall and his family for their fine company and delightful hospitality in Coral Harbour. Ken had the great fortitude to be patient and quiet when I crawled ever closer and closer to a huge walrus just to get my photograph. Thanks also to Adam Ravetch of the NGS for taking a break in filming walrus to take such excellent promo pictures of me on Coats Island.

In the UK there is Glyn Lovell and his wife Peggy at Nunavut Tourism UK. They organise the best possible evening at Spotlight Canada each year and have become good friends. Thanks also go to Jill White of Tourism Yukon UK for all her help and party invites and to Roger Harris and his staff at the Travel Canada Centre in London for lots of advice and for much needed assistance with pictures for talks when I had none. Teresa Cowan at the Canadian High Commission library at Canada House must not be forgotten. No book or research task was too big or too hard to do. A fellow Australian and product manager for Windows on the Wild, Russell Conchie, who has boundless enthusiasm for Canada and the north and all that she has to offer always came up with an answer when I needed one. Thanks Russell.

Nim Singh deserves special thanks. She still puts up with my regular phone calls wanting this and that bit of info and has been a godsend when organising any and all of my trips to the north and anywhere else in Canada. Some press officers are good at their job – Nim is one of those rare few who not only has lots of enthusiasm for Canada but actually has a great flair for the job and is consequently brilliant at it. The press office has produced exceptional results and much of the excellent promotion Canada has received here in the UK is down to Nim and her staff at the CTC. I still owe her a lunch. Someday Nim, I promise.

Others included in the thanks list are Judy McLinton of the Department of Resources, Wildlife and Economic Development in Yellowknife; Rick Boychuk and the staff at Canadian Geographic for their assistance with research material. Richard Lafferty, Colleen Bruce and the staff at North West Territories Arctic Tourism in Yellowknife for all their help and assistance and those others in NWT who helped me experience wood bison. I also want personally to thank Richard Hartmier and Adam Ravetch, two very professional photographers I met at different times in different places, whose passion for the north is reflected in their stunning work.

The plant section was written with the help of the Department of RWED in Yellowknife. My thanks to them for letting me copy from their excellent pamphlet *Trees and Scrubs of the Northwest Territories*.

I also owe a special thanks to all those unnamed people who provided hotel rooms, beds, meals, entertainment and conversation. I must thank all the barmen and women who helped pass away quiet nights and a couple of film makers/cameramen, whose names escape me, but who made long plane journeys less boring. Also there is a man called Buffalo in Dawson City, a couple of mushers, dog handlers and some excellent dogs all of whom added so much to my various stays. Above all I must thank all the Inuit, First Nations and European people without whose help this book wouldn't be possible and who make the north of Canada one very special place.

Lastly, I want to thank Hilary Bradt who gave me my first chance to delve into something more than just shooting pictures. I am specially grateful to Tricia Hayne who had faith in an obscure guide and convinced all of its worth. Without her this book would not have got off the ground. Thanks also to my guidebook editor Donald Sommerville and all the staff at Bradt who put up with endless requests to cater to all my needs.

This book is dedicated to my partner Debra who put up with a lot of nights alone while I sat at a computer after I had spent months away chasing walrus and other northern stars.

Introduction

If you were in the Space Shuttle looking down upon the Earth you would be greeted with a stupendous sight. Of the total area of land down there, not counting Antarctica, there is an estimated 26% of wilderness remaining. In the whole of North and Central America wilderness totals a more substantial 41% but in Europe there is only about 3%. Even so, in a world so obviously dominated by man and his creations, there is a part of this beautiful planet of ours where almost 80% of the landmass is wilderness, place where man and the other creatures gracing this earth compete on an almost equal footing. That place is Canada's far north.

Some parts of northern Canada are unimaginably harsh, barren and treeless, where almost permanently frozen tundra dominates over subarctic forest. Yet this is a place where mountains, glaciers, vast lakes and dynamic rivers mould and shape the landscape. Both summer and winter adventure activities occur throughout the region. There is a great abundance of wildlife here and the best viewing comes during the long summer days when the temperatures are acceptable and food is bountiful.

The northern territories of Canada are very wild, supremely beautiful and virtually untouched. This pristine wilderness accounts for almost 40% of Canada's land surface area yet it has only 0.33% of the country's population. The region is also, for the most part, populated by native aboriginal peoples.

For man to exist in this unkind environment, survival became the imperative and adaptation was vital. The people of the Yukon and the other two territories that constitute the north of Canada, the Northwest Territories and the recently created Nunavut, have developed a unique disposition towards their land. A combination of isolation, enhanced by a harsh environment, and the knowledge that they live in an area of absolutely pristine wilderness has led people here to think of themselves only as 'northerners'. This also applies to the neighbouring American state of Alaska. Anyone coming from anywhere else is deemed to be an 'outsider'.

Until recently only Canada's native First Nations and Inuit peoples thought of themselves as permanent residents here. Although explorers, whalers and fur traders have had a large impact on the native population since the late 16th century, most Europeans came somewhat late to the north. It wasn't until well into the 20th century that they had any effective influence on the Arctic Archipelago, even then mainly coming to work in the north but returning to the south to live out their final days. J B McGeachy, a personality from the golden days of Canadian radio once remarked, 'We sing about the north but we live as far south as possible.' Brian Moore, the Canadian novelist, thought that, '… the north is all important to the Canadian's self-image if only because its brooding presence over the land is a warning that Canadians have not yet conquered their universe.' Today more and more people are becoming enamoured with the north's isolation and have created a more permanent European population, if only a small one.

Stretching from the imaginary line of latitude known as the 60th Parallel that also indicates the northern limits of Canada's provinces; the northern territories extend to within 800km of the North Pole and from the Atlantic Ocean west across to the Pacific. A third ocean, the Arctic, links Alaska to Greenland via the islands of the Arctic Archipelago, and connects Canada to Siberia and northern Europe through the ever-moving pack ice that surrounds the North Pole.

There are no mythical creatures here like Big Foot or the Yeti, yet wildlife is bountiful. The Arctic region is much like a desert only colder. It is one of the driest climates on earth. On first appearances it appears to be quite desolate but on closer examination and with a little patience and determination all will be revealed. Whether you're an animal or a traveller everything here is about survival. As the saying goes, 'Any fool can be uncomfortable!' The right gear and a little knowledge about the correct behaviour in the presence of wildlife will help you get the most out of your wilderness experience. Remembering that you are a guest in someone else's home, whether animal or human, will lessen the impact you have on their environment. It will also enhance your experiences.

Far northern Canada, particularly above the Arctic Circle, is an expensive place to travel to. There are few, if any, roads and most of what you use, eat and live in has come there the hard way or by plane. Unlike the south where most things can be had just by clicking one's fingers, in the far north the sheer isolation dictates that only the bare necessities are available. Culturally things are also very different. The climate ensures that things don't quite happen as fast as outsiders would usually expect. Bear with it. The experiences you will come away with will far outweigh the lack of outstanding cuisine, five-star accommodation or a convenience store just around the corner.

Weather-wise, the Yukon and the more southerly parts of the Northwest Territories have a milder climate than the more northerly areas. Their good network of roads allows greater accessibility, giving you much more freedom to roam at will and sample all that the north has to offer.

I have included Alaska, albeit briefly, within the bounds of this guidebook, since only an international boundary separates Alaskans from northern Canadians. This US state is as much a part of the overall region as any of the three Canadian territories and one shouldn't discriminate because of an imaginary line drawn on a map.

I hope that by coupling factual information with good background knowledge this book will give you a sense of the region's rich heritage and manage to nudge your curiosity. I would like to let the geography and the history of the north's peoples help you develop an understanding of this vast landscape and at the same time set the scene for further personal exploration of a land that is populated more by wildlife than people.

Part One

Background Information

Arctic fox

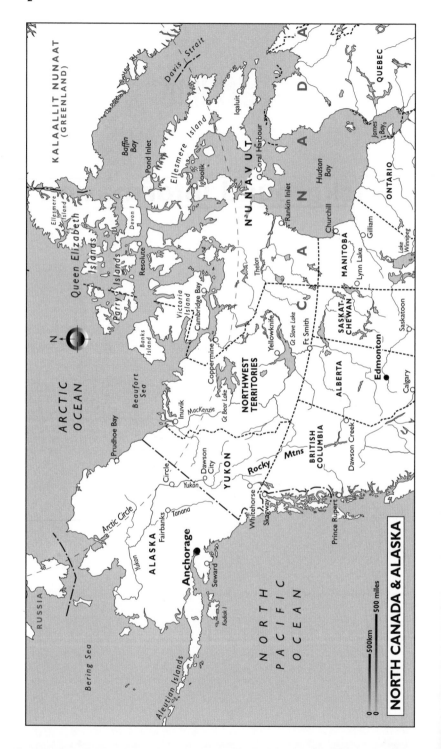

NORTH CANADA & ALASKA

General Information

GEOGRAPHY

This book deals with northern Canada and Alaska. Geographically speaking we are considering all the lands of the North American continent north of the 60° latitude. That encompasses the three Canadian territories of the Yukon, the Northwest Territories (which may or may not be renamed as the Western Arctic at some point in the future) and Nunavut, the newest territory designated within the Dominion of Canada, and the state of Alaska which is part of the United States of America. Throughout this book I shall refer to the area as 'north of the 60' because to all intents and purposes we are considering the same geological, geographical and climatic zone even though we are dealing with two politically separate nations.

It is only people who make a land different with different needs, perceptions and expectations. Yukoners and Alaskans share a similar habitat and feel very much akin to each other. The Northwest Territories has only recently been split (April 1 1999) into the two separate territories of Nunavut and NWT, principally on ethnic grounds. Only time and patience will tell whether the split will work and whether the Inuit of Nunavut will succeed politically and economically in their own right.

The degree of isolation sets the north apart from the rest of Canada. It depends on the heartland for capital and expertise and its future development is dictated by core economics. The north is a truly dependent region because most of its everyday needs and the majority of its labour force come from the south. What markets there are for its products are also in the south. Even the Inuit and the First Nations people, who in some places still maintain a lifestyle independent from the rest of Canada, have on the whole accepted or succumbed to a creeping modernisation relying on outside resources and technology.

The northlands define Canada and are as much a part of Canada's makeup as any of the lower provinces. Although the north may lack unity in its physical and cultural character it does have its role or function in Canada as a whole. The north sets Canada apart and helps create the country's national identity and sense of self. Without the north Canada would appear like a miniature United States and be lost in the greater scheme of things. With the north Canada has developed a distinct sense of being that sets it well apart from the United States and helps afford it a strong position when all the nations sit down to discuss subjects of world importance.

PHYSICAL CONDITIONS

In so large an area, some 5.44 million km^2, physical conditions vary widely. Although all types of relief are found, most people simply think of this region as a singularly cold and barren expanse. In actual fact there are significant differences in climate and vegetation within the north, all of which govern the use of the northern lands.

In terms of the physical environment the north comprises two separate regions: the Northwest and the Arctic. Differences occur in climate, geology and vegetation and I shall deal with each in turn, albeit briefly.

Climate

Next to politics and religion the weather is the world's most talked about subject. And so it should be, because the climate affects our daily lives far more than either politics or religion – at least in the long term.

The climate of northern Canada may be considered to be in two distinct zones. Simply put, these are:

1. The northern fringe of the continent, an area of polar climate that finds its counterpart in northern Siberia. Summers bring a brief surge of growth of tundra plants, but are too short and cool for tree growth; no month has an average temperature above 10°C. Precipitation is meagre and generally below 25cm annually but sufficient for tundra growth in summer and for shallow snow cover during the very long and cold winter.

2. The subarctic, the region of the great boreal forest, dominated by polar continental air, especially in winter. Winters are long, bitterly cold, and relatively dry – snow cover is not deep, but is of long duration. Summers are short, but with long, often warm days. Precipitation is low to moderate, but sufficiently effective, given the temperatures, for tree growth.

There are four seasons in the north, just as there are in temperate latitudes, although the further north you go the winters get longer and summers shorter while autumn and spring resemble more of a freeze-up and a thaw than distinct seasons in their own right. Having said that, parts of the Northwest Territories and much of the Yukon have quite visible seasons although winters are still quite long and summers relatively short. When describing their climate Yukoners say, 'We have eight months of winter and four months of poor dog-sledding', and the saying fits.

Another factor to consider in the equation when travelling in the north is the position of the Arctic Circle and how it relates to the number of hours of daylight there may be at any particular time of year. The Arctic Circle is an imaginary line drawn on the earth's surface at latitude 66° 33' N. It defines the most southerly point at which the sun remains below the horizon for the whole day during the winter solstice (December 22), and at which it is visible above the horizon all day long during the summer solstice (June 21). Hence, much of northern Canada is sometimes called the 'Land of the Midnight Sun'.

Visitors need to remember, however, that, while the sun may be shining all day long in mid-summer, the temperatures can still be near or below freezing.

ANNUAL CLIMATIC CHART

	Average high/low (°C)		Average hrs daylight	Average rain (mm)	Average snow (mm)
Yukon					
January	−14.4	−23.2	5.25	0.2	23.0
February	−8.2	−18.2	7.5	trace	13.5
March	−1.5	−13.1	10.25	trace	16.9
April	5.7	−6.1	13.5	1.0	9.8
May	12.7	0.4	16.5	11.8	2.9
June	18.1	5.1	19.0	30.3	0.9
July	20.3	7.6	20.0	38.5	trace
August	18.3	8.2	17.5	38.1	1.1
September	12.2	2.2	14.25	30	4.8
October	4.3	−3.1	11.25	7.5	18.7
November	−6.4	−13.7	8.25	1.2	25.5
December	−11.7	−20.2	5.5	0.3	25.1
NWT					
January	−24	−32.9		0.1	19.0
February	−21.6	−31.6		nil	15.6
March	−15.4	−27.5		nil	14.0
April	−4.3	−16.1		0.8	13.1
May	7.2	−2.9		9.4	9.7
June	17.3	−6.4		21.5	1.3
July	20.2	10.0		34.5	0.2
August	16.9	7.7		40.1	2.0
September	8.8	1.3		19.9	7.2
October	−1.8	−8.0		8.3	28.3
November	−14	−22.5		0.3	28.6
December	−20.8	−29.6		0.1	21.0

	Average temp (°C)	Average hrs daylight	Average high/low (°C)		Average hrs daylight
		Nunavut	**Alaska**		
January	−25.8	6.1	−11.7	−19.0	6.34
February	−26.8	8.8	−10.3	−17.0	8.86
March	−23.5	11.7	−5.9	−14.8	11.44
April	−14.7	14.4	0.8	−8.1	14.59
May	−4.2	17.9	9.1	0.2	17.38
June	3.4	19.2	14.5	6.0	19.57
July	7.7	18.8	16.7	8.3	18.58
August	6.8	16.0	14.9	7.1	15.70
September	2.3	13.0	10.3	−4.9	12.71
October	−4.9	9.9	1.4	−4.9	9.91
November	−12.7	7.0	−6.6	−13.7	6.96
December	−22.1	5.1	−10.6	−17.6	5.02

Cloudy days will seem warmer, but clear nights, irrespective of the time of year, will be decidedly cold. The weather is changeable, fickle and unpredictable. Be prepared.

All climate figures (see box on previous page) are quite generalised as the weather is by no means consistent, but they will give you an idea of what you may expect in the pre-planning stages of your journey in the north.

Geology

As most of the Northwest is made up of the northward extension of the Cordillera and the Pacific Coastlands, it is mountainous, whereas the mainland Arctic, which is underlain by the Laurentian shield, is of a more gentle relief.

During the late Cretaceous period there was tremendous mountain building going on in the western half of the North American continent. It resulted in a great uplift of the underlying sedimentary beds. This was accompanied by volcanic activity, folding and faulting. Erosive agents in the Tertiary period led an intensive attack on these mountain ranges and thousands of feet of sedimentary cover eroded away leaving the Precambrian floor exposed. Today this area is called the Rockies and extends from 35°N in the United States to the Liard River in Canada. Other ranges then extend this line via the Brooks Range into Alaska.

The Laurentian or Canadian Shield is a block of metamorphosed Precambrian rock covering more than 2½ million km² of eastern Canada. This wide area of ancient rock has been severely compressed and contorted, exposing a large variety of minerals. A long period of erosion culminating in severe glaciation has converted the shield into a rough plain that dips below younger formations south of Hudson Bay. There are two extensions that expand southward into the United States but for all intents and purposes the Laurentian shield is purely Canadian.

Among the most decisive shapers of the geology of North America were the periods when three-quarters of the landmass was covered by ice. Glacial erosion smoothed the rough edges of the continent and altered its drainage patterns. This glaciation can be considered in two parts: the Laurentian Ice Sheet and a separate system of glaciers known as the Cordilleran System.

The Laurentian Ice Sheet probably originated around Hudson Bay and from there spread across eastern North America. Geologists think that it originated as a series of valley glaciers that grew slowly until they altered the climate sufficiently to increase their own expansion. Expansion tended to be in the direction of the prevailing precipitation – westward. Much of this glaciation was erosive, with little glacial depositing anywhere on the Laurentian Shield. Scouring altered the relief, removing soil and often changing the drainage pattern in the process. The result is quite visible today with a barren infertile surface and a maze of swamps and lakes. This is obvious from any flight across the north where, on a clear day, a quick look out of the window gives an uninterrupted view of endless lakes and brown, almost vegetation-free, landscapes.

The Cordilleran System, with its higher precipitation, covered almost the whole of western Canada and Alaska, and remnants of that glacial period are still visible to this day in Kluane National Park in the Yukon and Wrangell-St Elias National Park in Alaska.

Vegetation

Vegetation in any ecosystem is the product of the geology and the climate of that particular system. Rock types, soil types, relief and the prevailing weather all influence, in their own way, the vegetation growing in a particular region.

Soil types are confusing. It is very scientific, but for those interested, most of the soil types found north of the 60 are classified as inceptisols, that is spodsols (northern podsols), lacustrine clays and sands of former glacial lakes and areas where glaciers have swept away the soil altogether. Some people may know them as brown forest, sol brun acide or humic gleys. Technically speaking, inceptisols are wet or frozen according to season and have little or no horizon of accumulation. Where drainage has been altered by glaciation, swamps or muskegs have been formed and these often have a thick peat cover to a depth of a metre or two in places. Rates of decomposition are slowed because of the low ambient temperature and most of the organic matter is held in 'cold storage'.

Much of what we see north of the 60 is boreal forest or tundra. Tundra vegetation consists of heaths and mosses and stunted varieties of trees like willows, and follows roughly the boundary of the climatic region I earlier identified as the polar climate region. The governing factors here are the lack of summer heat, dryness of the Arctic climate and the presence of permafrost in the soil. There is a transition belt of vegetation about 150–200 km wide before the boreal forest becomes the mainstay of vegetation. That line, which is known as the treeline, extends from a point on the MacKenzie Delta to the middle of Hudson Bay and on into northern Labrador.

Boreal forests consist mainly of spruce, white birch, balsam and poplar trees. This zone extends across much of North America. The tall mountains only break it in Canada on the Yukon/Alaska border. The Rockies are generally tree covered on their middle slopes. The lower levels are characterised by scattered and bushlike pinyon and juniper scrubs encountered between 1,200m and 1,800m. The treeline depends on slope and exposure but is usually between 2,750m and 3,350m with alpine meadow and bare rock above it.

Permafrost

Permafrost occurs where the ground is permanently frozen to a depth that may exceed 450m in the extreme north. A small surface layer will thaw in summer but this may only be to a depth of 25cm or so. Permafrost affects farmers trying to conduct what little agriculture is possible, miners in search of mineral wealth and civil engineers dealing with roads, sewerage, water and housing. The problems with permafrost result not from the fact that the ground is permanently solid, but because it is iron hard only in winter while in the summer it becomes soft and waterlogged to a certain depth because the lower layers of frozen soil impede drainage. This creates logistical problems to be overcome before any summer work can be conducted or any structure built.

Agriculturalists are the worst effected by permafrost but other factors limit the development of a sound agricultural base in the north. Lack of summer heat and near drought conditions play their part. Precipitation has a seasonal distribution – it usually comes too late in the summer to be of use to farmers – and the amounts are relatively small: 10–20cm per annum. Lack of top soil adds to the dilemma. Also, in some parts where the temperatures are favourable and the rainfall is the same as elsewhere, like the MacKenzie Valley, the region unfortunately has higher evaporation levels.

Thus the north suffers a triple drawback in its use of land: lack of usable soil, lack of sunshine and lack of growing-season rainfall.

This is just a brief glimpse at the natural geography of the north as a whole – there is more detail later in specific sections. I have tried to give a general picture. A beautiful landscape is a stunning sight. A little knowledge about how it was formed, what makes it unique, and how the sum of all the little parts that have created this wonderful vista help turn a scene worthy of a picture into something alive and kicking and decidedly more interesting.

HISTORY OF THE NORTH
Early exploration

It seems that the first explorer to venture north toward the Arctic region was a navigator called Pytheas sailing out of the Greek colony of Massilia (modern-day Marseilles) in about 325BC. What is left of his journals found in ancient books indicate that he sailed north and reached a land he called Ultima Thule. The little that can be gleaned from these journals reported that the people here produced honey and that the nights were very short in summer. The Irish monk Dicuil who 'discovered' Iceland in AD825 thought he had reached Thule. Modern opinion suggests that the ancient civilisation of Thule is more likely to be where Trondheim in Norway is now.

Next in the exploration stakes is a matter of conjecture. It seems that Pytheas met some people (Keltoi) on the islands that the Greeks called Alba (Britain). According to his records he landed somewhere in the Hebrides after sailing north up the west coast of Britain from Cornwall past the Isle of Man to what he called the Ebud Islands. The people he found here traded in walrus tusks and sailed in skin boats, not wooden ones like the Greeks although the design and rigging may have been similar. These Albans took him to an island called Tilli (probably Iceland) and back home again and he tells us no more of them. It is possible that the Albans sailed as far as Canada, or at least Greenland, when the world was a warmer place. Constant invasions by Norse, Romans and Celts could have forced the Albans to flee west in their skin boats and they may have arrived on the shores of Canada. Whether it is true or not it certainly makes a good story.

The first serious exploration north that we do know about was by the Vikings. It is known from the sagas that a Viking called Ohthere (or Ottar) sailed north around the tip of Scandinavia past North Cape and discovered the 'White Sea'. Danes had certainly settled in Iceland by the late 9th century. Another Dane called Eric the Red, who was banished from Iceland for being a bad boy, sailed with 25 ships (he arrived with four) and established two colonies on Greenland in the late 10th century. These lasted until the end of the 15th century when they suddenly vanished off the face of the Earth.

Recent archaeological evidence suggests that at that time there was a very severe mini-Ice Age. The agriculturally minded Vikings, with their crops, sheep and cattle, failed to adapt to Inuit ways of survival, and cold weather and failing harvests helped disease and starvation take their toll. Those not already dead might have attempted to sail away, perhaps to America, and perished en route. No one knows. So far there is no definite evidence that they landed anywhere else in the Northern Hemisphere to establish any form of settlement. If they had chosen to live like the Inuit by hunting the abundant wildlife – fish and seals – or by changing fashion from their normal woollen clothing to animal skins in order to combat the extremes of the cold they might have survived to this day.

Now I know that Scandinavia, Iceland and Greenland have little to do with Arctic Canada. But, as the First Nations people and the Inuit had no written language, they kept no records, so the European thirst to explore the Arctic region seems a good place to start when trying to discover the early history of Arctic Canada. The Vikings set the pattern for Columbus. He knew that they had sailed west and found land. In the days when most sailors believed the world was flat, he had to convince his crew that they would not fall off the edge. To this end he had a navigator on board, a fisherman, who had actually been to the land of the 'red man' (there is a grave in a churchyard in Galway that claims this).

Europe in the time of Columbus was fighting endless wars. Spices – the only means of preserving food before the invention of the refrigerator – travelled to Europe over the dangerous land route from Asia. Every territory the spices passed through demanded a toll to ensure right of passage, or else stole the spices outright and sold them to a third party. This raised the prices of spices available in Europe. Since the Ottoman Turks' conquest of the Middle East in the middle of the 15th century the land route was completely disrupted. Columbus was searching for a sea route west to the spices when he bumped into the Americas. It was not long before everyone was chasing rainbows dripping pots of gold by hunting out that elusive sea route around the American continent. A route west to the Pacific around Cape Horn at the foot of South America was found quite early in the story (Ferdinand Magellan in 1521) but many still believed that a shorter route could be found to the north – the Northwest Passage.

It would take Europeans another 400 years to find a way across the north but by then its only useful purpose existed in the minds of those explorers who sought to be the first to find the way. The moving pack ice and the weather were not on their side. Only time and advances in technology would secure an avenue across the north of a land that became known as Canada.

England's Henry VII sent John Cabot off in 1497 in the *Matthew* but he only got as far as Newfoundland, yet the Northwest Passage had by then captured the imagination of many of the world's explorers, pirates, buccaneers and sea captains; Sir Francis Drake, Jacques Cartier, Sir Martin Frobisher and Captain James Cook to name but a few. Hunting gold, furs and fame, they all tried and all met with failure, some disastrously.

Sir Humphrey Gilbert wrote a treatise on the passage that was like a guidebook for others to follow. He drowned attempting the route in 1583. Henry Hudson was set adrift with his son in 1611 by his own mutinous crew when his discovery of Hudson Bay led to an icy entrapment which barred the way west. With each passing expedition more knowledge was acquired about the passage. Hundreds of voyages over hundreds of years by land and by sea added to what was already known. Explorers such as John Davis, Sir William Baffin, Sir John Ross and Sir William Parry went by sea; Henry Kelsey, Samuel Hearne and Sir Alexander MacKenzie travelled overland. All failed; all had their problems.

The worst disaster and probably the most famous was Sir John Franklin's expedition in the two ships HMS *Erebus* and *Terror* both of which vanished in 1845. These ships were specially reinforced to withstand the crushing power of the ice and had the latest technology for vessels at that time – propellers driven by a 20 horsepower dismantled railway steam engine. The crews, 129 officers and men, were all handpicked for the expedition. There were three and a half years' worth of supplies and the ships had a library of some 2,900 books. Fortnum & Mason supplied much of the food. No expedition had been better equipped – or so everyone thought.

Although the expedition used fresh supplies they relied heavily on canned goods as a backup food source. Napoleon had tried canned rations for his troops when he invaded Russia in 1812. This was cutting edge technology at that time. Unknown to Napoleon the cans contained too much lead. His troops were slowly poisoned, making many of them unfit for battle. The Russian winter did the rest and that is history.

By 1845 technology had improved since Napoleon's day, although canning was still deemed new technology. As a cost-saving measure the Admiralty accepted the cheapest supplier's quote on basic provisions. After Franklin's disappearance there was much speculation about what actually happened to the expedition. There were even rumours of cannibalism. It is now believed that the tins may have been sealed with cheap solder containing excessive amounts of lead, poisoning the men who ate from them.

The fate of the expedition is contained in a message now on display in Britain's National Maritime Museum in Greenwich. There had been several rescue and search expeditions mounted to find Franklin and his crew. The last and final expedition was organised and financed by his wife, Lady Jane Franklin, in 1857. In April 1859 this expedition, under Captain McClintock, found a note in a metal box under a cairn at Victoria Point on the northwest coast of King William Island overlooking Victoria Strait. It said:

'April 25, 1848, HM Ships *Terror* and *Erebus* were deserted on April 22, five leagues NWW *[sic]* of this, having been beset since September 12, 1846. The officers and crew consisting of 105 souls under command of Captain F R M Crozier landed here. Sir John Franklin died on June 11, 1847, and the total loss by deaths in the expedition has been, to this date, nine officers and fifteen men.'

The message was signed by the captains of the two ice-locked vessels. On the top right hand corner of the note was scribbled 'and start back tomorrow 26th for Back's Fish River'. That was the last heard of the expedition.

Cannibalism was a myth started by John Rae, a Hudson Bay man, who apparently disliked the Royal Navy for some reason. Rae's credibility may be judged by the fact that, although he was only two days' travelling away from the survivors (some Inuit had sold him some of the crew's effects and told him where they were), he chose to go to England and claim the prize for discovering Franklin's fate.

Although an autopsy performed on two of Franklin's men exhumed from the permafrost in 1984 indicated high levels of lead in their bodies, there is little evidence to indicate that the cans were responsible. It seems that the food had become putrid. A batch of the same cans had been left behind in the victualling yard and had to be removed because of the stench. Scurvy and bad food would have seriously affected the men, leading to illness and exhaustion.

More recent evidence would suggest that the local Inuit were an aggressive lot. Thanks to many previous ships being abandoned, the Inuit had access to metal for weapons and in their state of ill health and exhaustion Franklin's crew were no match in battle for the Inuit. The crew would have split into small parties to search for help, making them easier targets for the aggressive Inuit. Everything was against the survivors – the weather, scurvy, exhaustion and the Inuit. It was a losing battle all round. It is no wonder they perished. Franklin and his crew typify the mettle of the explorers of the Northwest Passage. Their achievements should be celebrated.

But the way through the ice and over the north had still not been found. Although by this time no useful commercial purpose would have been served by finding a route around the north, in terms of exploration and science the Northwest Passage still had plenty to offer. It was an explorer's dream.

Finally, in 1906, after an arduous three-year voyage, the Norwegian explorer Roald Amundsen succeeded in a converted 47-tonne herring boat, the *Gjöa*. The first single-season transit of the passage was achieved in 1944 by Sergeant Henry A Larsen of the RCMP.

Today we know that opening the Northwest Passage to international commercial sea traffic could have worldwide economic significance, though the high costs of strengthening ships to withstand the ice, and the possibility of high insurance premiums would make it expensive as a trade route. Weighed against this, the savings in time and distance travelled would be substantial. Journeys from Britain to Japan would be almost halved from the 23,500km route around Africa to less than 12,500km through the passage.

Large deep-water vessels too big to pass through the Panama and Suez Canals would almost certainly find the route profitable.

Although many countries, including the United States and Japan, say that the Northwest Passage is international waters, at present Canada holds sway over the Arctic Islands. Canada's only quibble in opening up the passage to serious international commerce is, in light of the *Exxon Valdez* incident, whether shipping companies will co-operate with Canada's rigid pollution-control regulations.

Whalers and sealers

Explorers don't go anywhere without a serious purpose, whether it is to discover new lands, search out new trade routes, or chase rainbows. The exploration of the north was no different. Not only was the search on for a new route to the Indies by seeking the Northwest Passage but much of the establishment, mapping or charting of the initial routes was achieved by those bent on purely commercial gains. These men were in search of whales.

Earliest evidence of whaling goes back to the Inuit in about 3,000BC and it has continued in remote cultures ever since. The Japanese used nets, but the Aleuts used poisoned spears when hunting the smaller whales that were easily beached when they came close to shore to breed in sheltered bays. Coastal Native Americans also developed whaling techniques but these tended to be purely seasonal. The most prolific of these traditional whale hunters were the Inuit. Using sealskin boats and toggle-headed harpoons attached to long hide ropes towing inflated sealskin floats, they became adept at hunting the larger whales. When the animal tired it would be killed by lance. In Europe the Nordic peoples hunted the smaller species, and Iceland had laws that dealt with whaling as early as the 13th century.

Commercial whaling, as opposed to whaling to meet basic survival needs, probably began with the Basque people of Spain in the Bay of Biscay as early as the beginning of the 12th century. They hunted black right whales when they came to the bay to breed. Being docile and slow-moving they were easily hunted from rowing boats from which they were speared, played like fish and then lanced to death. When dead they floated (hence the name – from being the 'right' whale to hunt) and were towed ashore for processing. When serious ocean-going ships were developed in the 14th century, the Basques, having eliminated right whales from Europe's west coast, ventured further afield, eventually, by the early 16th century, crossing the Atlantic to Newfoundland and Labrador waters in search of the leviathan.

While the Basques were learning the ropes of practical whaling, northern Europeans were creating and developing the much-needed markets. By 1610 the English Muscovy Company, using Basque whalemen, had ventured into Arctic waters and began exploiting the whales around the bays of Spitsbergen. They were followed almost immediately by the Dutch who, with better business sense and a slight touch of violence, broke the English monopoly on whaling in the north Atlantic. They established a land-based whaling station on Spitsbergen nicknamed 'Blubbertown' in 1619. During its heyday during the 1630s and 1640s there were over 150 men servicing the whaling ships which hunted Greenland right, or bowhead, whales throughout the Arctic.

Two British whalers who had a major influence on northern exploration in the late 18th and early 19th century were a father and son, both called William Scoresby, from Whitby in Yorkshire (another great seafaring explorer, Captain James Cook, also came from there). Scoresby senior was a farmer's son who became a first-class navigator and, amongst other aids to navigation, invented the crow's nest to help his ships find their way through the ice. He was the first to suggest using sledges to reach the North Pole. Bill junior went to sea whaling with his father at the tender age of ten. He had inherited his father's talent for navigation. In 1806 the Scoresbys reached 81°21' N off Spitsbergen, the furthest north yet sailed by anyone. By 1822 Bill junior had mapped the east coast of Greenland in detail. The Scoresby family were the first successfully to mix commerce with exploration.

Another famous whaling navigator and pilot was William Baffin. He first headed north in 1612 in search of the Northwest Passage. He was considered the most exceptional navigator of his time, calculating longitude whilst underway. His instruments were crude; the sextant had yet to be invented and the chronograph was not even a thought, yet Baffin managed incredible accuracy with an astronomer's quadrant and the latest almanac to work out mathematically his position at sea on a heaving deck. He was never more than a single degree out. His drawings, sketches and ethnological observations provide the most accurate descriptions of whaling and exploration of the time.

It was a mini-Ice Age in the latter part of the 17th century that put an end to commercial whaling in Spitsbergen. Not to be beaten, the unperturbed whalers took their ships and moved into open water where the whales were processed alongside the boats. Blubber was flensed (stripped) off the whales and stored in barrels. The carcasses were then abandoned. By the 1690s Dutch and German domination of the north Atlantic whaling scene ceased and, to service its accelerating Industrial Revolution, Britain took over once again as Europe's principal whaling nation.

British whalers ventured forth from the American colonies and by 1712 had changed tack and now hunted sperm whales for the more industrially suited oil. New ships with furnaces on board allowed whalers to venture further and further afield moving whaling into the rich grounds of the Pacific and away from the north Atlantic. Yet between 1791 and 1911 whalers managed to take about 28,000 bowheads from eastern Arctic waters. As stocks of one species were depleted the whalers moved on to another species in another area: Spitsbergen in the 17th century, Greenland in the early 18th, then the south Atlantic and on to the Pacific. In the 20th century whalers headed to the Antarctic and hunted the vast populations of blue whales. Faster ships and new weaponry allowed whalers to chase the faster swimmers like minke and sei whales which were previously beyond the hunting capabilities of men in small boats.

The discovery of underground petroleum in Pennsylvania in 1859 put the first nail in the commercial whaling coffin although it continued through the 20th century until most usable whale species were on the verge of extinction.

Commercial whaling is now banned throughout the world but a few nations still maintain small commercial operations for 'scientific' purposes.

Sealers were much in the same vein – commercially motivated. Seals were a valuable source of fur, oil, meat and hides. Harp seal pups, in particular, were sought after for their extra fine fluffy white coats that were quite valuable to the fur trade. Fur seals were hunted for their pelts; elephant and monk seals for their blubber. Sealing declined worldwide after the end of World War II when international agreements set about conserving many seal species from extinction. It is quite possible that several species probably disappeared during 400 years of unrestricted hunting, but seal populations now seem on the increase.

Another animal pursued for its commercial value since Roman times is the walrus. Old 'toothwalker' was not only valuable for its exceptionally tough hide, blubber and meat but its tusks are made of ivory, giving hunters that additional commercial incentive to seek the animal. Hunting was limited because the animal spent most of its life in winter on ice floes. In summer limited beach landings made them difficult to get at; also the populations were smaller than most seal species.

Today commercial whaling serves no useful purpose. Enough whales die stranded on beaches to fill the need for edible delicacies worldwide. Science has allowed us to produce the products we need, of even finer quality, from other more easily obtainable resources, much of which can be found in far greater quantities – namely oil. We can also manufacture more cheaply many of the natural bi-products of whales than the continued hunting of live whales could ever achieve. This is before we even consider the implications of hunting an animal to the brink of extinction through over-fishing.

Britain and America gave up serious whaling in the mid-19th century for several reasons. Despite the growing potential of mineral and vegetable oils whale oil was still in high demand as a lubricant. Technological advances didn't improve the diminishing returns on their investments by British and American whalers. More efficient harpoons, rocket harpoons, 'dart' guns and grenade-type explosive heads failed to improve on the old-fashioned way of causing haemorrhage by lancing the animal with a spear when it came to speeding up the death of a whale. New technology was more likely to frighten the animals off than speed up their capture. On a more financial note, with right whales nearing extinction, neither country could find a profitable means of pursuing any alternative whale species.

Whale hunting still continues in the north amongst the Inuit and other native peoples. They are still allowed to hunt whales without too many restrictions beyond acquiring a licence. Sometimes these old hunting societies occasionally carry out unnecessary recreational hunting under the guise of promoting cultural survival and the excuse is based on the attitude that if you don't practise a skill, it dies. Unfortunately, many of the young Inuit (and I can rely only on my personal experiences of native hunts here) tend to depend on firepower rather than on the skill and cunning of the older generations for whom hunting with primitive weapons was the only means of survival. Much of the blame for this must lie at the feet of Europeans who exploited for financial gain the abundance of whales, seals and other marine mammals in the 18th and 19th centuries. Whaling as an Inuit tradition became more complex when it became intricately linked with more modern European commerce. The Inuit found either that they could not compete on the same scale or that there were so few animals left for them that hunting whales was not economic under any terms, either survival or commercial.

Moratoriums, legislation, laws and the scarcity of prey have caused the Inuit to hunt very few animals these days and the skills necessary, like many other Inuit traditions, are dying out. In a more modern world, survival – what the Inuit term 'The Great Necessity' – isn't dictating the need to hunt such large animals any more and because there is little commercial requirement for their produce the only thing left to consider is whether the hunting of whales is critical to cultural survival.

In 1996 a case in point occurred which caused much furore not only within the Inuit community but from the anti-whaling fraternity as well. Many Inuit were divided on the subject of this particular hunt. Some saw it as symbolic of the creation of Nunavut and a search for the sense of purpose, of community, and of dignity that traditionally defined Inuit society. Others took a more realistic approach, saying that for a modern thinking society to resurrect the culture of yesterday by killing an animal is nonsense – it is just killing something for killing's sake.

During negotiations between the Canadian government and the representatives of the Inuit people in the run-up to the 1993 Nunavut Land Claims Agreement, the Inuit fought for and obtained the right to hunt bowhead whales subject to approval by the Canadian Department of Fisheries and Wildlife. Approval was accordingly given in 1996 to take one bowhead whale in the waters of Repulse Bay. Thirteen men from across Nunavut participated in the hunt. The hunters were selected by local political organisations to represent each of Nunavut's three regions. They were either flown or boated in for what was to become an event. Whale hunts usually follow the tradition that they are carried out by men from the same community. This ensures that every man is familiar with every other man and his individual capabilities. However, for most of the hunters involved in this particular hunt it would be the first time any of them had met. Too many politicians and Inuit in important positions went on the hunt and there were too few skilled hunters present. All in all the local community played a very minor role in the hunt, although it did have the honour of providing the hunt captain, 72-year-old Abraham Tagornak.

It took three days before they found their whale, and it took 14 harpoon and countless bullet wounds before it succumbed. A harpoon had pierced its lung, causing the dead animal to sink, and it was lost for several days. When the slowly decaying leviathan eventually refloated due to a build-up of gases, there was little time left to cut it up and distribute the carcass effectively to all 29 Nunavut communities as planned. Sadly most of the 45-tonne animal went to waste. The ravens had a good feed. In the high Arctic summer the carcass quickly became rotten and after about four days of lying on a beach the local community was paid to dispose of the remains. Any of the meat that could not be stored was put on melting ice floes far out to sea while the bulk of the carcass was burnt where it laid. The skull of this particular animal now lies at the foot of the Arctic Circle monument outside Repulse Bay's airport.

These days a whale's real value lies in its being alive and being a whale, doing whale things, in a whale way. I have sea-kayaked with orcas in British Columbia; followed gray whales in a Zodiac inflatable off California; watched sperm whales dive for giant squid off New Zealand; and sailed with sei and minke whales off the Hebrides in Scotland. Whale-watching is one of the greatest joys that any traveller can experience in this wonderful natural world of ours. Through the efforts of tourist organisations some people who, because of where they live, would never have the opportunity to see one of these magnificent creatures in its natural environment, benefit immensely from seeing whales in their natural state. I would put it close to swimming with dolphins and seals as one of the all-time great experiences to be had. I know of no-one who has not been moved for a lifetime by the experience. Whales may be being exploited once again but at least they can swim away without fear of being pursued literally to death.

Northern Canada has some of the potentially best whale-watching on this planet, yet this is an almost completely untapped resource. The remoteness of the region sees to that and I hope the situation stays that way for a long time to come yet.

The fur trade

Two French Canadians, Pierre-Espirit Radisson and his brother-in-law Médard Chouart, were having lunch in Oxford with the King, Charles II. The year was 1666. Radisson, who claimed to have lived with the Huron since he was 15, spins a thrilling story about life north of Quebec in what we now know as the Northwest Territories. Tales of derring-do so fantastic that the King had Radisson write it all down. His theme was that the Indian nations had a fortune in beaver furs and were ripe for the plucking. Fur-felted beaver hats were the fashionable rage of all the dandies in London that season. London hatters could not keep up with the demand but Europe had wiped out most of its fur-bearing mammals; down hadn't been heard of and hollow-fill fibre hadn't been invented so fur was the only solution to the cold crisis hitting the streets of London. The two French-Canadians knew where to find it.

The King sent the two fortune hunters off in the royal ships the *Eaglet* and the *Nonsuch* to Hudson's Bay in search of this unseen wealth. They wintered in Canada and returned with a very lucrative haul of prime beaver pelts that made the King's eyes sparkle and the London social scene buzz with excitement.

On May 2 1670 the King set up the Hudson's Bay Company (see Hudson's Bay Company).

For the next two hundred years the Honourable Company bled the continent of North America dry in its desperate need to supply furs to the markets of Europe. That was until Albert, the Prince Consort of Queen Victoria, changed the fashion to silk toppers and the bottom dropped out of the industry in a bad way.

Yet the fur trade, for all its bad points, generated a great deal of exploration, much of it in the need to find more and more resources to feed an ever growing market, though there was a touch of 'what's on the other side of that hill' syndrome.

Of all the men who went in search of furs and wealth, two of the early fur-trader explorers stood out from the crowd. They were daring, brave, resourceful and very inquisitive and they crossed the Canadian wilderness in search of new sources of furs and in turn discovered a land of immense wealth and diversity. These two men wrote the book for future fur-trading exploration and at the same time mapped completely uncharted territory. Their names were Samuel Hearne and Alexander MacKenzie.

Hearne was a natural explorer: resourceful, mild mannered, a teetotaller, a self-taught artist, a lover of birds and animals and, above all, a zealous hiker. He thought nothing of trudging for months on end with only a rucksack full of books for company. Between 1769 and 1772 he covered almost 5,000 miles across the treeless tundra of what is now Nunavut and he was the first white man to gaze upon the Arctic Ocean.

Hearne came to Canada as a mate on a HBC whaling sloop in 1767. He arrived at Fort Prince of Wales near Churchill, Manitoba, in 1769 and came under the watchful eye of the Governor of the HBC post, Moses Norton. He prepared himself for his role as fur-trader by camping out with the First Nations, shooting game and racing after moose. Good health was needed for the task ahead. Norton's instructions to the young Hearne were simple. He was to drum up trade among the Chipewyan people of the northern hinterland, keep an eye out for the North West Passage, and track down an El Dorado of copper rumoured to exist at the mouth of the Far-Off-Metal River that emptied into an unknown ocean. Hearne was just 24 years old.

A couple of false starts and a poor choice of guides led to him hiring, in December 1770, a Chipewyan called Matonabbee and his merry little band. Everywhere the two went Matonabbee took with him his seven wives. He thought that the reason for Hearne's failures on previous trips was that he had had no women to carry his packs. He deemed women suitable only for lugging packs, pitching the tents, keeping them warm, and mending clothes for the hunt. The other advantage Matonabbee saw in his wives was that they could cook. Self-sufficient as Hearne was, he eventually came to depend on Matonabbee and his band for sustenance and, as he put it in his journals, 'good cheer'. He was always amazed at their physical abilities. They could reportedly tramp 60 miles a day on a diet of melted snow and a pipe full of tobacco. Bearing in mind that the First Nations scornfully called the Inuit *eskimantsik* 'eaters of raw meat', Hearne often relished uncooked Indian delicacies like unhatched snowbirds, a savoury haggis of kidneys gobbled steaming out of a freshly killed caribou, and unborn beaver torn from the belly of its mother. He thoroughly enjoyed the Chipewyan's company.

Hearne's little party reached the banks of the Coppermine River on July 13 1771 where, after a minor altercation (Hearne called it a massacre) with a local Inuit group, his party followed the river down to the Arctic Ocean, arriving on July 18 1771. He claimed possession of the coast on behalf of the Hudson's Bay Company. He found little copper worth worrying about and headed for home via the Great Slave Lake in the Northwest Territories. In the end he considered his stupendous feats as fairly poor. He remarked that, 'The continent of America is much wider than many people imagine, as to a passage through the continent of America by way of Hudson's Bay, it has been exploded.'

Hearne died destitute in England in 1792 aged 47 years. He had just sold the rights to his masterly journal to a publisher for £200. He had been retired from his position as head of the Hudson Bay Company in Canada in 1782, for being too timid in the face of overwhelming odds (the French forced him to surrender Fort Prince of Wales when a 74-gun battleship blew the fort to bits and took Hearne prisoner).

Matonabbee hanged himself on hearing of Hearne's dismissal. Hearne commented that, 'This is more to be wondered at as he is the only Northern Indian who, that I ever heard, put an end to his own existence.'

Six years later one of Matonabbee's little band acted as guide for another fur trade thrust into the interior. This time the explorer was Alexander MacKenzie.

MacKenzie was born in Stornoway, Lewis and Harris, Outer Hebrides, Scotland, in 1755 and emigrated to America in 1779 where he joined Hudson's Bay Company's rival, the North West Company. MacKenzie was a new breed of explorer, not only tough, but also a business executive, and the complete opposite to Hearne. He quickly rose through the ranks of the Nor'westers to become one of the partners in 1788.

The ambitious MacKenzie and his cousin were given carte blanche to develop the company's newest outpost called Fort Chipewyan on Lake Athabasca, in 1788, in the province we now know as Alberta.

On June 3 1789 he set out with four paddling French *voyageurs*, two with their wives, and a German. Also with the group was a party of Chipewyan Indians who would act as guides, interpreters and hunters for the party. They were led by a guide called English Chief (because he had learnt English whilst travelling with Hearne) and his two wives. This was a business trip so the three yellow birchbark canoes were loaded with blue beads, mirrors, knives and other trading goods. The *voyageurs* were said to be able to manage 100 miles downstream or 30 miles upstream a day.

It took MacKenzie and his party 102 days to follow the course of what is now the MacKenzie River, 1,770km to the Arctic Ocean and back. They traded goods for beaver furs and urged the natives to bring their pelts along to the new trading post on Lake Athabasca. MacKenzie, unlike Hearne, never liked his native companions nor those he visited.

In MacKenzie's favour he was a methodical geographer. He discovered petroleum at what is now Norman Wells but for all his acute business sense he never dreamed of the wealth that 'black gold' would bring; he was only interested in beaver pelts.

MacKenzie was back in Fort Chipewyan on September 12 1789 having called his great discovery the River of Disappointment – a splendid highway to nowhere. Four years later he headed east over the Rockies and found the Pacific Ocean. His inscription, painted on the southeast face of a rock jutting into Dean Channel, said, 'Alexander MacKenzie, from Canada, by land, the twenty-second of July, one thousand and seven hundred and ninety three.' He had made the first crossing of the continent of America by land, in effect a North West Passage. He returned to England when his Nor'wester partners thought the land west of the Rockies commercially valueless. He was knighted for his efforts in 1802 and died in 1820. Before he died he predicted that the fur trading companies would go bankrupt. He was right. In 1821 the two rival companies, the Nor'wester Swashbucklers and the humble Honourable Company were compelled by market forces to join hands under the banner of the HBC.

Furs are still sold today but in ever decreasing numbers. Exotic furs can still be a sign of wealth but are proving less and less functional and certainly less fashionable and socially acceptable. Fur traders may have opened up the Canadian wilderness but they have left it relatively intact. The next great surge into the wilderness came with the scent of gold, and Canada was sitting on the largest reserves ever known in the world.

Hudson Bay Company: The Company of Adventurers

Every where you go throughout the north you'll hear mention of the Hudson Bay Company. It was everywhere. There has never been a business empire like it. HBC's territory once covered more than a twelfth of the earth's surface and was at its height ten times larger than the Holy Roman Empire at the peak of its influence. Its dominion stretched from London, across Canada, down to San Francisco and across the Pacific Ocean as far as Hawaii.

The company was founded on May 2 1670 as the 'Company of Adventurers of England Tradeing into Hudson's Bay'. King Charles II granted a charter to Prince Rupert and 17 fellow investors for an:

> 'Expedicion for Hudson's Bay in the North west part of America for the discovery of a new passage into the South Sea and for finding some Trade for Furrs Mineralls and other considerable Commodityes and by such theire undertakeing have already made such discoveryes as doe encourage them to proceed further in pursuance of theire said designe by meanes whereof there may probably arise very great advantage to us and our Kingdome.'

Eighteen men and one woman eventually joined Prince Rupert in the Hudson's Bay Company including Sir George Carteret, thought to be the richest man in Britain at the time (he rescued the Royal Navy when Charles' coffers ran dry), and Sir Christopher Wren.

The charter gave the company sole and full rights to govern what was to be known as Prince Rupert's Land. It also gave full rights to pursue the fur trade on any river, creek, stream, strait or sound that fed Hudson's Bay (the name was change by the Geographic Board of Canada to Hudson Bay in 1900). Today that would be all of present-day Manitoba, Saskatchewan, Alberta, the Northwest Territories and Nunavut. It was a free-enterprise dream ticket.

It built forts, had private armies, and encouraged the native population to bring furs into the forts for sale. At one point it even had its own currency, HBC tokens, in which furs and services were paid for and which could only be redeemed in Hudson Bay stores. HBC had the market cornered. The only competition was from the French who came out of Montréal with a company called the North West Company. Their people were called Nor'westers. Both British and French interests ran high as they both sought to exploit the rich fur-bearing mammals of Canada. Competition was fierce and posts sprang up all over the place, not only around Hudson Bay but throughout the interior. Competition was so fierce that something resembling a guerrilla war ensued which in the end proved unprofitable for both sides.

By 1821 the Hudson's Bay Company had amalgamated with the North West Company, its chief rival for furs, and, through 173 posts, gained control of more than 3 million square miles of land and all the rights to the fur trade of British North America west of Upper Canada. In the first instance it was fur that put Canada on the map. It was the first serious income-generating business spanning the continent and for over two hundred years it thrived.

It was a change in fashion that began its demise. Prince Albert, Queen Victoria's consort, appeared in public in 1854 wearing a top hat not of beaver but of silk. The fashion for less expensive headgear swept European society and started a decline in the fur trade. Colonisation, nationhood and the demand of settlers to be able to farm their best land brought the HBC monopoly to an end. The public's boredom with beaver fur hats which were the mainstay of the fur trade, and the introduction of fur farms producing speciality furs, turned the HBC fortunes on their head.

The first permanent trading post and main depot of the HBC in Canada was known as the York Factory and it was established at the mouth of the Nelson River south of where Churchill is now in Manitoba. The post was named after the company's governor, the Duke of York. The word factory came not because they manufactured anything here, but because this was where the company factor lived.

The fur trade was all but finished by 1870 and had been North America's first transcontinental enterprise. With its decline the HBC got involved in merchandising and retail, feeding and supplying those farmers who had purchased all the company's best land. Within ten years HBC's shareholders were raking in the dividends again. HBC had shed its fur-trading monopoly to become Canada's largest private landlord.

For 249 years ships sailed annually from London to the York Factory until in 1931 the last supply ship sailed out of London. The York Factory was still trading strong in 1936 but by 1957 the trade had all but vanished and the HBC finally closed its famous headquarters. In 1987 the HBC was Canada's ninth-largest company employing over 40,000 people with an annual revenue of nearly CAD$6 billion.

Today in most of the communities throughout Nunavut the distinctive white and red buildings have stood the test of time. Once the distinctive and visible symbol of a grand old trading establishment, they are used as storerooms, schools or museums for the local region. Some are just broken down old shells waiting, once again, to be given a lick of paint and assigned a useful purpose. They are truly an endearing icon of a once very prosperous north.

The Hudson Bay Company sums itself up like this:

> 'What began as a simple fur trading enterprise evolved into a trading and exploration company that reached to the west of Canada and the United States, south to Oregon, north to the Arctic and east to Ungava Bay, with agents in Chile, Hawaii, California, and Siberia; a land development company with vast holdings in the prairie provinces; a merchandising, natural resources and real-estate development company and, today, Canada's oldest corporation and one of its largest retailers.'

Klondike gold stampede

The Klondike gold stampede, more than any other event in recent history, has brought Canada to the world's attention. It had such a significant effect on the north that without it Canada's northern regions would have remained a complete backwater.

On August 17 1896 a Californian named George Washington Carmack, his wife Kate who was the daughter of a Tagish First Nation chief, and his two Tagish First Nation brothers-in-law Keish, known as Skookum Jim Mason, and Káa Goox, known to Europeans as either Dawson Charlie or Tagish Charlie, discovered gold in Rabbit Creek. This should have been nothing of importance because the hills of the Yukon were crawling with prospectors at that time. What made it so prominent was the volume of gold retrieved. The Klondike still contains plenty of gold, but it is now much harder and more expensive to extract.

By the winter of 1896 about 300 men were working the Bonanza Creek. The rush continued with men arriving by dog teams and on snowshoes. On January 6 1897 500 claims had been staked.

The extreme isolation of the Yukon and Dawson meant that word of the strike would not reach the outside world until the first stern-wheelers came upstream after the spring melt of 1897. Some 80 prospectors left Dawson with anything from $25,000 to $500,000 in gold stuffed into metal boxes. At St Michael on the Alaskan coast they transferred to two steamers, the *Portland* and the *Excelsior* bound for Seattle and San Francisco. The *Excelsior* docked first on July 14 1897 and the word was out. Thousands watched as the *Portland* docked and newspapers claimed 'a ton of gold' being unloaded. The resulting 'gold fever' swept across the United States and the rest of the world.

All in all about 100,000 people joined the stampede to the Klondike, about 40,000 of whom made it to Dawson. Most of the claims had been struck by then so most of those arriving worked for other miners. The Klondike was the most peaceful of the world's gold rushes mainly due to the efforts of the North West Mounted Police who allowed none of the gun-related violence that plagued other big strikes.

By 1898 the rush for gold was well and truly over. A new strike near Nome in Alaska prompted a mass exodus from Dawson. Some $50 million worth of gold had been taken out of the ground by then. The Klondike would yield another $50 million over the next five years but by 1899 gold was mined commercially by technologically sophisticated machinery and the small time amateur prospectors had left. The Klondike today still gives up about $65 million annually but at $375 to $400 an ounce it is about 20 times the amount paid during the Stampede.

North West Mounted Police

Much of northern Canada was opened up by patrols of the North West Mounted Police. It later became the Royal North West Mounted Police. They were the predecessors of today's Royal Canadian Mounted Police. These patrols were used to assert Canadian sovereignty over a vast area of wilderness. They would blaze trails, establish forts and supply routes, collect customs duties and protect the aboriginal people against injustices from fur traders, whalers, prospectors etc and to some degree apply, by a combination of tact, diplomacy and firmness, what Canadian laws were applicable throughout such a remote region.

Established in 1873 the North West Mounted Police, as they were called then, was a small para-military police force of 150 men recruited to maintain order in the western lands after Canada bought from the Hudson Bay Company all the land north of the US border from the Great Lakes to the Rockies. This purchase was made with the aid of a £300,000 loan from the British government.

A sudden large influx of settlers into this vast and sparsely populated area deemed it necessary for the Canadian government to provide some form of law enforcement to maintain the peace and protect traditional native lands. The government was a little concerned that many of these settlers might not have respect for native rights and wanted to find a better way to deal with the land settlement question alongside treating the aboriginal peoples fairly. It was intended that the force would be disbanded as soon as the territory became settled with people who had respect for more traditional institutions.

Within a short period of time the force was expanded to 300 men. They covered the vast area on horseback or dog team and wore the now famous red tunics. By 1883 the force numbered 500 men and had been given the duty of maintaining peace during the construction of the Canadian Pacific Railway. They also established close relations with the natives and negotiated land settlements and peace treaties. After the 1885 *Métis* uprising the NWMP was increased again, to 1,000 men.

When the full-scale gold rush began on the Klondike in 1898 the potential for violence was quite formidable. The NWMP saw to it that the gold rush was an orderly affair. At this time they were also used to maintain Canadian sovereignty over the Yukon against American expansionist ideas.

One Superintendent Samuel B Steele called Skagway 'a little better than hell on earth'. In early 1897 Steele posted several Maxim guns to keep law and order at the top of Chilcoot and White Passes. In response the US Army sent in a detachment of 200 soldiers to Skagway and demanded the NWMP withdraw from the summits of the passes. Steele refused. In the end Steele and the US Army colonel negotiated an agreement whereby the summits would be recognised as a temporary boundary. He established a customs post to ensure that all the prospectors had a year's supply of provisions before allowing them to cross the frontier into Canada. The sight of a tattered Union Jack and blurred outlines of a NWMP sentry standing over a Maxim gum must have been a formidable sight to all those miners crossing into Canada in search of gold. Two months later the US Army eventually backed off.

Between February and June of 1898 Inspector Robert Belcher collected $174,470.32 in tolls at the customs posts. Often the NWMP were asked to provide change for the pettiest sums but the NWMP were noted for their honesty and fairness to all and were respected for it. Steele by this time was enforcing the law in Dawson. He enforced a 'no open carrying of firearms' policy, regulated the prostitution trade and prosecuted the bootleggers. In the end he was nicknamed the 'lion of the North' and when he left Dawson in 1901 the town lined the shoreline to bid him farewell and presented him with a purse of gold nuggets in appreciation for his service to the town.

After the gold rush the NWMP moved further north and continued to maintain Canada's sovereignty from other European expansionist notions and to stem the reported abuse of the native peoples.

In 1904, King Edward VII awarded the 'Royal' term to their name in recognition for their services to the crown. By 1920 the RNWMP had become the Royal Canadian Mounted Police and was officially expanded into the national police force.

Today the force numbers some 16,000 men and women plus civilian support. Throughout its history it has always emphasised the peaceful settlement of disputes, using guns only as a last resort.

The Dominion of Canada

By 1867 Canada was tiring of British rule and the folks out there were hinting at independence. Britain had lost the rights to America in 1776 when the American Revolution occurred and they didn't want the same to happen with their territories to the north. Canada on the other hand had seen the weaknesses in America's style of federalism that had led to the conflict known as the Civil War and didn't wish to make the same mistake. They decided on a cabinet system of government where residual powers were given to the central government rather than the new provincial governments, where criminal law was made a federal jurisdiction, and where central authority was stressed. There was a determination to construct a strong national state whose essential purpose was to grant regional and minority rights. They wanted to govern themselves with a constitution similar in principle to that of the United Kingdom.

After a lot of discussion Britain's Parliament acted and passed a bill called the British North America Act (1867) giving control of Canada to a central government with limited powers and similarly delegated powers to the provinces. This legislation created the Dominion of Canada. An amendment to the BNA Act in 1871 gave Ottawa the right, after negotiation with the appropriate authorities, to incorporate into Canada the northern half of North America stretching to the North Pole and excluding only Russian Alaska.

Rupert's Land had become known by then as the North West Territories and Canada wanted to strengthen its hold over the north by including that territory within the Dominion. To most people in Canada at the time NWT was a foreign land with very few people, a primitive lifestyle and no law enforcement but Canada was desperate to solidify the Dominion because there was fear at that time of American encroachment. Canada struck a deal with the Hudson Bay Company that allowed Canada to buy back the NWT from them with a loan from the British Government of £300,000.

When the Dominion of Canada was formed in 1867 it consisted of Ontario (West Canada), Quebec (East Canada), Nova Scotia and New Brunswick. Manitoba joined on July 15 1870 and, once the deal was done with the British Government and the Hudson Bay Company, the Northwest Territories followed suit the same year. British Columbia joined on July 20 1871 along with Vancouver Island; Prince Edward Island came on board on July 1 1873. The Klondike Stampede forced Canada to create a new territory within the domain of the Northwest Territories called the Yukon in 1898 in the face of continued expansionist ideas from the Americans. This helped strengthen Canadian sovereignty over the vast wilderness area of the NWT that bordered Alaska. On September 1 1905 both Saskatchewan and Alberta joined. Newfoundland and Labrador entered the 'union' on March 31 1949 and the Northwest Territories was once again divided, with the creation of Nunavut, on April 1 1999.

The BNA Act of 1867 became Canada's 'constitution' with certain amendments until Canada wrote its own Constitution Act in 1982. Time made the union stronger and eventually 'Dominion' was dropped from the title.

The north today and in the future

For all the reasons stated above about the physical conditions of the north, an expansion of the very limited agricultural base does not seem likely. Without a serious and almost immediate climatic change, agriculture will remain a minor concern north of the 60. Because many of the communities are so isolated, the only viable markets are likely to be local ones and these are, at this point in time, very small.

The largest northern development to date has been in the mining industry. Ever since the great gold strike of the Klondike, precious metals, coal and petroleum have been the basis of mineral exploration. Alexander MacKenzie found 'black gold' seeping out of the rocks near Norman Wells back in the 18th century but failed to realise its potential at the time. In such a vast area the mineral wealth has hardly been tapped and holds much for the future. Oil companies are searching the offshore waters of the Beaufort Sea for additional reserves. However, the physical problems are horrendous. The ever-moving polar ice perched on a sea frozen for much of the year rubbing against land-based icefields that are normally stationary runs havoc with drilling rigs, crushing them like matchsticks as both fields thaw and the edges rub together. Solutions, such as creating artificial islands to support the rigs, are in use but the problem of transporting the oil and gas south either by pipeline or by icebreaker remains to be solved.

Mining exploration communities litter the north. Only ghost towns now exist where once great rigs hammered and thumped surrounded by temporary communities to house the workers. All the building supplies had to be brought in, making this some of the most expensive exploration on earth. To create any town in the north calls for huge investment in construction, insulation and services, and permanent settlements occur only where a variety of minerals can be found so that the life expectancy of the community is considered to be long term. Mining alone is unlikely to be the future of the north as many of the communities' existences begin and end with the mine.

Water is one of the great resources of the north, particularly along the Yukon and MacKenzie Valleys. But these are remote regions and, as with mining, the problems of financing schemes and marketing the power will have to be overcome and this isn't likely to be easy. As technology improves, populations won't be needed to run the schemes except during the construction phase so communities will once again be temporary.

Forestry has been a great provider in the past, making a valuable contribution to the north in terms of employment and road building which helps to open up remote areas. But the problems occur when forestry runs up against conservation interests. Will the great resources be replenished? What methods are in place to restrict the pulp industry from polluting an area of almost pristine wilderness? I should think that the forestry-producing industries will want to expand in the future and they will state that they will make a valuable contribution to the north. Sadly, at what cost to the environment?

During the Cold War the north came into its own. A line of early warning radar stations was set up at American expense and with Canadian permission as a defence against supposed Russian attack from across the North Pole. These DEW line stations opened up the north and created permanent settlements and communities that are the mainstay of the extreme northern region today. Now that the Cold War is over, if we expand this 'strategic' industry further into the world of modern communications these small but necessary communities might grow with the ever-expanding communications industry. The world is becoming a smaller place because of the expansions in the communications industry and this in turn should have long-term benefits for the north.

The other service industry that should reap huge benefits for the communities of the north is tourism. Although still in its infancy, the potential for expansion is massive. Transport and tourism go hand in hand. Expand a road or rail network and the flow of tourists will increase. The mining and forestry industries have made advances into the north, increasing the transport potential to market their goods. At the same time they opened the gates to allow better access for tourists. The mining and strategic industries open up an extended air network in the north, also opening up the remotest areas to tourism. It is now possible to fly almost daily to any one of Nunavut's 28 communities. You can drive on an excellent road or series of roads from British Columbia to Inuvik in NWT via Whitehorse and Dawson in the Yukon. At the same time you can head north into Alaska along the AlCan Highway. A road is currently under construction from Fort Simpson, NWT, down the MacKenzie River to Inuvik at its mouth near the Arctic Ocean.

Mass tourism is a long way off, if at all. And it is not what the north needs, as it is unlikely ever to become the basis for a regional economy nor create regional centres. If the people of the north can harness the potential of tourism and develop programmes centred round local natural resources for both winter and extended summer periods, then there will probably be a marked growth in development. At the moment the system is overtaxed in summer and underused in the winter.

The main problems hindering a serious increase in the flow of tourists to the north are:

- The extremes of weather make timetables appear unfeasible for any serious winter tourism.
- The demands and expectations of the travelling public who would be interested in what the north has to offer need to become more flexible.
- The skills necessary for effective tourism at both a management level as well as with on-the-ground staff need to be improved and come in line with current levels in the rest of the world.

The last two can be improved upon. The first is in the lap of the Gods. Tourism is the largest expanding service industry and the north has the potential to reap the rewards. Time and some serious investment will create the demand. The people are already there.

Natural History

For all its apparent bleakness northern Canada is intensely rich in wildlife. A great profusion of mammals, birds, plants and insects occupies the whole region and many species travel the full length of the continent, as in the case of migratory birds. Some insects have been known to migrate, certainly across North America. The Monarch butterfly is a particular case here – it migrates from Mexico all the way north and well into Canada. Other creatures are less far-travelled but are still found across a variety of ecosystems and climate zones.

Whatever your take on natural history, whether you are a keen 'twitcher', a nature photographer or just someone with a broad interest in the natural world, there is something in the north for you to see. This is not meant to be a complete treatise on the natural history of the north, there are people out there far more qualified to talk and write on the subject than I am and there is a large range of already published material on the various aspects of natural history. What I hope to achieve here is to give you a small taste of what can easily be seen and where to look for it. Hopefully, it will help you get all the more out of your wilderness experience.

What follows on from here is by no means a complete list of mammals, birds and other creatures that inhabit the north of Canada. There are checklists in the appendices for those interested, though they are for specific areas. They can be taken as generally usable for different areas where critters in residence have a similar habitat.

I have tried to put together a list of some of the more easily seen, more common, bigger and better known creatures. In general they are the species that I have either had experience with and actually seen, wanted to see or just think they are pretty important to the environment – not that the ones who have been left out are not, but there is only so much space. As I am not a biologist, a scientist or other suitably qualified person able to discuss such things at length, I have only tried to give a fairly general treatment of the species you might either come across by accident when in the wilderness or by intention whilst on an organised tour. The content is my own drawn from actual observations, experiences and information gleaned from the various guides whose opinions I respect. Sometimes what is written here is a personal interpretation of information found in reference books and seen through the eyes of a photographer.

A little knowledge of what you are looking at makes the animal or bird or whatever far more interesting than no knowledge at all. With tourism in its infancy in the north many of the guides lack any serious in-depth knowledge of their animals, or they do not know what tale to tell or how to tell it to the benefit of clients. This is no bad reflection on the guides as that situation will change with time and I hope that everyone reading this will, for the time being, be gracious and accept this temporary lack of serious educational information. Great hunters do not necessarily make informative wildlife experts without the need of some extra tuition.

I had to draw a line somewhere between deciding which animals could be classified the big, middle or little creatures of northern Canada. My categorisation may not agree with everyone else's but I have worked it like this: the big animals are the ones that are easy to see; the smallish ones are easy to see but require more observational expertise. The little critters are just plain hard work because they are so small and tend to be heard but not seen because they live in the undergrowth, up trees or wherever. These guys take time, skill, and acute observation and, above all, they require far more patience to see than the bigger animals do. Fortunately, the outcome, I feel, is just as rewarding.

LARGE LAND MAMMALS
Muskoxen

Muskoxen (*Ovibos moschatus*; order *Artiodactyla*; family *Bovidae*) or *Umingmak* ('the bearded one' in Inuktitut) came to North America about 90,000 years ago when the Bering Straits were actually a land bridge between Siberia and North America. When the glaciers of the last Ice Age covered North America, muskoxen retreated to ice-free islands in the northern Arctic. These islands were known as 'glacial refugia' and extended all the way to Greenland. When the glaciers eventually retreated at the end of the last Ice Age muskoxen returned and spread throughout the north across Canada to Alaska. Today they are mostly found on the Arctic islands of Banks, Ellesmere, Melville, and Victoria. On the mainland they are found in substantial numbers in the area north of the Great Bear Lake up to the Arctic coast; in the Queen Maud Gulf area and in smaller numbers in the Thelon Game Sanctuary and southwest to Artillery Lake. Populations are estimated at 80–90,000 animals in Arctic Canada and the easiest place to see them is at Cambridge Bay on the southern tip of Victoria Island (see page 225). Single animals, usually bulls, and small herds are seen throughout the year only a few kilometres outside the community.

These delightful animals are gregarious by nature, living in loosely attached groups and small herds controlled by a dominant bull or cow. Herd sizes vary with the time of year, the weather, food resources and the threat of predators. Sometimes, usually in the summer, bulls may be found wandering around singly or in pairs. The well-known muskoxen wall is the animal's reaction to a threat to the herd. The dominant bull stands at the front in the centre of the herd with the cows closing ranks behind and surrounding the calves. This characteristic defensive formation presents a line of horns toward the foe and, in a well-organised herd, is extremely effective. Wolves in particular will attack any animal that charges out from the protection of this defensive wall.

Animals found alone, or those that become separated from the herd, are prone to attack if they encounter wolves. A full-grown muskox can easily defend itself for some time against wolf attack, but wolves have a lot more stamina and will worry the animal with intermittent attacks until the muskox tires. If it fails to elude its attackers it will eventually fall prey to the wolf's persistence.

Although they are about the size of our average domestic cattle their thick woolly coat makes them look much larger. An underlay of extremely fine, short hair provides the muskox with its exceptional protection against the extreme weather that the north has on offer. Calves are usually born in April after an eight-month gestation period. Bulls stand at about 1.5m and weigh on average 340kg; cows are about a third smaller. The horns on bulls usually reach 60cm but the largest found were on a bull near the Perry River area. They measured 80cm tip to tip.

These animals are regularly hunted and have a wariness of humans and can be dangerous if approached too closely, especially during the 'rut' or mating season during August and September. Yet, on hot summer days you may find that they prefer to remain sedentary for most of the day, just grazing on the lush summer vegetation. Their unique coats tend to make the animals overheat with too much physical exertion and they can often be approached quite closely.

Main natural predators are wolves although polar bears and barren-ground grizzlies would not be opposed to taking a calf.

Dall's sheep and Stone's sheep

Anyone trekking in Kluane National Park in the Yukon should be treated to a sighting of Dall's sheep on any of the mountain slopes. Their white coats stand out spectacularly against the summer browns and greens of their alpine habitat. The rams have large curled horns making them a delight to any photographer.

American mountain sheep are either classified as bighorn (*Ovis canadensis*) or thinhorn (*Ovis dalli*; order *Artiodactyla*; family *Bovidae*) and among thinhorn sheep there are two sub-species – Dall's sheep (*O. dalli dalli*) and Stone's sheep (*O. dalli stonei*).

Dall's sheep are found in Alaska, the Yukon, western Northwest Territories and the extreme north-west of British Columbia. In the Northwest Territories they are found in the MacKenzie Mountains west of the MacKenzie River and in the Richardson Mountains west of the Peel River and the MacKenzie Delta. Dall's sheep are ideally suited to the cold with a coat of fine hairs under an overcoat of hollow hairs that provide excellent insulation against the ravages of their alpine habitat. Their hooves have a soft pliable centre surrounded by a hard rim giving them a solid grip on rocks and making them agile and graceful climbers in their rugged mountain habitat.

Natural predators include wolves, grizzly and black bears, wolverine and golden eagles. Their diet consists mainly of grasses and sedges with flowers and the leaves and stems of some scrubs in summer and mosses and lichens in winter. Being typical sheep they need to rest between feeding to ruminate or chew their cud. Minerals from mineral licks are an essential part of their diet. Hunting of Dall's sheep is permitted, mainly for trophy animals, but the numbers involved are small. The MacKenzie Mountains population is estimated at 15–20,000 animals. In the Yukon there are an estimated 19,000 Dall's sheep, mainly in Kluane NP.

Stone's sheep are found only in the most southern mountainous areas of the Yukon and into northern BC. They are slightly smaller and more greyish, rather than pure white, in colour. For the most part the untrained eye will not be able to differentiate between the two species.

Bison

Bison (order *Artiodactyla*; family *Bovidae*) are the largest terrestrial mammals in North America. There are two sub-species but it is the forest dweller that belongs in this part of the world and he is the wood bison (*Bison bison athabascae*). Slightly taller but less stocky than his cousin the Plains or American bison (*Bison bison bison*) the wood bison stands about 1.8m at the shoulder and bulls may weigh as much as 1,000kg. Cows are a little more than half the weight of bulls. The main differences between the two sub-species are a more pronounced hump and less hair on the head and throat of the wood bison. A woolly undercoat overlaid by longer guard hair makes them resilient in cold climates but summer insects aggravate all bison. They have sensitive eyes, nostrils and almost hairless flanks and they are plagued throughout the summer by hordes of mosquitoes, black flies and 'bull dog' horseflies. I came across an old bull in MacKenzie Bison Sanctuary who was driven to distraction by the insects and was forced to seek relief on the breezy main road between Yellowknife and Fort Providence – a dangerous place for him to be. True relief would only come with darkness.

Bison have a keen sense of smell but poor eyesight though they can see movement up to a kilometre away. Sitting quietly and very still at the edge of the forest I have had bulls walk right past me without knowing I was there.

Three things affect bison populations – disease, predators and, oddly, drowning. The diseases are those of cattle – brucellosis, tuberculosis and anthrax. Anthrax occurs naturally but the other two were introduced by transplanted plains bison in the mid-1920s. Wolves are the major predators taking calves and sick or injured adults and occasionally healthy adults if the situation arises. Drowning is unusual because bison are good swimmers but they get caught out by freak flooding or by falling through weak spring ice on the lakes. Although wood bison are on the endangered list there is some hunting allowed, but the quota is strictly regulated with none of the animal being wasted. Oddly, the best place to see wood bison is along the road between Rae-Edzo and Fort Providence as you pass through the 10,000km² MacKenzie Bison Sanctuary. Here there is a stable population of about 2,000 animals who regularly wander along the open stretches at the side of the road. I should think that the breeze here gives the animals some relief from the annoying insects.

CANADA'S REINDEER

Just out of interest, there are reindeer herds in Canada. They were introduced from Siberia into Alaska between 1891 and 1902 and herds now found in NWT are from this stock. Reindeer differ from caribou by having shorter legs, a broader back and a slightly different gait. Reindeer calve earlier, rut earlier and there is evidence that they are more fertile than caribou (twinning, although rare in caribou, is not uncommon in reindeer).

Caribou

There are four distinct sub-species of caribou (order *Artiodactyla*; family *Cernidae*) in Canada. Their importance to the welfare of the native peoples gets a fuller treatment in Chapter 3 (see page 70). Suffice to say here that the survival of Canada's native peoples is a direct result of the abundance of caribou throughout the land; in all the caribou hunts I have been on, nothing – and I mean nothing – is wasted.

Caribou are related to the reindeer of Europe and the four sub-species in northern Canada have overlapping but relatively distinct ranges. The barren-ground caribou (*Rangifer tarandus groenlandicus*) has a range that extends from the taiga forests and tundra of the mainland Northwest Territories across to Southampton, Coats and Baffin Islands. Grant's caribou (*Rangifer tarandus granti*) are found mainly in Alaska and the Yukon Territory with some members of the Porcupine herd wintering in the northwest corner of the Northwest Territories. Peary caribou (*Rangifer tarandus pearyi*) range throughout the Arctic archipelago and the woodland caribou (*Rangifer tarandus caribou*) are found throughout the boreal forests of the MacKenzie Valley and the forests and alpine tundra of the MacKenzie Mountains.

A herd's individual name is usually related to the location of its calving grounds. For example the Bluenose herd calves around the Bluenose Lake some 200km north west of Coppermine in the Northwest Territories and the Qamanirjuaq herd gives birth near Lake Kaminuriak west of Rankin Inlet. The four major herds are Bluenose, Bathurst, Beverly and Qamanirjuaq, with other distinct populations known as the Northeastern Mainland, Boothia Peninsular, North Baffin, South Baffin, Northeast Baffin, Southampton Island and Coats Island herds.

The caribou has lots of different names, from *tuktuk* given by the Inuit to *ekwe* by the Slavey First Nations. Adult males stand a little over a metre tall and weigh about 140kg, but lose about a third of this weight during the mating season. Size varies between sub-species with the woodland caribou the largest whilst the Peary caribou are the smallest. The exceptional warmth of a caribou's coat is down to the individual hairs of the coat being hollow. The air cells in the hairs act as an insulator, trapping body heat. Caribou also have the largest antlers in relation to their body size of any deer species and, like all deer, these are shed and regrown each year.

ANNUAL CARIBOU ACTIVITY CHART

March and April	Caribou cows begin to migrate north to calving grounds. Herds sometimes migrate 700km. Bulls follow slowly.
June	Calves are born usually within the first two weeks.
July	Herds congregate to reduce annoyance from insects and begin migration south again. Numbers may exceed 10,000 animals.
August and September	Herds disperse as food becomes abundant and insects less annoying. Migration continues south.
October	Rut begins. Lasts for several weeks. Winter arrives in the north. Migration arrives in winter feeding grounds near the treeline.
November to March	Herds spend their time in the southern winter feeding grounds. Diet is mainly sedges, lichens and evergreen leaves where the snowfall is the lightest.

For many years the government and the hunters have blamed the wolf for any reduction in the caribou herd populations. They have systematically tried to decimate wolf populations throughout the north and, by so doing, remove one of the natural predators from the ecosystem and the food chain. It is only natural that the premier predator in the north would prey on the most abundant animal resource within its territory, ie: the caribou. Yet wolves also eat mice, lemmings and squirrels. This is most obvious during the denning period when these smaller mammals are more abundant in the immediate vicinity of the area where the pups are born. Similarly, at this time of the year the caribou have headed north to their calving grounds mainly to avoid wolf predation on their young calves. It is a common process seen throughout the natural world; it allows the re-establishment of predator and prey populations, thus maintaining a healthy environment all round.

Bears, being opportunistic feeders, will also take caribou but those taken are usually frail and/or injured animals, or calves separated from the herd. Caribou, when migrating, can manage up to 65km a day at a steady walking pace of about 7km/hr. They are excellent swimmers with their hollow hairs providing excellent flotation.

The chart above gives an idea of the caribou's annual cycle as they migrate to and fro throughout their territory.

Moose

Moose (*Alces alces*; order *Artiodactyla*; family *Cervidae*) are the largest members of the deer family. Males stand about 2m high and weigh as much as 850kg. Cows are the same height but weigh considerably less. The body is bulky with a disproportionately large head in both sexes. Long legs allow the animal to wade through deep snow, dense ground cover and fallen trees. Moose have a distinctive palmate or 'open hand' antler and, as with all deer, these are found on the males only. Unlike most deer, however, moose prefer a solitary life, only getting together to mate or sometimes as a survival measure against extremes in the weather.

Moose are unpredictable because, although they have excellent hearing and smell, they have poor eyesight. When threatened, they retreat into the woods until the danger passes by. If the threat continues they will blindly crash through the woods in an effort to escape. Thick hides and warm coats with two layers of fur insulate them against the cold.

During the rut between late September and early October bulls become more unpredictable. Both sexes call to each other. Females are sexually mature at 18 months of age and although males mature at about 2½ years there is usually a dominant male order so bulls rarely breed before they are 5 or 6 years old. Cows seek seclusion to give birth, usually lying down and, unlike other deer species, calves are helpless for several days after birth and are kept isolated and guarded during that time. Moose calves grow quickly because of the high fat content of their mother's milk so that in their second month they gain a kilogram or more in weight each day.

Timber wolves are the moose's most serious predator but in thriving populations wolves act more as herd cleansers, taking the old or diseased animals and the weakened or undefended calves. Any adult moose can easily handle a lone wolf and it usually needs a considerable pack to pull down and kill a large moose. Moose are a frequent target for hunters. A licence is required.

American elk

Your chances of seeing elk are very slim but, having said that, you are just as likely to see one crossing the road as you drive around the north as you are in the wilds. Elk, who are also known as wapiti, were once common throughout North America but are now confined to the Rocky Mountains and forests of northern Canada. They are more readily found within the bounds of the national parks.

The elk (*Cervus canadensis*; order *Artiodactyla*; family *Cervidae*) is the second largest living deer in North America, only out-sized by its cousin the moose. Males stand at about 1.5m tall and weigh anywhere between 250kg and 500kg (average 295kg). The males have very large antlers (up to 1.2m across) making them a prize trophy for hunters. This large animal provided the First Nations peoples with a large supply of meat and, amongst other uses, they also used the hides to cover their boats.

Elk congregate in large bands in the winter but disperse into small herds in the summer. Bulls compete for the right to have a harem and the rut begins in

August. Fawns are usually born in May or early June after a 249–265 day gestation period. Twins are rare.

Main predators are, in order of the number of elk taken, man, wolves, mountain lions and grizzly bears. The natural predators take mainly calves and, oddly, prime bulls. It seems that the bulls get so weak through lack of eating when claiming females for their harems during the rut that they become easy prey during the winter when food is scarce. Females may live to 24 years in the wild but males rarely attain the age of 14 owing either to starvation or predation by wolves who seem to kill most bulls at their absolute prime – about seven or eight years. Fawns are weaned by four months but predators will have taken one third of those born in any year by this time. Another third will be lost to starvation by the following spring. Sexual maturity comes at 16 months for both sexes but females do not usually breed until their third year and bulls are not strong enough to take a harem until they are five or six.

Bears
Bear behaviour and habits etc are covered under *Bears: General safety* (see page 124) so they get limited treatment here. Bears are from the order *Carnivora*, family *Ursidae*. Four species are found in the north. The **black bear** (*Ursus americanus*) is common throughout all of forested North America. There are four distinct populations of **grizzly bear** (*Ursus arctos horribilis*) in northern Canada, based on the ecosystems that they live in. The four classifications are Arctic coastal grizzlies; Arctic mountain grizzlies; northern interior grizzlies and barren-ground grizzlies. Habits vary slightly and are a product of their individual ecosystems. These bears generally prefer open country to thick forest. Some colour variations may occur but they all have a distinct back hump and upturned snout and older animals have a silver tip to their fur giving them a grizzled effect. The Kodiak or coastal **brown bear** (*Ursus arctos middendorffi*) is a sub-species of the grizzly bear and is found only in Alaska on its islands and along the south coast. The **polar bear** (*Ursus maritimus*) is the largest land predator on earth. Polar bears are serious carnivores and not omnivorous, as the other bears found in North America are. This is a product of their environment, there being little else for a polar bear to eat but meat. Polar bears, followed closely by grizzlies, are the most popular land mammals sought after by wildlife enthusiasts to view in their natural environment next to whales of any species. Bears have no natural predators other than man and themselves.

SMALL LAND MAMMALS
The wild dogs
The various types of wild dog treated here are from the order *Carnivora*, family *Canidae*.

Wolves
All domestic dogs have probably stemmed at one time or another from wolves. Wolves are found only in the northern hemisphere and have at one

HOW WOLVES WERE CREATED

In the beginning of time there was only a man and a woman on earth. When they asked Nuliayuk, the great female sea spirit who created everything, what they should do for their needs, she reached into a huge hole and pulled out the caribou. The caribou supplied all the Inuit needs but eventually they killed off all the best animals leaving only the sick and weak ones behind. These animals bred and created inferior animals that were no good to the people at all. So they went back to Nuliayuk who created everything and asked what to do to solve the problem. She gave them the wolf. His job was to get rid of the unhealthy animals so the caribou would grow strong again.

time or another inhabited every type of ecosystem but tropical forests and true arid deserts. Their range, although once extensive, is now primarily limited to Alaska and Canada in North America with small pockets in Mexico, Minnesota, and the US Rockies (mainly within the bounds of national parks) and isolated pockets in central and southern Europe, Scandinavia, the Balkans, and Russia. There are only two species in existence – the grey or timber wolf (*Canis lupus*) and the red wolf (*Canis rufus*) of south central United States.

In Canada a wolf pelt is worth about $300 or $350. It is probably the best fur for the trim on a parka hood, as warm breath falling on it does not turn to ice as it does on synthetic materials. Sadly, I have found that wolves are often shot for the sake of shooting, rather than for the money the pelts bring. I have heard that northerners think of wolves as useless animals and will shoot a wolf on sight. Many will go out of their way to shoot them. Wolf hatred is endemic and much of it is based on hearsay, legend and fear. Little is based on pure scientific fact.

In bygone years the government blamed the wolf for the reduction in the caribou herds – and one would expect that the premier predator in the north would prey on the most abundant animal resource within its territory. This is only partly true. Wolves also eat mice, lemmings and squirrels during the denning period when these smaller mammals are more abundant in the immediate vicinity of the den than their usual prey, the caribou, who have headed north to their calving grounds particularly to avoid wolf predation on their young calves. It is a common process seen throughout the natural world that allows the re-establishment of predator and prey populations thus maintaining a healthy environment all round.

If the Inuit tale above is even close to the truth then I find that the systematic decimation of wolf populations throughout the north and, subsequently, removing one of the natural predators from the ecosystem and the food chain a very poor state of affairs. The excuse is always money but superstition, primordial fear and just plain ignorance all contribute to these executions.

The current policy of the various Departments of Renewable Resources is that there will be no wolf control whilst the bison, moose and caribou populations are not threatened by wolf predation. The problem is that the government wants to maintain the prey animal populations for human consumption and you cannot have some wolf interfering with that. Controls currently on hunting restrict taking a wolf to wintertime when the animals are not denning and the pelt is in its prime condition. The only figures I have are a little dated but indicate that the Northwest Territories (when NWT and Nunavut were still combined) harvested 600–800 wolves annually, mainly for their hides or to use the fur for home-made winter clothing like parkas and mittens.

Wolves are fairly resilient creatures, though, and can survive the pressures of hunting and trapping, providing they have plenty of prey available. At the moment the caribou and other game animal populations are fairly stable but should that change for the worse then the immediate response will be a cull of the wolf packs. The outcome will be detrimental to the whole ecosystem with man trying to influence nature for his own ends. There is a lot of wolf research happening at the moment and the management of the wolf populations is closely linked with the management of the game animal populations. I am thankful that the wolf is such a strong survivalist.

I hope I might be forgiven for my stern words here for, in all my visits to the north, I have never been blessed with a wolf sighting, never mind getting a photograph of the animal. When I was on the Dempster Highway north of Dawson City in the Yukon, beleaguered by a flat tyre, a chap heading south stopped and said he had seen a wolf that day when he had a similar demise. He said it just stood there in the middle of the road watching him replace his tyre and then just trotted off across the tundra. I could sense the huge joy this guy got in just seeing a wolf and I am sure a wolf sighting would be the highlight of any wildlife experience in Canada. One day I will get lucky and get my audience with a wolf.

I have a friend, Chuck Hume, who is an elder in the Champagne Aishihik clan of First Nations in the Yukon. We were sitting outside his cabin at Klukshu near Haines Junction a couple of years ago enjoying a beer or two after a trek up to Gopher Mountain near Kluane National Park. A bear passed by chasing a salmon in the stream outside his front door and Chuck spoke to it. When I asked him what he said to the bear he replied, shrugging his shoulders,

> 'Oh! nothing important. I always speak to bears and wolves when they pass by my cabins. My people think it's bad luck to talk behind a bear's back or speak ill of it, so I do it because it's good manners.'

After another sip he said,

> 'But it's only the wolves that answer me back.'

Although wolves will feed on hares, foxes, beaver, deer, small rodents, muskrat, birds, fish, eggs and small quantities of vegetation depending on the time of year, area of their range and availability, the main prey of all the groups is the larger game – bison, moose and particularly caribou. There is only one species of wolf in northern Canada but there are three distinct groups and they can each be distinguished by their behaviour and distribution.

Animals in the first group are known as **Arctic wolves**. These animals live on the Arctic islands and their primary prey is caribou, muskoxen and arctic hares. They generally have whitish fur to blend in better with their surroundings. **Tundra** or **caribou wolves** are the wolves that travel above and below the treeline on the mainland of Northwest Territories and Nunavut. They den near the treeline but do not maintain specific territories because their main prey, barren-ground caribou, has a migratory disposition and there is no point in defending a territory that does not have an adequate year-round supply of prey. The last wolf group are the **timber wolves**. These wolves are found below the treeline and in the mountains of NWT, the Yukon and Alaska. Their prey is mainly the non-migratory species like bison and moose. These wolves usually have a strict territory and its size will depend on the size of the pack, density of prey animals and time of the year (winter ranges are usually larger because of greater prey dispersal). Just as an example here the Alaskan winter range for a breeding pair of wolves would be 100km^2 yet a pack of ten would require a range of 12,000km^2 in the same environment. Timber wolves' fur, though usually grey, may be brown, reddish brown or even black.

Wolves are intelligent, social animals who usually live within a social pack environment consisting of an alpha (breeding, dominant) pair and their offspring of various ages. Packs actively defend their territories and move and hunt mostly at night.

A particular behaviour of wolves that everyone recognises is their howling. It seems to be a means whereby one animal communicates with another, perhaps calling for a lost pup or just gathering a pack together for a hunt. Some people, though, think that maybe wolves just enjoy howling. Researchers have attested to this saying that they have seen wolves obviously enjoy a good howling session with one wolf beginning the proceedings and the others following suit at a slightly different pitch. This produces the wild harmony that is so familiar to us all.

Wolves mate in late March and the pups arrive about 63 days later. Pups are born in an underground den dug out by the female. Where there is permafrost dens are in rock caves, sandy riverbanks or eskers. (Eskers are long, linear ridges of glacial-deposited rock material that are prominent topographical features on the tundra and may vary in shape and be up to 30km in length.) Wolves reach breeding age at about two and adults who become sexually mature will often split from their natal pack to form their own.

Foxes

Two species occur in the north with slightly overlapping ranges. The **Arctic fox** (*Alopex lagopus*) is the smaller of the two and is found only on the Arctic tundra but is circumpolar in that respect inhabiting North America, Asia,

Europe and Greenland. They inhabit both inland and coastal terrain and they are the only canid that changes the colour of its coat in summer. Arctic foxes live primarily on lemmings but will hunt arctic hares, squirrels (in summer), and ptarmigan. They also take carrion, following wolves to obtain scraps or polar bears for their seal leftovers.

Cubs are usually born in May or June and litters are on average six puppies. Both parents raise the young. They go their own way at about four months old. They have no natural predators but are wary of wolves and polar bears.

The **red fox** (*Vulpes vulpes*) is the most widely distributed carnivore on the planet occurring across most of North America, Europe and Asia. Its range in Canada extends to the Arctic islands and this is where its range overlaps that of the Arctic fox. Red foxes are omnivorous but prey mainly on mice. During the summer their diet will include vegetation, insects, birds' eggs and berries. They will also scavenge for carrion as well as garbage. Such dietary versatility is why the red fox has such a wide distribution. Reproduction is similar to the Arctic fox and both animals live about four years.

Coyote
One other species of the dog family found in North America and quite common is the coyote (*Canis latrans*). Larger than a fox but smaller than the wolf the coyote is frequently seen around towns, picnic grounds and campsites being less wary of man. A coyote will often turn up for a handout. The coyotes' diet is mainly meadow voles in the summer and wolf carrion in the winter although, when hunting in packs, they are quite capable of bringing down an elk, sheep or deer struggling in the deep snow. The species often mates for life with pups being born in late April or May after a gestation of 60 days. They are fully-grown at a year old and have attained the ripe old age of 18 years in captivity. They will breed with domestic dogs and wolves. The coyote is an extremely adaptable animal and, although heavily hunted across North America, their numbers seem to be on the increase.

The wild cats
Three species of wild cats (order *Carnivora*; family *Felidae*) are found in the north.

Cougar
The biggest cat is the cougar (*Felis concolor*) and sightings of these animals in northern Canada are an extremely rare occurrence. They have been seen in the MacKenzie Mountains in NWT and the mammal list for Kluane NP in the Yukon acknowledges the cougar, but this is not the traditional range of the animal. Sightings are more common in the Canadian Rockies of Alberta and British Columbia. The cougar is often called the mountain lion or, more correctly, puma. It is found right across the Americas but is strictly a wilderness animal.

Wary of man and solitary except when breeding they have vast territories of up to 200km² or more, depending on the time of year. Male territories usually overlap the territories of three females. Males weigh about 70kg with females about 30% smaller. Their main prey is mule deer but they will also take white-tailed deer and elk. Males have a taste for moose calves and yearlings. Domestic livestock rarely form part of a cougar's diet as their wariness of man keeps them away from areas where these animals are found. Females come on heat at anytime but usually breed in Canada between March and June. The male leaves after mating and gestation takes 90 days with litters averaging two kittens. They stay with their mother until about 15 months old when they set off and find their own territory. Adults are sexually mature at about 30 months. Hunting of cougars was prevalent in North America until the 1960s, but they are now protected in most places.

Lynx and bobcat

I have put these two animals together solely because they are so visibly similar that unless you see either of them up close or standing side by side you will have difficulty distinguishing which species you are seeing. Bobcats (also known as wildcats) are less common than lynx in northern Canada, though they can cope with open spaces and the presence of man much better than the lynx.

Lynx (*Felis lynx* or *Felis canadensis*) are like cougar – quiet, elusive and, above all, solitary by nature. Lynx are completely intolerant of human activity, avoiding settled places and even highways, yet sometimes you get lucky. I was fortunate enough to glimpse a pair at the edge of Dezadeash Lake in the Yukon when Chuck Hume and I were fishing for lunch one summer's day. They emerged out of the light forest at the lake's edge oblivious to our presence on the lake. They frolicked at the water's edge for only a few seconds before one of them spotted us and then they vanished instantly. When Chuck and I arrived at the spot where they were there was no sign that they had even been there.

What distinguishes the lynx from the **bobcat** (*Felis rufa*) are the ear tufts, which are longer in the lynx and far more pronounced. A lynx has a greyish coat whereas the bobcat is tawnier and more spotted and the tail of the lynx is shorter. Lynx are the larger of the two species by about a kilogram in weight and 7–10cm in length. They hunt the same territory and similar prey. The lynx is ideally suited to the northern environment with thicker fur, long legs and broad, well-furred paws allowing it to hunt its preferred prey – the snowshoe hare. They are found below the treeline in the boreal forests of NWT and the Yukon. Territories vary between 12km² and 25km², although a shortage of prey will extend these limits. When hares are scarce, lynx will eat voles, mice, squirrels, grouse and ptarmigan. Breeding season is mid-March to early April and gestation lasts about nine weeks producing a litter of two to five kittens. The kittens stay with their mother for their first ten months then find home ranges of their own. Lynx live about five years in the wild with starvation the biggest killer. The population of lynx is linked directly to the fluctuations in the population cycle of snowshoe hares.

OTHER SMALLISH MAMMALS
Wolverine

I caught sight of a wolverine once during the Yukon Quest International Dog Sled Race. It had been during a break between the mushers departing Whitehorse and arriving in Dawson for the layover. Chuck Hume and I had been out for a couple of days checking his cabins on snowmobiles. It had been a good excursion and we had seen otter, mink, fox and moose by the time we were heading home. The wolverine looked like a big fluffy black ball of fur leaping and bounding up the mountainside above the river we were following. I originally thought it was a bear but, as Chuck pointed out, its gait put that idea in its place – bears do not leap and bounce through the snow.

Wolverines (*Gulo gulo* or, sometimes, *G. luscus*; order *Carnivora*; family *Mustelidae*) are superb hunters with teeth resembling those of an African hyena for strength and bone-crunching power. They inhabit sub-alpine and alpine zones in any habitat anywhere in North America, Scandinavia and Europe. Their main diet in Canada is made up of marmots, beavers, porcupines, muskrats and carrion but in Europe they have been known to kill reindeer.

Very little is known about these amazing little animals because of their solitary nature and the extent of their home ranges. Young are born sometime in the spring and stay with mum for their first year. One male will tend to several females on overlapping territories but has nothing to do with raising the cubs. Sexual maturity for females is about 15 months and 2–3 years for males. To the best of my knowledge no one is sure as to what age they live.

They have only one predator – man. A wolverine's pelt is highly sought after for its magnificent fur. Chuck says it is the best fur of any of the forest animals. Wolverines are related to weasels, stoats, ferrets, otters, minks and raccoons. Constantly on the move, wolverines have territories as large as 1000km^2 or more. They are known to the native peoples as the 'skunk-bear' because of the musk they deposit on everything they touch. They have no fear of man, although they are wary of us, and frequently ransack cabins in their endless search for food – if they can get in. Their Latin name *gulo gulo* means 'glutton glutton' and that's enough said about their eating habits.

Otters

Only one species of otter (order *Carnivora*; family *Mustelidae*) is found within the realms of this book. The **river otter** (*Lutra canadensis*) is found throughout the forested north where there are rivers, streams, lakes and ponds. Their diet is mainly fish but they will eat clams, muskrats, small rodents, amphibians, and insects. Sometimes they will take very young or enfeebled beavers. Otters love sliding and I have seen them regularly sliding along the snow-covered banks of streams in winter. They race across the snow for several paces then flop onto their bellies and slide perhaps 6–8m to their obvious delight – and mine.

Otters are technically busy breeders; right after one batch is born they start another. Fortunately otters only have a single annual litter. This is due to delayed implantation of the embryos in the womb meaning a gestation period of maybe a year. Litters are usually small consisting of 2–3 youngsters and mum kicks dad out while she weans the kids. Otters stay together for a long time and families are usually close. Sexual maturity in females is reached at about two years but males have to wait until they are six or seven.

Beaver

This little fella (*Castor canadensis*; order *Rodentia*; family *Castoridae*) is the largest rodent in North America weighing up to 20kg. Active all year round, you will see him in the summer in lakes and ponds of his own making, usually in the late afternoon and early morning as he is mainly a nocturnal animal. In winter, with ponds frozen over and lodges buried under heavy snowdrifts, the beaver remains out of sight. Just like the ones depicted in the cartoons beavers chop down trees with their teeth. They are bark-eaters and their particular favourites are willow, birch, balsam poplar, cottonwood and aspen. They also eat seeds of some water plants, leaves and twigs as a last resort if they get hungry. Beavers need about half a hectare of aspens to support them for a year and they can bring down a tree 25cm in diameter in just a few minutes. Lodges are the result of damming streams and are not completed until the pond reaches its maximum size. Meanwhile beavers live in burrows along the stream's banks. Beavers are slow and awkward on the ground but extremely agile in water. The ponds provide them with a medium which they use to reach their feeding grounds while remaining safe from predators.

Someone once aptly described a beaver's lodge as akin to a castle complete with moat. When the food supply dwindles the beaver and his family move on. They are known to destroy the lodge and breach the dam in certain areas before doing so, returning the stream to its natural state and restoring the balance within the ecosystem. Natural predators are grizzly bears, wolverines, wolves, coyotes and lynx and otters will sometimes prey on the young. Beavers breed in January and February and gestation is 3½ months. There is one litter of kits born each year, which usually numbers four but can be as many as eight. The young leave their parents in their second spring when they are a little over a year old and go on to live about 12 years in the wild.

Muskrat

Although only about half the size of a beaver the muskrat (*Ondatra zibethicus*; order *Rodentia*; family *Muridae*, sub-family *Cricetinae*) is often mistaken for one because, to the inexperienced eye, it looks similar at a distance. The muskrat is really a water vole with a rat-like tail whereas a beaver has a large flat tail. It swims by whipping its tail back and forth churning up the water. A beaver's tail lies flat when swimming, leaving a smooth wake. Capable of remaining submerged for up to 15 minutes, the muskrat eats cattails (or bullrushes), tubers, sedges, freshwater clams, frogs and salamanders. Like beavers, muskrats build lodges but they do not build dams. They do not store food in the winter like beavers and they do not hibernate either. Their main predators are otters, mink and any wild dog species. Muskrats breed in the spring with a litter of 3–7 young born after a 25–30 day gestation period. Lifespan is about three years in the wild for those that make it to adulthood. Sexual maturity is reached at about 12 months

THE LITTLE CRITTERS

There are several species from this family in the north. Wolverines have already been discussed because they are a little too big to be classified as little critters, and otters, beavers and muskrats all live in water so I have kept them together for ease, disregarding their sizes, because they share the same habitat. Confused – you'll sort it out!

Of all the little fellas you may see the **marten** (*Martes americana*) is the most common in forested areas. Sometimes known as the pine marten or American marten, to the fur industry he is also known as a sable. He is around all year in montane and the lower subalpine forests. About the size of a house cat, he feeds on red-backed voles, deer mice and snowshoe hares throughout the year, birds' eggs and insects in summer, berries late in the summer, and opportunistically birds, squirrels, shrews and carrion. Diet varies with prey population cycles but these energetic little fellas need about three voles a day to remain healthy. Their home ranges vary from 1.5km² to about 15km² depending on whether the animal is male or female. Ranges overlap with the opposite sex but martens do not share territory with adults of the same sex.

Although good climbers they hunt mostly on the ground. Martens are unable to store fat so they must hunt throughout the winter. To save energy they hunt in the warmest part of the day; catch larger prey that will feed them for several days; avoid hunting in extreme weather conditions and make use of other animal's trails through the snow.

Martens are secretive and wary of humans. They are difficult to see but, as often happens with various animals when you are sitting quietly around a campfire, one may wander into your camp. It will be quite curious as to what this new animal in its territory is and spend a lot of time checking you out. Remaining perfectly still and quiet will get you the full search treatment and I have had them come as close as to sniff my boots. Although populations are strong the marten is one of the popular fur-bearing mammals hunted extensively in the north.

Another common fur-bearing mammal more famous than the marten is the **mink** (*Mustela vison*). This guy is found most along creeks and lake shores and seldom in the forests and mountains. Mink are great fishers and very adept swimmers on a par with the otters. They are only small – about 18cm long – and hunt mainly at night, catching small fish, muskrats, water voles, frogs and other water life. They live in burrows along riverbanks often wrested from beavers or muskrats, which is no mean feat considering how tough these two are.

These little animals breed in the late spring and early winter, with kits, as the young are called, arriving late in April or early May. Litters are usually about five youngsters and they are born blind and deaf. They are weaned within a few days of opening their eyes and follow their mothers around until the autumn. They mature at about a year for females and 18 months for males.

They are easiest to spot in the winter because, like martens, they do not change the colour of their fur to match the white snow.

Now I like the **Arctic ground squirrel** (*Spermophilus parryii*; order *Rodentia*; family *Sciuridae*). The Inuit call them *sik-sik* because the name is like the sound they make when aggravated. Sadly, Inuit children persecute these little guys and they are the brunt of all the jokes on the tundra. They are the only tundra mammals truly to hibernate in the winter. Sik-siks become torpid rather than dormant like bears do. Their heart rate, breathing and metabolism almost stop but somehow they manage to survive in this state without freezing to death. Most small mammals have a high surface-to-volume ratio so they must remain active to survive the Arctic winter. Sik-siks, who live in large busy colonies throughout the Arctic tundra, can store large amounts of body fat built up during the autumn. They also lay in a store of food to tide them over for the first few weeks of spring when they initially wake from their deep winter sleep.

They are very common on the mainland and I am told they can be found on some islands but I have not noticed this. Their diet is mainly berries, plants, leaves, roots and seeds. They will eat meat – males have been known to be cannibalistic and eat young sik-siks. They, in turn, are preyed upon by grizzly bears, wolves, foxes, wolverines, owls, hawks, falcons and eagles though not all at the same time. They are probably the only mammals never to see night-time, resting during the cool late evening hours and are at their most active during the heat of the day.

Sitting anywhere on the tundra you can be assured that one will pop up in front of you, then disappear, only to surface behind you yelling abuse all the time. He will spend as much time checking you out as you will him, only he is the one making all the noise.

There are no true rabbits up north, only hares. The best known and most common is the **snowshoe hare** (*Lepus americanus*; order *Lagomorpha*; family *Leporidae*). Found throughout the wooded areas of the north, this hare moults twice a year. In the summer they are brownish in colour with white belly and in winter they are white all over except for the tips of their ears which are black. Mostly nocturnal, snowshoe hares weigh about 1.5kg and are preyed upon by owls, wolves, foxes, weasels, lynx, martens, mountain lions and coyotes. They are prolific breeders, often with two litters a season, each of 2–4 leverets. Snowshoe hares provide many of the predators with a ready supply of meals, although there are usually more hares than the predators can gobble up in any one season and numbers fluctuate annually with population explosions frequent. The yearly survival rate amongst hares can be anywhere in the range 10–50% and depends on the population cycle and number of predators within a particular area.

SEA MAMMALS
Seals
There are three families of the order *Pinnipedia*; *Phocidae* or true seals, *Otariidae* which includes fur seals and sea lions, and *Odobenidae* or walrus. True seals have hair on both sides of their flippers, no external ears and hind flippers that

cannot rotate forward. There are fives species in the waters of northern Canada. The most common are the ringed seal (*Phoca hispida*), the harp seal (*Phoca groenlandica*) and the bearded seal (*Erignathus barbatus*). Two other species the harbour seal (*Phoca vitulina*) and the hooded seal (*Cystophora cristata*) are not common and you are not likely to see them.

Ringed seals are by far the most common and are found throughout the oceanic waters of the Yukon, Northwest Territories and Nunavut. They are so named because of the circular marking on the backs of the adult animals. This is also the smallest seal in the Arctic. Adults weigh about 70kg with females slightly smaller than males, and cubs weigh about 4.5kg when born. Population estimates indicate about one million live in Canadian waters. Primarily solitary animals, ringed seals sometimes travel in loosely organised groups. Their diet consists mainly of the larger shrimp-like crustaceans, Arctic cod and other small fish and planktonic krill. Seals generally fast during breeding, moulting and basking. They can go for a month without sleep. Most feeding dives last about three minutes, although they can remain submerged for up to 45 minutes and dive to depths of 90m.

One pup is born, usually on stable ice in a den, between mid-March and early April. The female nurses pups for about eight weeks. When the ice breaks up the cub is abandoned. Ringed seals sexually mature at between five and ten years and have been known to live for 43 years. Their main natural predators are polar bears, arctic foxes, wolverines and sharks, although walrus have preyed on them occasionally. Some 26% of pups are killed in their dens and they are the main source of food for polar bears, which kill a seal on average every 6½ days.

When basking on the ice seals will raise their heads every 26–30 seconds for about seven seconds as they check their surroundings. They will heed warnings from other seals and quickly head for the safety of the water through breathing holes in the ice.   '

They are vital to the culture of the coastal Inuit. Ringed seals are a source of heating oil and skins and their meat provides much of the coastal Inuit winter nutrition.

The **bearded seal** is the largest seal found in northern Canadian waters. Adults weigh about 250kg and blubber accounts for almost 40% of their weight. Population numbers about 300,000 animals in Canadian waters. Usually solitary animals, they are permanent dwellers of the Arctic. Their diet consists of bottom-living organisms: worms, crustaceans, crabs, clams and fish such as Arctic cod, flounder and sculpin. Feeding dives as deep as 220m have been recorded. Breeding information is similar to ringed seals but the weaning period is a lot shorter, 12–18 days. Bearded seals are important to the Inuit. The hide is extremely tough and flexible and is used for lines, kayak coverings, traces and *kamik* (boot) soles. The meat is eaten but the liver often contains toxic levels of vitamin A. Bearded seals are found in all Canadian Arctic coastal waters.

Harp seals are so named because of the large horseshoe-shaped patch on the back of adult animals. The pups have a soft, white woolly coat for about the first week or so of life and this was sought after by fur traders. Their diet

HUNTING HARP SEALS

The harp seal is one of Canada's most controversial wildlife species. A commercial hunt used to be conducted in the Gulf of St Lawrence in March before the seals began their migration north. This hunt focused largely on 'whitecoats' of the week-old pups. Emotional campaigns promoted by animal rights groups brought an end to this hunt in the 1980s. These groups claimed that the hunt was inhumane (the methods used were economically sound but barbaric in practice) and that the seals were declining in numbers (harp seals are the most abundant in the world – northwest Atlantic populations are estimated at 1.3 million animals). Following intensive lobbying, what was then the European Economic Community banned the import of harp and hooded seal skins in 1983. Though aimed at stopping the killing of seal pups by Newfoundlanders, it also had a detrimental effect on the already economically disadvantaged Canadian Inuit.

Seal hunting is of paramount importance to the continuation of the Inuit's resource-based way of life. Seals are hunted for food, and their skins provide material for clothing. The sale of sealskins prior to the EEC ban netted the Inuit communities of Canada about $500,000 annually. Today this figure is below $30,000 and alternative employment for these hunters is either limited or non-existent.

Canada's Seal Protection Regulations currently allow unrestricted harvesting of seals by the Inuit and limit non-native Canadians to hunting seals for domestic use only. Sealing is part of the Inuit heritage. Sustainable utilisation is compatible with an ecologically conscious world.

consists mainly of marine fish like Arctic cod and crustacean macroplankton. Main predators are polar bears, orcas, sharks and man. Pups are born between late February and early March, mainly in the area of the Gulf of St Lawrence. Mothers abandon the pups after about two weeks of feeding on rich butterfat milk. Restlessness and hunger force the young seals into the water where they start by feeding on krill.

Walrus

The scientific name of the walrus (*Odobenus rosmarus rosmarus*) (order: *Pinnipedia*; family: *Odobenidae*) comes from the Greek *odous* meaning a tooth and *baini* meaning I step or I walk. Hence they are known as 'toothwalkers'. They have been seen to drag themselves along the ice using their tusks which are actually overdeveloped canine teeth. The **Atlantic walrus** or sea cow is the species seen in Canadian Arctic waters and is also found throughout Canada, Scandinavia and Russia. The second species is the **Pacific walrus** (*Odobenus rosmarus divergens*) which is found in Alaska as well as the eastern coasts of Siberia and the Bering Sea. The word *rosmarus* comes from the *rossmaal* or *rossmar* which is Scandinavian for walrus (the old English name was *horschwael*, meaning 'horse-whale'). In some places, such as Lapland, they are called morse, from *mors* (Lappish) meaning a walrus.

These are the most amazing pinnipeds I have ever seen and certainly one of the most remarkable animals of the north. I have spent many enjoyable hours sitting on haul-outs with walrus though they are very smelly. Take any opportunity you can to see them – you will not be disappointed. The Inuit regard this animal with awe and consider it to have supernatural powers and human attributes so it is well established within their folklore. They are huge animals with males weighing up to 1,400kg and attaining a length of nearly four metres. Females are slightly smaller, weighing just under a tonne. Walrus have a very thick hide and possess a special heat regulation system whereby, when the animal is warm, as when resting on a haul-out, it shunts blood to the outer skin and blubber to allow it to cool off. When immersed in water it draws blood away from the outer body, maintaining heat. In this heated state their eyes are bloodshot and the skin is pale and almost white. But it is the tusks that are the walrus' most amazing physical feature. These are large canine teeth that protrude from the upper jaw and can grow to 60cm in length. The tusks are mainly for show and social interaction between animals and not to dig up clams, their main source of food. They are used for defence, maintaining social order and for displays of aggression between group members. They are often used to create breathing holes in the ice.

Walrus are gregarious creatures and, although they look ungainly on land, can travel quite considerable distances. Unlike seals their front and rear flippers are also developed so that they can actually walk. Hence the ancient Greek name of 'toothwalker'. All seals propel themselves through the water by swimming with their rear flippers and using the front ones as steering arms. A walrus, on the other hand, uses its rear flippers as a rudder and its front flippers like oars, rowing itself along.

Walrus are found in the Arctic waters of eastern Canada, Greenland, Norway and Western Russia. Their traditional range extended as far south as the Gulf of St Lawrence, Cape Breton Island, Sable Island and the southern coast of Nova Scotia to the Bay of Fundy. They were also found in most parts of Hudson Bay and James Bay but by the mid-1800s they were eradicated from south of Labrador and the southern reaches of Hudson Bay. Today you can find them around Coats Island, Southampton Island, Baffin Island, Ellesmere Island and west as far as Prince of Wales Island.

Their diet consists of creatures found along the sea floor of Arctic waters. Their favourite foods are bivalve molluscs – clams and mussels – but they will also eat sea-worms, crabs, squid and snails. The Inuit say that old rogue males sometimes eat seals that they have either killed or found dead.

Sexual maturity is reached at four for females and six for males. The males form loose harems during the breeding season in April and May. Gestation is 376 days with calves born before early May. They stay with their mother for up to three years and depend solely on milk for the first year but are weaned by the end of the second. Their natural enemies are polar bears and orcas. You can always tell when a dead walrus has been taken by a polar bear. There's a small hole where the bear has had to chew through the very tough hide to get at the flesh and soft organs. Bears prefer young animals as they are easier to eat.

I met a film-maker, Adam Ravetch, from the National Geographic Society, off Coats Island one summer in Nunavut. He was completing a new film on walrus and wanted a shot of bear taking a walrus. There was a bear there the day he arrived and it had just killed a young walrus. Adam said he got the sequence of the bear on the kill but missed the actual hunt and, unfortunately, he had not seen a bear since. He had been waiting three weeks when we met.

Adam eventually got his shot. He told me later that, a couple of days after we had first spoken, a bear swam up to the walrus haul-out he was watching and apparently climbed right over all the walrus to get at a young one, getting tusked a few times along the way. He then killed the walrus of his choice and dragged it all the way back across the group, continuing to get tusked, before swimming back to shore to consume the animal. I cannot wait to see the film.

Whales

There are only three species of whale (order *Cetacea*) resident in the Canadian Arctic waters: the beluga (*Delphinapterus leucas*), the narwhal (*Monodon monoceros*) and the bowhead (*Balaena mysticetus*). Killer whales or orcas (*Orcinus orca*) are occasionally seen in the Beaufort Sea, and are rare but regular visitors to the eastern Arctic. Some other species do migrate as far as the southern limits of Davis Strait but that is not within the scope of this book. Both the beluga and the narwhal are toothed whales of the family *Monodontidae* and are closely related and similar in size – smallish by whale standards.

Belugas are also called 'white whales' and the name is derived from the Russian for white and refers to the colouration of their skin. New-borns are, however, brown and juveniles are grey and do not turn white until their fifth year. Belugas can be anything up to five metres in length and weigh as much as 770kg. Females are smaller than males. Belugas are the most common whale in Canadian Arctic waters. Females reach maturity by five, males by eight. Conception occurs in early May and calves are born 12 months later. Lactation lasts about two years and females produce a single calf once every three years. The western side of Hudson Bay is the best place to see belugas, particularly when the ice has melted and the females are searching for warm shallow rivers to give birth. Belugas have no true natural predators other than man, with the odd animal being attacked by a polar bear or orca. Belugas feed on benthic or bottom-dwelling fish and invertebrates.

Belugas were hunted extensively during the whaling period (see *Whalers and Sealers,* page 12) but stocks seem to be recovering in places. Only subsistence hunting by Inuit and Dene First Nations is permitted. There are quota restrictions in some communities. Belugas are migratory having summer and winter ranges.

Narwhal is an old Norse word meaning 'corpse' and it refers to the adult colouration of these mammals. They are white-grey with dark grey blotches. This mottled grey colour is absent in the young narwhals. The tusk for which the animal is famous is really a tooth and is found only in adult males. It is an erupted incisor tooth on the left side of the upper jaw. It has no obvious function though it may be a secondary sexual characteristic. There is evidence that males use the tusk in aggressive encounters with other males, such as disputes over females.

Narwhals reach a length of five metres and the tusk may be as long as three metres. Females are smaller than males, which may weigh as much as 1,200kg. Although having a more restricted distribution than belugas, narwhals are migratory in their habits. They spend winter around Baffin Bay and the northern Davis Strait. In summer they head further north following the break-up of the pack ice. They are rarely found south of the Arctic Circle. A small number do winter in Hudson Bay. Best places to see narwhals are off the northeast coast of Baffin Island, in the Repulse Bay area and around the northern end of Southampton Island.

Diet consists of molluscs, crustaceans and fish, including arctic cod, squid and shrimp. Narwhals inhabit deeper waters than their beluga cousins do and they are not usually associated with rivers. Their cycle of sexual maturity and breeding is similar to that of the belugas, but gestation is more like 15 months than 12.

Narwhals were not hunted as extensively as belugas but there was some trade in their horn. Current legislation limits hunting them to the Inuit for subsistence or domestic use only. The tusks are sometimes found for sale. A licence is needed to take them out of Canada, as is the case for walrus tusks.

Orcas are the 'wolves of the sea'. All marine animals take shelter when they are about. Hunting in packs of anything between three and 40 animals they take seals, fish, squid, seabirds and other cetaceans. It is thought that the summer distribution of belugas and narwhals is down to the arrival and presence of orcas within their winter ranges.

One hunting technique is to dislodge basking seals from ice floes by turning them over from underneath and attacks on narwhals and belugas are well known. Orcas will often drive pods of belugas towards shore and into the waiting arms of Inuit hunters. I have heard of this before in Australia off the New South Wales coast where for many years an orca called 'Old Tom' and his pod would herd sperm whales into Twofold Bay near the town of Eden towards waiting shore-based whalers. In return the orcas got a piece of the spoils.

Orcas are the most awesome of the world's whales. A true dolphin of the family *Delphinidae* and the largest of its kind, the male orca can weigh as much as 20 tonnes or more and be up to nine metres in length. Their reputation for ferocity is unequalled in the cetacean world and their sleek black bodies with distinctive white patches and dorsal fins that may be two metres in height on the mature males only add to the mystery surrounding orcas. Native people hold them in awe and call them 'blackfish'. They feature on totem poles and in legend as the guide of the afterworld and they are probably the most studied cetaceans in the world, being one of the most widely spread. They prefer cool temperate waters and, probably because of their tall dorsal fins, avoid the frozen seas of the north, usually arriving only in the summer hot on the tail of the migrating herds of smaller whales and seals.

One calf is usually born after a 16-month gestation period in November or December. Pods have a matriarchal structure with mothers accompanied by daughters and followed by young sons. Orcas are not hunted in Arctic Canada because of the fear they inspire in northern communities.

The **bowhead whale** was one of the first animals to be exploited by the Europeans and was the most intensively hunted of all the Arctic species. That was because it is a 'right whale' and a slow traveller. This big animal was therefore an easy target for whalers under man and sail power and valued for its high yield of whalebone and blubber. It was also known as the Greenland right whale.

Attaining a length of 20m and weighing as much as 50,000kg, it has the thickest blubber of all the whale species. Little is known about this whale's population dynamics and biology. Sexual maturity is reached when the animal reaches about 15m in length and it is suspected that it may live as long as 50 or more years. A single calf, about four metres long, is born in March or April after a 10–12 month gestation period. Calves nurse for about 14 months. Bowheads are gregarious creatures living in small groups. Their food is mainly the crustaceans called krill that are sifted out of the ocean near the surface and caught in baleen plates inside the mouth. There may be 650–720 baleen plates inside each whale. A huge tongue then separates the krill from the plates and moves the trapped prey to the gullet.

Hunting of bowheads is banned in Canada except under special permission issued by the Minister of Fisheries and Oceans (see also *Whalers and Sealers,* page 12). There are an estimated 7,800 bowhead whales in the western Arctic population and that population appears to be on the increase. However, with only one calf born to each breeding female every three years or so, this increase is very slow. The once plentiful stocks of Hudson Bay and the eastern Arctic now number only a few hundred animals. The bowhead is still on the endangered species list. The US government and the International Whaling Commission (IWC) permit the Alaskan Inuit, Aleuts and Native Americans to conduct a limited subsistence hunt of the western bowhead population. At present this hunt is considered safe and does not endanger the species. According to the Alaska Department of Fish & Wildlife, numbers of eastern bowhead whales are actually on the increase and all harvesting is strictly monitored.

ARCTIC BIRDS

Approximately 280 species of birds have been recorded in northern Canada, about 45% of Canada's total. Some 70 of these species nest exclusively north of the 60th Parallel. Of these species eight are listed as threatened or endangered: the Caspian tern, ivory gull, Ross' gull, trumpeter swan, peregrine falcon, American white pelican, Eskimo curlew and whooping crane. The north provides indispensable breeding grounds in a variety of ecosystems for these species as well as attracting birds from six continents travelling through more than 30 countries to breed here.

The best birdwatching season is the spring when millions of songbirds, shorebirds, waterfowl and seabirds arrive in Canada's north to breed. Most of the species come from their wintering grounds in southern North America and the coastal offshore waters of the northern Atlantic and Pacific Oceans. Some species, like the sanderling and the ruddy turnstone migrate up from South America and the Arctic tern comes all the way from Antarctica. The northern wheatear returns to Canada from Asia via Alaska and the common ringed plover comes from southern Europe via Greenland.

The Canadian Wildlife Service has established more than 100 Migratory Bird Sanctuaries and 45 National Wildlife Areas across Canada in addition to the national parks and world heritage sites established and managed by Parks Canada. There are currently 16 Migratory Bird Sanctuaries in the north (see box, page 54). To give you an idea of how important they are: Dewey Soper Bird Sanctuary is home to one of the largest colonies of lesser snow goose; Queen Maud Gulf Bird Sanctuary protects over 90% of the world's Ross' gull population; and Bylot Island Bird Sanctuary protects over 35% of the greater snow goose population. The sanctuaries of Queen Maud, Dewey Soper and McConnell River have been designated 'Wetlands of International Importance' under the Ramsar Convention (for more information, see www.ramsar.org).

There are some excellent bird guides to Canada and North America available and with so many species to cover I have not the space to do all the birds found in the north justice here. I have included some of my favourites, notably the birds of prey, as they tend to be the most exciting and watchable to non-birdwatchers and some of the more common birds usually seen in most places.

Raptors

Birds of prey are the polar bears and the wolves of the sky. They are sleek, fast and efficient and they prey on birds and mammals alike. Birds of prey have always been favourites of mine. There is something magical watching a falcon

THE RAMSAR CONVENTION

In 1976 the United Kingdom ratified the Ramsar Convention on Wetlands of International Importance, Especially as Waterfowl Habitat (HMSO,1976), so called after the meeting venue of Ramsar in Iran. Contracting parties are required to promote the conservation of listed wetlands. More generally parties are exhorted to plan the wise use of wetlands in all areas of policy planning and formulation. Where listed sites are involved, damaging development can proceed only in the urgent national interest. The criteria used to identify Ramsar sites depend on factors such as the number of waterfowl they support and complementary criteria for non-bird sites are currently under discussion.

dive from up high on to its prey in a feat of aerial combat that would make any fighter pilot proud. Majestic, and purveying a sense of awesome power, they are probably the most difficult birds to observe close up.

Imagine how we see everything. Our bifocal vision sees the world in 3D and our brain constantly reassesses the information our eyes send to it allowing us to form an accurate picture of the world around us. We have good vision near and far with wide peripherals, left to right and top to bottom.

Now, think of what it's like to be looking through binoculars. Images appear more like in 2D only. There is no peripheral vision to speak of but we can see very faraway objects as though they are quite close. It seems as though you could reach out and touch them. Children, when first using binoculars, often try to touch what they see in front of them and are disappointed when it is suddenly not there. This is how raptors see – in binocular vision. Obviously, it helps them detect prey from great heights, but as they approach they must constantly refocus and the information they receive diminishes as the prey gets closer. Vision like this is great during the final attack when pinpoint accuracy is needed, but terrible should you also want to see what is going on around you. With birds of prey it is a bit of a pay-off between one and the other.

When you approach a normal bird with vision similar to ours it can reassess its position and decide to leave when its personal space is truly invaded and danger seems inevitable to the little creature. To a hawk, eagle or falcon its telefocal vision does not allow it that privilege. Like kids with binoculars for the first time, everything appears to a bird of prey as really close, so close that they think they could touch it and in the eyes of a bird of prey that is too close for comfort. Not only are its eyes constantly refocusing on your approach, in the same way as they would when the bird is hunting, the peripheral dimensions it sees are becoming smaller and smaller with each approaching step, and so the bird becomes agitated and unsure about its surroundings. Its instincts take over and it flies away to escape to a safer position, even though you are not really that close to the bird. Similarly, slow movements will appear quite sudden to a hawk because he naturally sees everything in blown-out proportions. It is no wonder the bird heads for a distant tree or, in the case of the tundra of the north, a distant rock.

Raptors and other predators have always been considered by man as competitors in the search for food and therefore hunted mercilessly, or alternatively are captured and persuaded to do the work for man in return for food. Captured birds have it relatively easy in that hunting is done in conjunction with man and his other hunting animals like dogs and on the off days the bird still gets fed without doing any work. She just loses her freedom in the process.

Where a bird has been deemed a competitor she has been poisoned, shot or trapped, in some cases, to near extinction. Man eventually discovered that this relentless slaughter to save a few chickens, lambs and other livestock also caused an increase in the other critters that destroyed precious crops – the rodents, insects and birds. Research showed that healthy domestic livestock was rarely taken by birds of prey. Animals eaten had usually died of natural causes or had been preyed upon by bigger and less efficient mammalian hunters. The birds were probably feeding on carrion and got the blame for the death of the animals concerned. Some prejudices still exist but public attitudes have changed with education and the sight of a raptor flying free is an added bonus to any outdoor adventurer and should be considered as a symbol of the wild and unspoilt lands of northern Canada.

Woodland hawks

Their short, rounded wings and long tails distinguish woodland hawks and give them added manoeuvrability in forested areas as they dodge branches in their pursuit of small birds, squirrels and mice. They will often be seen sitting on an exposed branch in the forest waiting for their prey to appear. Two species are found in the north, both are true hawks.

The **goshawk** (*Accipiter gentilis*) is the largest true hawk in North America and is distinguished by light grey underparts and striped dark grey back. Eyes are a bright yellow colour usually with a light white strip just above the eye. This is a successful forest hawk with large broad wings well adapted for manoeuvring through the trees. Goshawks prey on lemmings, squirrels, hares and grouse. Nests are usually built in the tallest trees in the forest and a clutch of two to three eggs is laid in mid-June. Young fly at 45 days and survival rates among young birds reflect local prey abundance. Most goshawks migrate south to milder southern climes in winter but a few birds stay resident, usually in the Yukon and NWT.

The **sharp-shinned hawk** (*Accipiter striatus*) is the other true hawk. Smaller than the goshawk and rustier in colour it prefers to nest in conifers. Main prey is small woodland birds, supplemented by small rodents. This uncommon bird winters in Mexico. Its numbers have been dramatically reduced over the last 30 years by pesticide concentrations in the food chain.

Soaring hawks and eagles

These heavily built raptors have broad wide wings and fan-shaped tails which allow them to soar on the air currents in search of their prey. They have powerful beaks and feet and hunt in more open country than the true hawks.

The largest and most common of the soaring hawks is the **red-tailed hawk** (*Buteo jamaicensis*). Found throughout the whole of North America, this rusty brown bird lives on a diet of voles, lemmings, hares, insects and carrion. Females lay 1–3 eggs in May with young leaving the nest at 43 days. Red-tailed hawks in the north migrate to southern Canada and the USA in winter.

Similar in size is the **Swainson's hawk** (*Buteo swainsoni*) but this bird is uncommon in NWT and the Yukon. Two eggs are laid in a stick nest in small deciduous trees in May and the young fledge 28 days after hatching. Diet consists of rodents, hares and insects. Swainson's hawk over-winters in Argentina.

The **rough-legged hawk** (*Buteo lagopus*) is a common inhabitant in the mountains and tundra of mainland NWT and Nunavut and the southern reaches of the Arctic Archipelago. Adult plumage is variable but displays usually a dark patch on the belly and a light tail with a dark edge. This bird nests on ledges or on the ground and may maintain several nests which it alternates over several years. Two to three eggs are laid in late May and young are fed lemming and voles. The bird's relatively small feet prevent it capturing larger prey. Young fledge at 41 days and the birds over-winter throughout the USA. Population size depends on the lemming population cycle.

The two eagles are the golden eagle (*Aquila chrysaetos*) and the bald eagle (*Haliaeetus leucocephalos*).

The **golden eagle** takes four years to reach its mature plumage with its distinctive golden shine on the neck and head. It has large powerful feet allowing it to prey on hares, ground squirrels and occasionally newborn caribou calves. Females lay 2–3 eggs on a cliff side nest in late May but usually only the first chick to hatch survives to fledge at 77 days. There are some permanent mature golden eagles resident in NWT in the MacKenzie Mountains but most migrate south and over-winter in southern Canada and the USA.

The pure white head of the **bald eagle** helps it stand out amongst the raptors of North America. Similar in all aspects to the golden eagle, bald eagles also eat fish and can be seen along any river and lake during the salmon-spawning season waiting for an easy meal. Other prey includes hares and these birds are not beyond feeding on carrion or stealing food from ospreys. Best seen in the Yukon and southeastern Alaska near Haines, where, in the Chilkat Bald Eagle Preserve, hundreds of birds congregate in September waiting for the spawning salmon.

Harriers

The **northern harrier** (*Circus cyaneus*) is also known as the marshhawk and is the only harrier found north of the 60 in the Yukon, Alaska and NWT. Males are slate grey in colour and they are distinguished from Swainson's hawk by a white patch on their rumps. The female is brown in colour to remain camouflaged in the scrub while she sits on her nest. Usually 4–6 eggs are laid in late May and young fledge at 37 days. They are fed on mice, frogs, small rodents, birds and insects found on the marshes. Birds winter in southern Canada and the USA.

Osprey

The **osprey** (*Pandion haliaetus*) is similar to the soaring hawks in size but builds a stick nest on isolated trees, cliff pinnacles and poles near rivers and lakes. Three eggs are laid in June and adults are tireless fishermen, often diving under the water to catch their prey. Young fledge at 50 days and birds migrate as far south as Peru in the winter. Although uncommon in the north there are a few birds around Yellowknife where special nesting boards have been erected on poles to avoid unnecessary deaths due to birds using power poles as nest sites. The osprey population is small because of high pesticide levels in fish from insecticides sprayed onto crops and the run-off polluting the waterways.

BIRD MIGRATION SITES

Site	Size (km²)	Featured bird species
Kendall Island	606	7,500 lesser snow geese, greater white-fronted geese, Brant, tundra swans
Anderson River Delta	1,083	8,000 lesser snow geese, 2,500 Brant, greater white-fronted geese, tundra swans
Cape Perry	3,800	Thick-billed murres (100% of the western Arctic population)
Banks Island No 1	20,500	200,000 lesser snow geese, 100,000 king eiders, Brant
Banks Island No 2	142	25,000 lesser snow geese, Brant
Seymour Island	8	300 ivory gulls (12% of the Canadian breeding population)
Queen Maud Gulf	62,782	90,000 Ross' geese, 100,000 lesser snow geese, Brant
Bylot Island	10,878	45,000 greater snow geese, 320,000 thick-billed murres, 46,000 black-legged kittiwakes
Dewey Soper	8,160	450,000 lesser snow geese, 50,000 Canada geese, 1,600 Brant, Sabine's gulls, red phalaropes
Cape Dorset	259	5,000 common eiders
East Bay	1,166	42,000 lesser snow geese, 6000 Brant, king eiders, tundra swans
Harry Gibbons	1,490	200,000 lesser snow geese, Brant, Canada geese, Ross' geese, tundra swans
McConnell River	330	260,000 lesser snow geese (includes geese nesting near the sanctuary)
Akimiski Island	3,367	Hundreds of thousands of migrating geese, ducks and shorebirds
Hannah Bay	295	Hundreds of thousands of migrating geese, ducks and shorebirds
Boatswain Bay	179	Thousands of migrating geese, duck and shorebirds

Habitat types

Delta, estuary, tidal flats,
marshes, wetlands, tundra

Delta, estuary, flood plain,
tidal flats, wetlands, tundra,
open spruce forest

Limestone cliff, polynya

Tidal flats, sedge lowlands,
river valleys, wetlands

River valley, coastal lowland,
polynya

Reef-like island, raised beaches,
ponds, pack ice

Lowlands with rock outcrops,
beach ridges, drumlins,
sedge meadows, wetlands

Lowlands, cliffs, polynyas,
mountains, glaciers

Sedge lowlands, tidal flats,
wetlands

Rocky coastal islands,
lowland ponds

Sedge lowlands, tidal flats,
raised beaches, coastal waters

Sedge lowlands, tidal flats,
river, ponds

Sedge lowlands, tidal flats,
river, ponds

Tidal flats, eel-grass beds,
muskeg, spruce forest

Tidal flats, coastal marsh,
muskeg, spruce forest

Tidal flats, coastal marsh
and spruce forest

Comments

The lower MacKenzie delta
is an important waterbird staging
area during migration

There have been several
sightings of the almost extinct
Eskimo curlew

Only thick-billed murres colony in
the Western Canadian Arctic

Largest lesser snow goose colony
in western Canadian Arctic

Area used primarily for moulting

Canada's northernmost bird
sanctuary: 30 species recorded

One of the largest migratory bird
sanctuaries in the world. RAMSAR
site

The Lancaster Sound area provides
prime habitat for seabirds and
marine mammals

In 1929 Dewey Soper first
discovered the nesting ground of
the blue-phase Lesser snow goose
at this location. RAMSAR site

Eider numbers have declined due to
harvest of birds, eggs and down

White and blue phases of the
Lesser snow goose nest in most of
the eastern Arctic sanctuaries
including this one.

Harry Gibbons was an Inuk who
guided early biologists to this area

111 birds species recorded.
1,000,000 geese stage in the area
during the migration. RAMSAR site

Important staging area during
the spring and autumn migrations

Important staging area during the
migration. The sanctaury spans the
Nunavut–Ontario border

Important staging area during
the migration. The sanctuary spans
the Nunavut-Quebec border

Falcons

Gyrfalcons (*Falco rusticolus*) are the world's largest falcon and are found throughout the Arctic regions. Plumage varies from dark grey in the mountains to almost white in the tundra of the Arctic Archipelago. Gyrfalcons do not build a nest but use a disused cliff-face nest of other species like ravens or golden eagles. Usually 2–4 eggs are laid in April in the MacKenzie Mountains and in May elsewhere and are incubated by the female. Primary prey is ptarmigan, but they will eat lemmings, ground squirrels, hares and other birds. Birds nesting near the Arctic coast will prey on seabirds. Young fledge at 47 days. Some birds follow the migrations south to the boreal forest in search of ptarmigan; others stay with the wintering birds. Numbers seem to fluctuate around local resident populations of prey. Gyrfalcons are the most highly prized by falconers. In the Middle Ages only a king or an emperor could fly one. Even today this bird retains a high status in the world of falconry.

Much better known is the **peregrine falcon** (*Falco peregrinus*). Slightly smaller in size with a dark grey back and distinctive sideburns, the peregrine falcon epitomises the hunting bird. Fast and sleek, diving from great heights with closed wings, decapitating its prey with a single blow from its hind talon. It is one of the most spectacular sights in the animal kingdom. The thrill of these birds on a hunt has made them highly sought after by falconers' worldwide. Numbers went into serious decline for many years because of their ingestion of DDT-contaminated prey. They now seem to be on the increase after exhaustive efforts made by conservationists and scientists alike. Peregrine falcons are found throughout the north, except on Ellesmere and the most northerly islands of the Arctic Archipelago. Usually two to four eggs are laid in May in a shallow scrape on a cliff edge. Young fly at 39 days.

About half the size of the peregrine is the **merlin** (*Falco columbarius*). Males are a blue-grey whilst females are in contrast with a dark brown plumage. Nesting sites vary from cliff edges to used nest sites of other birds. Either four or five eggs are laid in June and incubated by the female. Young fledge at 28 days and they over-winter in Central and South America. Once common on the taiga, the merlin's reproduction rate has also been reduced by pesticide-contaminated prey.

The smallest of the falcons is the **kestrel** (*Falco sparverius*). This delightful little bird is often seen hovering over a field spying out prey from amongst the grass. Diet consists of small rodents and insects. Unlike other diurnal raptors the kestrel is a cavity nester. The female lays two to three eggs in late May and young fledge at 28 days. Birds migrate south and over-winter in southern USA and Mexico.

Owls

Just as hawks, eagles and falcons patrol the skies during the day, we assume that owls are mainly night time hunters and therefore extremely difficult to see. An owl's vision varies slightly from that of other birds of prey. Firstly, the eyes are in the front of the head not at the side. The eyes are fixed in their sockets so an owl must move its head to look in a different direction and, with rare exceptions, there is no ridge of feathers above the eyes to shade their vision from the sun. An owl's big eyes let in more light (about 100 times that of a daytime hunter) and with 14 vertebrae in their necks owls can swivel their heads through 270° in either direction. What allows owls to hunt so well in the dark is not their big eyes, however, it is their acute hearing. In some owl species this is so focused that they can hunt in total darkness. Most owls, though, hunt using the pre-dawn light or at last light in the evening.

There are six species found in the north. They are the great horned owl (Alaska, Yukon, NWT), long-eared owl (NWT), boreal owl (Yukon, Alaska, NWT), northern hawk owl (Alaska, Yukon, NWT), snowy owl (all of the north), short-eared owl (all of the north), and great grey owl (Alaska, Yukon, NWT). Of all these species the last three are the ones you are most likely to see. They are part of a group of owls known as 'hawk owls' because they tend to hunt primarily during the day and are relatively tame and common.

The **great grey owl** (*Strix nebulosa*) is scarce in boreal forests preferring dense conifers. It hunts from a perch in deep woods and open forest areas and is usually seen hunting during the daylight hours of the Arctic summer. This is a large bird (standing about 70cm) but its actual body size is quite small, most of its bulk being feathers.

The **snowy owl** (*Nyctea scandiaca*) can be seen anywhere on the open tundra during the summer. Its white coat forces it to stand out against the green background. Lack of trees and more pronounced perches causes this bird to rest on rocky outcrops and small knolls to spy out its prey, usually lemmings and other small rodents, and birds, mainly waterfowl. This is one of the few owls with a feathery ridge above its eyes to shade out the sun.

The **short-eared owl** (*Asio flammeus*) is not found as far north as the snowy owl but is the only other owl species that lives north of the treeline. Habits are similar, as is prey. Colouration is a pale tan rather than white and the bird is smaller in size (about 38cm). However, it is its flight that is its most distinguishing feature. It bounces along quite low to the ground when hunting.

Seabirds

The most common seabird in the north must definitely be the **thick-billed murre** (*Uria lomvia*). Often seen alone or in small flocks flying close to the water's surface, these sleek little birds nest in vast colonies on rocky coasts and cliffs. They can be found all year round on the east coast of Canada and the Arctic Islands as far west as the western edge of Hudson Bay and all along on the west coast of Alaska. Their range does not extend to the inland waters of Hudson Bay but there is a large colony on the west side of Coats Island.

Another seabird you are quite likely to see is the **Arctic tern** (*Sterna paradisaea*). They are abundant in the Arctic in summer having migrated to Canada all the way from Antarctica. Terns fish by diving into the sea while airborne (plunge-diving) and they also catch insects. They tend to nest on beaches in large colonies, which makes them vulnerable to aerial predators like gulls. Human impact on their nesting sites is limited because of the north's isolation.

Waterbirds

The **tundra swan** (*Cygnus columbianus*) is probably the most numerous swan species in the north and is often confused by inexperienced twitchers with the trumpeter swan (*Cygnus buccinator*) although it is a smaller bird. Often seen flying in single line or V-formation when migrating. Found in large flocks during the winter and when migrating, this bird's habitat is shallow fresh water, especially coastal estuaries with nearby grainfields. Trumpeter swans breed in the north but winter in southern North America.

The bird symbol of Canada must be the loon. The **common loon** (*Gavia immer*) is found on the face of the one dollar coin (called loonies) and is quite numerous throughout Canada. It nests on islands and shores of the northern lakes just after the summer thaw. This is a shy bird and difficult to approach. It is distinguished from the two other common species of loon by the green gloss on its head feathers. The **Pacific loon** (*Gavia pacifica*) has a soft grey head with a striped throat and the **red-throated loon** (*Gavia stellata*) has a soft grey head with a striped back of the neck. The red throat is difficult to see and is only found on mature males. The ranges of all three species are similar but the red-throated loon is uncommon in Yukon and only found along coastal reaches in Alaska and the common loon is rare amongst the Arctic Islands.

Forest birds

There are lots of ground dwelling birds in the north but for most people they are too small to notice when walking along a trail. A couple of birds that are common in the northern forests of Alaska, Yukon and the southwest corner of NWT are the spruce grouse and the white-tailed ptarmigan.

The **spruce grouse** (*Dendragapus canadensis*) is best observed in the autumn when the male cockbirds are busy courting the hens. A male clears himself a space on the forest floor, puffs himself up and does a little dance that is quite a merry affair to watch. Usually the best clearings are on the trails and that means you are likely to see them as you walk along through a quiet bit of forest. You can get quite close, as the cock is so preoccupied that he does not notice you and if he does spot you he will not go far from his bit of territory.

The **white-tailed ptarmigan** (*Lagopus leucurus*) is equally common in the same region. This particular bird turns white in the winter and, as it is quite unwary about his surroundings, it needs the camouflage to survive. The summer plumage is mottled brown with strong white underparts and well-feathered feet. The grouse's feet are uncovered. Both birds appear to be of a similar size although the ptarmigan is the smaller of the two. Both birds are generally ground feeders but the grouse will flee to the safety of a tree when in danger and feeds on pine needles during the winter.

NORTHERN PLANTS

Northern vegetation comes in two distinct regions: the vegetation found north of the treeline, and those trees, scrubs and plants that occur south of the treeline. The problem here is in defining the treeline. In some instances it is defined as the northern boundary of trees that grow more than five metres in height; others say it's where the forest meets the tundra in some hazy blending of patches of forest interspersed with tundra and *vice versa*. The treeline commonly drawn on the map of Canada is a distinct line of artificial construction that represents something that in reality is quite fuzzy. Add to this the effect of climate changes that cause this line to become even more fuzzy and you have something that is physically undefinable but still occurs on maps. Confused – good!

The northernmost tree found in Canada is a spruce called **krummholz**, the name for a small, gnarled species that grows so slowly and is so bent by the fierce Arctic winds that it never grows taller than most scrubs.

Now, trees are not affected by cold, and in fact it is colder in the forests of northern Canada than out on the tundra, yet the trees in the forests are tall while the trees on the tundra are small. The answer is simple and it is all down to the sun. To grow, plants need to photosynthesise, that is to receive warmth from the sun to energise the plants' cells into growing. Now, there is plenty of sun in the short Arctic summer to stimulate growth, so why does it not happen? The answer concerns the angle of the sun in relation to the earth's surface. If plants get plenty of sun but do not warm up first, because the sun's angle to the earth is too low, photosynthesis does not occur. Where new tissue therefore grows so slowly the plant cannot afford to waste energy on growing tall and must put all its energy into producing the essentials for life. These are the leaves, so the plant will not starve, and the roots and other underground parts to store the energy necessary to sustain it during the long period of winter. Wood, which helps trees stand upright and gives them strength and rigidity, is a bit of a luxury when a plant needs to supply what energy it does receive from the sun to its leaves and roots to continue to exist. So plants, trees and scrubs do not grow very tall.

One other thing affects a tree's ability to grow tall: permafrost. The closer that the permafrost occurs to the surface the shallower a tree's roots will be. Roots give a tree holding power in the soil. Therefore the depth of usable soil beneath it is another limiting factor in a tree's height.

Many of the trees at and above the treeline reproduce by cloning. This region is often too cold for trees to reproduce using the common method of producing seeds and scattering them upon the ground. Seeds are just too unlikely to get a foothold on the soil or get beneath it to germinate and develop. Cloning is where a branch of a tree or scrub will droop to touch the ground. A root system then develops and a new trunk grows above the new roots. When this is established the original branch dies off. The result is a completely new independent tree once the connecting branch has died. These trees are genetically identical and in this way may produce large stands of trees that grow without cones or their secure seeds. Trees like this can go on producing in a cold climate where growth from a seed is no longer possible, although the original tree must have begun from a seed at some time. Forests created from clones are usually completely destroyed in the event of a fire, as there is no source of seeds to establish new growth.

The forces that act upon vegetation in the north, the limited sun, the lack of warmth and permafrost are all reasons why when you travel further and further north the trees become shorter and shorter until they no longer resemble trees. It also explains why the 'treeline' can be a fuzzy state of affairs and defining its position at all is something of a mystery. At the end of the day it is only a line drawn on a map and must be taken for what it is – an estimation of where the forest ends and the tundra or treeless barrens begin.

Beyond the northern forest the tundra begins. Low-growing plants like scrubs, herbs (non-woody types) mosses and lichens continue on well past the edge of the forest and remain as before. Only the trees change. They grow smaller and smaller, eventually disappearing. As the temperature drops and the climate becomes harsher so the plant species diminish and vegetation becomes sparser. There are over 400 species of plants at the treeline. This reduces to about 50 on the most north-westerly of the Arctic islands.

Just as the sunlight deficiency leads to the treeline the same applies to the scrubs in turn leading to a scrubline. At this point water is extremely limited. Over much of the Arctic Islands annual precipitation (rain and snow) is less than 10cm a year. Much of the ground is covered by rock and only the hardiest of little plants establish themselves in the cracks and fissures where they shelter themselves as much as possible from the ravages of the weather. This region makes up what we call a true 'polar desert'. There are some grasses and sedges that flower during the brief summer if at all, otherwise it is only mosses and lichens, if there are any plants at all.

Vegetation in the forested zones

The two most important trees at the treeline are the **black spruce** (*Picea mariana*) and the **white spruce** (*Picea glauca*). Both of these trees are hardy with low root systems and are well adapted to resist the prolonged cold. Both are evergreen and dominate the forests immediately south of the treeline. Another fairly common conifer is the **tamarack** (*Larix laricina*) but this tree is deciduous and loses its leaves in the autumn.

There are three subarctic hardwoods here. The **balsam poplar** (*Populus balsamifera*) is the only broadleaf tree in the region. It is so named because of the scent given off by its resinous buds. In the western Arctic it can be found on the gravelly shores of the lakes and rivers draining into the Beaufort Sea, making it the most northerly growing tree on continental North America. Moose eat the twigs and leaves. Beaver, porcupines and hares like the bark and grouse eat the buds. Its close cousin is the **trembling aspen** (*Populus tremuloides*) which does not grow as far north and is so named because of the sound coming from the leaves in any slight breeze. This tree is the favourite food of the beaver. The third hardwood is the **paper birch** or white birch (*Betula papyrifera*). Its name comes from its former use in making baskets and paper bark canoes. Some botanists refer to this tree as the Alaska birch (*Betula neoalaskana*) because they consider it a separate species to the white birch found further south in more temperate zones. To the inexperienced eye both these species look the same. The differences are that the Alaska birch is not as tall and the leaves are more triangular in shape. These species of tree are both found in similar areas and are a popular food source for a variety of animals; moose eat the twigs in winter, small birds and rodents eat the seeds, and grouse and ptarmigan eat the buds.

Vegetation in the tundra zones

There are three major tree types that grow north of the treeline. The **green alder** (*Alnus crispa*) is found as far north as the Beaufort Sea but only on the mainland. This bushy scrub forms dense thickets in some areas and is common in all forests of the north preferring low, moist sites along rivers and creeks. Sometimes it is found along rivers in the treeless tundra. The **dwarf birch** (*Betula glandulosa*) is found on the mainland, Banks, Victoria, and Southampton Islands and around the southern tip of Baffin Island. The dwarf birch is a bushy scrub with many branches densely covered in small round leaves. This tree inhabits the low-Arctic tundra and is often found in thickets formed on peat bogs.

The northern range of some 40 different species of **willows** (species *Salix*) extends as far north as a line extending west from the northern tip of Baffin Island. These species are generally indistinguishable to the untrained eye but are easily separated from other tree varieties. The leaves are pointed at both ends and are long and narrow. They tend to grow along streams or in areas where the soil is moist and are among the few woody trees to survive in the treeless tundra. Willows provide browse for caribou, muskoxen and hares and the buds are the principal winter food for ptarmigan.

One of the great joys of the Arctic tundra is the beauty of the abundant **flowers** that burst forth in the summer. The profusion of colour is for the benefit of the insects that pollinate the flowers and not for we humans but the flowers are not to know that. Arctic flowers do not bud and flower in the same short summer season but bud in the late summer and over-winter ready for the first rays of the sun next summer to bring forth the blooms. This ensures that every flower has the longest possible warm season.

Flowers attract insects by their colour and reward them with pollen and nectar to feed upon. In return the unsuspecting insect takes pollen from one flower to another – thus cross-pollination occurs. The insects most useful here are flies and bumblebees. By flies I mean all insects with only two wings and this includes gnats, midges, blackflies and mosquitoes as well as the common housefly. The cross-pollination fertilises the seeds; the sun warms everything up and the seeds ripen. Plants can then reproduce. It all sounds simple and it is.

Do not expect to see the blazing carpets of flowers you might find in temperate zones or flowers of a grandiose size. What you will see is the full range of colours from whites and yellows through to blues, purples and reds and loads of wonderful scents, all designed to attract those vital insects in such a very short summer.

For those of you seriously interested in flowers I have listed some popular guides to aid those intent on identifying flowers in the bibliography (page 269).

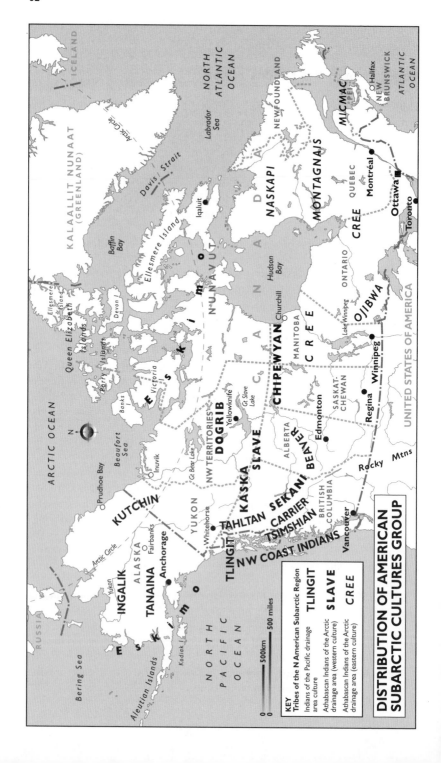

DISTRIBUTION OF AMERICAN SUBARCTIC CULTURES GROUP

KEY
Tribes of the N American Subarctic Region

Indians of the Pacific drainage area culture **TLINGIT**

Athabascan Indians of the Arctic drainage area (western culture) **SLAVE**

Athabascan Indians of the Arctic drainage area (eastern culture) **CREE**

The People

The first humans arrived in North America during the Pleistocene Epoch between 1,600,000 and 10,000 years ago. There is some doubt about the precise date but most experts accept that the earliest inhabitants arrived in North America after the last glacial period, somewhere between 35,000 and 20,000 years ago. Some authorities disagree, however, and speculate that habitation may have begun as early as 60,000 years ago. Speculation and guesswork is how archaeologists start and then they get down to the serious research and digging. What is generally believed is that the site of entry into North America was via a land-bridge which formed as glaciers advanced and sea levels fell in the area that divided Asia and America. We now call this place the Bering Strait.

The ancestors of the Native Americans were nomadic hunters of Asian-Mongoloid stock who migrated over the Bering Strait land-bridge probably during the last glacial period between 20,000 and 35,000 years ago. They, like their predecessors, shared with their Asian contemporaries such cultural traits as the use of the dog, the use of fire and various rites, although they had not yet discovered the wheel and the plough. These prehistoric settlers belonged to a number of separate traditions yet they had similar economies despite many environmental differences. The three societies were the Paleo-Indian hunting societies of the West, the Great Plains, and Eastern North America. Their major source of food was meat and they used animal hides for clothing.

Some 12,000 years ago North America was quite temperate, although there were still some glaciers about. The native peoples spread far and wide across the Americas and it is certainly known from archaeological evidence that man had travelled to the far south of the Americas. A site at Palli Aike on the Straits of Magellan has yielded a radiocarbon dating of a culture about 8,000 years ago. But by 4000BC the food-collecting cultures had become well adapted and specialised in their ways of life which suited their local environment.

THE FIRST NATIONS
These subarctic cultures or groups occupied a physiographic zone called taiga, a land of coniferous forests criss-crossed by many rivers and streams. Natural resources included the wood of spruce, alder and tamarack, and the game animals included moose, caribou and beaver. Basic diets were meat supplemented by fish and berries; skins provided the clothing. Snow-covered

ground led these people to adapt to fur garments, sleds, ice chisels, and snowshoes. Yet they failed to develop the wheel and, as hunter-gatherers, had no use for the plough.

There are two broad groups of First Nation Peoples (the Canadian expression equivalent to Native Americans) in modern northern Canada, distinguished by their language structure. They are the Northwest Coast First Nations and the tribal groups belonging to the Athabascan First Nations. You may also come across a third group who speak the Algonquin group of languages further east towards Québec, Manitoba and Ontario, but in general these people are a little out of this book's territory.

Northwest Coast First Nations

The Northwest Coast First Nations occupy a thin strip of land and the off-shore islands from Yakutat Bay in the northeast Gulf of Alaska south to Mendocino in California. They are the most delimited cultural group of Native Americans. The Coast Range flanks this thin strip of land down past British Columbia and into Washington State, USA. The coastal forests are dense with predominantly coniferous trees: spruce, Douglas fir, hemlock, red and yellow cedar and, on the far south coast, redwood. These forests support a wide variety of fauna. The waters of the coast are filled with a large range of fish species including five species of salmon, herring, oil-rich 'candlefish' or eulachon (a fish that is so oily at spawning time that it can be dried and burned as a candle), smelt, cod, halibut, and plenty of molluscs. It was on this harvest from the sea that these groups primarily depended. The Northwest Coast was once the most densely populated area of native peoples in North America. It is estimated that 129,000 people lived on the coast at the dawn of the historic period (1800–50BC). Archaeological evidence suggests that this number would be the maximum the region could support without improvements in the available and already complex technology.

The only tribe or clan you are likely to meet in northern Canada and Alaska is the northernmost clan of this group, the **Tlingit**. They include various Alaskan groups and those in the southwest corner of the Yukon. They are speakers of the Tlingit language and there are 14 territorial tribes. Tlingit groups are organised into two divisions called *moieties* with each individual being assigned at birth to his mother's affiliation. *Moieties* are subdivided into clans whose members trace their relationship to a legendary common ancestor. The basic social unit was, however, the lineage of people through maternal descent. Lineages were politically independent but with their own chief who had no overall tribal authority. Lineages might cooperate during a war and one or more lineages might unify to form large villages. Each lineage owned and exploited land for economic importance and functioned together as a basic ceremonial unit.

As an example of this *moieties* system, I would like to use my friend Chuck Hume (his First Nations name is Kosh-Klux). Although his grandfather was a Scotsman, his grandmother was of the First Nations, which confused me a little when we first spoke about these *moieties*, but as everything passes down

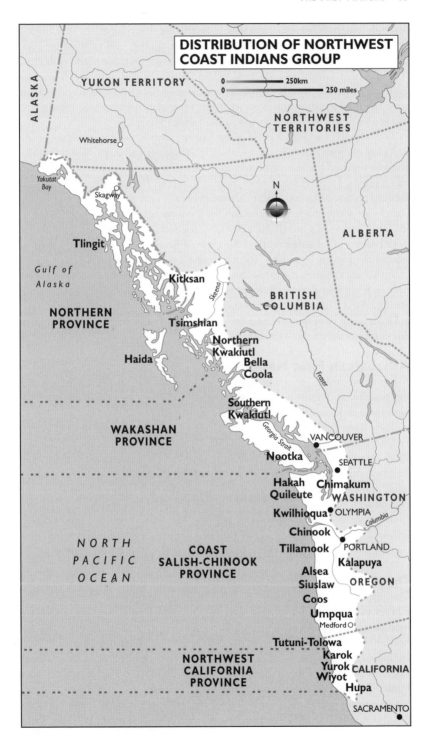

DISTRIBUTION OF NORTHWEST COAST INDIANS GROUP

0 ————— 250km
0 ————— 250 miles

ALASKA

YUKON TERRITORY

NORTHWEST
TERRITORIES

Whitehorse

Yakutat
Bay

Skagway

N

ALBERTA

Tlingit

Gulf of
Alaska

Kitksan

Skeena

BRITISH
COLUMBIA

NORTHERN
PROVINCE

Tsimshian

Northern
Kwakiutl

Haida

Bella
Coola

Fraser

Southern
Kwakiutl

Georgia Strait

VANCOUVER

WAKASHAN
PROVINCE

Nootka

SEATTLE

Hakah
Quileute

Chimakum
WASHINGTON

Kwilhioqua

OLYMPIA

Columbia

Chinook

NORTH
PACIFIC
OCEAN

COAST
SALISH-CHINOOK
PROVINCE

Tillamook

PORTLAND

Alsea
Siuslaw

Kalapuya

OREGON

Coos

Umpqua

Medford

Tutuni-Tolowa

Karok

NORTHWEST
CALIFORNIA
PROVINCE

Yurok
Wiyot

CALIFORNIA

Hupa

SACRAMENTO

through maternal lineage, somehow it eventually made some sense. Chuck's father belonged to the killer-whale clan and his mother was of the frog clan. Chuck himself is from the crow clan and his wife is a member of the wolf clan. It is all about family relationships where cousins, aunts and uncles are not quite recognised as family members but those of the same clan are. A person may not marry within the same clan but inter-clan marriages can and were used to strengthen alliances between the various groups.

The Tlingit economy was based on fishing, usually salmon, with some sea and land mammals also hunted with harpoons, nets and traps. Wood was the primary material for manufacture and was used in houses, canoes, utensils and other goods. Large houses were built near secure fishing grounds with safe landing places for canoes. Houses were generally occupied only in the winter with tribes scattering to hunt and fish for the summer. The Tlingit are famous, like all Northwest Coastal First Nations, for *potlatches,* which are ceremonial distributions of gifts that marked the cycle of rituals. Often they were used to mourn the passing of a chief. Today they are a good excuse for a party.

These are the major groups and everyone belongs to one or another. You may hear different names but territorial land is the best indication of what group a First Nation person belongs to. I have found all First Nations take pride in being who they are and are very willing to tell their story, but politics does raise its ugly head sometimes.

Athabascan First Nations

There are six main groups of Athabascan First Nations in Alaska, Yukon and the Northwest Territories. Like all First Nations there are numerous clans all with their own names but this will give you an idea.

They form two groups. The first of these, the Chipewyan, Slave, Dogrib, Yellowknife and Beaver First Nations, inhabit the area drained by the MacKenzie River system. These people's culture is simpler and less sedentary than their western counterparts. The other group, which inhabits the area whose rivers drain into the Pacific Ocean, comprises mainly the Kutchin First Nations, along with other smaller tribes such as the Carrier, the Tanaina and Ingalik. Traders were attracted to these regions during the fur trade years and missionaries followed the traders as they opened up new areas. Many of the old beliefs and customs, fortunately, persisted well into the second half of the 20th century.

The Chipewyan

The most numerous group of Athabascan-speaking First Nations is the Chipewyan. They inhabit a large triangular area of northern Canada with a base along the 1,600km Churchill River and an apex some 1,000km to the north. This land is boreal forest divided by patches of barren ground. There are lots of independent bands and these nomadic people followed the seasonal migrations of the caribou, their main source of food and clothing. They also hunted bison, muskoxen, moose, waterfowl and fish.

Chipewyan culture is most noted for its ruthless attitude to survival. Only the fittest survived. The strongest men overlorded the weak, pilfering their goods and seizing their women. Women were usually no better off than beasts of burden who were married in adolescence and used to pull toboggans and sleds or carry packs. The weak and aged were left to die by the trail if they could not keep up with the group. Murder was, however, considered abhorrent. They had a general belief in visions, guardian spirits and dreams, in the powers of the medicine man to cure or cause disease, and in deliverance to a happier place after death.

When the Hudson Bay Company started trading at the mouth of the Churchill in 1717 the Chipewyan turned to hunting fur and being the middlemen in dealings with a number of western tribes. They exploited everyone for huge profits. A smallpox epidemic in 1781, other diseases and malnutrition, and the decline of the fur trade reduced their numbers until there are only about 5,000 remaining in Canada today.

The Slave

Around the shores of the Great Slave Lake and the basins of the MacKenzie and Liard Rivers lives a group of First Nations called the Slave or Slavey. Other names are Awokanak and Etchareottine. The Slave name comes from the Cree nation who often plundered and enslaved them, and this name became familiar usage with the English and French. The group had a general reputation for timidity or pacifism whether they deserved it or not.

Like most other Athabascan tribes the Slave are separated into a number of independent groups, loosely organised and led by nominal leaders. These groups are usually associated with specific hunting territories. Disputes were settled by a council of hunters, and women and the aged were treated with respect and kindness which seems to be atypical of Athabascan tribes. The Slave inhabited forests and hunted moose, woodland caribou and other game for food but also relied on fish. Animal skins provided most of their domestic needs. The dwellings were bush-covered tepees in summer and rectangular huts made from poles and spruce branches in winter. They believed in guardian spirits, in the power of their medicine men, and in an undefined life after death. A common practice on the deathbed was to confess all sins. It was thought to delay the process of dying.

The Dogrib

Another group around the Great Slave Lake is the Dogrib or Thlingchadinne. They inhabited the forests and barren ground between the Great Slave Lake and the Great Bear Lake. The name Dogrib is an English adaptation of their own name Thlingchadinne or 'dog-flank' people, referring to their fabled descent from a supernatural dog. Dogrib are traditional hunters and fishermen subsisting mainly on barren ground caribou that were trapped and speared. They lived in skin-covered tepees, although they sometimes built wooden and brush-covered lodges in winter. Women were better off than in other tribes but the aged and infirm were often left to die. Chief enemies were the Cree, Chipewyan and Yellowknife. The Dogrib eventually massacred all the Yellowknife in the late 18th and early 19th centuries.

The Dogrib remained relatively isolated until the 20th century when improved transport and communication facilities brought them in contact with other parts of Canada. They number about 1,200 today.

The Yellowknife
The Yellowknife were a tribe who shared a similar territory to the Dogrib between the Great Slave and Great Bear lakes. Their name derived from their use of yellow copper for tools. In language and culture they are almost identical to the Chipewyan. Their destruction at the hands of the Dogrib in retaliation for early raids and harassment has left them numbering only about 500 today and they now tend to count themselves as Ojibwa.

The Beaver
Another small group of First Nations people from this part of Canada are called the Beaver and they inhabit the mountainous riverine areas of northern Alberta. The gun-toting Cree, seeking furs for the European trade, drove them westward from their traditional grounds. Their name comes from their main site, Tsades, or the River of Beavers, now called the Peace River where the remaining members of the tribe live today. The Beaver were a scattered, nomadic tribe of independent groups with their own hunting territory. They hunted moose, caribou, bison and beavers. Dwellings were skin-covered tepees in winter and brush-covered lean-tos in summer. They travelled mainly by canoe. They also believed in a guardian spirit and an afterlife.

The Kutchin
The Kutchin inhabit the basins of the Yukon and Peel Rivers in eastern Alaska and the Yukon Territory. This is an area of coniferous forests interspersed with open barren ground. The word Kutchin means 'people' and is given to those distinct tribes who collectively have as much in common linguistically as culturally. The social organisation is unusual in that each tribe is divided into three exogamous castes or subdivisions where there is no recognised rank or heritable status. Men became chiefs through demonstrations of leadership or prowess. A warlike people, the Kutchin were ruthless in battle, taking no prisoners or slaves and mercilessly killing men, women and children alike. Men were hunters and fishermen; women were obliged to do all the daily chores and portage and had no part in decision-making. The old, sick and those unable to help themselves were customarily put to death.

The Kutchin were most influenced by the Inuit with whom they traded and fought. They borrowed the Inuit's cultural habit of caribou-skin clothing, most notably hoods and mittens, some of their hunting weapons and dog sleds. They also shared customs with their relatives to the south, decorating clothing with paint and beads, putting feathers in their hair as well as face painting. Housing was generally dome-shaped, and made of natural materials like the boughs of firs etc and were covered with snow in winter. A small smoke hole at the top ventilated the lodge. The Kutchin are well known for their feasts, games (mainly wrestling), singing and dancing. Of the 2,000 or so remaining now, they are the tribe most influenced by the European way of life.

Algonquin-speaking First Nations

The Algonquin-speaking natives inhabit the eastern subarctic. These groups include the Naskapi of northern Québec, the Cree, and the Ojibwa who replaced the Cree from west central Ontario and eastern Manitoba after the beginning of the fur trade.

First Nations peoples today

The First Nations number a little over half a million people or about 2% of the Canadian population. They tend to live on reservations and unfortunately suffer from high unemployment and poverty living, as often as not, off federal hand-outs. Although their lot has improved over the past couple of decades very few have fully integrated into modern Canadian society. Their traditional livelihood of hunting moose, caribou and other big game animals or fishing for salmon has gone and the old practical skills have fast disappeared. Until recently many of their traditional ceremonies had been banned in an effort to subjugate the native population into accepting European ways. For many years any practice of their culture was suppressed. As a result, incidences of alcoholism and substance abuse is higher amongst First Nations people than with the European population.

Today the government is learning, and there has been a revival of native culture. I suspect that the money that tourism attracts and a subtle changing in European attitudes towards the native population is bringing all this about. Many native groups have negotiated settlements over the mineral rights on their lands held by treaty, and this in turn has raised the living standards of these groups. Some crown land has also been returned to the original native inhabitants as part of aboriginal land rights claims.

Many wilderness guides are First Nations and I would highly recommend travelling with one to anybody exploring the wilderness, should the opportunity arise. They are better tuned in to the environment, see things with more open eyes, and are less in a hurry so they spend more time showing and explaining things that catch their eye. Some of the more mature guides still remember the old ways and I've spent many a night listening to tales, myths and legends about the world according to the natives. It's extremely entertaining. Story-telling is an art form that we have tended to lose in the age of television. I have the advantage of choosing my guides as I usually work on a one-to-one basis when photographing the wilderness and prefer the more congenial and silent company of a native person. As guiding is still considered a menial task and the natives have always led the European around since he first arrived on North American shores and, with conventional employment still somewhat closed to the First Nations, your chances of having a First Nations guide are quite high. Take advantage and enjoy the company. Both you and your guide will gain something from the experience.

Caribou and the native peoples of the north

Caribou are probably the most important food source for all the indigenous peoples of the north. They have been for centuries. Long before the Europeans arrived life in the north was closely tied to the caribou. Because they occur in such vast numbers across the entire region, they are an important legacy of the north. As such, caribou are the 'lifeblood' of the northern peoples. A vast amount of research has gone into the caribou in order to maintain them as the major part of the northern way of life today.

Prior to the Europeans' arrival, the indigenous peoples, both First Nations and Inuit, lived almost exclusively by hunting and fishing. For those people who lived within the range of the migrating caribou, the caribou became the focus of many of their activities.

Meat, blood and stomach contents provided their food; antlers, bones and sinew created their tools, ornaments and weapons; caribou skins provided shelter, clothing and bedding. The nomadic movements of the various tribes and groups were harmonised to coincide with those of the caribou. Caribou even figure in Inuit and First Nation religion and mythology. Life for the northern peoples appears to have been completely merged with that of the caribou and the other animals that sustained them. And rightly so – survival depended on it!

All edible parts of the caribou were consumed. Bones were broken up and boiled to release their grease; meat was either boiled or roasted. In winter the surpluses were frozen for later consumption; in summer meat was smoked and/or sun-dried. Dried meat was pounded into a powder and mixed with caribou grease and berries and stored in skin bags for ease of transportation and future consumption. The stomach contents provide a source of edible vegetable matter.

Skins provided the coverings for teepees and were made into thongs. Thongs in their turn were used for ropes and snares. Skins were used for containers and all manner of clothing from moccasins on the feet to sleeping robes for nightwear. It is estimated that each person needed about 20 skins a year for clothing. This provided two suits of moccasins, a robe,

CARIBOU PARTS CLASSIFIED BY FOOD GROUPS

Milk and milk products
soft end of bones
stomach contents
intestines

Meat and alternatives
meat, heart, liver, kidneys,
brain, blood

Bread and cereals
heart, liver, kidneys
bone marrow
intestines and
web covering stomach

Fruits and vegetables
stomach contents
eyes, liver

KEY NUTRIENT SOURCES IN CARIBOU

Animal Part	Nutrients
meat	protein, fat, iron, vitamin A, riboflavin, niacin
organ meats (heart, liver, kidneys)	protein, iron, vitamins A & C, riboflavin, niacin, thiamin (liver also contains calcium)
blood	iron, protein
bone marrow	fat and small amounts of iron, thiamin, riboflavin, niacin, vitamin A
intestines and web stomach covering	fat, iron, riboflavin, niacin, calcium
stomach contents	calcium, vitamins A & C, fibre, riboflavin, niacin, and carbohydrates
back fat (tallow)	fat, vitamins A, E, K
soft ends of bones	calcium, phosphorus
brain	fat, protein, vitamin C
eyes	vitamin A

shirt, cap, breech cloth, leggings, and mittens. Clothes were generally made from skins obtained in the late autumn when they were at their prime. Skins for summer clothing were shaved; those for winter had the hair left on. With the Inuit, clothing was doubled layered for protection against the cold. The outside layer had the hair left on but turned out and the skin only scraped. The inside layer had the fur turned inward and the skin was softened.

The bone and antlers made arrowheads, spear heads and knives. Fine bones were used for needles for sewing. Wide flat bones were made into hide scrapers. Inuit also made harpoon heads and fish hooks from bone. Antlers were used for combs. The teeth were used for amulets for good luck on the hunt and were sewn into the breast of the hunter's inner coat.

You can see by the above table and the one on the previous page why the caribou was so important to the survival of the indigenous peoples. The animal provided everything they needed for a healthy diet eaten, either cooked as in the case of most First Nations or raw as in the case of the Inuit.

THE INUIT
Where did the word Eskimo come from?

The word 'eskimo' is a Cree First Nations word for the Inuit meaning 'eaters of raw meat'. The early explorers, who obviously knew no better, adopted it. The term at the time was quite relevant as the Inuit did eat raw meat. It was a dictate of survival in a land where there were no trees for firewood nor grasses to make fire with except during the short summer when food was either cooked for immediate consumption or preserved by sun drying or smoking. Today the Inuit still eat their meat raw. It is often considered a delicacy today and it is eaten with relish when very fresh. The meat doesn't go off in the cold climate and many of the Inuit I have been with eat dried meat as a snack in the same way that we would eat a biscuit. Some thought it the only way to eat meat and detested the taste of the cooked stuff.

Much of the goodness in meat is destroyed when it is cooked. The Inuit got all they needed, nutrition-wise, from raw meat because all the vitamins and minerals are still in the flesh and have not been cooked out. One case in particular is scurvy, the plague of seamen on those early long voyages. The search for a cure was the subject of much exploration in the 18th century. Although the Inuit's diet was exclusively meat and fish, scurvy was unknown amongst the people. They must have got all the vitamin C they needed from raw meat. It is a pity those early sailors didn't take advantage and do the same thing. Going native would have saved many a seafaring life. The Inuit aren't alone in being 'eaters of raw meat'. The Ethiopians eat raw meat with chilli powder sprinkled liberally on it. They think it a delicacy and eat it on special occasions. The Japanese eat raw fish in *sushi*, as we also do now. The French have *steak tartare*.

You will be offered raw meat often by the Inuit. They will offer *muktuk* or raw whale blubber as well. It is a personal choice whether or not you want to eat it and no-one will be offended if you decline. They will just look at you as if you are stupid to turn down such a fine offer and then immediately think that there is more for them.

Most of the Inuit cook their food these days, on kerosene and other more modern stoves, although I found this more common with Inuit in the field in Greenland than I did in Nunavut. There is still no nutritional waste as the fluid used for cooking is also consumed.

Inuit beginnings

The Inuit are relative newcomers to North America. Research has indicated that the Inuit and their ancestors have been in continuous habitation of the Arctic regions for a little more than 4,000 years. The original people came from the west via Alaska and are divided into two groups: Pre-Dorset (in southern Nunavut) and Independence I (in Northern Nunavut). At that time North America was much warmer. They lived in skin tents year round, wore skin clothing, travelled on foot and probably had dogs and a small boat similar to a kayak. They hunted everything except bowhead whales. These paleo-eskimo people adapted to climate fluctuations but when the big freeze came about 2,700 years ago there was a rapid transition in the lifestyle that was so dramatic that archaeologists gave the culture a different name and called it the Dorset culture. The bow and arrow disappeared from the culture, as did dogs. New tools appeared, houses changed and hunting techniques modified. They developed a rich artistic tradition. Despite no dogs nor the use of large boats, it seems the Dorset travelled widely and traded over long distances.

The climate changed again about a thousand years ago and once more grew warmer. A new group appeared from Alaska with dogs, boats and sledges. They could cover great distances faster than the Dorset people. These migrants were called the Thule (too-lee) people and are the direct ancestors of today's Inuit.

Archaeologists can't find any evidence of contact between the Dorset and Thule people, but Inuit oral history tells of a people called Tuniit or Tunijuat who occupied the land before their descendants came. Eventually the Dorset people disappeared. The Thule people hunted bowhead whales and society was structured on the leadership of the whale boat captain. These people adapted to regional differences in resources and altered their social organisation to suit.

The Inuit's lifestyle was altered forever with the arrival of Europeans. Explorers, whalers and traders made sporadic contact with the Inuit, which had little impact on Inuit culture. When the whalers came in force in the 1820s things altered. The whalers depleted bowhead stocks, concentrated the Inuit into areas surrounded by whalers, and introduced diseases that had devastating effects on Inuit populations. It is a time marked by many rapid changes in material culture, religion and social structure.

The Inuit groups

The various Inuit groups don't consider themselves different from one another. They are all Inuit, which in Inuktitut, the language of the Inuit, means 'the people'. But there are regional differences in Inuit. The Inuit today have either travelled about naturally or else were born where they are now and they and their ancestors have always lived in the region.

A couple of exceptions to that are the communities of Cornwallis and Ellesmere Islands. The Canadian Department of Northern Affairs in the 1950s forcibly moved Inuit from Inukjuak, Québec and Pond Inlet to the islands where the Government said there were plenty of natural resources and that the move would be good for the Inuit. This bleak relocation programme was really a gross oversight by the Canadian government. Under the pretence of improving the life of these southern Inuit, what the government was really trying to do was help reinforce its sovereignty over the islands of the High Arctic. These Inuit from the south were in a totally alien environment and barely survived. But survive they did, at the communities of Grise Fjord and Resolute Bay.

In general, most Inuit have always lived on coastal fringes. They hunted marine mammals and fish and for those on islands that had resident caribou or who lived on the coastal edges of the Canadian mainland hunted caribou in the summer when the animals migrated north.

One exception to this is the inland Inuit of Baker Lake. They hunt caribou during the summer migrations and fish but being 260 km from the sea means that they take no marine mammals. The hunting methods vary slightly, and the kayaks are shorter and made from wood rather than whalebone and are covered with caribou skin rather than seal. However, this is basically a regional adaptation.

Another group with a distinct name is the Copper Inuit from around Kugluktuk, so-called because they made use of locally available copper for weapons and tools rather than the more traditional bone and antler implements. Netsilik Inuit of King William Island are famous as seal hunters, hence their name. The Arviligjuaqmuit Inuit of Pelly Bay are named after the Inuktitut word for bowhead whales – *arviligjuaq*.

One group of Inuit no longer exists. The Sallirmiut Inuit inhabited a small area called Native Point about 60km southeast of Coral Harbour. They were supposedly direct descendants of the Thule or Dorset people and lived in complete isolation, culturally distinct from all other Inuit communities. It seems that diseases, contracted most likely from a whaling fleet, killed off all of them in the winter of 1902/3.

The Inuit today

For those of you who will inevitably ask the question, 'Do Inuit still live in igloos?', the answer is yes. The word *igloo* in Inuktitut means house or dwelling. The ones made of snow and ice that we normally associate with the Inuit are rarely built today, although the Inuit will build them for visitors if asked and the conditions are right. Most Inuit now live in proper houses or bungalows in communities like the rest of us, as they no longer live a purely nomadic life. That said, they do go off for days on end hunting; some use modern tents while others use old established sod and earth huts that have been used for centuries in traditional hunting grounds and are rebuilt each year as and when needed.

The Inuit need little excuse to go hunting and relish the chance to pursue anything suitable for the table. Traditionally this would be seals, caribou, muskoxen, whale and walrus although most Inuit respect the moratorium on whales. After the misfortunes of the Repulse Bay hunt in 1996 most Inuit I have spoken to see no commercial advantage in hunting whales at the moment and they are aware that the communities would benefit more from the tourism in promoting the live animal. That said, if bowhead stocks ever reach their old levels I'm sure that hunting them would be back on the agenda. Inuit, who come from a whale-hunting tradition, still see it as their right to kill the animal for food. Fortunately for the whales, hunting takes a lot of organisation and skill. Anyone with the experience needed is becoming rather old and the traditional skills may disappear with the passing of time.

In just a couple of generations the Inuit of Nunavut have gone from 'igloos to skyscrapers'. This rapid change has caused some underlying problems. The old social order had changed too rapidly for some people. Opportunities were limited for employment in the first instance; work was a misunderstood ethic; education was seen as an anathema. Years ago children as young as five were often taken from their families and sent to schools in the bigger towns and cities. They weren't allowed to speak Inuktitut, only English. When they came home they were strangers. They wore different clothes, spoke a different language, had haircuts. They had been forced to accept a different culture and in the process had lost sight of their own. This led to a somewhat confused society that turned to alcoholism, substance abuse and self-destruction. Nunavut has the highest suicide rate amongst any group of people worldwide. This cultural gap seems to be affecting the young more than the old. As children they are taught the old Inuit ways but then they have to compete in a more modern world. Education is still substandard amongst the Inuit, with many children seeing no point in going to school or being taught by Western teachers who have little or no understanding of Inuit ways and culture. School often just seems a wasted exercise that someone in Ottawa says they must do.

Things are improving. There are more cross-cultural marriages. More European people from the south, who originally came to the north to work and then returned south on retirement, are now staying to make the north their permanent home. Education standards are lifting and there are more and more trained Inuit teachers. Inuktitut is being taught in the schools as the main language of education. The formation of an Inuit government will provide greater opportunities for Inuit children to receive a higher education. The Inuit are beginning to understand the value of education; it is no longer just a word.

Today more Inuit are returning to their traditional skills and having a major re-learn. They have formed educational committees, alcohol and drug education groups, hunters and trapper organisations, social committees and other self-help groups to improve their lot. The Inuktitut language is flourishing once again and many new terms have entered its vocabulary to reflect the Inuit's move into the modern world.

Work, too, is no longer just a word. An Inuit friend of mine used to drive trucks in Iqualit and got paid for it. He thought it was fun and couldn't understand why he got money for it; the government had always paid his family to give up the nomadic life and come to live in the town. One day when he was at home, someone asked him, 'Why aren't you at work?' He replied that he didn't do work. It was only when they said that driving the truck was work and that was why he got paid that the concept of work finally dawned on him. To him it was just a meaningless European word that had no equivalent in Inuktitut. It was something that the *Kabloona* did.

The youngsters today are struggling to see an immediate future. Unemployment is still relatively high amongst the Inuit and, at the moment, non-Inuit people are still filling all the best jobs. But things are changing. Inuit are learning the skills necessary to establish a modern Canadian Territory where they will become a vital part of the bigger Canadian picture. The establishment of Nunavut has given the Inuit something to believe in strongly. Their self-esteem and dignity has been given a boost. There is lots to do and much learning to be done in the process, but it will be done, and it will be done in a very Inuit fashion. Only time will tell more of the future of Nunavut.

THE COMING OF NUNAVUT

On April 1 1999 something almost alien to most European thought occurred in Canada. The Canadian government went out on a serious limb and was the first national government to grant autonomy to an indigenous race based on ancient land claims.

The Nunavut Land Claims Settlement was proclaimed at Kugluktuk on July 9 1993 after 20 years of negotiation and hard work. It was the first time a sovereign nation reached a land claims settlement with an aboriginal group anywhere in the world. And there was no violence associated with the settlement at all.

Oil exploration was creating an economic boom in the High Arctic. With little oil elsewhere in Canada the government looked to the land north of the 60 for its oil and gas reserves. There is great potential in the offshore waters of the Arctic and the east coast of Canada and these regions were a federal responsibility. This intense period of exploration made the Inuit realise how little control they had over their own traditional lands. They discovered that the federal government and big businesses could do what they liked on Inuit land without a by-your-leave from the Inuit leaders of the time. The Inuit decided that they had got to get themselves together politically.

Large discoveries of oil in Alaska and the Beaufort Sea in 1976 created a flurry of exploration activity with talk of pipelines, supertankers, giant submarines and flying tankers to take the oil out. The energy crisis that had begun in the early 1970s was over but oil prices had dropped and stayed low. This made transportation of oil from the reserves of the High Arctic economically unfeasible. The uncertainty of the oil business in Canada was further complicated by the problem of who actually owned the land and the resources on or under it. The discovery of serious oil reserves in Alaska had led the federal Government of the USA and the state of Alaska to sign an agreement with the aboriginal peoples of that state over land rights. It was the first of its kind and, although limited, the Inuit saw that there was a real possibility that they could negotiate a treaty for northern Canada.

Precedent was set in British Columbia in 1973 in what was called the Calder Case. Chief Calder of the Nishga Indians of northwest British Columbia went to court to review the existence of 'aboriginal rights' claimed over lands historically occupied by the Nishga. The decision of the Supreme Court of British Columbia acknowledged the existence of aboriginal rights in Canada. The government on the other hand had dismissed any suggestions of land and other rights of aboriginal peoples. Public awareness and publicity eventually forced the Canadian government to take the issue seriously and go to the negotiating table.

At this time there were some young, well-educated, politically activated Inuit emerging from the sidelines. They researched land claims, raised funds and got organised. The first steps toward an autonomous Nunavut had begun.

In 1971 the Inuit Tapirisat of Canada was formed. Its responsibility was to pursue and negotiate land claims for the Inuit of Canada. It was decided that an overall land claims programme for Canada was impossible at the time. Bringing the federal government, provincial governments, and the Inuit from three different jurisdictions together at the same time was just too difficult. They therefore decided to negotiate regional rights one at a time. In 1973 the first land claims agreement was settled between the province of Quebec, the federal government, the James Bay Cree and the Inuit of Nunavik. This was followed in June 1984 by the Inuvialuit Settlement that included the Inuit of

Western Arctic and Dene tribes of the MacKenzie Delta. They felt it necessary at that time to negotiate a separate treaty from the land claims of Nunavut.

In 1982 the Tungavik Federation of Nunavut was incorporated to pursue the land claim rights on behalf of the Inuit of Nunavut taking the mandate from the Inuit Tapirisat of Canada. Thirteen years of intense negotiations followed. The talks were slow because the Canadian government had no real land claims policy; they had never discussed offshore rights or the sharing of royalties or even thought about self governing institutions being given any sort of real regal power. The Nunavut Inuit claims were a much broader and more liberal land claims policy than had been previously negotiated under the narrow aboriginal rights that existed in the 1970s. A publicly televised Conference of First Ministers on Aboriginal Rights educated Canadians as to what was at stake. Increased public support forced the federal government to become more willing to discuss broader issues. In 1990 they all reached an agreement-in-principle which was followed by two more years of negotiations.

Finally in September 1992 an agreement was signed, and ratified by 84.7% of the Inuit beneficiaries two months later. The treaty was seen as a benchmark for aboriginal matters throughout the world. The accord gave the Inuit majority control over their future including:

- Inuit owned lands measuring 355,842 km^2 with mineral rights over 35,257 km^2 of that land
- Capital transfer payments of $1.1 billion over 14 years beginning in 1993
- A share of federal government royalties from oil, gas and mineral development
- The right to harvest wildlife on lands and waters throughout Nunavut
- The right to first refusal on sport and commercial development of renewable resources in Nunavut
- A wildlife management board to promote and serve the long-term economic, social and cultural interests of the Inuit harvesters
- Procurement preference policies that ensure federal government and territorial government contracts awarded for Nunavut-destined projects will see increased participation of Inuit firms (providing training and education where necessary). Also, the labour force hired must reflect the proportion of Inuit in Nunavut
- Inuit Impact and Benefits Agreements (IIBAs), negotiated in advance of major development projects (such as mining development) that could have a detrimental impact or provide benefits to the Inuit

The Nunavut Land Claim Agreement changed the map of Canada and has now changed the course of life for the Inuit in Nunavut.

The arrival of Nunavut
From the time that land claims were started between the federal government and the Inuit, the idea of creating a new territory was always on the agenda. The Inuit not only wanted to settle the land claims question, they wanted a new political entity for themselves.

The idea was to split the Northwest Territories into two new territories. The federal government examined the idea as far back as 1965 and 1966 but put it on the backburner for ten years. When the Inuit eventually pushed the idea again, the territorial government was against it, wanting more power to devolve from federal government rather than devolve from the territory as a whole. A vote on the subject of division in April 1982 had a high turnout of Nunavut voters (90%) but a low one from the NWT. The overall result was 53% for division and 47% against. The Inuit had won the first hurdle.

The next problem was the boundary and a line was decided. This was again put to the voters in 1992. Once again there was a high turnout in the east and a low one in the west but the boundary was ratified and hurdle number two was overcome. Final agreement on land claims reached the home stretch.

In September 1992 the Inuit leadership and the Indian and Northern Affairs Minister, Tom Siddon, met. The Inuit held out for the creation of Nunavut saying they wouldn't sign any agreement until the question of autonomy was resolved. The minister made a few phone calls and the government of Canada committed itself to the idea of creating Nunavut. The Inuit had overcome all the hurdles and the agreement was signed and ratified by the Inuit. The Nunavut Act was passed by parliament in June 1993.

On April 1 1999 Nunavut became the first territory to enter the federation of Canada since Newfoundland joined in 1949. Nunavut is subject to the Canadian Constitution and the Charter of Rights and Freedoms and will be a public government with all of its citizens having the same rights. This will reflect in the reality that the population of Nunavut is 85% Inuit.

THE EUROPEANS

When the Europeans first arrived in northern Canada in the 16th century it was only really in search of a quicker route to the Indies. In the beginning of the 17th century, though, a small pocket of Europeans settled on the east coast of what is now the United States. About the same time King Charles II granted the charter to the Company of Adventurers to explore and exploit the area they called Rupert's Land which is now called Nunavut. The native population at this time was somewhere around 5 million throughout North America and included some 3,000 Inuit in the far north. Canadian native populations were a little more than a million at most.

An invasion of other peoples comes in two forms. The first is an all-out invasion subduing peoples by force of arms and overwhelming numbers. The second kind is the subtler version whereby the invader is far superior technologically but vastly inferior in numbers. The invader gains the upper hand by stealth, diplomacy and persuasion.

The first settlers in North America were poorly equipped for the environment and lacked the necessary survival skills to be truly successful in their new land. Fear of the native population and fear of asking for help nearly led to their demise. Somehow they survived. The subsequent settlers of Canada took up the lessons learnt by the first settlers with poor survival skills in the USA with gusto adapting native skills where necessary and being willing

A PERSONAL REFLECTION ON THE INUIT

Most Inuit I met didn't wear skins any more, preferring more modern-style clothing. Seal meat is still a favourite food amongst the Inuit as is caribou, fish and any other animal that we would class as 'country fayre' or food off the land. The sale of animal skins was an additional means by which the Inuit could earn extra income related to what to do for a living or a means of providing food for their families. (See box, *Hunting harp seals*, page 45.) They still need to buy bullets, boats, fuel and building materials (most Inuit live in communities and not the traditional nomadic life) to exist in a more modern and realistic world. One politician, Peter Ernerk, a deputy minister in Nunavut's new government, was heard to comment that, 'We've come from the igloo to high-rise in a very short time.' He's worried that the Inuit are going through changes at a pace that is hard to handle.

We don't live in the same world as the Inuit. Nor have we undergone the immense and very rapid changes in our lifestyle that the Inuit have. As far as I can see, the rest of the world isn't interested in fur, in general, because the campaign against the killing of fur-bearing animals has been effective in stopping all but the extremely rich selecting fur for cold-weather clothing. In most cases fur is no longer practical and there are many man-made materials that are almost as good.

To live in our world the Inuit have found it necessary to adopt some of our ways. Before, their life was a matter of survival, taking what they needed from whatever source was available. Today some of those needs have changed to wants and that change costs money. Clothing is a perfect example of one of the wants and needs syndrome. Modern clothes don't come as part of any animal you have killed for food, but instead are displayed on a rack in the Northern Store. Education and association with a completely different society with different aspirations, wants and needs have altered the Inuit outlook on things. Inuit children are growing up in a different world from the one in which their parents grew up.

During this transition from 'igloo to skyscraper' we must accept that Inuit need to retain some of their traditions and must be able to profit from them until they themselves find a new direction in a world that we consider normal. It will come, because the Inuit are the most adaptable people on this planet. To have survived 3,500 years in the Arctic environment is testament to that.

to enlist the help of the native peoples as they slowly and subtly took control of the land.

When the British and French fought for control of Canada during the Colonial Wars Native Americans were encouraged to take sides. This was where diplomacy came into its own. Each native group saw advantages in whichever particular side they took, realising that there were economical gains to be made. It is possible that they knew that this was a subtle invasion over which they would have little control in the long term and wanted to have a deciding hand in who would eventually have control over their destiny. At the end of the day the Europeans had, since they first arrived, a commanding position over the North American native peoples. In terms of relative technology, a different approach to life and the planet's resources, the Europeans were, to the chagrin of the native peoples, always going to win.

European habitation of the north has always been fairly scant. In 1866 the population of what was then British North America was about 3 million people. Of those some 2½ million lived in the St Lawrence–Great Lakes area. There was a small European enclave at the Red River but beyond that were just a few thousand Métis (descendants of indigenous women and fur traders) and aboriginal inhabitants of the prairies, forests and the icy wastes of Rupert's Land and the Northwestern Territories. Over the Rocky Mountains the 10,000 or so Europeans were outnumbered three to one by the natives.

Only primary resource industries were any basis for settlement in the north; the fur trade, the fishery and timber trade, a little agriculture and, in the far west, gold. These resources brought people to the wilderness and sustained them there but their numbers were tiny compared to the rest of Canada. Settlement was, for many years, actively discouraged in the north. The fur trade relied on unspoilt wilderness to achieve the best results. The commercial demands created a nomadic populace until the gold strike on the Klondike in the Yukon. This heralded a period of exploration for the mineral wealth of the north, which although expanding the European population didn't greatly affect their numbers. Most of the population was, in actual fact, still fairly transient, with many coming to the north to work and then returning to the south to live out their final days.

A few major towns were established around the mining communities like Dawson City and Whitehorse. Yellowknife in Northwest Territories didn't become a sizeable town until the 1930s. Most of the other towns today were only little settlements based around the Hudson Bay Company trading posts that were scattered throughout the north. As these trading communities were in actual fact regional centres actively engaged in the fur trade, the need for an expanding settlement was deemed unnecessary.

Canadian immigration, although it consisted of mainly British and French persons, also reflected a wider European make-up of Germans, Dutch, Greeks, Italians, Lithuanians, Poles, Ukrainians, Norwegians, Russians and Swedes. There was even a sizeable Chinese and Japanese population in the south of the country. Yet immigration northward was only managed at a trickle. In the north Europeans have always been in the minority and represent only about 25% of the population although this varies from town to town and region to region. Much of it is still fluctuating and transient.

As the north grows and expands, many of these people of European descent will stay and make the north their home but the bedrock of the population will always be indigenous.

Part Two

Practical Information

Beaver

Grizzly bear

Planning your Trip

CHOOSING WHAT TO DO

Northern Canada abounds with wilderness activities. You can either experiment with a new activity in a fresh environment or enjoy your favourite adventure in a different destination. Some wildlife enthusiasts will opt for the best animal viewing irrespective of how distant and remote the location. Those seeking adventure activities may also be influenced by where they would like to visit rather than the activity itself. For example, you can dog-sledge anywhere but going to the North Pole carries more of a buzz when you come home to tell the tales, lies and legends. What I would like to do here is give those readers who are new to wilderness activities a few ideas of the options available and where best to see certain species of wildlife. Although many of these activities and animals are found in most places, some places are better geared than others for certain pursuits. It may take you several visits to fulfil this list.

Ten best outdoor activities
Glacial viewing
Catch a light plane out of Haines Junction and fly over the St Elias Mountains. This area of Kluane National Park is the largest non-polar icefield in the world and includes the 65km-long Lowell Glacier, the Steele Glacier which once advanced 11km in only four months, and the Kaskawulsh Glacier which drains into both the Yukon River and the Pacific Ocean. A one-hour flight out of Haines Junction can be arranged for about $90.

Whitewater rafting
There are some great whitewater rafting rivers in northern Canada but the best is probably the South Nahanni River in NWT. It has been called the purest, wildest and most spectacular whitewater river in the world. Spectacular mountain scenery, deep river canyons and excellent wildlife viewing make the trip brilliant. Journeys are anything from three weeks out of Moose Ponds to 10 or 12 days from Virginia Falls. Most outfitters will spend only four or five hours each day on the water, allowing plenty of time to view the wildlife and do some exploring. Outfitters can be found in Fort Simpson.

Dog-sledging
This old method of transport is one of the best outdoor activities I've ever experienced – but you have to like dogs. Perhaps the greatest experience is to

sledge all the way to the North Pole. Journeys start in Resolute and take about 16 days. You fly in and out of Iqaluit, then on to Resolute, returning from the North Pole by Twin Otter.

Aurora borealis
This atmospheric anomaly can be seen anywhere north of the 60th parallel. It doesn't occur every night but it is frequent. A clear night well away from the bright city lights will give you an excellent view of the display. Yellowknife has a couple of hotels that have special viewing rooms to watch the show in comfort. I once saw it from 31,000 feet when flying home. When I questioned the pilot about not telling the passengers of the view out of the window the captain said, 'We like to keep some things to ourselves.' I don't blame him!

Hiking
The best hiking or trekking in the north has to be through Kluane National Park in the Yukon. It's easy to reach, the trails are well marked, the routes are comfortable to do, the facilities are excellent, the rangers informative, and the scenery takes a lot of beating. There is plenty of wildlife along the way and the park HQ and ranger posts will supply bear-resistant food caches.

Snowmobiling
Try this out of Pond Inlet on Baffin Island, Nunavut, to the edge of the pack ice. Walrus, polar bear, seals, birds, narwhals and orcas – the lot as far as marine mammals and birds go. There are limited facilities in Pond Inlet which can only be reached by air.

Gold mining
Only one place and that's Dawson City at the junction of the Yukon and the Klondike Rivers. It was the site of the world's greatest gold strike and there is plenty left – it's just hard to get at. There are plenty of facilities in town and someone will sort you out with a bit of panning.

Sea kayaking
Sea kayaking among the fjords of Ellesmere Island in Nunavut is spectacular. Nights are spent on shore camping in tents and the marine life abounds. Walrus and seals are everywhere and some kayakers have been lucky enough to see wolves chasing arctic hares amongst the lush summer flowers. Ellesmere Island can only be reached by plane out of Resolute. You must be self-sufficient.

Horse trekking
I tried this out of Haines Junction and not being a horsy person I actually found it a buzz. A horse, having a more acute set of senses, sees things before you do and alerts you to the fact. While trekking the mountains and forests to the east of the St Elias Mountains my companions and I saw in one day a moose and calf, a grizzly bear feeding on berries and lots of grouse doing their

Previous page Bull muskox, Cambridge Bay, Nunavut (GR)

Above Walrus, Nunavut (GR)

Below Walrus on haulout, Walrus Island, Hudson Bay, Nunavut (GR)

Above Polar bear (MT)

Left Arctic ground squirrel or sik-sik, Baker Lake, Nunavut (GR)

Below Wood bison, Fort Providence, Northwest Territories (GR)

Above Dawson City, Yukon (GR)
Right Gold buyer's sign, Dawson City (GR)
Below Old buildings, Dawson City (GR)

GOLD DUST BOUGHT AND SOLD

mating display. We caught fresh fish for dinner and slept above the treeline in cool, crisp mountain air. Couldn't be better.

Driving
If you head north along the Dempster Highway out of Dawson City in the Yukon you are travelling on the most northerly road in the world. The road is paved but not covered in tarmac and the journey from Dawson to Inuvik in NWT takes two days with an overnight stop at Eagle Plains in Yukon and a ferry across the MacKenzie at Arctic Red River. The landscape is superb, the driving is easy and there's plenty to see along the way. Although the road is open most of the year the best time is in August or September when the autumnal changes begin. The colours are out of this world. A four-wheel drive vehicle is not necessary but is advisable, as is a second spare tyre. Fuel is limited so be prepared.

Ten best wildlife viewing sites
Polar bears
Easily the best viewing is around Hudson Bay near Churchill, Manitoba, in October and November when the bay is about to freeze over again for the winter. Churchill is known as the 'polar bear capital of the world' and it is easy to see why. Dozens of bears have wandered up from the south of the bay in search of the first freeze over. For some reason the bears congregate around Churchill in Manitoba. The local outfitters are geared up for this event and most will almost guarantee seeing at least one bear if you go out in a special purpose-built vehicle called a tundra buggy. These vehicles stand 10ft (3m) tall on huge rubber tyres and provide a safe and secure environment for viewing polar bears at close range. All this is done in a certain amount of comfort. This is also a good spot to see beluga whales as the estuary of the Churchill River is used as a breeding ground. Churchill can be easily reached by plane or train. Another excellent place to view polar bears is Wager Bay in Nunavut. Here there are plenty of bears, but you must fly in and the facilities are more limited than in Churchill.

Wood bison
There are two parks in the Northwest Territories that have good populations of wood bison. Wood Buffalo National Park straddles the border of the NWT and the province of Alberta. Guides and outfitters can be organised from Fort Smith but the animals are a hybrid breed of wood bison and plains bison. MacKenzie Bison Sanctuary near Fort Providence in NWT is far better with a small herd of about 2,000 animals that are a pure, untainted group. However, I have had the best viewing along the main highway between Fort Providence and Yellowknife. Both parks can be reached by plane or by road. Limited facilities are available.

Grizzly bears
The best place is Dalton Post on the Tatshenshini River during August, September and October when the bears come down from the hills to feed on

the spawning salmon. With three species of salmon running the river, the extended season offers plenty of opportunities to see bears. There are also some bear watching hides in the area. Outfitters can be found in Haines Junction, Yukon, which can be reached by road or air.

Dall's sheep

Kluane National Park in the Yukon is the place. The nearest town is once again Haines Junction. The park headquarters are in town and there is plenty of accommodation. Access into the park is by foot. Local outfitters can help, alternatively see the park rangers.

Muskoxen

Without a doubt you must visit Cambridge Bay for this. They are on the edge of the town most days and are relatively timid in summer just before the rut. Cambridge Bay is a regional centre and well supported with facilities. Local outfitters can organise your viewing.

Walrus

Walrus are quite common but difficult to reach in the north. One good way is to take a boat out of Coral Harbour and go south to Coats Island and Walrus Island in the north of Hudson Bay. There are good facilities in Coral but accommodation is limited.

Birds

Bylot Island is a new sanctuary 25km north of Pond Inlet on Baffin Island in Nunavut and is the place to go for birds. Some 300,000 thick-billed murres and 80,000 black-legged kittiwakes make the cliffs on the island their summer breeding home. It also has the world's largest colony of greater snow geese. Along the floe edge you might also see walrus, orcas, bowhead whales, narwhal and five species of seal. Outfitters from Pond Inlet, which can only be reached by air, can get you there but facilities are limited.

Narwhal and bowhead whales

The waters around Repulse Bay are the summer home for narwhals and bowhead whales. Belugas are also here, as well as four species of seal. The local hunters and trappers organisation can organise boat trips. Accommodation is limited.

Caribou

Caribou are common throughout the north and there are some fairly big herds once the migration has got going. The best place to see caribou easily is east of the Thelon Game Reserve near Baker Lake. Outfitters can be found in Baker Lake to take you up the Thelon River to where the caribou are. There are good accommodation facilities in Baker Lake. The town can only be reached by air or by boat from Rankin Inlet.

Moose
Two Moose Lake along the Dempster Highway 102km north of Dawson City is the place. Moose are elusive animals but are often seen here feeding on the aquatic plants along the lakeshore. Accommodation is in Dawson City and the lake can be easily reached by road from either Dawson or Whitehorse.

WHEN TO GO
Although northern Canada is a year-round destination, many of the sights you might want to see are seasonal. Wildlife, in particular, has seasonal patterns and to get the best viewing you must take advantage of those windows of opportunity. Most organised tours do just that and only depart at the best viewing times. If you are travelling on your own, you must do your homework beforehand and make sure you are in the right place at the right time. A study of tour operators' brochures will tell you the best time to be somewhere to see your choice of wildlife or outdoor activity. Please bear in mind that, in some towns and communities in the north, accommodation and other facilities are limited and need to be booked well in advance. The same applies to buying a seat on an aircraft; flights to some destinations are not daily and are regularly booked up by the local inhabitants.

TOURIST INFORMATION
UK
The **Visit Canada Centre** in London has closed and there is now only a telephone service. Their number is 0906 871 5000 (calls cost 60p/min at all times). With this 24-hour service you can either leave your name and address so they can supply a general information pack on Canada, or alternatively you can speak to an advisor between 09.00 and 17.30 Mon–Fri.

USA
Canadian Embassy 501 Pennsylvania Ave NW, Washington DC, tel: (202) 682-1740
Consulates General 1 Marine Midland Center, Ste 3000, Buffalo, NY 14203-2884, tel: 1-716-858-9501; 600 Renaissance Center, Ste 1100, Detroit, MI 48243-1798, tel: 1-313-567-2340; 550 S Hope St, 9th Floor Los Angeles, CA 90071-2627, tel: 1-213-346-2700; Concourse Level, 1251 Ave of the Americas, 22nd floor, New York, NY 10020-1175, tel: 1-212-596-1600; 412 Plaza 600, Sixth & Stewart Sts, Seattle, WA 98101-1286, tel: 1-206-443-1777

Rest of the world
Australia Consulate General of Canada, 5th Level, Quay West, 111 Harrington Street Sydney NSW 2000, Australia; tel: +61 2 364-3000; fax: +61 2 364-3098
France Canadian Embassy, 35 Avenue Montaigne, 75008 Paris, France; tel: +33 1 44 43 29 00; fax: +33 1 44 43 29 94
Germany Canada Tourismusprogramm, Postfach 200 247, D-63469 Maintal 2, Deutschland; tel: +49 6181 45178; fax: +49 6181 497558; email: Canada-Info@t-online.de; web: http://www.dfait-maeci.gc.ca/~bonn/Tourism/eto2main.htm
Italy Via Vittor Pisani 19, 20124 Milan, Italy; tel: +39 2 67581; fax: +39 2 6758-3900

Japan Canadian Embassy, 3-38, Akasaka 7-Chome, Minato-ku, Tokyo 107, Japan; tel: +81 3 3479-5851; fax: +81 3 3479-5320
Korea Canadian Embassy, 10th Floor, Kolon Building, 45 Mugyo-Dong, Jung-Ku, Seoul 100-170, Republic of Korea; tel: +82 2 753-2605; fax: +82 2 755-0686

Canada
Canadian Tourism Commission, 8th Floor West, 235 Queen Street, Ottawa, ON K1A 0H6; tel: +1-613-946-1000; web: www.travelcanada.ca
Northwest Territories www.nwttravel.nt.ca; emmail nwtat@nwttravel.nt.ca
Nunavut www.arctic-travel.com/www.nunatour.nt.ca; email nunatour@nunanet.com
Yukon www.touryukon.com; email info@yukontour.com

RED TAPE
Visas
Citizens of Britain and Ireland are not required to obtain a visa for Canada. You may be asked to provide evidence that you are a genuine visitor and satisfy the immigration officer at the port of entry on arrival in Canada. You may be asked to prove that you have sufficient funds to maintain yourself during your stay and have an onward or return air ticket or evidence of such in your possession. These types of entry requirements are fairly standard throughout the better-off countries as a measure against increased illegal immigration. It is all straight-forward and painless and genuine visitors will receive a warm welcome. Passports must be valid for the duration of your stay plus one day. British subjects and overseas citizens who are subject to UK immigration control do require a visa to visit Canada. Visas can be obtained from the Canadian High Commission, Immigration Division, 38 Grosvenor Street, London W1X 0AB telephone 0891 616644 (24hr/premium rate numbers – calls cost 60p/min) they are open 08.00–11.00 Mon–Fri. Those who wish to study, receive employment or emigrate to Canada must obtain all the necessary paperwork from the Canadian High Commission before entering Canada.

Customs and currency regulations
Visitors to Canada may bring the following free of import duties if for personal use and not for others or for sale in Canada.

- Personal effects such as clothing, articles of personal adornment, toilet articles and sports equipment
- 200 cigarettes; 50 cigar/cigarillos; 200 grams tobacco; 200 tobacco sticks
- One 1.5-litre bottle of wine or 1.4 litres of spirits or other alcoholic beverage or liquor or 24 x 355ml of beer or ale. Drinks containing 0.5% of alcohol by volume or less is not classified as an alcoholic beverage so quantity limit applies. Minimum age in Québec, Manitoba and Alberta is 18 years, and 19 years elsewhere.
- A small amount of perfume for personal use.

There are no restrictions on the import or export of either local or foreign currency if declared.

Gift exemption
Visitors may bring to Canada gifts free of duties to the value of $60 per gift. This does not include alcoholic beverages, tobacco products or advertising material.

Medical insurance
There is no reciprocal medical treatment between Britain, Ireland and Canada. Although the facilities are excellent, they are expensive. You should obtain adequate insurance before leaving home to cover all eventualities. See insurance and other health measures under the section on health, page 109.

GETTING THERE
By air
From the UK
The following airlines fly out from the UK for Canada. None fly direct to the north but instead use the major gateway cities of Montréal, Ottawa, Edmonton, Toronto and Vancouver.

Air Canada (0870 524 7226) flies to Edmonton, Montréal, Ottawa and Vancouver from Heathrow. They also fly from Glasgow to Vancouver via Toronto in the summer.
Canadian Airlines (0345 616767) flies daily to Vancouver, Montréal and Ottawa three times a week from Heathrow.
British Airways (0345 222111) flies daily to Montréal and Vancouver and from Birmingham to Toronto via New York.
United Airlines (0845 844 4777) flies to Vancouver via connections in the States on a daily basis.
KLM (0870 575 0900) also connects London to Montréal and Vancouver via Amsterdam.

From Australia
Cathay Pacific, **Canadian Airlines** and **United Airlines** fly from Sydney to Vancouver direct on a daily basis. United Airlines also fly from Melbourne to Vancouver on a daily basis.

From the USA
Canadian Airlines, **Air Canada** and **most US airlines** offer daily flights from over 20 US ports to Vancouver and Montréal in Canada. There are also flights to Halifax, Calgary and Edmonton.

From Europe
KLM (see above)
Lufthansa flies from Frankfurt to Montréal and Vancouver.
Air Canada flies from Frankfurt to Edmonton, Montréal, Ottawa and Vancouver and from Paris to Edmonton, Montréal, Ottawa and Vancouver.
British Airways flies from Frankfurt to Montréal and Vancouver and from Paris to Vancouver.

United Airlines flies to Vancouver.
Air France flies from Paris to Montréal.

Flight specialists
UK
Flight Centre tel: 0990 666677. 13 stores in UK (440 in UK, Canada, South Africa, Australia and New Zealand)

US
Ticket Planet website: www.ticketplanet.com
Travel Mood 214 Edgware Rd, London W2 1DH; tel: 020 7258 1234

By road
All the major cities in Canada are accessible by road from elsewhere in Canada. Only Whitehorse and Yellowknife can be reached by road from British Columbia and Alberta. The Dempster Highway goes all the way north from Whitehorse to Inuvik in NWT via Dawson City. The Alaska Canadian Highway (AlCan) allows you to reach Fairbanks and the rest of the state from Whitehorse and all points south. Other than these few roads the north is accessible by air only.

Several bus companies have scheduled services throughout the north with services from the Yukon to Vancouver, BC, and Edmonton, Alberta, six days a week. The Alaskon Express/Gray Line Yukon runs regular services between Whitehorse and Tok, Fairbanks, Anchorage and Valdez in Alaska. Gray Line Alaska runs a daily service between Skagway and Whitehorse from mid-May to mid-September (www.yukon.net/westours). Greyhound Lines of Canada runs passenger services to the north (www.greyhound.ca). Gray Line Canada website is www.grayline.ca. Schedules and fares are available at all the websites; you can even book your tickets if you have dates.

Tour operators offering journeys to the north
UK
All Canada Travel & Holidays tel: 01502 585825; email: mail@all-canada.com web: all-canada.com
AmeriCan Adventures tel: 01892 512700; email: amaduk@twins.co.uk web: www.americanadventures.com
Animal Watch tel: 01732 741612
Arctic Experience tel: 01737 218800. Yukon only
Arcturus Expeditions tel: 01389 830204: email: arcturus@btinternet.com
Bluebird Holidays tel: 0990 320000 or 0870 700 0500; email: sales@bluebird.uk.com
Canada 4 U tel: 01502 565648; email: sales@canada4u.co.uk; web: www.canada4u.co.uk
Canadian Connections tel: 01494 473173
Dsicover the World tel: 01737 218801; web: www.arctic-discover.co.uk
Experience Canada tel: 01323 416699; email: experience.hols@btinternet.com; web: www.experienceholidays.co.uk
First Call (London) Ltd tel: 020 8500 0011; email: firstcall@btinternet.com; web: www.firstcalltravel.com
Frontiers Adventures tel: 020 8776 8709. NWT and Nunavut only

Frontier Canada tel: 020 7757 2000; brochures: 020 8659 5636; email:sandra@whistler.demon.co.uk; web: www.frontier-ski.co.uk

Globespan Group Plc tel: 0990 561525; email: gatwick@globespan.co.uk

Go Fishing tel: 020 8742 1556; email: sales:go-fishing-worldwide.com web: www.go-fishing-worldwide.com

Hemmingways tel: 01737 842735; email: hemmingways_limited@compuserve.com; web: www.hemmingways.uninet.co.uk

The Imaginative Traveller tel: 020 8742 8612; email: info@imaginative-traveller.com; web: www.imaginative-traveller.com

The Independent Traveller tel: 01509 618800

Jetsave Ltd tel: 0870 848 7019; web: www.crystalholidays.co.uk

Jetset Europe Plc tel: 0870 700 5000; email: res:jetset-europe.plc.uk; web: www.jetsetworld.com

Kuoni Travel tel: 01306 742888; web: www.kuoni.co.uk

Naturetrek tel: 01962 733051; email: info@naturetrek.co.uk; web: www.naturetrek.co.uk

North American Highways tel: 01902 851138; email: american@btinternet.com web: www.northamericanhighways.co.uk. Yukon only

North American Holidays tel: 01892 619000

Page and Moy Travel tel: 0870 010 6373

The Polar Travel Company tel: 01364 631470. NWT and Nunavut only

Saga Holidays tel: 0800 414383

Shearings Holidays tel: 01942 829800

Spirit of the West tel: 01892 619000

Tailor Made Travel tel: 01386 712000; email: sales@tailor-made.co.uk; web: www.tailor-made.co.uk

Titan Hitours tel: 01737 760033

Travel 4 tel: 0870 155 0066

Travelbag tel: 01420 88380; email: freequotel@travelbag.co.uk

Travelpack tel: 0870 574 7101; web: www.travelpack.co.uk

Travelpath tel: 0990 168508; email: colin@path.woden.com

Trek International Travel Ltd tel: 01295 256777; email: postmaster@trekam.demon.co.uk; web: www.trekamerica.com

Vacation Canada email: vacationcanada@btinternet.com; web: www.vacationcanada@btinternet.com

Wildlife Worldwide tel: 020 8667 9158; email: sales@wildlifeworldwide.com; web: www.wildlifeworldwide.com

Windows on the Wild tel: 020 8742 1556; web: www.windows-on-the-wild.com

USA

Adventure Alaska Tours Arkansas; tel: 1-800-365-7057

Alaska Travel Adventures Redmond, Washington; tel: 1-800-323-5757

Collette Tours Pawtucket, Rhode Island; tel: 1-800-248-8943

Cosmos/Globus Littleton, Colorado; tel: 1-888-218-8665

Journeys International Inc 107 Aprill Drive, Suite #3, Ann Arbor, MI 48103-1903; tel: 1-800-255-8735/734-665-4407; email: info@journeys-intl.com; web: www.journeys-intl.com

Mountain Sobek Travel 6420 Fairmont Avenue, El Cerrito, California 94530; email: info@mtsobek.com; web: www.mtsobek.com; UK/Europe office tel: 01494 448901; email: Sales@mtsobekeu.com; Australian office tel: 02 9264 5710; email: Adventure@africatravel.com.au
Princess Tours Seattle Washington; tel: 1-800-426-0442

Canada
Ecosummer www.ecosummer.com; email: trips@ecosummer.com

GETTING ABOUT
By air
There are three major airlines that cover the north. Which airline you take depends on your destination. Flights are not necessarily daily and seats are limited as most of the aircraft is turned over to cargo. Some of the flights offer only the lightest of refreshments and limited in-flight services. Don't expect anything flash, even though the cost of the flights is excessive.

Air North www.airnorth.yk.net or www.yukonweb.com/tourism/airnorth. Imuvik/Whitehorse links. Schedule and charter service between Yukon, Alaska and NWT.
Alkan Air www.yukonweb.wis.net/tourism/alkanair. Charter flights, sightseeing tours and air ambulance service.
Calm Air www.calmair.com. Website has flights, schedules and web airfare specials. Charter and scheduled services within Nunavut. Flies to Thompson, Winnipeg and Churchill to Rankin Inlet, Coral Harbour, Chesterfield Inlet, Whale Cove, Repulse Bay, Baker Lake, and Arviat.
Canadian North/Canadian International Airlines www.cdnair.ca. Charter and scheduled flights throughout Nunavut and NWT. Flies from Edmonton through connections on Canadian flights from Ottawa, Toronto, and Vancouver to Fort Smith, Hay River, Yellowknife, Norman Wells, Inuvik, Cambridge Bay, Iqaluit and Resolute.
First Air www.firstair.ca. On-line booking service for scheduled and charter passenger flights to and within NWT and Nunavut. Flies from Ottawa, Montréal, Iqaluit and Yellowknife to Whitehorse, Fort Simpson, Hay River, Fort Resolution, Kugluktuk, Holman, Cambridge Bay, Resolute Bay, Taloyoak, Gjoa Haven, Pelly Bay, Naanisivik, Pond Inlet, Igloolik, Hall Beach, Coral Harbour, Cape Dorset, Clyde River, Broughton Island, Pangnirtung, Kimmirut and Kuujjuaq. It also connects Winnipeg, Inuvik, Rankin Inlet and Edmonton using NWT Air.
NWT Air www.nwtair.ca. The regional carrier of Air Canada features a flight timetable database.
Trans North Helicopters kluanetours@yukon.net. Offers a helicopter charter service.

It's a complicated network and there are numerous little regional charter services that use small aircraft to get you to some of the more isolated communities. To give you some idea, when I last travelled around the north I had 16 flights in 16 days on all three airlines at some time or another; to reach somewhere distant I often needed to catch up to three flights in any one flying day. In addition it needed three different flights to get home from Yellowknife via Edmonton and Vancouver and two flights to get to Iqaluit via Ottawa. My schedule didn't allow me the luxury of catching the most direct service. Sometimes it is easy, but often it is rather longwinded to get anywhere.

By road (see also page 90)
Websites
Gray Line Yukon www.yukon.net/westours. Bus services and tours throughout Yukon.
Greyhound Lines of Canada Ltd www.greyhound.com. Schedule services between towns and cities in NWT

Car rentals
Auto Wohnmobile RV Rentals www.yukontour.com
Avis Car Rentals www.Avis.com

WHAT TO TAKE
Most outfitters will supply any localised special needs as far as **clothing** goes. On a pre-booked journey any special needs should be indicated on the company's pre-departure information; if you have any queries ask the company – there is nothing worse than arriving somewhere strange and finding you need to buy something in an unfamiliar shopping environment. Personally, I always feel more comfortable in something I'm used to and I am very personal about my sleeping bags.

Be prepared. The weather in the north is very fickle and can change without much warning. Just because you are travelling in the middle of summer doesn't mean a blizzard won't happen. You don't want to be caught out with nothing warm to wear. Don't forget something in case it turns extremely cold and don't forget the rainwear, plus woolly hat, gloves, thermal underwear and warm socks.

A three-season **sleeping bag** would be adequate for the summer and I have one that has no zips so it packs up small. For arctic conditions I have a US Army Arctic sleeping bag. It is big, bulky and cumbersome, but it really is warm and I have slept in the open in well below freezing temperatures and have been as warm as toast. I picked it up in an outdoors shop.

Sturdy **boots** are suitable for most conditions but in winter buy yourself a pair of fabric-topped snowmobile boots with insulated liners made by a company called Sorel or the like. They aren't cheap (about $200) but can be purchased anywhere in Canada and they keep your feet warm. You can buy them rated down as far as –100°C. Arctic military boots are probably the best, but people in the know snap them up as soon as they become available. Another boot I have heard recommended is the 'shoe-pac' boot or bushboot. These have leather tops and rubber bottoms and a wool insulator inside. For indoor use I have a pair of insulated booties that I wear in camp or inside a cabin. These are lightweight and filled with down and they make me look like Herman Munster. They keep my feet warm inside my sleeping bag and pack down to almost nothing. Sandals and open-type flip-flop shoes are completely unsuitable in any weather and condition. Watch what the locals wear and emulate them.

Insects are a problem in the summer so remember to be prepared either with lots of suitable and **strong repellent** or with clothing designed to keep off the little pests.

If you wear **contact lenses** take along a pair of spectacles as well. Dusty conditions may make wearing contact lenses uncomfortable. If you take any special **medication** it is better to take more than adequate supplies of it from home, along with a doctor's letter explaining what it is and what it is for in case you need to replace it or justify having it to a customs official.

The last two things I never forget to take are a trashy **book** for when I want a quiet moment or need to fill one and some **music**. I have my own desert island discs – six pieces of music that suit my moods when I have them. These two are the only luxuries I afford myself as my **cameras** weigh a ton and take up vast amounts of space (see page 101 for photographic supplies and tips). Remember, any fool can be uncomfortable; a clever person takes advantage of an uncomfortable situation and turns it into five-star luxury.

MONEY MATTERS
All prices in dollars given throughout this book are in Canadian (not US) dollars, unless stated otherwise.

Exchange rates
While this book was in preparation in the spring of 2000 exchange rates were as follows £1 = $CAD2.30.

Taxes
Canada is great for taxes. These are applied to goods for sale and for services such as restaurant, hotel and motel bills. The price quoted is usually without the various taxes added and this is done at the point of sale. Non-residents are eligible for a refund on most of the taxes but it is quite a time-consuming process when departing Canada for home. Allow plenty of time if you wish to obtain a refund on all the extra taxes and ensure that you keep all the valid receipts.

First, there's a national Good and Services Tax (GST) currently levied on all goods and services at 7%. This is a similar tax to VAT in Britain. BC, Saskatchewan, Manitoba, Ontario, Quebec and PE Island levy a Provincial Sales Tax (PST) on shop-bought items, food and hotel and motel rooms. The level of PST may vary between provinces but it is nominally somewhere between 5% and 12% and is redeemable when you exit Canada. Currently the northern territories charge no PST at all. Finally, Nova Scotia, Newfoundland & Labrador and New Brunswick have what is called a harmonised tax (HST), ie: where GST and PST are combined, at 15% on accommodation, goods and services.

You qualify for a refund if:

- You are not a resident of Canada
- You have the original receipts for goods, each individual receipt shows a minimum purchase amount (before taxes) on which you paid GST/HST of $50
- Your purchase amounts (before taxes) of eligible accommodation and goods on which you paid GST/HST total at least $200

To claim a rebate you need form GST176. Proof of export is required and visitors leaving through a Canadian customs post need to have their goods inspected and the receipts stamped. Certain participating duty-free shops can refund the taxes immediately up to a maximum of $500. However, the Canadian customs officers will have to stamp the receipts and the visitor will have to complete form GST176 and mail it back to Canada for the refund. The cheques are in Canadian dollars. It's all a bit of a pain but some people like to make the effort.

Currency
The Canadian dollar ($) is divided into 100 cents (¢). Notes are in the following denominations: $1,000, $100, $50, $20, $10 and $5. Coins come in $2 and $1 (known locally as a loonie) and 50¢, 25¢, 10¢, 5¢ and 1¢.

Carrying money
When travelling anywhere abroad the safest way to carry money is in the form of travellers' cheques. However, in the far north many hotels and restaurants will only accept cash and in many small communities there aren't any banks, so a combination of cash and travellers' cheques is advisable. Sterling is not readily changeable except in banks but US dollars are. There are money changing facilities at all international and the larger local airports. All international credit cards are accepted in most places, the exception being some of the smaller communities in the far north. VISA, Mastercard/Access, Diners' Club and American Express are in general use but check first with the establishment what they accept.

Banking
Normal banking hours in Canada are 10.00–15.00, Mon–Fri with extended hours in some locations. Trust companies and credit unions often have longer opening hours.

Tipping
Tips and service charges are not usually added to the bill in Canada. Usually, a tip is expected to the value of 15% of the bill. This applies to barbers and hairdressers, taxi drivers, bellhops, doormen, redcaps (porters), etc. Porters at airports and railway stations expect $1 per item of luggage and tipping your waiter or server in a restaurant or bar is standard practice.

ACCOMMODATION

Hotel, motel and budget accommodation in the north is often scarce. The big cities like Whitehorse, Yellowknife and Dawson City have a reasonable range of accommodation from budget hostels to well-serviced 3- and 4-star establishments. But as the destinations get smaller so the choice begins to dry up until, in some of Nunavut's communities, there is only one form of visitor accommodation in the town. Nothing is cheap, with most reasonable places costing up to $100 or more per night. The advantage here is that the cost usually applies to the room not the number of beds in it. In many northern communities the hotels will have very limited bed space as well, and single rooms or single supplements are not necessarily available. You may find that, after being out all day, you have a new roommate when you return to your hotel. It is a fact of life and unfortunately you will have to live with it. Consider it a part of the northern experience.

If you are suitably attired, camping may be an option. A few northern communities that have road connections and all the major towns have camping sites or RV (Recreational Vehicle) sites; in addition there are a few along the major highways that may be free.

FOOD AND DRINK

Canadian restaurants compare favourably with those in the UK in terms of variety of meals and types of menu. You can eat three meals for as little as $30 per day. The quantities are sometimes larger than we would expect to see here. Some breakfasts, in particular, are enormous. A hearty (enormous) breakfast can cost as little as $5. Lunch may be $7–12, while dinner can be had for $18–30. All this depends on your taste and wallet. Some of the restaurants in the smaller communities have a fixed menu at a fixed price and usually don't cater to vegetarians. Often meals are included in the price of the hotel and are at set times. Check when you check in. As far as alcohol goes, there are plenty of bars in most towns and restaurants usually serve alcohol with meals. Bar and 'pub' hours are usually fairly liberal. Some restaurants have an excellent variety of wines available, selling European, American and Australian wines, but anything imported is expensive. Canada does produce some excellent wines of its own and they are well worth trying if they are on the wine list. Laws prohibit a person drinking until he/she is 18 or 19 years of age depending on the province. Some communities have a 'no alcohol' policy.

SHOPPING

There are some fine Canadian and native handicrafts to be bought as souvenirs in Canada. Aboriginal art and novelties, moccasins and other items of clothing are available. Pottery, jewellery, woodcarvings, glassware, and knitted or hand-woven goods are also good buys for those at home. Most stores are open daily from 09.00 to 17.30 or 18.00, and until 21.00 on Fridays. In some municipalities local by-laws have extended the opening hours during the week and on Sundays. Small local stores remain open until late and on Sundays for groceries, personal items and newspapers.

Clothing sizes

Where possible try on everything before you buy because, no matter what happens and how accurate the sizes may be, some variations do occur from one manufacturer to another. With the exception of men's shirts, which appear to be standard throughout the world, the chart below will help when selecting any items of clothing you may wish to buy.

Adult women's sizes

Canada/US	8	10	12	14	16	18	20	
UK	6	8	10	12	14	16	18	
Europe	38	40	42	44	46	48		

Sweaters and blouses

Canada/US	30	32	34	36	38	40	42	44
UK/Europe	36	38	40	42	44	46	48	50

Women's shoes

Canada	4	5	6	7	8
Europe	37	38	39	40	41
UK/Europe	4	5	5½	6	7

Adult men's sizes

Suits

Canada/US/UK	34	36	38	40	42	44	46	48		
Europe	44	46	48	50	52	54	56	58		

Men's shoes

Canada/US	6	7	8	9	1	11	12	13	14	15
Europe	39	40	41	42	43	44	45	46	47	48
UK	5	6	7	8	9	10	11	12	13	14

NATIONAL HOLIDAYS

All the usual holidays occur in Canada plus a few national days. They are:

New Year's Day, January 1st	Labour Day, September 4
Good Friday	Thanksgiving, October 9
Easter Sunday	Remembrance Day, November 11
Easter Monday	Christmas Day, December 25
Victoria Day, May 22	Boxing Day, December 26
Canada Day, July 1	

Some provincial holidays that may effect you when visiting northern Canada are:

Alberta	Alberta Family Day, February 21; Heritage Day, August 7
British Columbia	British Columbia Day, August 7
NWT/Ontario/Manitoba	Civic holiday, August 7
Yukon	Discovery Day, August 21

Some of these days are subject to change without notice but they give you a general idea of what holidays occur when. Remember that if a holiday falls on a weekend then the following Monday will be a holiday.

ELECTRIC CURRENT

Electricity in Canada is supplied at 110 volts AC at 60Hz. Europe is 220 volts AC at 50Hz. Adapters are required to use appliances like hairdryers and shavers.

MEDIA AND COMMUNICATIONS
Telephone

The international dialling code for the UK from Canada is 011 44, then the STD code (less the zero) and then the number. Cheap rates apply 18.00–09.00 local time. For Directory Assistance dial 411. To get a number outside the local area code dial 1 + area code + number. To connect to the operator dial 0. For the emergency services dial 911.

To dial Canada from the UK dial 001 then the area code, then the number. Many Canadian public call boxes use pre-purchased phone cards as well as coins and credit cards. Phone cards are available at convenience stores, post offices, newsagents, supermarkets etc.

Emergencies

In case of emergency dial 911 for the emergency services. If the line is unobtainable dial '0' for the operator and asked to be connected to whichever service you require.

Standard time zones

In the winter months without daylight savings applied the times zones are;

Standard Time	GMT –3$\frac{1}{2}$
Atlantic Standard Time	GMT –4
Eastern Standard Time	GMT –5
Central Standard Time	GMT –6
Mountain Standard Time	GMT –7
Pacific Standard Time	GMT –8

Daylight saving begins on the first Sunday in April when the clocks are advanced by one hour. They revert to standard time on the last Sunday in October.

Newspapers

There are no national Canadian newspapers as such, but many of the big journals are available throughout the country. In some communities they may not be current as they only arrive with an incoming flight. Having said that the best choices are the *Globe* and *Mail* out of Toronto, or the *Vancouver Sun*.

Television

Canadian law prescribes a minimum of Canadian content on all television stations. The Canadian Broadcasting Corporation operates both television and radio stations and its news service is reputed to be more impartial and international than the American services frequently found on the cable or, as in the north, satellite networks. Some scheduling is devoted to Inuit and native language broadcasts with Nunavut getting, if it hasn't already, its own nation-wide channel. There is a national weather forecast channel that I have found superb and many of the CBC stations broadcast BBC programmes as well. The choice is greater than in the UK but much of it is, sadly, very Americanised.

Postal services
Canada Post is a crown corporation and is therefore often slow and inefficient. I have had things sent from Canada that have taken months to arrive so I have little faith in a speedy delivery. Not every community or town has a post office as such and they certainly aren't as numerous as they are in Britain but many hotels and some shopping centres have postal counters from where you can send that much-awaited letter or postcard. Proper postal services are available in all the big cities like Whitehorse and Yellowknife. There are numerous small businesses that offer fax facilities, and cyber cafés and outlets offering Internet services are becoming more frequent.

FISHING AND HUNTING
Fishing
Federal, provincial and local laws govern all sport fishing in Canada. All non-resident anglers over the age of 16 years require a licence. In the Yukon licences are obtainable from Department of Renewable Resources offices, the Whitehorse District office of the federal Department of Fisheries and Oceans, most highway lodges, sporting goods stores and convenience stores and some offices of the RCMP. In the NWT and Nunavut they are available from any Resources, Wildlife and Economic Development office (Department of Sustainable Development in Nunavut); any Department of Fisheries and Oceans office; most sport fishing lodges, sporting goods, hardware and convenience stores; and certain offices of the RCMP. National parks are not covered by any of the territorial fishing licences so special permits are required if you intend to fish within the bounds of any of these areas. These can be obtained at the national park offices for an additional nominal fee and are valid for use in all the national parks throughout Canada.

In the Yukon a licence costs $35 for the season; $20 for six days; and $5 for one day. In Nunavut and the NWT a licence costs $40 for a season and $30 for three days. Licences must be carried on your person at all times whilst fishing. At the time of purchasing your licence you will be provided with a booklet describing seasons, weight limits, gear restrictions and fishing method restrictions that are applicable to each territory. In the Yukon you must also have a valid Salmon Conservation Catch Card if you want to fish for salmon. All details of the salmon caught are recorded and this card must be returned to the Department of Fisheries and Oceans by October 31 each year. The cards cost $50 for non-residents over 16 years of age.

Special permits are also required to fish in Tatlmain and Wellesley lakes in the Yukon and Great Bear Lake and within the bounds of the Inuvialuit

Settlement Region in NWT. These licences are free but to fish these waters without one is illegal. They are available at the Department of Renewable Resources offices in the Yukon; or the Resources, Wildlife and Economic Development offices in NWT. In Nunavut there may be special terms and conditions that apply to sport fisherman within certain areas of the Nunavut Settlement Area under the Nunavut Land Claim Agreement. The local Renewable Resource office can help here.

Sporting fish include Arctic char, Arctic grayling, all species of trout and salmon, northern pike, walleye, burbot and whitefish.

Hunting

I doubt that hunting comes within the scope of this book and some readers may be abhorred by the thought of killing animals for sport but it is ingrained in Canadian life amongst the resident population, particularly in country and wilderness areas. I also feel that some big game hunters may read this guidebook for additional information on the area that they intend to visit and, although I may not agree with their particular sport, it is a reality in northern Canada, not an exception. Hunting is something readers will meet right the way across Canada, so I have provided it for information only. I apologise if it causes any reader distress or offence.

All but aboriginal peoples are required to pay for a fixed-fee licence to hunt in Canada. These are purchased at Renewable Resources Offices, Government Administration buildings, territorial agents and certain sporting goods stores. Most game is monitored. Some species require you to produce evidence of the kill in person so that all the necessary permits can be issued and the hides and/or trophy heads tagged etc before they can be sold or exported. Hunting is seriously regulated throughout Canada and massive fines can be incurred by anyone found breaking the ground rules. Game meat, or 'country fayre' as it is called in Canada, is popular food and is sold everywhere. In the northern territories it is the only available source of meat as the usual beef and lamb costs too much to transport so far from the sources of production.

ARCTIC PHOTOGRAPHY

Northern Canada is rugged and unpredictable wilderness. The scope of that wilderness is beyond most people's comprehension. It is frighteningly brilliant and its awe-inspiring landscapes quite simply free the soul. I get a real rush of adrenaline when I am out there. Sometimes I get so excited out there in the wilderness with so much going on that I fumble; I have dropped lenses when trying to change to something more suitable to the task; on occasion I have even forgotten to put film in I have been so taken aback by my surroundings. That low-level sun does something magical to all it falls upon.

Beauty aside, everything I do and everything I use are just tools for doing my job as a photojournalist. Fortunately for me, I still get as excited as a young schoolboy with a new toy when someone comes up and says that there's muskoxen on a hill just outside town and I realise that the sun is just going down and the light is perfect. Or maybe they say that there are polar bears raiding the garbage tip and would I like to take a look? My passion for photography instantly gets the better of me and I'm swinging my bag into the truck and climbing aboard before I've even thought about what I'm going to do.

I try to interpret what I see for the benefit of others. The wilderness experience is so rewarding, particularly when the autumnal light is playing. I tend to shoot a wide variety of shots from travel to close-up and, of course, wildlife. I would suggest that you always try to put the images in perspective and give them a sense of place. Autumn is the best time as the animals are in their prime and the landscape at its most colourful. It is also the time when the weather is the least predictable. Still, if the weather is not right, wait a while and it is likely to change, although time has not always been on my side when I've been on assignment in Canada.

Arctic photography presents its own problems and rewards the further north you go. Extended travel in the Canadian wilderness can mean photographing in all seasons and weathers. There might be 'eight months of winter' but that short four-month window of spring, summer and autumn means the long-term traveller has often to change tactics and techniques.

Equipment

The Arctic north above the tree line offers little or no cover so if it's wildlife you want to photograph getting close is almost impossible. Most wildlife photographers in the north find that a 1,000mm lens is the minimum length required for a decent close-up image. They are almost impossible to hold still and focus. Their aperture is so wide, probably $f5.6$ or $f8$ at best, that a fine grain quality film such as Fuji Velvia results in such slow shutter speeds that the photograph won't work without a tripod. Wildlife photography is as much about luck and being in the right place at the right time as it is about being a skilled photographer. If time permits I always use a tripod; it's often deemed the only difference between an amateur and a professional.

I work almost exclusively in 35mm but I do use medium format if time and the assignment permit. The reproduction quality is better in the larger format. I usually carry two Nikon bodies, one with a motordrive and a number of dedicated lenses ranging from a 28mm to a 300mm telephoto. Depending on the job I may carry a 400mm with a 1.4x or 2x teleconverter but I sometimes have to consider the weight problems here. A tripod is useful and I have one called a Benbo Trekker which opens up to suit all angles and situations; I find it far more useful than the conventional even three-legged types. All my lenses are fitted with Skylight UV filters and metal lens hoods. I carry a small Sekonic light meter that that can measure ambient and flash readings in both incident and reflected modes. I don't need anything flashy here, just something that's compact, accurate and robust. A couple of flashes complete the kit. All this is carried in either an over the shoulder bag or a photo-rucksack, depending on what's required. As my means of transport vary from car or truck to all-terrain vehicles, snowmobiles, dog-sledges and horseback I try to be as weight conscious and space conscious as possible. At the end of the day I still have to carry it all.

In the modern world of fast autofocus cameras any of the newer cameras will stand up to the rigours of Arctic conditions. Autofocus and motordrives will be a bit slow but if you follow the tips I have laid out below there shouldn't be too many problems. Two lenses, such as a 28-80mm zoom and a 70-210mm zoom will adequately cover most situations in most weathers. A polarising filter is an added bonus but use a linear type rather than a circular one. If you heed the advice below you can achieve some stunning results with them.

Film

Choice of **film** can be either a personal or a monetary thing. Whether you buy print or transparency depends on what you want to do or achieve. Sometimes the only film available at the time in whatever brand you can get is the only choice you have. Otherwise you can pick and choose and pay whatever you like. Quality is another thing and professional level films are not cheap no matter where you travel. I stock up before I go with all that I think I will need. With practice I generally guess the right amount but sometimes I misjudge and need more film. Wherever I have found a good supply I have listed the shops in their respective towns, but do not count on either a wide variety or film with lots of life left on it. With re-supplies coming either by plane or once a year by boat it will inevitably be very expensive.

Some people get really personal and use only the film that they are most familiar with and get the best results from. I do not blame them and their results will be consistent. You may be like me and be influenced by what a film achieves visually. I use one type of film or several different films to suit the available lighting situations and what effects or results I want to achieve when the shoot's over.

In general, I use a mixture of Fuji Velvia and Provia 100 most of the time. I carry several rolls of Kodachrome 200 for the slightly warmer colours it portrays and some Fuji Provia 800 for very low-light situations. I do experiment with film types, particularly when a new film comes on the market. I take copious notes and details with new films and compare the results to what I'm currently using on the editing light box when I return home. I am interested only in strong, rich colours and pin sharp images. I avoid cheap or unknown brands of film irrespective of who produces the film because I cannot guarantee the same quality every time I press the shutter. From the films listed above you can see that I am very particular and I need a lot of convincing to try something new.

I only shoot transparency, which is what my editors and clients require for use in publications and brochures. In a normal week on assignment I allow 50 rolls of film but I do have many hungry editors to feed. Film is kept in a soft cool bag or icebox all the time and only removed as and when needed. I usually take out a day's supply the night before when the temperature is at its coolest. Icepacks are used when they are available or I have use of a refrigerator to re-freeze them. All rolls are numbered and the place where they were shot written in my notebook. I trust nothing to memory.

Technicalities

In the extreme north the sun is either not visible at all or it is there all the time. During the 'midnight sun' of the summer solstice the sun actually revolves around your head and sunset just melts into the dawn. It is confusing for those of us who only recognise a sun setting in the west and getting up in the opposite eastern horizon the following dawn. I always keep a compass handy just so that I can keep my head about me. A shot may be better tomorrow when the sun is somewhere else and the background more picturesque. I am always making notes in case I return to the same spot again.

Polarising **filters** are a bit of a disadvantage in winter if not used correctly; many people overuse the polariser in pursuit of strong rich colours. Besides, losing a couple of F stops in low light conditions, they affect the way the image is recorded. Snow and ice have colour, depth, texture and integrity of light. What it looks like depends on the angle of the light in relation to the land, the intensity of that light, and the colour with which the light washes the surrounding scene. Polarising filters at their extreme cause snow to go a muddy grey in colour causing a nice crisp scene to look rather bland. Full manual control (linear type) allows the trade-off somewhere between that deep, rich, blue sky and bright vibrant colours we all want and snow that has some shape and feeling to it.

Photographing wildlife

Wildlife photography is best in the early morning and late afternoon when the animals are feeding. They are at their most relaxed, the light is at its best, and there are additional atmospheric conditions, such as mist and fog, for instance, that can only add to the quality of the image. Good images require dedication and long, unsociable hours. A good shoot is hard work and very hectic as everything seems to be happening at once. Contrary to popular belief, photographers do not lead 'the life of Riley'.

Quite often Canada's wildlife looks pretty docile: elk and moose grazing contentedly in a forest, bears picking berries or looking preoccupied with feasting on salmon, etc. Do not ever forget that these are still wild animals and must be treated with respect.

People are always drawn toward predators. There is something about an animal that eats other animals for food. Please take no chances when photographing Canada's larger animals, particularly the predators. You would not get out of a car in Africa amongst a pride of lions, yet so many people try to get close to a big bear in North America. These are dangerous animals so treat them with caution.

It is not only the predators that are dangerous. The grazers and browsers are too. An elk's antlers are sharp and can gore a man to death. The same applies to moose. Both animals are particularly dangerous during the rut when there is fierce competition for the right to mate with the females. Everything is considered a threat at that time. Moose also have a powerful kick that can easily break a limb. These animals are the heavy weights of Canada's wildlife with a male moose weighing almost a tonne. Do not take chances and get too close just for the sake of a picture!

If you see an animal you wish to photograph do not approach the animal directly – even the little ones. Heading straight for them only leads to trouble. Aim for where the animal is heading. Be obvious and take your time. Be aware that animals need personal space just like we do. If the animal sets the limits of that personal space, usually a couple of hundred metres, and you maintain those limits, it will leave you alone and not consider you a threat. Move slowly and positively. Do not be erratic in what you do – it only raises the animal's awareness of you. Break the rules the animal has set down and it will do one of two things: it will run away or it will attack. Neither are acceptable and show bad judgement on your part. Remember whose environment you are in in the first place.

When approaching an animal, do not act like a predator but remain obvious and in the open. Let the animal see you. Keep downwind if possible, as it is preferable that the animal sees you first. Catching your scent before catching sight of you will most likely cause the animal to flee immediately without you getting close to it. A hungry predator, like a bear, may consider you their next course for dinner and hunt you intentionally if you are unaware of the bear's position. Under such circumstances you are in serious danger (see *Bears: General safety*, page 124).

Most animals will avoid confrontation. Physical confrontation between animals may lead to injury and/or death for either of the animals, thus lessening their long-term survival chances. They will usually either approach or mock attack to bluff their way out, or flee to what they would consider a safe stopping distance. Do not pursue the animal but back off. It may change the rules of engagement to your disadvantage the second time round. Come again another day or find yourself another animal and do not make the same mistakes again.

When near an animal, talk softly in a low, calm and assured voice. Do not whisper, talk loudly or allow too much emotion in your voice (we all get excited near wild animals and the adrenaline does start pumping, but try to be calm). Do not change the tone or level of sound but talk all of the time. Constantly reassure the animal that you are no threat. We humans have a wonderfully calming voice if we try, and animals recognise this.

A word of caution: if an animal gets fidgety or nervous – you are too close. Back off slowly. Restore that safe personal distance or, better still, leave and try again later. Remember, it is their environment and you are the guest.

Photographic tips for northern adventurers
- If you are new to photography, practise how to use your camera before you leave home. Do not forget to take your camera's instruction book with you; it is a wonderful aid to the memory.
- Always keep your camera padded in a tough, weatherproof bag when not in use. A bag containing silica gel, available from most camera stores, will help keep out moisture but in the dry climate of the north this is pretty pointless.
- Where possible, clean your camera daily. Avoid excessive use of lens cleaning solutions as they may break down the lens' delicate coatings.

Clean the inside of the back and behind your lens with a small battery-operated vacuum cleaner. A blower will only force dust further into the works.

- Protect the front of your lens with a Skylight (1A) filter. At high altitudes use salmon-coloured UV filter to reduce the bluing that occurs due to the increase in ultraviolet light in the thin atmosphere. Avoid excessive use of polarising filters in snow and ice conditions. Snow and ice have texture that is important to the picture. Too much polarising turns all that into a grey mush.

- Put in fresh camera batteries before you go on your travels and always carry a spare set in your bag. Modern SLR and compact cameras with built-in flashes consume a lot of power, so more than one spare may be required. Extreme cold weather lowers a battery's efficiency and it loses power quickly, so keep batteries warm in your pocket until they are needed. In most circumstances the preferable solution would be to keep the whole camera in a strong weatherproof bag out of the cold, keeping it, the batteries and the film warmish. The main drawback here is that you may be keeping everything too warm, causing condensation to build up every time you take the camera out. Different professional photographers take different approaches to this problem. On a personal note, my cameras are my tools of work, so being immediately usable is more important to me than my cameras' long-term protection. So in extremely cold weather I do not let the camera warm up at all. It stays outside the tent or building but sheltered from the weather in its bag. The camera is maintained at an ambient temperature all the time and avoids condensation build-up but is secure from the extremes of the weather. I keep my film with the cameras, as it does not need to be kept warm. I always take the batteries inside the tent. My cameras are cleaned every day, sometimes twice a day, religiously, whilst on assignment. I am more likely to wear out a camera before the rigours of the weather effect it. If something goes wrong with a camera I have at least one spare, usually two. As a final resort, I will probably fix it because I carry the tools to do so. I do not expect you will be afforded that luxury.

- If you must take your camera inside a house or building, put it inside a sealable plastic bag and suck all the air out of it. Then go inside. All the condensation will form on the inside of the plastic bag and not on your camera. After about 30 minutes you can remove it from the bag. Repeat the scenario before heading outside again.

- After you have decided how much film you think you will need for your journey, go out and buy twice that amount. It is better to have more than you need than to find out that you have not enough to capture that wildlife shot you'd been waiting for all day. Film is likely to be cheaper at home and you will have more choice.

- If you are photographing from a vehicle and the engine is running, make sure your camera's shutter speed is at least 1/500th of a second to eliminate any vibration.

- Learn to use your camera with two hands. One hand focuses and the other one holds the camera – all at the same time. Both hands should be under the camera, not on top of it. At no time should any one hand not be in contact with the camera. Imagine the body as a tripod with elbows tucked well in and everything in balance. Keep your trigger finger on the button at all times when taking a photograph. Speed in shooting is essential for that ultimate wildlife photograph. It is better to waste a shot than to have waited and missed it altogether. By practising before you leave home you will improve your chances of getting that stunning shot. Modern auto-focusing cameras are excellent, but if something goes wrong and you have to do it all manually – be prepared.
- Relax! Breathe normally and try to ignore all that adrenaline running around your body.
- Under normal circumstances 100 ASA film is quite adequate for most situations.
- Choice of film is a personal preference. Please bear in mind that most photographic libraries require transparencies but your exposures must be absolutely spot on. Print film is more tolerant and good photographs can be obtained when the exposure is not quite right.
- Never take your film out of the boxes or canisters until you want to load it. These are factory sealed and are subsequently weatherproofed. Avoid direct sunlight when loading and although a darkened room is often recommended it is not necessary.
- Cold weather makes film brittle. If winding on by hand, go slowly. Cold also causes static electricity which in turn creates streaks across the film. Once again, wind film on slowly (cold weather will normally make motordrives and autowinders run slowly).

The best camera tip ever

Being out there with all those wild animals is absolutely wonderful. I have a passion for photography but every now and again I stop and put the camera down. Sometimes I spend days without actually taking a picture. All too often I see the world in rectangular format limited by the frame and the constraints of taking a photograph. But memories go beyond the limits of film. I get excited when on assignment by everything that's happening around me, not just by what I see through a viewfinder.

At some time during your journey put your camera away and enjoy Canada and her wildlife for their own sake. You will be disappointed when you get home and find that, although you shot some great photographs, you missed the entire atmosphere that comes with travelling. Canada should be seen in its entirety not just through the lens of a camera. Remember that a picture may trigger a memory but if you have not had that memory in the first place the picture just remains a picture.

The climate is extremely dry the further north you go and the conditions cause the skin to become dry and sometimes painful. Each night rub a little moisturising cream, such as E45, into your hands, feet and on your face before going to sleep. They will love you forever.

If your fingers are cold do not take your gloves off and blow on them. The moisture from your breath condenses on your fingers and assists in the freezing process. The best solution is to fling your arms about your body warming up the arm muscles and subsequently your hands. Movement is the best way and the same applies to the feet. Make sure your boots are not too tight; you need to be able to wriggle your toes to keep them warm, especially if you are dog-sledging where your feet tend to be quite stationary for long periods of time.

Harp seals

Health and Safety

with Dr Felicity Nicholson

HEALTH

An awareness of health concerns that can seriously effect your journey into northern Canada is important. Some things are common anywhere in the world, but others are specific to conditions north of the 60. I have given the special issue of bear hazards a section on its own; in any wilderness area bears can be a problem. Avoidance is the key to good health. In any remote area help and access to proper medical facilities is not just around the corner but may be several days away and problems are generally easier to avoid than they are to treat. Cold is the biggest concern and can occur at any time of the year. A certain amount of preparation can help but being thrown into −31°C will be a shock for anyone. The two major cold concerns – hypothermia and frostbite – are covered in the section under survival. The rest are covered here.

Travel insurance

Anyone travelling anywhere in the world outside their own country would be advised to take out some form of travel insurance. Emergency transport home and medical expenses are obviously important. Full coverage is best and it should include all the activities you plan to undertake in Canada; check your policy's small print to ensure that you are covered if you are whitewater rafting or canoeing, skiing, mountain climbing, dog sledging or snowmobiling, or travelling in small aircraft or by boat. Does it cover you for emergency evacuations by helicopter if necessary? A cover of at least US$1 million for medical emergencies and evacuation would be the minimum expected.

Allow for all eventualities. It's no good having a policy for 31 days, missing a plane, and then having an accident requiring assistance on day 32. The policy will obviously be invalid and insurance companies are not flexible in these matters. The cost of helicopter rescue and emergency treatment for a major accident could be financially crippling to you and your family back home.

Water sterilisation

There are more things in water than just bugs. Providing a safe and plentiful supply of water will not only prevent dehydration but will avoid those annoying stomach disturbances that can spoil any journey. Canada and Alaska are often portrayed as places with almost pure water supplies but, even in the poorly inhabited north, water pollution can still be a problem. Contamination from the industrial effluent of paper and pulp mills, and municipal sewage for small communities can effect any seemingly pure water source. That mountain stream may look beautiful but what is going on upstream from you is what is really important.

Treat all water with suspicion, particularly near habitation, and that means camping sites, logging camps, mining exploration camps, mountain huts, ski resorts and hunting and fishing camps.

Some water will want filtration. Sediment from high mountain passes and glaciers finds its way into streams and these minute particles play havoc with your bowels. Boiling water supplies is really only effective at sea level. The higher up you go, the lower the temperature at which water boils, so reducing its effectiveness.

The most problematic organism in Canadian inland waters is a protozoan called *Giardia lamblia*. It causes an unpleasant and debilitating gut problem known as Giardiasis or locally as 'beaver fever'. As its local name suggests, beavers carry it, so you need to be vigilant downstream from beaver ponds. Dogs, cattle, horses and muskrats can also carry it. Unfortunately, it is also carried by man, and is one of the greatest health concerns in remote communities. It is thought to survive better in cold clear water so purification is recommended for all natural water except melted snow. Remember that just because water comes out of the ground as a spring does not necessarily mean it is pure. Rocks do not filter water, nor do they take out any bacteria or any other organism.

Water purifying tablets work providing either that you do not need to filter or that you filter first. There are several on the market which have varying degrees of effectiveness. It is probably a good idea to purchase locally, as you will get the most effective for the area. I carry tincture of iodine as it doubles up as an antiseptic for minor cuts, but it is not particularly effective in extremely cold water.

There are lots of water purifying devices available on the market. I find them bulky to carry and time-consuming to use but they are very effective. They must be used strictly according to their instructions; keep any inlet and outlet hoses in separate marked plastic bags. Do not mix any container used for purified water with unpurified water. Be strict about keeping them separate (this will apply mainly to walkers and climbers who may carry water to camp before purifying it).

Traveller's diarrhoea

You can get loose bowels just from changing the type of water you drink or the place you get it from. By loose I mean one or two uncomfortable sessions on the toilet during the day or night and it is all over. Traveller's diarrhoea becomes serious when you are going five times an hour, every hour, all day. Anywhere you go in Canada the health and hygiene standards are usually quite high, so food poisoning is no more likely than in any other civilised place on the planet. Any loose session is likely to be a minor slip in someone's hygiene methods, or contaminated water, explained above.

However, dealing with any form of diarrhoea is relatively straightforward. Fluid loss is an inevitable consequence, so replacing lost fluids is vital. Putting a little rehydration salts in with your water will help things along nicely. They can be purchased in ready-to-use sachets (eg: Electrolade or Dioralyte) or you can make your own by putting 40g of sugar and 3.5g of salt into a litre of purified water.

If absolutely necessary, take Lomotil or Imodium. These drugs slow down the bowel's constant movements and allow the body to get on with treating itself. Giardiasis requires prompt treatment so it is helpful if you are able to recognise the symptoms. These include stomach cramps and greasy bulky stools accompanied by 'eggy' burps. Go as soon as possible to medical help for antibiotics. If you are a long way from help and suspect giardiasis, then you can self-treat with tinidazole (2g in one dose washed down with lots of water and repeated one week later if it fails).

Dehydration

The body loses water naturally in several ways. The most obvious methods are sweating and urination, but the body also loses water through evaporation from the skin (known as insensible perspiration) and evaporation from the lungs where air breathed out has been moistened by water in the lungs themselves. A completely inactive body can lose up to a couple of litres of water a day so you must be aware of your water intake and loss at all times in order to maintain sufficient levels.

It is possible that an unaware person could lose a lot of water unnoticed. This is significant in winter and at high altitudes when you are breathing in cold, dry air. Loss by sweating may not be apparent because in a cold, dry climate sweat evaporates almost instantly and does not remain on the skin to assist cooling as it does in hot climates.

A simple way to check fluid intake and loss is to watch the colour and quantity of urine passed. The darker it is, the more dehydrated you are. Any quantity less than half a litre indicates dehydration. Any drinks containing caffeine, such as coffee, tea and cola, and all alcoholic drinks, are diuretics and cause the body to pee more than necessary and not retain the fluids. Best drinks are water, weak juices, and herb teas. Force yourself to drink all the time. We often get too busy to drink when on holiday, even if at home we have regular tea breaks. I always restrict my consumption of alcohol when I am on assignment. I cannot work with a fuzzy brain. In most northern communities alcohol is either forbidden or in limited supply and extremely expensive solely because of the anti-social aspects related to its abuse.

Altitude sickness

The effects of altitude sickness are well documented in any book on mountain climbing or mountain medicine and first aid but for some reason people get it wrong. Either they do not read the books or they do not take in the advice or they push their luck at high altitudes. Some people's determination to climb a mountain overcomes their good sense and they carry on regardless.

Acclimatisation, or spending a reasonable time at altitude to get used to it all, is the key although for some people acclimatisation is ineffectual – they just cannot go to high altitudes. Altitudes over 2,500m (8,000ft) affect everyone. In the north high altitude is complicated by temperatures and climate more so than in areas like the Himalayas because these adverse weather conditions still continue at lower altitudes. For most people travelling to the north, altitude is not even on the agenda; it is just for those who wish to pursue mountain activites which will be mainly in the Yukon and Alaska.

Treatment for any altitude-related illness is immediate descent; as little as 500m will help. Arctic conditions will not help the situation. Denali in Alaska is relatively popular and you may find other climbers en route to assist, but in the rest of the region it is unlikely you will meet anyone to help.

Competent local mountain guides are in the best position to understand the effects and symptoms of altitude sickness and not be fooled by other physical conditions the victim may exhibit. Rely on their judgement.

Some of you may have heard of (or be advised to take) a drug called Diamox (acetazolamide). This drug has found favour among some doctors in reducing the likelihood of developing altitude sickness. Symptoms of AS could include, headaches, fatigue, shortness of breath on exertion, nausea and vomiting, dizziness, tingling in the extremities and in more severe cases breathlessness at rest. Diamox may effect some people in a similar way so you should try it least two weeks before you go when you are at sea-level. Take 250mg twice a day for two days to see if it suits you. If it does then you need to take a five-day course of the drug at the same dosage, starting three days before arriving at 3,500 metres and for two days after.

Sunburn

This is a real health problem in the north. A clear, unpolluted atmosphere allows the sun's strong UV rays to reach the earth's surface more easily. The ozone depletion does not make things any better. Weather forecasts on suspected sunny days often have an ultraviolet warning index:

low – skin burns in 60 minutes
moderate – skin burns in 30 minutes
high – skin burns in 20 minutes
extreme – skin burns in 15 minutes

Burnt shoulders make carrying a pack impossible; burnt lips make eating and drinking difficult and at higher altitudes the effects of burning can worsen.

Heavy use of sunscreen is the easiest solution, or covering up from top to toe in a sun-protective fabric. Cotton is only equivalent to a Sun Protection Factor (SPF) of around 8–15. Do not forget to put suncream on as well as cover up. Do not forget the ears and the top of your head if, like me, your hair is thinning. Remember, the effects of the sun are compounded and increased by the reflection factor of the snow. It comes at you from two directions and it can be fierce. Fog and overcast cover offer little protection from the sun's rays and I have known people to be burnt on completely sunless days.

Other problems besides sunburn occur with too much exposure to sunlight. Eye irritations can put your trip in jeopardy; snowblindness will put an end to your journey. I wear high altitude sunglasses. These make everything look yellow but they cut even the strongest UV without affecting normal vision. I also have a pair of 100% UV goggles that fit around my head with an elastic strap. Sunglasses with sidepieces and nose coverings should be looked at seriously. You may look silly but who cares if you are protected.

Minor cuts and bruises

Minor cuts and bruises are more of an annoyance than a problem. In the cold they do not heal very quickly and in the case of bruising it seems to take forever for the stiffness and pain to go away. More care than normal should be used when handling sharp objects. Coldness makes you less supple and co-ordination deteriorates slightly.

The biting bugs

Anywhere in the world that you sleep on the ground in the wilderness you will be bitten by some ground-hovering insect going about its business. Sleeping on the open hearth of a forest floor is an automatic invitation for ticks and other ground-dwelling parasites to deem you a host for a while. Ticks carry a variety of diseases that can be serious, such as eastern equine encephalitis and rocky mountain spotted fever; ticks may also carry a spirochaete called *Borrelia burgdorferi* which causes lyme disease.

Check even your most private parts for infestation, particularly those parts that are constantly moist with perspiration. I usually give myself a good body inspection every time I have a bath in a stream or river as you never feel ticks until they have well and truly made themselves at home in your skin. There are plenty of 'old wives' tales' about removing ticks and the like. The twisting method is best. Remember to ensure that you get the head. Pull the tick off gently, giving the body a little twist. Try not to crush the body, as this tends to squeeze the intestinal juices and body fluids back under your skin. Burning ticks off with a still-hot but not alight match head or by putting a drop of lighter fluid on the animal will cause the tick to regurgitate its disease-ridden cocktail of stomach fluids before releasing itself. However you do it, ensure that the wound left behind is thoroughly cleansed with antiseptic to avoid infection.

The biggest problems in the north are mosquitoes and blackflies, which are a nightmare to all mammals in summer no matter what repellent you use, cover up with or put on. Accept it. The caribou travel hundreds of kilometres to the north to escape the unwanted attentions of the mosquitoes and blackflies of their winter forest habitat. That's how bad they can be.

Blackflies are the worst. Their bites bleed, itch, produce lumps and become easily infected. Blackflies get everywhere – into your nose, eyes, ears, mouth, and inside your clothes; they are extremely uncomfortable. Mosquitoes are just annoying and their bites are itchy. About the worst thing the mozzies can do is spread equine encephalitis, but it is not common. Personally I just hate the noise of one buzzing in my ear. It drives me to distraction!

There are four defences against unwanted insect attention. They are: avoid bug times; avoid bug areas; use insect repellents; use suitable clothing and equipment such as tents.

Insects are seasonal. In the mountainous regions of the Yukon, NWT and Alaska, bugs can be avoided by going above the treeline. In Nunavut you are safe if a reasonable breeze is blowing. Early morning and late evening seem to be the worst times for mosquitoes and the middle of the day for blackflies. A cold spring delays the insects' hatching time and a wet summer prolongs the time they are around. In the far north there are no insects while the snow is about; the water needs to warm up before they hatch. They are not very keen on the cold so their season is actually a good deal shorter than those that live further south in the forested areas.

Mosquitoes breed in standing and poorly drained water. Avoid wet places with ponds of stagnant water. Windy places are ideal. The breeze disturbs the attractions that the human body puts out so insects cannot home in on you. A good stiff breeze also makes flying difficult. Steer clear of areas of light forest and tall grasses during the day to avoid the attentions of blackflies.

Bite prevention

There are lots of **insect repellents** on the market. A journey into any pharmacy will show you this. Insects locate their warm-blooded prey by detecting water vapour, carbon dioxide, scents, chemical attractants and the infra-red radiation we naturally omit. Insect repellents work by emitting a vapour that confuses the insects' ability to spot dinner. I have found that anything based on DEET works for me. Unfortunately some people cannot wear DEET and it has a detrimental effect on all things plastic and some synthetic materials. Bug Guards (DEET-containing wrist and ankle bands) are sold which claim that the chemical does not have direct skin contact and therefore may be worth trying for those with sensitive skin. Otherwise, failing these then natural repellents such as Mosiguard can be used but tend to be less effective than DEET- containing ones. Burning mosquito coils at night helps but the perfume they use to disguise the smell of burning cow dung attracts the unwanted attentions of bears (burning actual animal dung outside your tent works much better than commercially bought coils but the smell is awful). I would rather not have a curious bear in my camp unexpectedly. It all becomes something of an experiment as to what works for you and your natural aroma.

Wearing **protective clothing** depends on you. Extra clothing can prove to be too hot in summer when the insects are at their worst and where there is no breeze to blow them away. Some specialist shirts are truly effective when impregnated with repellent as well. I use a shirt made by a company called Bugwear in Scotland. It is lightweight, well meshed and the hood has a zipper so I can quickly take pictures before being eaten to death. I need to use a repellent on my hands in particular, otherwise I have to resort to gloves in areas of really bad infestation. No matter what piece of clothing you use to keep out the insects it will sometimes be hot and tedious to wear. Dressing in that overall cover-up takes a bit of getting used to when insects are still buzzing around just outside.

First aid kit

There are no hard and fast rules about what should be carried in a first aid kit, but generally only carry what you are comfortable with using. There is no point in carrying a vast array of antibiotics if you don't know how to use them, unless you will have medical advice en route and you won't have easy access to medical facilities. It is sensible to carry paracetamol, aspirin and Imodium; optional are antibiotics, for example, tinidazole for giardia.

The following are also useful: a pair of small scissors, tweezers, a digital thermometer, a small suture clamp and a couple of hypodermic needles (they're sterile and sealed should I need one for a blister or splinter). I have suture silk and steri-strips for the more serious cuts and a few plasters of various shapes and sizes. I also carry a small bottle of iodine, which is used as an antiseptic and as a water purifier.

Somewhere in my pack I'll have lots of triangular bandages and a few compressed, sterile wound dressings. You should only carry these if you can use them. I have found over the years that the worst things I need to attend to on me are a few minor cuts and splinters, a dose of the squits and the odd headache. Should I come across an emergency roadside or mountain-top situation I need to be able to do several things: stop serious bleeding, ease broken limbs, and cope with the biggest problem in any trauma situation – shock. Anything less dangerous and non-life threatening can wait for proper medical attention. In a modern place like Canada I can go to a doctor or pharmacist and get what I need for a few pence rather than carry it around with me all the time. Sunburn protection can be purchased anywhere in Canada.

Do not get carried away with too much kit. You still have to carry it and when you bring it home unopened you will wonder why you took it in the first place. A first aid kit should contain what you would normally find in the bathroom cabinet at home. You know what it is and what it is used for.

You are familiar with these items and are happy to use them with confidence. Anything else is in the territory of a well-trained doctor. Remember, a little knowledge and a big kit is dangerous. A good basic knowledge and a small kit is life saving and this is why I feel everyone should do some basic form of first aid training. You may need to save your own or someone else's life some day.

For information on hypothermia and frostbite, see *Chapter 6*, pages 122–3.

SAFETY

Personal safety comes in two parts: first, where you are responsible for your own personal security, and, second, your own personal safety within someone else's environment.

Personal security

You can expect that in wilderness country in Canada and Alaska you will be alone or with your immediate companions. The further away from civilisation (ie: motorised transport), the safer you will be and the less likely it is that you will encounter people who may cause you problems. However, there are some 'strange individuals' living in the wilderness who may or may not have a dubious past and be decidedly unfriendly towards other humans. Local knowledge will tell you where they are and how to avoid contact with them. Be aware that substance abuse is rife in some remote areas; people may behave strangely and unexpected violence may result. The wide-open wilderness does hide some disturbing realities. Should you stumble across a patch of funny grass hidden in the bush – leave immediately. The owner may not appreciate your uninvited attentions.

Poaching is big money, both for meat and body parts, and the criminal element has a big hand in it all. Should you accidentally happen on such a thing – leave. If contact is unavoidable, show a lack of interest or lack of awareness and get the hell out of there. When you feel yourself safely away, report the incident to the nearest RCMP depot. Hunters may consider a piece of land their patch. Land-owners are sometimes a little belligerent to strangers because of abusive behaviour from hunters, party-goers and off-road louts.

Man is the most dangerous animal on earth. He is even more dangerous when he has big, motorised toys and firearms. The situation gets worse if alcohol is involved. In the era of 4x4 vehicles it is too easy to drive into the middle of nowhere, get smashed, and then return to civilisation in an inebriated state.

Recreational motorboaters can be a problem if you are in a kayak or canoe. They may not see you and, even if they do, lack of consideration, bad manners, irresponsibility or plain stupidity are all factors that make big boats dangerous towards small ones. At the very least make yourself visible with bright-coloured clothing and fluorescent strips on your paddles.

Be exceptionally careful in the backwoods during the hunting seasons. Some irresponsible shooters will fire at anything that moves irrespective of whether they can see it or consider it a legitimate target.

Water safety

Once the ice has thawed boating is a serious activity in the north. When on any stretch of Arctic water in a small boat always wear a survival suit. The bigger mother boat should always have enough for everyone on board. Always wear a lifejacket. I know they are uncomfortable and cumbersome, but inland rivers are wild and unpredictable and you will have no hope of putting it on after you are tossed into a wild and freezing river. When canoeing or kayaking, be aware of other boats. They may not see you. If you go kayaking or rafting with an outfitter and they do not give you a safety lesson, ask for one. It is in your interests to know the procedures and to feel reassured that the outfitter knows what he is doing. Once again, always wear lifejackets and use helmets in any rough whitish water. Canadian law requires every boat to carry a PDF or personal flotation device (that's a lifejacket to you and me) for every person, something for bailing out and a whistle or other device for signalling. See that yours does! And as for any outdoor activity, remember to tell someone your plans, and never go alone.

For information on bears, see page 124.

Wilderness Survival 6

The saying I strictly adhere to when I travel is called six Ps – Prior Preparation and Planning Prevents Poor Performance

I feel it is self-explanatory and it applies to all things, whether you are travelling in a car, by plane, by ship or off trekking in an unfamiliar wilderness area. This is not a guide to physical survival techniques. The best suggestion I could make there is to buy a copy of John Wiseman's *SAS Survival Handbook* (HarperCollins, London 1986, £14.99) if you are that way inclined. They do not come any better. The bibliography at the back of this book lists several other good books on outdoors and wilderness activities all with region-related techniques for those who are into serious survival activities. Here, I would just like to look at common sense solutions should you, by some stroke of fate, require some basic skills to enable you to hold up and survive for a couple of days until help arrives. If you follow my plan of the six Ps and follow the guidelines set out below then survival should not become an issue.

Survival is about being positive and sensible. Avoid trouble in the first instance. When tackling new tasks or regions where you find yourself on unfamiliar ground, do not get carried away. Limit yourself to what you know you can do. Exceeding your personal limits only courts disaster.

Two things kill people in a survival situation – panic and fear combined and a loss of your own personal sense of self worth. Panic and fear will always come hand in hand. They bring along with them poor judgement, mistakes and ongoing disasters. If the panic stops, then the rest will disappear. Fear, on its own, can sometimes be a healthy thing in a survival situation because it does help to focus the mind.

Loss of the sense of personal self worth kills more people in a survival situation than panic, because they just lay down and wait to die. Usually they are within imminent sight of rescue and safety. If you do not help yourself – and you can trust me on this one – in a desperate survival situation you will die. A calm, positive and sensible approach to your situation and surroundings, a belief in yourself as a person and that you *will* be rescued will see that you get to tell everyone at home the stories, tales, lies and legends rather than have them read about it in the papers.

Let us look at a list of things I think you should carry with you at all times when in or passing through wilderness areas. I have these in my camera bag along with a couple of home comforts like teabags and small packets of sugar.

These odd extras may seem a strange thing for a photographer to carry but I can always find boiling water but not necessarily good teabags. The sugar is a little treat to myself because I have a sweet tooth.

I always carry a small pencil and a sheet of paper. I may want to leave a message somewhere to tell someone where I am going or that I called and when I expect to be back. In a small, sealable plastic packet I carry several waterproof matches and the side of the matchbox to strike them on. Handy if I want to make a fire and, as the matches are waterproof, I will be able to make a fire in almost any weather. A couple of condoms may seem strange thing for a photographer to carry but they do not take up much room. Besides their intended use, they are small and lightweight and will stretch extremely well to weather-proof my equipment and will, in an emergency, expand to carry quite a considerable amount of water. I also take a bar of rich cooking chocolate. It tastes terrible but is so high in energy that a small amount will take away the hunger pangs. Avoid carrying sweet things that contain lots of sugar. Sugar will only make you hungry.

The most important item in my little survival kit is a Swiss Army knife or other multi-tooled knife. I have the model that has a pen, tweezers, a toothpick, and a corkscrew plus all the usual tools. Make sure your knife has a piece of string attached so you can secure it to your person. Long-term survival would be impossible without one and short-term survival would be more uncomfortable than necessary.

Alongside my Swiss Army knife in my camera bag I carry a compass. I do this as a matter of course. As a photographer, I find a compass quite useful. It can tell me where the sun is going to rise and set when I am in unfamiliar territory. And when the sun is not visible in the sky or at such a low angle as to make its position confusing, a compass lets me know in which direction I am travelling. Next to the Swiss Army knife, a miniature compass is probably the most important item you can carry in the wilderness. It can tell you which way you are going should you have taken a wrong turning. You can tell someone which way you went if you leave a message with your pencil and paper. Most importantly, it will give you a feeling of comfort because you will know where you are heading and that you are doing something positive to help yourself.

Another useful item I always have is a piece of string or nylon fishing line. String can be used to secure light timbers for a makeshift shelter, or perhaps suspend something in a tree. Its uses are limited only by your imagination. Fishing line is the best substitute for a piece of string because it not only packs smaller, it also fulfils the same tasks. Additionally, it can also be used for what it is designed for – to catch fish – if you can devise a hook of some sort or if you have one with you.

All this takes up a minuscule amount of room and, if you keep it all with a small first-aid kit (see page 115) somewhere accessible but secure, in something you carry with you at all times such as a daypack, camera bag, bumbag etc, you cannot go wrong. You will now be prepared for any amount of survival necessary should fate so befall you.

CAR TRAVEL

There are some particular points to bear in mind when travelling about the wilderness in a car or 4x4 vehicle.

- Always know where your jack and spare tyre are. In some North American vehicles they are stored underneath the car on a winch system. These are sometimes difficult for the inexperienced to get at. Also, familiarise yourself with the workings of the jack. Again, North American systems are different from those commonly found in Europe.
- Always fill up the vehicle when the fuel-gauge indicates half full. Fuel stations are usually long distances apart and some maintain strange hours. Although most stations now have smart-card type pumps that allow 24-hour fuel, these do not always work in the middle of nowhere. There is nothing worse than having an RCMP officer pull up to see what is wrong when you are stopped at the side of the road and having to tell him or her that you ran out of fuel in the middle of nowhere. No-one driving in Canada's north should do such a silly thing in front of a RCMP officer. Such stupidity really annoys them.
- Drive slowly and allow yourself plenty of time to get where you plan to go. The scenery is stunning so make the best of it.
- The people of the north are delightful and friendly. If you are stopped by the side of the road they will automatically stop to see if you are OK. Do the same. Besides, it is always a good excuse for a chat.
- If you break down *do not leave your car*. Staying with the vehicle is the safest place to be. There are not many roads in the north so someone will come along eventually. Help may not be quick in coming but it will come. Most distances to the next or last town will be well beyond reasonable walking distance. Any wild animal that may cross your path will avoid passing or ignore a stationary car and, in severe and/or quickly changeable weather, the vehicle is usually the warmest place to be.

ON THE TRAIL

Imagine driving to the car park at the start point of a trail to a well-known beauty spot. You park the car, get out your daypack with your little survival kit, the thermos and a packed lunch and head off up the trail for an enjoyable picnic off-the-beaten-track. The sun is shining and it is a warm pleasant day. It is a delightful thought.

A couple of hours later you have found a nice secluded spot with a stunning view and set out your picnic. Sounds wonderful. Now, imagine a sudden storm appears on the horizon and it is heading your way. You quickly pack up the picnic and race for the car. You forget that it took you nearly three hours to get where you were, the rain is pouring down, the trail is slippery and you are are not too sure of your way. Your wonderful day has suddenly got scary.

You eventually find your car and are none the worse for wear besides being soaked through to the skin and very cold. Next time you go out, you will remember to pack the rain gear as a precaution and wear a stouter pair of boots. This may be a scenario and I may have made it up, but think about it. It could be real enough.

Things get serious when everything gets out of hand. Be prepared on the trail, whether it is only a short day trip or a journey involving several days. Northern Canada's weather is unpredictable at the best of times. Sudden storms can come from nowhere and catch you out. Blizzards can occur in the middle of summer.

In most Canadian national parks you must report to the park headquarters or a ranger's post before entering that particular park. Usually it is to pay the entrance fee, get some free local advice and collect your food cache if you are in bear country. For the rangers it does one other important thing: it helps them to help you. They will know where you are going, how long you are staying and when you are expected back. If something untoward happens to you they will at least know where to start looking for you.

Whenever you go into any wilderness area always tell someone where you are going and when you expect to be back. If no-one knows you are out there, no-one knows to come looking for you when you do not return. It is common sense but you would be amazed at the number of people who venture into the wilderness without telling anyone where they are going. Some of them do not make it back.

Getting lost

Most people get lost on the trail by taking unknown shortcuts. The trail you are following turns left, say, and you think it should turn right. So you decide to nip off the corner. After 20 minutes of uncontrolled bush bashing, you still have not found your trail and you suddenly realise that you have been past this spot before. You are lost. Do not go off on sessions of uncontrolled bush bashing. Trails usually go around obstacles like cliffs, big trees, detouring around a gorge or lead to a safer stream/river crossing. If you must nip off the corner use a compass and plan that shortcut properly. If it proves unsuccessful then you can work out where you are and retrace your steps back to the original trail, having only wasted a little of your time.

Most trails follow practical lines of topography. They may follow ridgelines or go along valleys, or maybe they follow a stream. The terrain will decide the remedy. If you are in open country, stop and have a serious look about. It should be obvious where you went wrong and where you should be. Some other landmark may present itself that you can accurately distinguish on your map. Head for it. Follow streams downhill. Somewhere along the way you will meet another trail, people or a road.

Maybe the trail splits and you are unsure which fork to take and it is not represented on the map. Try one fork and see if it works out. If you got it wrong do not take a shortcut. Turn around and return the way you came until you reach the spot where the trail forked. Then follow the other trail. Simple, but many people get it wrong.

If an accident occurs

In some wilderness areas you may be in a party of people and an accident occurs, or you may come across someone who has had an accident and is unable to help him or herself. What do you do? Having some knowledge of first aid would be invaluable here. A basic course is well worth doing and relatively inexpensive.

Firstly, stay calm and appear confident. You will be a great sense of comfort to the person who is injured. Before you do anything, assess the situation. Reassure the injured person. Remember, never, ever put yourself in any danger when trying to assist someone else. Two injured people are no good to anyone. Apply whatever first aid you feel is required by the situation. Comfort the injured person at all times. Keep them warm and rig up some form of shelter if possible to protect the patient, and possibly yourself, from the weather.

At some point you or someone else will need to decide whether to await a rescue or initiate one. If it is you who has to go for help, make sure the injured person is comfortable, sheltered and prepared to wait. Accidents are strange things and cause some unexpected and abnormal reactions in people. After an accident some people have a fear of being alone and cannot be left in that state. You must decide. Responsibility can sometimes be a difficult burden to bear particularly when someone else's life is on the line.

The next thing you need to do is determine where the person is to be found. Make notes on terrain and distinguishing landmarks; describe the place to yourself so you can describe it to rescuers. You may not be returning. Write it all down. Be very accurate. Leave a note with the injured person saying where you are going for help. Do not rely on them to pass it on orally. Carry all the injury details with you. This will help the rescuers decide on a course of action.

On the way to get help go slowly. Negotiate difficult terrain patiently. Hurrying may cause another mishap. Remember, the injured person is depending on you to get help. If you are in a party, two people should always go for help if possible and someone must remain with the patient. This is not always possible. Whatever decisions you make will be the right ones – confidence will succeed on the day.

One other decision you may have to make is whether the injured person can walk or be carried out. The answer is sometimes yes and sometimes no. If the person can walk without too much difficulty and the distances are not too far then effecting a walk-out is a good choice. Why burden the rescue services and the taxpayers with an unnecessary helicopter rescue? On the other hand, society may be a lot more burdened if the walk-out goes wrong. If the injury is serious, then the injured party must stay to await rescue. Never carry a seriously injured person out. Much is made of improvised solutions to moving wounded people, some of them quite ingenious, but most professional rescuers think that a non-walking injured person should be moved only as far as shelter, if at all. In this way rescues can be initiated earlier and it is much more comfortable for the patient.

Hypothermia

The *Oxford Dictionary* describes hypothermia as 'the condition of having an abnormally low body temperature'. Put more simply, hypothermia is the body's failure to produce enough heat to keep its internal organs at the proper temperature. We once called it 'exposure'; fatigue, hunger and the body having insufficient insulation from wet clothing or not enough clothing in adverse temperatures usually brings it on. Hypothermia can occur in the middle of summer if all the conditions are right.

When you are tired, hungry and thirsty the body's metabolic heater does not always work as well as it should. The body is a superb natural machine but it does need fuel to operate. When you are cold the body generates more heat to compensate for the loss due to physical effort and your surroundings. If rest appears a long way off, and you are hungry and thirsty, and the body is failing to keep the inner bits warm enough, hypothermia results.

The body's first reaction is to slow down the circulation in your hands and feet. You put on a warm jacket, hat and gloves and you feel better. Moving more quickly will generate more heat and things will improve. You will tend to shiver at this time. That is the body's evolutionary bit kicking in to stoke those inner fires and get you where you're going.

Normal body core temperature is 37°C. As your temperature drops towards 35°C you start to shiver. By the time the core is at 34°C you will have become uncoordinated and be apathetic and sluggish. By the time it hits 32°C you will be stumbling all over the place and you will not be able to use your hands. At 30°C true hypothermia sets in and shivering stops. You will not be able to walk any more, you will behave irrationally and you will be seriously confused by all around you. Once your temperature drops below 30°C death is knocking at the door. You will be semi-conscious and hardly breathing. Your pulse will be almost indiscernible. At 28°C your heart stops.

If you deal with this at the shivering stage the situation should not get any worse. If you are just shivering put on more clothes, a hat and gloves. If you are shivering and you are wet, change into the driest clothes you have and, if possible, eat and drink something. You will not feel like it, but force yourself. Stop and rest if your camp is a long way off, or speed up and warm up if it is close.

When you reach camp you must warm up – not heat up. Do things slowly. Build a fire and put on dry clothes. Eat, drink and sleep, for tomorrow all should be well. If camp is a long way off and the hypothermic person, who from now on we will call the victim, cannot go any further, then stop and camp early. Find what shelter you can and build a fire slowly, gradually building up the heat. If you cannot light a fire, head straight for civilisation. The victim's life will probably depend on it.

Let us assume you have a tent and the rest of your camping equipment with you. Get a tent up. Put the victim in dry clothes. If no dry clothes are available strip the victim of his wet clothes and get him into his sleeping bag. If he cannot generate enough heat of his own someone has to strip down and get in beside him. Social taboos are out the window at this point. Skin to skin contact is one of the best ways to warm a hypothermic body. Work at keeping up the fluid levels by drinking warm, but not hot, drinks like chocolate or very weak tea and but never drink alcohol. (Do not drink coffee – it is a diuretic and reduces the body's ability to process fluids. The victim may also feel the need to pee resulting in additional fluid loss.)

A word of warning here. Do not warm a hypothermic person up rapidly. Cold, poorly oxygenated blood returning to the heart may cause fibrillation (a random twitching) of the heart, resulting in death. For the same reason do not rub the limbs. Put the victim in a sleeping bag and increase the insulation. Keep up the warm fluids and let him/her warm up slowly. If the victim is at this extreme point, help should be sought and the victim got to a hospital as quickly as possible where the rewarming can be done internally.

On a final note, it seems that some 'dead' victims with no discernible heartbeat have recovered from severe hypothermia. It would appear that the body goes into some form of suspended animation. There is an old medical adage that goes something like this: 'No-one should be considered cold and dead before that person has actually been warm and dead.'

Frostbite

Frostbite is the killing of the body's cells by freezing them. You cannot become frostbitten at temperatures above freezing, but frostbite can develop without any signs of hypothermia. It normally affects the fingers and toes and, more rarely, the nose, face and ears.

Once you have experienced frostbite you are forever susceptible to it so avoid that first encounter. Wear gloves, hats, boots and warm clothing suitable for the lowest temperatures you are likely to meet. Do not wear metal earrings or metal framed glasses. Frostbite can occur where metal touches the skin. Signs of frostbite are telltale white patches on what should be normal, healthy pink skin.

There is no pain associated with getting frostbite, only in re-thawing the appendage. I once got frostbite on Mount Kilimanjaro in Africa. It was not that I was unprepared, but my gloves had become wet and my group encountered a blizzard near the summit. My hands went rock solid. Thawing them out is akin to the feeling you get in your foot after you have been sitting on it awkwardly and have got up. Recovering from frostbite is similar only worse. I have never known such pain as when my hands were warmed in the armpits of my Tanzanian guide. I had no use of two fingers on one hand and three on the other for several months after. It was two years before my hands appeared to have fully recovered.

In the cold you should layer the hands like you would the rest of your body. I wear thermal inner gloves of silk under fingerless woollen gloves (I cannot take a picture with a thick glove covering the finger I use for the shutter button). I then cover all this with extreme-weather mittens with no fingers (the fingers' own warmth helps to keep them warm underneath, whereas fingered mittens keep the fingers separate and are less effective).

BEARS
General safety

All visitors to Canada's north are very fortunate that the region has a great abundance of wildlife in almost any wilderness area. A great part of journeying through Canada's superb landscape is the chance to experience much of this wildlife at close hand and to see the animals in their natural setting as they go about their daily business.

A most enjoyable part of any wilderness experience is unplanned encounters with wild animals. In general, all animals will avoid physical interaction if at all possible. Any animal injured in a confrontation with another animal (including man) will be less able than otherwise to find food, shelter and successfully raise its young. Confrontations do sometimes occur because these unplanned encounters often catch an animal off-guard, making its behaviour unpredictable to an inexperienced observer. The presence of young will heighten the animal's anxiety and make it all the more dangerous and unpredictable – especially if that animal is a bear.

Bears are an important part of the environment, not only as a wildlife resource and a vital part of the ecosystems found in the north, but they also play a significant part in the cultural and economic well-being of northern residents. Sighting a bear can be the highlight of any wilderness experience but an unplanned meeting may prove detrimental to your health.

As more and more people invade the bear's habitat, encounters between bears and people become more frequent. The bear is usually on the losing end of the equation, particularly when a bear's need for food leads it to investigate areas of intensive human habitation. Out in the wilderness the bear remains supreme. He is more powerful than a human, operates by a code that does not recognise human boundaries, and is usually propelled by an appetite less discriminating than ours. Therefore, when travelling in any of Canada's wilderness country, and this usually means bear country, you must be prepared to make concessions to your ursine neighbours and, above all else, show them the respect they deserve. Failure to do so will lead to you becoming one of a growing number of bear-caused death statistics or, worse still (for the rest of us), lead to the need for wildlife officials and rangers to partake in another unfortunate, difficult and sometimes dangerous situation where the bear needs to be removed from the environment. Transportation away from the area does not always work and, sadly, the bear must be put down. This is called nuisance-bear killing.

Safety is everyone's responsibility when in bear country. You will often hear the phrase – be bear-aware. Here are a few simple rules that apply everywhere that bears are to be found:

- be alert at all times
- respect all bears – they can be dangerous
- never approach a bear; use a telephoto lens when taking a photograph
- never feed bears – or any other wildlife for that matter
- have a plan of action that everyone in your party understands for dealing with the unplanned bear encounter

• if you are travelling with children, make sure you know where they are at all times

There are different rules for dealing with black bears and grizzlies (which are basically vegetarians and will not generally attack you) and polar bears (which are carnivores and will consider you legitimate food).

Black bears and grizzlies
Black bears
Black bears (*Ursus americanus*) are quite common and found throughout all of North America. They prefer forested areas with intermittent open areas for berries, shrubs and grasses, very rarely venturing north of the treeline and on to the tundra. It is important to note and remember that black bears can climb trees – very efficiently.

Black bears are sometimes confused with grizzlies because they may appear similar in size and colour. Black bears, though, are, in general, smaller in size and have a less robust build with flat shoulders and a straight muzzle. The claws are quite short and curved and males usually weigh about 100–150kg.

Black bears are omnivorous and highly adaptable in their food habits. Their diet varies seasonally and locally but usually consists of grasses, sedges, to some extent carrion, eggs from nesting waterfowl, fish, roots and tubers. In the late summer they feed almost exclusively on berries and fruits. They rarely dig for squirrels or marmots but do eat other smaller mammals like voles, lemmings and mice when they can catch them. They will prey on young moose, caribou or sheep but only if the opportunity arises. Black bears are not active hunters, preferring vegetable matter. Their adaptability makes them more vulnerable to human activity. Our garbage dumps and rubbish piles are seen as an easy source of food and, being more curious and adaptable than a grizzly, they quickly become accustomed to our human presence.

Grizzly bears
Grizzlies (*Ursus arctos horribilis*) inhabit predominantly open country from the high mountain ranges to the open tundra of mainland Canada, but they are also found in forested areas, particularly when they come down from their mountain retreats in search of spawning salmon. The grizzly bear has a cousin that is found in Alaska and it is known as the coastal brown bear or Kodiak bear *Ursus arctos middendorffi*. Adult grizzly bears cannot or will not climb trees.

Grizzlies have a stout, solid build, a massive head with an upturned snout and a prominent shoulder hump. The claws are about 6–8cm long and males can weigh as much as 300kg depending on where they live, the length of the summer season and how ample the food supplies are.

A grizzly's diet is very similar to that of the black bear with the exception that a grizzly bear is a fairly active, aggressive hunter and digs for squirrels, marmots, voles, mice and lemmings. They are opportunistic predators, taking moose, caribou, muskoxen and sheep should the occasion arise. They usually prey on the young, the old or the sick but they have been known to take full-grown mature animals that are quite healthy. This is usually a sign of some desparation as the chance of injury when attacking a full-grown moose or caribou is quite significant. Carrion also makes up a significant part of a grizzly's diet, particularly the carcasses of winter-killed animals, which provide a vital source of food before the spring vegetation arrives. Like the black bear, the late summer fruits and berries are its staple before the long winter sets in.

Bear behaviour

The lumbering gait of both species is quite deceptive, although quite comical to watch. They are capable of enormous feats of strength and can run much faster than humans. Both species swim well; black bears and young grizzlies can climb trees but adult grizzlies are less inclined to do so. Both species have an excellent sense of smell which helps them find food and warns them of impending danger. In both species hearing is good and eyesight is, depending on who you ask, anything from good to poor. Personally, I would presume all bear eyesight to be excellent. Both these species of bear are usually dormant (asleep but not truly hibernating) during the winter months and females in both species are considerably smaller than the males. In some places the ranges of black bears and grizzlies are combined or overlap.

A bear's reaction to a human encounter may be influenced by a number of factors and therefore makes the animal's behaviour somewhat unpredictable. Bears will avoid humans where possible, but animals which are old, sick, wounded and in pain, or starving may search aggressively for food around humans. These bears are dangerous. Any bear that has become used to people is also dangerous because it has learnt not to fear us and will assume us to be fair game.

All animals have a critical safe distance or space. Any encroachment on this space will either cause the animal to flee or, if the intrusion into its space is considered a threat, may provoke an attack. Any kind of female bear with cubs should be considered hostile and be avoided at all times. Bears are usually loath to leave their food until it is all eaten and may become aggressive if approached.

Bears do engage in predictable displays that are intended to scare away unwanted guests. They may huff, hiss, pant and growl. Once, whilst I was photographing walrus in Hudson Bay, I came across a polar bear resting deep in a cave. He or she sounded like a snake in a bad mood hissing and puffing with intermittent low growls – all very loudly. Although the bear did not want to engage my party physically, it was making the point very clearly that we should leave it in peace and quiet. Other threatening displays are a lowering of the head and ears laid back, stamping paws, mock charges but then stopping a few metres short or veering to the side. These mock attacks usually end up with the bear running or walking away but they do sometimes end up with the real thing the second time around.

If a bear is standing on its hind legs it is probably trying to catch your scent, work out who or what you are, and give itself time to figure out what to do next. Fortunately, bears do not charge on their hind legs so, if you see one in this pose, leave while the going is good.

The grizzly's reputation for ferociousness is well earned. If cornered, threatened, or even surprised, it will most likely become aggressive and stand its ground. The next defence will usually be to charge. Black bears are a little less aggressive and will usually flee, but they are a lot more curious and adaptable than grizzlies and quickly become accustomed to humans, particularly when it comes to easy food like human garbage. Treat them with extreme caution.

Finally, some bears have been known to stalk humans. Although the incidents are rare, some bears do consider we humans as fair game in the food stakes. They are usually old, sick or starving bears who cannot fend for themselves properly. The behaviour of a hunting bear and a threatened bear vary considerably. A hunting bear will not bother with displays and will show no fear whatsoever; nor will it appear annoyed. It will either walk straight up to you at a fast walk or circle you carefully, assessing the situation and making a plan. Your behaviour in such a situation will save your life.

Travelling in black and grizzly bear country
These few simple rules apply to anywhere where you might find wilderness in Canada. Most of you will probably travel within the bounds of Parks Canada's superb national parks system but as with all things that are common sense they can be applied to any wilderness area.

When travelling within the national parks system it is usual to check in and out with park headquarters or at a ranger's post. Some parks have visitor's fees which must be paid before entry and in parks where there are marked walking trails the rangers will usually provide you with bear-proof food caches if you do not have your own. These are sealable containers that are scent proof so they don't attract bears. They are usually stored up in trees. Basically they look like a round screw-top plastic jar about a foot in diameter and a foot long and are used to put fresh food in. The rangers at headquarters can usually tell you which trails are safest, where the bears usually are at that time of the year, and how to avoid a chance encounter. I have found all rangers in Canada's national parks enlightening, informative and willing to help you get the most out of your time in their particular park. Their advice should always be sought and taken wisely. They know their area and, in particular, their animals better than anyone else. No book can counter local experience but here are a few points for avoiding bear problems whilst on the trail:

- Travel only during daylight hours.
- Tell someone where you are going and when you expect to return.
- Watch for bear signs such as tracks, claw marks on trees, upturned earth, droppings that contain berries, hair or vegetation.
- Never approach a fresh kill. Upturned earth may indicate a buried kill. The bear will not be far away.
- Think ahead as you walk down a trail. Use binoculars to scout for bears. Be aware of your surroundings. If you see a bear in the distance, take action to avoid surprising it!

- Carry your food in bear-proof containers and avoid carrying food with strong aromas.
- Make noise where visibility is limited. Sing, talk or shout loudly to make any animal aware of your presence. Take into account the terrain. The wind and noise of water can disguise your sounds. Some people carry bells and airhorns in such areas.
- Women should try to minimise odours when menstruating through extra careful personal hygiene. Where possible destroy all sanitary materials in a hot fire. Avoid wearing scented cosmetics or anything else that has a strong artificial smell.

The following can be applied to any campsite whether you are walking a trail, whitewater rafting or canoeing, or perhaps horse trekking or fishing in a wilderness area. Care when choosing a campsite will offer a bear-free good night's rest. Where possible avoid the following:

- Places that are obvious bear feeding areas such as flood-plains, berry patches, recent burns, wet meadows or rivers and streams where fish are spawning.
- Places where bears have been a problem in the past. The rangers can tell you where these are if you are in a national park.
- Well-used or littered campsites.
- Places where bear signs such as tracks and/or droppings are evident.
- Sites with limited visibility or near rushing water which may disguise the sound of an approaching bear.
- Do not underestimate a bear's ability to find food. Without some careful precautions their sense of smell and relentless search for food will bring them straight to your camp irrespective of the time of day. So when in camp:
- Do not sleep under the stars.
- Keep the number of tents to a minimum. Keep them in a circle or a straight line with enough space between them to allow a bear an easy escape route.
- Keep cooking areas at least 100 metres from the sleeping areas but in an area that is visible from camp. The same applies to toilet facilities and food storage. Food caches should be at least 4m off the ground and suspended between two trees if possible. Caches should include all food, cooking utensils, clothes worn whilst cooking, anything with a strange smell that might attract bears such as toothpaste or detergent and all garbage that you cannot dispose of.
- Do not take any food into your tent.
- Avoid any scent of food on your person, clothing or tent. Keep the camp clean. Greasy smells are particularly attractive to bears.
- Destroy all garbage by burning it to ashes at least 200m from camp and bury the ashes at least 1m down if possible. Avoid burning garbage just before bedtime – it might attract bears whilst everyone is sleeping. It is better to be awake with a bear nearby than to be sound asleep and unaware of its presence. Pack out all unburned garbage with you when you leave

How to behave in the presence of a black or grizzly bear

There is no tried and tested blueprint on how to behave when you have an encounter with a bear. It will be different every time. Each bear will behave uniquely. You may surprise a bear at close quarters or find a bear that is not afraid of people. Common sense, knowledge of bear behaviour and good judgement will hold you fast. However, here are some guidelines that might help:

- Stop, stand still and stay calm. Assess the situation.
- If the bear is aware of you, help it identify you as a person. It may leave. Staying upwind will help it smell you. Talk in low tones and slowly wave your arms.
- *Do not run* from a bear unless you are sure you can reach a safe place before the bear catches up. Running may cause the bear to chase you, and a bear is much faster than you are!
- Always leave a bear an open avenue of escape.
- If you see a bear at a distance, alert the bear to your presence. Quietly walk back the way you came or make a very wide detour around the bear, watching it all the time. *Do not* get between a female bear and her cubs.
- If time, distance and circumstances permit, try to scare the bear. Many people in the Canadian wilderness carry a rifle or flares for protection against unwanted bear attention. If someone with you has a rifle, fire a warning shot, discharge a flare or use some form of noisemaker or airhorn.

In the case of a close encounter:

- Stand still and assess the situation. *Do not* shout or make sudden movements and avoid direct eye contact with the bear. It may provoke an attack. Even at 50m, even when a bear is displaying threatening behaviour, there is still probably time for you to avoid an encounter.
- Back away slowly. *Do not* leave any clothing or gear behind unless you are sure the bear is still trying to identify you. This will not work if the bear is following you. Leave food or an article of clothing only as a last resort.
- Climb a tree if one is available. You will have to go quite high up – more than 4m – grizzlies can reach that high. Remember that black bears can climb trees.
- If the bear is very close (less than 30m), it is usually best to stand your ground. Be prepared to shoot if you are carrying a firearm.

If a bear charges, it will be on all four legs. Many charges are bluffs; bears will often stop or veer to the side at the last minute. If the encounter looks like it is unavoidable there are three options open to you:

- Shoot the bear if you have a firearm
- Play dead if you are attacked by a grizzly; or
- Fight back if you are attacked by a black bear.

Playing dead

Do not play dead if attacked by a black bear. However, playing dead may prevent serious injury if you are attacked by a grizzly. By playing dead and protecting your vital areas a bear may deem you harmless and leave you alone. There are two recommended methods of playing dead:

- Lie on your side curled up into a ball, legs drawn tightly up to your chest with your hands and arms behind your neck.
- Lie face down on the ground with your arms over the back of your neck.

Stay in these positions. *Do not* resist or struggle even if the bear moves you – it may intensify the attack. Take a good look around cautiously before you move to be certain the bear has gone.

Fighting back

Unless a grizzly is actually hunting you he will attack you only if he perceives you as a serious threat. However, an attack by a black bear is, on the other hand, a predacious act. A black bear attacks because it sees you only as a source of food and the attack does not generally represent a measure of defence.

If a black bear does come at you or a grizzly considers you as its next meal and you do not have a firearm, do not play dead. Act aggressively. Defend yourself with whatever means you have available – sticks, rocks, logs – anything that will do as a weapon. You want to appear large, dominant and frighten the bear. Jump up and down, shout, wave your jacket around – use your pack to make yourself look larger than you are.

On a more pleasant note… The vast majority of serious wilderness travellers in Canada travel without the protection of a firearm. They rely on good bear-alert manoeuvres by keeping their camp clean and using their brains to avoid any unplanned encounters with bears. Bears are not a problem to get paranoid about. Learn about bears and their behaviour, seek good advice before heading out into the wilderness, keep your eyes and ears open and your brain in gear. The chances of ever seeing a bear by accident in the wilderness are quite small and the chance of one such encounter becoming a problem is even smaller, but encounters do occur. A bear incident may be exciting and something to talk about when you get home but it is the insects that are more likely to cause you more annoyance on your trip into the wilderness.

Polar bears

The polar bear is found almost exclusively above the Arctic Circle, from Anticosti Island in the St Lawrence to the mouth of the Yukon River in Alaska, including all the coastal areas of Hudson and James Bays and all the Arctic islands to the tip of Ellesmere Island. They are most common around the Arctic islands and around Southampton Island at the northern end of Hudson Bay. They are also common along Alaska's coast north of the Bering Strait, in Amundsen Gulf and the Beaufort Sea. It is estimated that there are about 50,000 polar bears within the ice-covered waters of the circumpolar Arctic. Canadian populations indicate somewhere between 7,000 and 10,000 animals. Throughout Canada they are common along the Arctic islands and the nearby coastal fringes but they are rarely seen on the mainland with the exception of the shores of Hudson Bay and, occasionally, the northern fringe of the Yukon.

They have sometimes been found up to 200km inland but as marine mammals they do not tend to compete food-wise with their nearest ursine relative, the open-tundra grizzly bear.

They are very different from black bears and grizzlies in that that are almost exclusively carnivorous. Man is seen as a very obvious source of food and we are, therefore, hunted by polar bears that have food on their minds. They do not hibernate but spend most of the winter on the pack ice hunting their natural prey – seals. As the pack ice melts polar bears are forced to seek the safety of land. Then their natural prey has the advantage of being able to see their white coats easily and, therefore, polar bears tend to go hungry for most of the summer.

Polar bears are excellent hunters and when stalking their prey are capable of getting very close before they pounce. This includes humans. They have an acute sense of smell and eyesight as good as any human's. Polar bears are good swimmers and have been seen many miles out to sea travelling between islands. They are quite capable of killing a fully-grown walrus (about two tonnes worth) though they do prefer the calves – it is less like hard work.

The most important point to remember here is that the polar bear is the largest non-aquatic mammalian predator on earth. Males can weigh anything in the range 350–650kg; females come in a little less at 150–250kg.

The females come into season in the spring and begin to adopt dens, when carrying young, off the pack ice somewhere on the mainland, usually by late August. A female will enter the den for the last time in late October or early November. By this time she has stored up the 200kg of fat necessary to carry off a successful pregnancy. Cubs are born anywhere between late November and the end of January. Depending on the latitude the mother and cubs will have left the dens by the middle of April and cubs remain with their mothers until they are about two years old.

Polar bear behaviour

Polar bears hunt seals in two ways – either by stalking or still-hunting. Although there are a number of variations on each approach, the general idea is much the same. When a bear first spots his seal hauled out on the ice, the bear stands absolutely motionless, watching it intently and assessing the situation. It seems to be deciding how to get close enough to charge. The bear, with its head lowered and sometimes in a crouched position as it nears its prey, will then walk very slowly toward the seal. Seals are usually quite alert on the ice; they raise their heads from time to time and have a look around for danger. Inuk hunters adopt seal-like mannerisms in their approach when hunting seals on the ice and I have used this technique quite successfully when photographing walrus on land. If you behave like them they think you are one of them and no threat whatsoever. Bears seem to have one advantage over us: their white coat is perfect camouflage. I once read that bears have been known to cover their black noses with their paws to disguise them. No-one I have talked to has ever seen this, so it may just be an old Inuit story to enhance the magic they sense in a bear's hunting abilities when telling their traditional tales.

At 20m or so the bear charges. Its speed is incredible. The seal will be grabbed by the bear's claws or teeth and dragged out of the breathing hole, bitten about the head several times and then pulled well clear before being eaten.

Bears are excellent swimmers and they have been known to stalk a seal from under the ice using ice holes for breathing and coming up right next to the resting seal. This aquatic stalk ends in a great eruption of water at the breathing hole as the bear explodes out of the hole and takes his prey, once again killing it by biting through its skull before dragging the carcass away from the hole to eat it. This is one reason why the Inuit do not like camping right next to the floe edge. Most stalking methods used by polar bears are a variation on these themes.

Still-hunting involves standing, sitting or lying motionless at a breathing hole and awaiting the arrival of a seal. It is assumed that the bear detects the scent of a seal on a favourite hole and just waits for it to arrive. Lying horizontal at the hole's mouth limits a bear's profile from view below the surface and is energy saving. It also means the bear is less likely to make a sound on the ice as this can carry vast distances under water, alerting a seal to the bear's presence. When the seal surfaces to breathe, a scene of peace and tranquillity leaps into a meshing of two bodies. The bear bites the seal on the head and flips it out of the hole before killing it and then dragging it away as before.

Bears also hunt baby seals under the ice. Seal mothers leave their pups on an ice shelf above the water line but below the upper ice level. When a bear smells a seal under the ice it quickly smashes its way through to grab the pup. The older a pup gets the quicker the bear has to be. Once the pup can swim it can retreat immediately into the water. I was amazed by tales of this sense of smell through ice but dogs have it too. On one occasion when I was in Greenland with some Inuit, we buried several seal carcasses in a snow hole to collect later. The Inuit left no marker to indicate where the site was. When questioned they said that the dogs would find it! No sooner were we returning past the same spot several days later than the dogs immediately dived to the side of the trail and commenced digging up the dead seals. Boas, my Inuit guide, looked at me and just smiled. My apparent disbelief must have been obvious at the time.

As the pack ice retreats with the onset of summer, bears must also retreat to solid land. This begins the general summer fast for the bears. Some bears will still be able hunt at seal and walrus haul-outs throughout the north, but for most bears the summer is a very lean time. Being wholly carnivorous and seals being much faster swimmers, polar bears have no option but to wait out the summer months until the seas freeze over again. It is at this time that bears are at their most dangerous to man. They are hungry and in a bad mood. Their fur, perfect protection against the Arctic cold, is now a burden, making them quite hot and bothered. Man would seem easy prey at this time. Our only advantage is that their normally perfect camouflage stands out against the brown and green background so surprise is not on their side.

By the end of summer and on towards late autumn bears are beginning actively to seek frozen seas. It is at this time that bears may begin to congregate in large numbers around towns looking for scraps. This congregation creates ideal bear-watching situations and has become one of the prime income earners for those living in the community of Churchill on the shores of Hudson Bay (see page 244). These bears are usually migrating north from the more southerly base of Hudson Bay in anticipation of a speedier freeze over at more northern latitudes.

Travelling in polar bear country

In the first instance all the rules for safety in polar bear country are exactly the same for any other bear. It is important to be bear-alert. The rules regarding camp layout, trail walking, food caches, etc are all the same. What is different about this bear is twofold – the environment and the animal. It is important to remember that this animal is a serious carnivore. It is for this reason that whenever you are in polar bear country, whether on tour or out with the Inuit, someone in the party should always be armed as a matter of course.

Polar bears generally hunt their prey by a combination of stealth and cam-ouflage. In a polar bear's eyes man is just like any other animal – a source of food. Being the largest mammalian predator means that polar bears have almost no natural fear of man, though experience usually teaches them other-wise. A bear that has no fear of man is not tame – it is dangerous. Polar bears are clever, cunning and will take great advantage of the environment.

In summer when there is no ice and snow about they can easily be spotted. Usually the weather is too hot for them to spend time hunting you seriously. They have enough trouble stopping themselves from overheating. This does not mean they will not attack if they see an easy meal. If the day is cooler than normal and you just happen to appear, a polar bear will not think twice.

The Arctic climate will sometimes make seeing a polar bear difficult. White on white is not easy to see past. Blizzards, snowstorms and fog all contribute to almost whiteout situations. The need to protect yourself against the ravages of the weather lessens the ability of your senses to operate to their greatest effi-ciency. If we cannot see or hear, we humans are almost defenceless in a polar bear's environment. The Inuit always had their dogs as an early warning system; in today's environment of snowmobiles we have lost that additional canine bear detector.

Polar bears are not scared off easily. If a polar bear does approach it is either curious or hungry. Assume it is hungry.

- Try to stay calm and assess the situation
- *Do not* run from a polar bear unless you are positive you can reach a safe place before the bear catches you up. Running will cause the bear to chase and he is a lot faster than you are.
- If you come across a bear by accident always leave the bear an avenue of escape.
- If the bear is aware of you, help it identify you as human. It may leave. Stay upwind if possible. Talk in low tones and slowly wave your arms about.

- If time and circumstances permit, try to scare the bear away by firing warning shots over its head, shooting flares at it, using noisemakers or by chasing it in a vehicle.
- In a close encounter act as non-threateningly as possible. Do not shout or make any sudden movements that might provoke the bear. Avoid direct eye contact. Back away slowly.
- If the bear is close (30m) stand your ground and be prepared to shoot it if you have a firearm.
- If you are unarmed and a bear attacks, act aggressively and defend yourself by whatever means available. Do not play dead. Jump up and down, shout, wave your arms. Fight back. Use your jacket or pack to make yourself look bigger than you are.
- If the bear continues the attack and you are forced to the ground, make every attempt to protect your vital organs. Curl up into a ball, hands clasped behind your neck, legs drawn up to your chest and your head buried between your knees. Stay in this position. Resistance may intensify the attack. Hopefully the bear will change its mind. If the bear does try to maul you, serious injury may be reduced or prevented by keeping still. Unfortunately, if this situation does occur I can offer no advice as to what to do. If you are alone you are unlikely to survive a serious polar bear attack. If you have company they might be able to draw off the bear and persuade it to flee or get a clean shot at the bear and kill it.

On a more positive note, people do survive serious attacks by polar bears. One old man, Moses Aliyak, of Rankin Inlet is known locally as the 'polar bear wrestler'. He has survived, I believe, three or four attacks. Inuit explain these things quite philosophically, saying that he once killed a polar bear without asking its permission. Now every time he encounters a bear it attacks him or those he is with. Someone is inevitably seriously hurt or dies but he, for some unknown reason, miraculously survives. I saw him in Baker Lake when he was accompanying the returning body of a local woman who was killed by a young bear when it attacked their party near Arviat south of Rankin Inlet a few weeks previously. The facts of the story got lost somewhere between the translation and the story telling but it seems that the bear had attacked their camp and Moses had gone to the aid of the woman. She was killed before he managed to fight off the bear and someone eventually shot the animal. Moses' injuries looked pretty gruesome with fresh cuts, scratches and claw marks about his neck and shoulders. He had obviously been in physical contact with a bear and, although some of these scars were not recent, I could not tell whether old age or past battles with polar bears actually accounted for his frail state.

Although there are numerous tales of polar bear attacks up north, unintentional or chance encounters are rare. They are uncommon because of the vast areas involved and the small populations. It is only when travellers seek out a polar bear's natural prey that these unintentional encounters do occur and most travellers and tourists are well protected by vehicles and/or armed guides.

Shooting a bear

Although this is not in the domain of normal wilderness trekkers and walkers, you may find yourself in the wilderness with a party; your guide will possess a firearm as a normal safety measure and, by stroke of misfortune, you may be required to use that firearm. So, the right moment to squeeze the trigger depends on your nerve, experience with a firearm, and how fast the bear is approaching. This decision can only be made by the person with the firearm and must be made quickly.

An accurate shot at close range has more chance of killing the bear than one fired from a long way away. An inexperienced person will also have more chance of hitting the bear when it is close, as the target will be bigger. Remember the first shot is the most important! If you must kill a bear, aim for the shoulder if the bear is broadside to you or the back of the neck between the shoulders if it is facing you. Avoid head shots. Bears have pretty thick skulls and a headshot may not kill it! *Do not* stop to check your shots – keep firing until the bear is still. Always try to kill a bear quickly and cleanly – a wounded bear is a very dangerous animal.

If you do kill a bear in self-defence, you are legally required to report it to the authorities. The hide and the skull (or lower jaw) are the property of the government so it is in your interest to let the local park warden or Renewable Resource Officer in that area know at the first opportunity.

The Gateway Cities

INTRODUCTION

One of the problems associated with flying such a long way to the north is not only the distances travelled but also the time it takes to get there, from Europe in particular. Flights usually arrive late in the evening Canadian time and onward journeys are usually first thing in the morning, requiring most visitors to spend a night in one of the gateway cities – Vancouver, Edmonton, Ottawa, Winnipeg or Montréal. With such long-haul journeys to Canada many of you may like to take in a day's break from all this flying so I am going to touch lightly on the gateway cities. Other guidebooks will cover them in more depth if you really want to explore these cities but I have tried to keep everything fairly simple and centralised for your convenience.

I have no personal preferences as to which city is the best; I have stayed in whichever one was most convenient to my destination. They all have their own personal flavour, sights and styles. I have always enjoyed what little time I have spent in them and found plenty to do to occupy my waiting or rest days.

Getting around Canadian cities is easy. All have excellent transport systems with regular services to the airports and plenty of hotels. The choice will depend on your time limits, your budget and what you would like to see. It will also be influenced by what time your flight arrives and when your next flight north departs. It is no good arriving at midnight Canada time and having to find a hotel on the opposite side of town. The same applies if you are leaving on a very early morning flight and have to get to the airport at some ungodly hour, or if you are using a hotel that is so far out of town that having a full and profitable day in the city is made impossible by having to spend half your time travelling in and out of the centre.

Arrival

If your hotel has not already been booked there are booking facilities at all the international airports which offer a wide range of establishments to cater to all tastes. They will provide you with information on how to get there by bus, train or taxi, and all the usual maps. There are information desks at the airports that can provide you with maps and transport information if you want to go it alone. Most major hotels have a free shuttle service to and from the airport, and once again the information desk can point you in the right direction to catch these buses. And then there is the infamous taxi driver who will take you anywhere for a fee. All taxis are licensed and the fee controlled by a meter in the cab in Canada but rip-offs still do occur.

VANCOUVER

Vancouver is on the west coast of Canada in the province of British Columbia. It is a wide, well-spaced city that is neatly laid out and it is fairly easy to find your way around. Most of the sights worth seeing are downtown. There are also plenty of things to do within a short distance of the city and some great adventure-type activities for those with a little more time on their hands. Vancouver has a mild climate, even in the winter, because it is so close to the sea. Bear in mind, however, that it does rain a lot, so make sure you have an umbrella or raincoat conveniently to hand.

Getting about

The local **bus service** is called BC Transit. It operates regular services between 05.00 and 24.00, plus a late night 'Owl' service until 04.00 on some downtown and suburban routes. There is also the **Skytrain**, a completely automated light rapid transit system between downtown Vancouver and Surrey. The elevated 28km scenic route has 20 stops in all and, although escalators are needed to reach stations, all have wheelchair access. There is a **SeaBus** service that operates between Vancouver and the North Shore. The journey takes 12 minutes with sailings every 15–30 minutes. Most bus routes have vehicles equipped for wheelchair lift assistance. Fares on all three systems are on a three-zone basis starting at $1.50 and rising to $2.25 and $3.00. Discount fares of $1.50 apply after 18.30 daily in all three zones. They also apply all day Saturday, Sunday and public holidays. Timetables are available in any public library, Vancouver Info Centre and the various tourist offices around town. Or you can call customer information on 604.521.0400.

There appear to be two airports in Vancouver but they are in fact one. The International Airport (north side) is for all international and most domestic flights and a smaller local airport (south side) covers all the local BC destinations such as Victoria Island. The airport offers a wide range of flights to and from international and domestic destinations. To reach the north from Vancouver you can fly to Whitehorse in the Yukon, Edmonton in Alberta (onwards to Yellowknife in NWT), and Winnipeg in Manitoba (for polar bears in Churchill).

Where to stay

The establishments listed here are all under $100 per night and are all in the downtown area.

Buchan Hotel 1906 Haro St (tel: 604.685.5354)
Dominion Hotel 210 Abbott St (tel: 604.681.6666)
Kingston Hotel Bed & Breakfast 757 Richards St (tel: 604.684.9024)
Vancouver Centre Travelodge 1304 Howe St (tel: 604.689.7777)
YMCA 955 Burrard St (tel: 604.681.0221)
YWCA 733 Beatty St (tel: 604.895.5830)

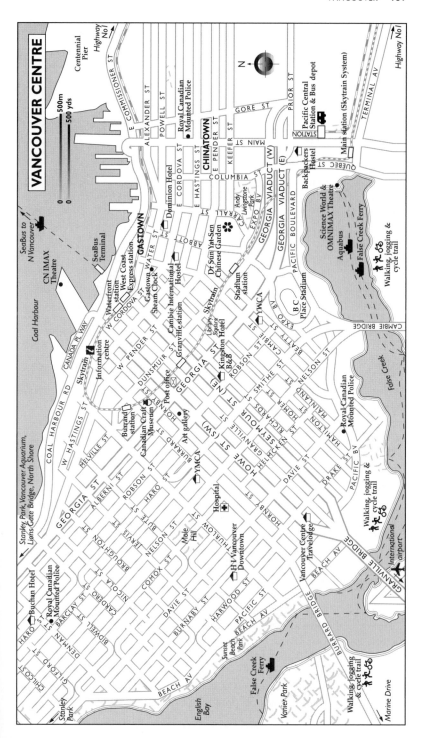

There are more expensive places to stay and there are a great many near and between the two sides of the airport for those just overnighting.

Hostels
Backpackers Hostel 927 Main St (tel: 604.682.2441)
Cambie International Hostel 300 Cambie St (tel: 604.684.6466)
Hostelling International – Downtown 1114 Burnaby St (tel: 604.684.4565)
Hostelling International – Jericho Beach (tel: 604.224.3208)

Where to eat
Vancouver is a gourmet's paradise with every type of cuisine imaginable. The following list is in downtown alone: five Californian restaurants, two Canadian, ten Chinese, 19 Continental, three East Indian, 18 family restaurants (these include McDonalds), one First Nations, three French, one Greek, one international, one Internet, 12 Italian, seven Japanese, one Mediterranean, nine North American, and four Northwest Coast. There are also Mexican and Spanish restaurants and restaurants that serve a style of food rather than a particular cuisine like bar & grill, steak & seafood, vegetarian and west coast menus. Some restaurants call themselves pubs or specialise in local seafood. All the fast-food chains are present in Vancouver and there are plenty of street-side cafés, snack bars and little men with trolleys serving hot dogs. I have no particular recommendations at all but the local seafood cannot be beaten and with five species of salmon passing through local waters' you will be spoilt for choice.

What to see and do
If time permits and you are in Vancouver during August and September head off to Victoria Island and Port Hardy/Telegraph Cove for a spot of **orca watching**. Boats go daily for a couple of hours and a sighting is usually guaranteed. There are daily flights to and from the south side airport to Port Hardy.

Other suggestions for things to do are to take a one-hour **horse drawn tour** through Stanley Park (tel: 604.681 5115), $12 for adults. Visit the **Vancouver Aquarium** (tel: 604.631.2549 – admission charges apply) or try **Science World BC** and **OMNIMAX Theatre** at 1455 Quebec St. There is also the multi-storey **CN IMAX Theatre** (tel: 604.682.2384) at the end of the Canada Place cruise ship terminal. The **Capilano Suspension Bridge** to the north of the city is open all year round ($6.60–$8:10 admission) plus there are all the usual half-day and full-day city tours, harbour tours, dinner cruises and the like.

I enjoyed the **Royal British Columbia Museum** on 675 Belleville St in Victoria on Victoria Island (tel: 250.387.3701) as a nice change to wandering around downtown Vancouver itself. To get there take the ferry from Tsawwassen outside town. The journey time is 1 hour 40 minutes and the walk-on fare is $6.00 (tel: call 604.656.0757 for ferry times etc). Ferries are usually every 30 minutes allowing you time to spend the whole day at Victoria if you wish.

EDMONTON

Edmonton is Canada's fifth largest city and the major gateway to the north. Edmonton can be looked upon as the technological and cultural centre of the province. It is a city of parks and is fairly well laid out on both sides of the North Saskatchewan River. The cultural facilities and the sporting facilities are the best in the province but you expect that from a city that has hosted the Commonwealth Games (1978) and the World University Games (1983). Edmonton's biggest attraction is the West Edmonton Mall, deemed to be the world's largest shopping and amusement complex.

Getting about

The airport is 29km south of the city. The big hotels all have free shuttle buses and there is a service called the Sky Shuttle that serves most of the downtown hotels for $11 one way or $18 for the round trip with door-to-door pick-up. These buses leave every 20 minutes. The airport is smallish but has all the usual car-rental booths, restaurants, a hotel booking service, and courtesy phones for the hotels. For those that need it there is a foreign exchange counter.

The **Edmonton Transit System** is the local bus service that links the city centre with the rest of Edmonton. The fare anywhere within the city is $1.60 at peak times (05.00–09.00 and 15.00–18.00) and $1.35 at all other times. There is also a day-pass for $4.25. For information on times, where to get passes and so on, dial (780) 496.1611. There is also an underground-overground system called the LRT that travels between the university and 139th St. Ticket prices are the same as for the bus system.

From Edmonton you can fly north to Cambridge Bay (NWT), Inuvik (NWT), Iqaluit (Nun), Rankin Inlet (Nun), and Yellowknife (NWT).

Where to stay

Once again I am only dealing with downtown:

Mayfair Hotel 10815 Jasper Ave (tel: 780.423.1650)
Days Inn 10041 106th St (tel: 780.423.1925)
Garden City Hotel 10425 100th St (tel: 780.423.5611)
Howard Johnston Plaza Hotel 10010 104th St (tel: 780.423.2450)
Inn on 7th 10001 107th St (tel: 780.429.2861)

There are **bed & breakfasts** scattered throughout the city which start at about $50 per night. There is a listing in the **free accommodation guide** available from tourist information centres. The **YMCA** is downtown at 10030 102A Ave (tel: 780.421.9622) but the **Edmonton International Hostel** is out of town in Old Strathcona at 10647 81st Ave (tel: 780.988.6836).

Where to eat

As one would expect, with a cultural capital like Edmonton there is plenty of variety in restaurants in the city. With over 2,000 restaurants to choose from you are, once again, spoilt for choice. The downtown plazas have food halls

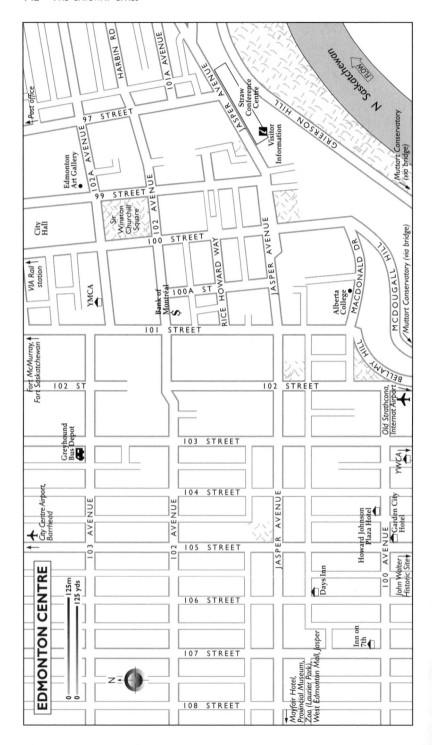

that fill with those who are after a quick meal, whether it is at lunchtime or for dinner. There are many fine restaurants in the same area. For selected cuisine try the **Old Strathcona area** with restaurants from all corners of the world. This has always been a bit out of my way, but I am told that the steak houses and family restaurants along the Calgary Way (Highway 2) are cheap and extremely good value and I intend to find out next visit. It's just a suggestion if you don't mind a bit of a journey to have your dinner.

What to see and do

The **West Edmonton Mall** has been billed as the 'greatest indoor show on earth' – as opposed to Calgary's greatest outdoor show, perhaps? The mall covers 483,000m², or 48 city blocks, and has 800 stores, 100 eateries, 19 movie theatres, the world's only indoor bungee jump and more submarines than the Canadian Navy. The amusement section has 27 rides including the mind bender – a 14-storey triple loop roller coaster and the 'Drop of Doom' where you are hauled up 13 floors and then dropped back to earth in seconds. Admission to the mall is free, though the rides are charged for. A day pass for unlimited rides costs $29.95 for adults and $21.95 for children. There is also a two-hectare water-park where the water temperature is set at 30°C – brilliant in the middle of winter. There are tropical palms, a beach bar and waves which resemble the real thing. There are 22 water slides to amuse you as well. Water-park admissions are the same as for the amusement park. The bungee jump costs $69.95 but for an extra 30 bucks you can have the T-shirt and the video as well. If you are only in town for the day this is the place to come. For those serious players there is a 355-room hotel called **Fantasyland** offering weekend packages.

WINNIPEG

Winnipeg is the fourth largest city in Canada and situated about halfway between the east and west coasts. The city derives her name from the Cree First Nation word 'Winnipee' meaning muddy water, and today the city considers itself the 'city of rivers'. Winnipeg has a large French community, the largest in fact of all western Canada, whose residents play a big part in the cultural life of the city. Situated in the Canadian prairies along the Trans Canada Highway, Winnipeg has a fascinating history and makes a wonderful place for a stopover en route to the north. It is also the stepping-off point for the polar bear capital of the world – Churchill, on the shores of Hudson Bay. The only disadvantage I find with Winnipeg is the weather. It is quite hot in the summer, very cold in the winter and sometimes rather windy. The city is often thought to be a miniature version of Chicago, being a mid-western, grain-producing, transportation hub that's rather breezy.

Getting about

The international airport is about 20 minutes outside town. As well as the usual taxis there is the Sargent No 15 bus that leaves the airport for the city every 20 minutes or so, at a cost of $1.50. The bigger hotels all have shuttle

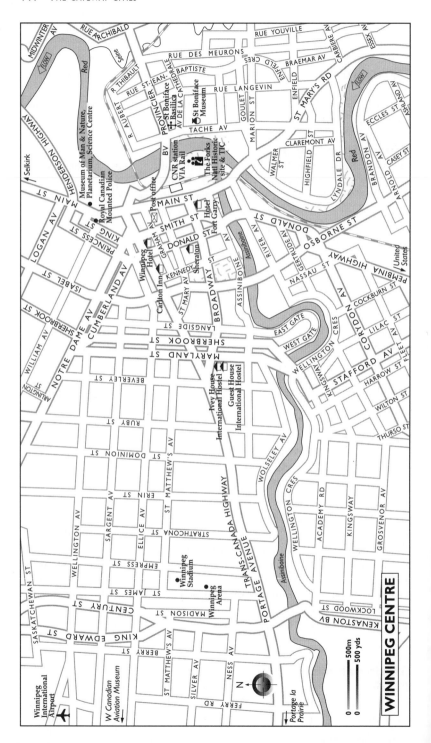

WINNIPEG CENTRE

buses. Local buses cost $1.50 per journey. If you need to change buses, get a transfer ticket from the driver or you'll be liable for another fare.

Where to stay

There are a couple of hostels and backpackers' establishments that are relatively central in Winnipeg. The **Ivey House International Hostel** (204.772.3022) at 210 Maryland St has a kitchen, and laundry, rents bicycles and costs $14–18 per night. The **Guest House International** (204.772.1272) is just down the road at 168 Maryland St and has all the same facilities including bicycle rental. Their rates are $14 for a single and $35 for a double.

Winnipeg has lots of B&Bs spread right across the city. The few mentioned here are centrally located and within easy walking distance of downtown and most of the sights. **Bunny Hollow** (204.231.1135) at 129 Tache Avenue and **Butterfly** (204.783.6664) at 226 Walnut Street are both clean, small and cosy B&Bs in private homes situated in very pleasant areas of town away from the main hustle and bustle. **Franz B&B** (204.774.3900) at 38 Alloway Avenue can cater for families as well as individuals and is very close to the downtown area. If you would like to stay in the French area of town try **Gate de la Cathédrale** (204.233.7792 at 581 rue Langevin) or **Masson's** (204.237.9230 at 181 rue Masson).

For those of you who want a serious budget hotel you might like to try the **Winnipeg Hotel** (204.942.7762) on Main Street but it's fairly basic at $25. In the middle range is the **Best Western Carlton Inn** (204.942.0881) at 220 Carlton St which is a good reliable choice.

At the top end there is the **Hotel Fort Garry** (204.942.8251) situated in an old historic building near the railway station at 222 Broadway. For those who really want to live in luxury there is always the **Sheraton** (204.942.5300) at 161 Donald Street.

Where to eat

Central Winnipeg has lots of restaurants and I have no favourites at all. A Winnipeg institution is **Rae and Jerry's** on Portage Ave that has served classic meat dishes for years. There are several places in and around town that are a combination of bar and restaurant in a decidedly modern atmosphere. Try **Earls** near the station on Main St or the **Chocolate Shop Restaurant** on Portage Ave. Two recommendations in the French quarter are **Le Café Jardin** and the somewhat more expensive **Le Beaujolais**. Both are in Boulevard Provencher.

What to see and do

The main **tourist office** is in the Travel Manitoba Centre in the Johnstone Building at The Forks (204.945.3777, or freephone 1-800-665-0040). There is a **Tourism Winnipeg information counter** at the airport that's open till late.

All Canadian cities are excellent for museums and the like, and Winnipeg is no exception. One museum well worth a good visit rather than a quick look is the **Museum of Man and Nature** on Rupert Street. There are lots of exhibits on nature, culture – both European and native, wildlife and, of course, geology. There is an admission fee and you can get a combined ticket that gets you into the **Planetarium and the Science Centre** as well. It's open every day in the summer but closes on Mondays between September and June.

For people watching, shopping or just taking in a coffee try **The Forks** behind the VIA railway station off Main and Broadway Streets. Parks Canada do walking tours or you can pick up a map and please yourself. The market building has lots of stalls, boutiques and galleries and there are plenty of cafés to rest in and enjoy the goings-on.

Annual events in Winnipeg include **Le Festival du Voyageur** in February when everyone dresses up in traditional costume for a huge winter street party. There's the **Winnipeg Folk Festival** in July with concerts and an international food fair. It is held at Bird's Hill Park outside town. **Folklorama** is the city's favourite event when everyone celebrates the city's ethnic origins. Two weeks of music, dance and lots of food in pavilions throughout the downtown area.

For those who want to explore the city sights from a boat there is a two-hour cruise that departs from The Forks wharf by The Forks Historical Site. The cruise is in a replica paddlesteamer and costs about $12 per person. They also do dinner cruises each evening which last about three hours.

OTTAWA

Ottawa is the capital city of Canada. It sits gently on the south bank of the Ottawa River but just over the other side is Québec so many people work in one province and live in the other. The largest employer is the Canadian government as you would expect with a capital city, but there are many big business interests in the city as well. Ottawa is a wide, spacious city with little heavy industry, making it a clean and extremely pleasant place to visit. Many of the local residents can be seen cycling or jogging the paths and parks of this unpolluted and comfortable place.

For tourist information try www.ottawakiosk.com.

Getting about

There is an **airport shuttle bus** that goes to and from the Château Laurier Hotel and cost $7 one-way, $11 return and runs about every half-hour for most of the day. The weekend timings are a little less frequent. Around town there is the **Ottawa bus service**. It runs a two-tier system (peak hours and off-peak hours) for fares ($2.00 and $1.30 respectively) and the tickets can be purchased almost anywhere, avoiding the need to search for small change when getting aboard. There is an all-day Tourpass available from the office of Ottawa City Transport at 1500 St Laurent (tel: 613.741.4390) which costs $5.00.

Ottawa is extremely bicycle friendly if you can get your hands on one. The **tourist office** (tel: 613.237.5158) in the National Arts Centre has a map showing all the paths and routes that you can take to see the city, plus all the usual city guides, accommodation guides and it can organise tours as well.

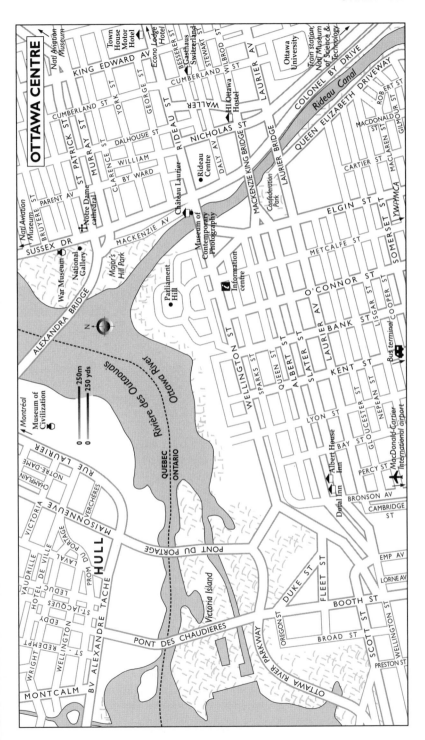

OTTAWA CENTRE

City maps are available free from the shuttle bus and at the tourist information booth at the airport.

Ottawa has flights north to Iqaluit (Nun) and Yellowknife (NWT).

Where to stay

Ottawa has the most famous hostel in Canada. The **Hi Ottawa Hostel** (tel: 613.235.2595) is situated in the old Ottawa gaol complete with the gallows out back. Located right next to the parliament building you couldn't be closer to downtown Ottawa. The **YM/YWCA** is at 180 Argyle Ave on the corner of O'Connor St. (tel: 613.237.1320). The tourist office can help with tourist homes and **bed & breakfasts**.

Some of the hotels in town that are less than $100 per night are:

Château Laurier (tel: 613.241.1414)
Doral Inn (tel: 613.230.8055)
Econo Lodge Downtown (tel: 613.789.3781)
Town House Motor Hotel (tel: 613.789.5555)

There are a couple of guesthouses downtown called the **Albert House Inn** (tel: 613.236.4479) and the **Gasthaus Switzerland Inn** (tel: 613.237.0335) with quite cheap and clean accommodation.

Where to eat

The best restaurants are across the river in Hull, but downtown Ottawa has some nice little establishments. Unfortunately you may find that the prices here may be a little higher than elsewhere. A couple of British-style places in the centre of town are the **Royal Oak** and the **Duke of Somerset**. They serve British beer and food. The **market** also has numerous eateries and is popular for breakfast, lunch and dinner, all in a busy market atmosphere. There is **Chinatown** to the west of the city centre if you like Chinese food. A recommended Indian restaurant is the **Sitar** on Rideau St, but it is apparently a bit pricey. There's a place called **Nate's** at 316 Rideau St which is a little Jewish deli that serves delicious snacks and light meals. It is open every day. All the major hotels have restaurants, generally with prices to match. I find that if I need to find somewhere nice to eat I can always ask the concierge at my hotel for a recommendation. They have invariably come up with something reasonable and close at hand that only the locals know about and the prices have always been quite reasonable.

What to see and do

Ottawa is museum capital of Canada. You could get museumed-out in a day here there are so many good ones. I take my pick and do one either side of lunch and expect to return to see them all over time. Pick of the crop are the **Museum of Contemporary Photography**, the **Museum of Civilization**, the **War Museum**, the **National Gallery**, the **National Museum of Science and Technology** and, lastly, the **National Aviation Museum**. All have something different; some have excellent interactive and interpretive displays and in the others one can just chill out in front of some stunning works of art.

There is an **Ottawa River cruise** showing you the historic sights of Ottawa from the comfort of a boat (Ottawa Riverboat Co. 613.562.4888 for times and pick-up points). In the entertainment stakes you might like to try something different. Just across the river in Québec the **Ferme Rouge Showtime Restaurant** (tel: 819.986.7013) has a cabaret. Speciality is seafood and it is only 20 minutes by taxi from the city centre. It can be lots of fun if you are in a group.

MONTREAL

The French-speaking capital of Canada, Montréal has North America's largest concentration of 17th-, 18th- and 19th-century architecture, with a bit of modern thrown in for good measure. Montréal hosted the 1996 Olympics and now has the claim to fame of having the largest pedestrian-only city centre in the world – even if most of it is underground. The city is a fascinating blend of English and French with the largest French-speaking population of any city in the world other than Paris (two-thirds of the population are French-speakers). The only thing wrong with Montréal, and everyone says it, is the winter. It can get down to a miserable –40°C with lots of snow. Fortunately you can get about the city on the underground system without ever having to step outside. Anyone familiar with Paris will find Montréal a doddle, the rest of us will just have to struggle with difficult French names.

Getting about

Montréal's problem is that the international airport, Mirabel, is 50km to the northwest of the city, making it a long journey into town. There is an **airport bus** from Mirabel to the downtown area. It takes about 45 minutes and costs $11.15 one-way; taxis will cost a huge $60 each way. The city has both a **metro** (underground) and a **bus system**. Tickets work equally well on both buses and the metro and cost $1.75 per journey. The metro is by far the easier to use and understand, and covers most of the city.

The only destination of concern to this guidebook you can fly to from Montréal is Iqaluit in Nunavut.

Where to stay

The best hotel in town is the **Queen Elizabeth Hotel**, 900 Réne Lévesque Blvd. Everyone has stayed here, from John Lennon and Yoko Ono to Nelson Mandela, Gérard Depardieu and Liberace. A stay here will send your holiday budget out of the window, but it is not often you get to hob-nob with the rich and famous. A more modest establishment is the **Hôtel de Paris**, rue Sherbrooke East (tel: 514.522.6861), or try the **Hotel Europa** (tel: 514.866.6492). Others are the **Days Inn Downtown Montréal Hotel** (tel: 514.393.3388) and the **Hotel Travelodge Montréal Centre** (tel: 514.874.9090). Hostels include the **Hostelling International Montréal** (tel:

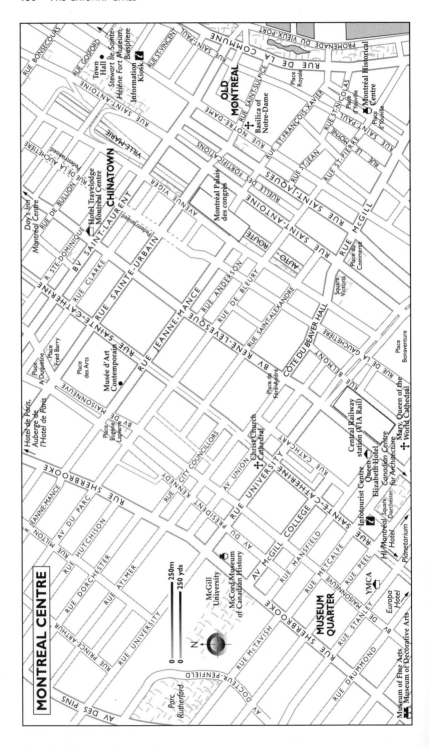

MONTREAL CENTRE

N

0   250m
0   250 yds

OLD MONTRÉAL

CHINATOWN

MUSEUM QUARTER

Town Hall
Stewart Île Sainte-Hélène Fort Museum;
Biosphere
Information Kiosk

Days Inn/
Montréal Centre

Hôtel Travelodge
Montréal Centre

Basilica of Notre-Dame

Montréal Historical Centre

Place Royale
Place d'Youville
Place d'Youville
Place du Commerce

Montréal Palais des congrès

Musée d'Art Contemporain

Place des Arts

Place Fred Barry
Place A. Duquesne

Hôtel de Paris,
Auberge de
l'Hôtel de Paris

Place Eugène-Lapierre

Christ Church Cathedral

Place du Frère-André

Square Victoria

Place Bonaventure

Central Railway station (VIA Rail)
Queen Elizabeth Hotel

Infotourist Centre

Canadian Centre for Architecture

Mary, Queen of the World Cathedral

HI/Montréal Hotel

Square Dorchester

Planetarium

McGill University

McCord Museum of Canadian History

YMCA

Europa Hotel

Museum of Fine Arts
Museum of Decorative Arts

Parc Rutherford

Streets

RUE BONSECOURS
RUE GOSFORD
RUE SAINT-ANTOINE
RUE SAINT-VINCENT
RUE SAINT-PAUL
RUE DE LA COMMUNE
PROMENADE DU VIEUX-PORT
RUE SAINT-SULPICE
RUE NOTRE-DAME
RUE SAINT-FRANÇOIS-XAVIER
RUE SAINT-NICOLAS
RUE SAINT-JEAN
RUE LE MOYNE
RUE ST-PIERRE
RUE McGILL
VILLE-MARIE
RUE DE LA GAUCHETIÈRE
RUE DE BULLION
R. STE-DOMINIQUE
BV SAINT-LAURENT
RUE CLARKE
RUE SAINTE-URBAIN
RUE SAINTE-CATHERINE
AVENUE VIGER
RUELLE DES FORTIFICATIONS
RUE SAINT-JACQUES
ROUTE AUTO.
RUE SAINT-ANTOINE
RUE ANDERSON
RUE DE BLEURY
RUE JEANNE-MANCE
RUE SAINT-ALEXANDRE
BV RENÉ-LÉVESQUE
CÔTE DU BEAVER HALL
RUE BELMONT
RUE DE LA GAUCHETIÈRE
MAISONNEUVE
RUE UNIVERSITY
AV UNION
RUE CITY COUNCILLORS
KENNEDY
PRESIDENT KENNEDY
RUE SAINTE-CATHERINE
RUE CATHCART
RUE SHERBROOKE
R. JEANNE-MANCE
AV DU PARC
RUE HUTCHISON
RUE MILTON
RUE AYLMER
RUE UNIVERSITY
AV McGILL COLLEGE
RUE MANSFIELD
RUE METCALFE
RUE PEEL
MAISONNEUVE
DE STANLEY
RUE DRUMMOND
RUE McTAVISH
RUE DORCHESTER
RUE PRINCE-ARTHUR
DOCTEUR-PENFIELD
AV DES PINS

514.843.3317); the **Downtown YMCA** (tel: 514.849.8393); and the **Auberge de l'Hôtel de Paris** (tel: 514.522.6861)

Where to eat

Montréal is considered the gastronomic capital of North America, although this may be just a bit of French snobbery. Having said that, the choice of cuisine is diverse, though much of it has a French flavour. Try the **Restaurant Chez Chez** (tel: 514.744.0590) at 1402 de l'Eglise, St Laurent for three courses for under $30. For cheap food served by rude waiters and a high cholesterol content to boot try **Schwartz's** (tel: 514.842.4813) at 3895 St Laurent. Saint Laurent Avenue is the place to go for food with every style from Indian, Thai and Greek right through to the most perfect French cuisine. There is everything from cappuccinos to sumptuous dinners.

What to see and do

Montréal is another city of museums and they have a museum pass (one day $15, three days $28) to help you along. For information about the pass call 514.845.6873. All in all there are some 19 museums on the pass varying from architectural masterpieces, places of historical reference, the arts and science. Try the **McCord Museum of Canadian History**, the **Canadian Centre for Architecture**, the **Museum of Decorative Arts** and the **Museum of Fine Arts**, the **Biosphere** and the **Musée d'Art Contemporain**.

The famous **Cirque du Soleil** comes from Montréal. If they are in town go and see the show – a lively blend of circus and street entertainment (tel: 514.722.3692).

Montréal now has an underground city. A network of corridors connects the bus stations and the metro with a variety of commercial and office buildings. Along these passageways are more than 2,000 stores, restaurants, cinemas and exhibition halls. Don't get lost is all I can say!

152

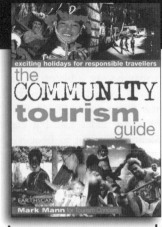

Part Three

The Guide

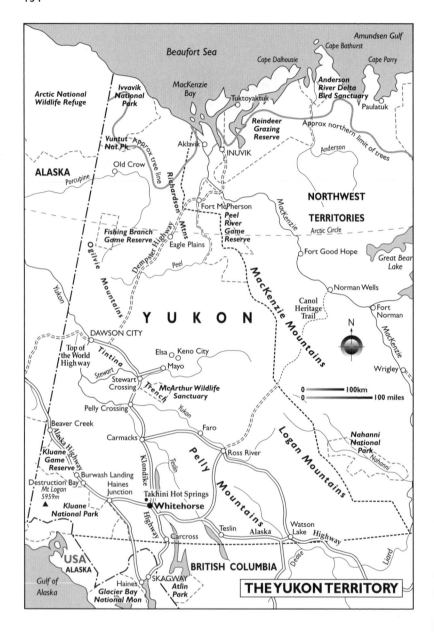

THE YUKON TERRITORY

The Yukon Territory

Of all the northern territories, the Yukon is my favourite, though I am not sure why. Maybe it is because the Yukon was my first experience of the north and somehow fulfilled my every perception of what the Canadian wilderness was all about. I have had more experiences of the Yukon and, although I have been made to feel welcome everywhere I have been in the north, the folk of the Yukon, the Yukoners, have made me feel especially at home.

The Yukon is the easiest of the three territories to get about with a fine network of roads including the most northerly road in the world, the Dempster Highway. Running from its junction with the Klondike Highway just outside Dawson City, the Dempster heads almost due north to Inuvik in Northwest Territories. Somewhere beyond Eagle Plains it passes the frontier into Northwest Territories, crossing the MacKenzie River at Arctic Red River at the head of the MacKenzie Delta, 62km east of Fort McPherson. Some sections of the road are fully sealed while others are well maintained, fully constructed though non-surfaced.

Travelling through pristine wilderness by road is one of the great joys of the Yukon. Most of the other two territories require a plane to get about and the world does not look the same from 6,000m. Whether it is through spruce and aspen forests or across the heath-covered open tundra along much of the Dempster this wilderness teems with wildlife and you will have as much a chance of seeing it from the side of a road as you will stalking it through the bush.

To give you some idea of the vast number of animals in the Yukon just quickly scan this list. The are an estimated 50,000 moose, 10,000 black bears, 7,000 grizzlies, 22,000 Dall's sheep and 3,000 Stone's sheep. There are about 160,000 barren ground caribou (the Porcupine herd) plus some 28,000 woodland caribou and between 4,000 and 5,000 wolves. The elk population is well monitored at 40 animals across the territory. There are about 400 bison in the area of Canyon Creek and 150 muskoxen on the Firth River in Ivvavik National Park. Of the other animals there are too many beaver to count, as also birds and fish. It is thought that there are a few cougars, flying squirrels and deer. Add to that list about 4,900 hunters, 50–60 biologists and 29,000 people and you have the sum total of the natural history of the Yukon.

YUKON FACTS

Area 483,450km², including 4,480km² of fresh water and 281,030km² of forested land. About 80% is classified as wilderness. Included in all this are three national parks, three territorial parks, five protected areas or sanctuaries, and six heritage sites.

Boundaries 60° North latitude bordering with British Columbia on the south; the western boundary is with Alaska at 141° West longitude; the northern boundary is the Beaufort Sea; and in the east the Yukon's boundary with the Northwest Territories follows a line from a point on the coast at roughly 136° 30' West longitude to the border with BC at 124° W/60° N in the south.

Geographical features Highest mountain is Mt Logan (5,959m)in the St Elias Mountains in Kluane National Park and Reserve; the lowest point is sea level on the coast at the Beaufort Sea.

Time Pacific Standard Time (GMT −8hr). There is Daylight Saving Time April to October (GMT −7hr).

Population 33,580 with 70% living in Whitehorse (24,000).

Capital Whitehorse.

Telephone area code 867.

Territorial status The Yukon became a separate territory of the Dominion of Canada on June 13 1898. It was established to help protect Canadian sovereignty from the flood of Americans arriving during the Klondike Stampede.

HISTORY

The Yukon is considered part of a lost sub-continent. This anomaly dates back to the last Ice Age when most of Canada was under huge sheets of ice and the Yukon, Alaska and Eastern Siberia remained glacier free. The sea levels were lower than now by about 125m and part of the floor of the Bering Sea was exposed creating a land bridge between Asia and the Americas. This ice-free area has been called Beringia and supported an astonishing variety of wildlife including the woolly mammoth. Three metres tall, these hairy humpback giants roamed the tundra for thousands of years. Their main predator was the scimitar cat that had a set of serrated upper fangs and was an agile and speedy killing machine. Another predator at the time was the short-faced bear. This animal was about 25cm taller than today's grizzly and was the most powerful land predator in North America during the last Ice Age. The third and most significant predator was man.

The New World's earliest inhabitants moved into Beringia about 25,000 years ago. They came following the vast herds of woolly mammoth and giant bison. Well adapted to the hunter-gatherer role, these first people eventually out-survived the animals they preyed upon and are the ancestors of today's First Nations people.

Yukon had no European population until Robert Campbell of the Hudson

MOUNT LOGAN

At 5,959m above sea level, Mount Logan is the highest point in the Yukon and Canada. Mount Logan is part of the St Elias Mountains. The mountain is the world's single most massive block. Until 1992, Mount Logan' height had been estimated at 6,050m. A team of scientists ascended the mountain and, using highly accurate GPS satellite technology, officially declared its height to be 5,959m on July 1 1992.

Bay Company established a fur-trading post at Fort Selkirk at the junction of the Pelly and Yukon Rivers near modern day Pelly Crossing in 1848. The idea was to disrupt the monopoly on fur-trading of the north-west interior then held by the Chilkat people of the Alaskan coast, providing an alternative market for the Yukon First Nations to sell their furs. The Chilkat pillaged the post on August 19 1852 but, for some reason, left the Europeans alone. The abandoned post was later burnt to the ground by local First Nations people to extract the metal fittings for use as tools.

Although the HBC withdrew from the Yukon for decades Fort Selkirk came back into prominence when an independent operator called Arthur Harper erected a new post on the same site in September 1889. The post was still prominent when the Klondike Gold Strike began being used as a stopping point for those stampeders coming down the Yukon River to Dawson. Although the Yukon Field Force established its headquarters here in 1898 and Fort Selkirk was often thought of as the first capital of the Yukon, it fell into disuse at the end of the Klondike rush when everyone headed for Nome in Alaska in search of new gold in 1899. The HBC did eventually return in 1938 and continued to trade at Fort Selkirk until the steamboat traffic down the Yukon River ended in the 1950s.

The Yukon was not high on the Canadian Government agenda until George Dawson, the director of the Geological Survey of Canada, led the Canadian Yukon Exploration Expedition in 1887–8. Mining and prospecting had replaced fur trading as the economic lure of the Yukon. Prospectors had been filtering into the territory from the rushes in British Columbia and south-eastern Alaska over the Chilkoot Pass and coming down the Yukon River into the Klondike Valley.

Gold!

Of all the events that have occurred in Canada's history and particularly that of the north, only one event has really captured the imagination of the whole world. That event was the Klondike Gold Stampede of 1898. When gold was discovered in the quantities that the Klondike yielded the whole face of the territory changed. No longer was it the exclusive preserve of the First Nations, the fur traders and a few wily old prospectors. The discovery of gold opened up the north to people from ordinary ways of life and altered the Yukon for ever. It all began like this.

On August 17 1896 a Californian named George Washington Carmack discovered gold in a small tributary of the Klondike River called Rabbit Creek. He was with his wife Kate, the daughter of a Tagish First Nation chief, and his two Tagish First Nation brothers-in-law Keish, known as Skookum Jim Mason, and Ḵáa Goox̱, known to Europeans as Tagish Charlie or Dawson Charlie. It had all begun some days before when our little group went fishing for salmon along the Klondike River. George was intending to cut some trees from the banks of Rabbit Creek to float down to a mill at Forty-mile Creek to make a bit of money. The mill paid about $25 per thousand feet.

Robert Henderson, a Nova Scotian who had been prospecting for 25 years all over the world but had not struck it rich, also figures in the story. He approached George's fishing camp at the mouth of the Klondike River where it runs into the Yukon River. (The Tr'ondek Hwech'in people of the han language are named after the Tr'ondek or Klondike River. Tr'ondek is named for the traditional stones – *tr'o* – which were used to pound stakes into the river bed to construct salmon fish traps.) George was not really interested in gold but listened when Henderson told him of a possible strike up the Klondike River. What spoiled the conversation was when Henderson, as he was leaving, said to Carmack, 'There's a chance for you, George, but I don't want any damn *Siwashes* (Indians) staking on that creek.' That comment rankled Carmack and he decided to go and find a creek of his own that he could share with his relatives. It would turn out to be just that simple. Henderson and Carmack met up again a couple of days later and promised to share finds if either of them got lucky, but Henderson's previous comments still annoyed Carmack and his First Nation friends.

That night they headed back to their fishing camp on the Klondike but ended up camping near a fork in the Rabbit Creek. The little group had been reconnoitring for trees as well as doing a little gold panning along the way. Little did they know that they were camped on the richest gold bearing ground in the world – several million dollars worth.

Myth, legend and hearsay all tell different tales about who found the gold first. Skookum Jim and Tagish Charlie both claimed that Carmack was asleep at the time of the find. They shot a moose and were cleaning the dishpan in the creek behind their camp when they made the find. Carmack says it was he who happened upon a protruding rim of bedrock and pulled out a thumb-sized piece of gold. Whoever it was in reality what they found was gold lying thick between the flaky slabs of rock like 'cheese in a sandwich'. A single pan yielded about a quarter of an ounce, worth about $4 then, and every pan had its quarter ounce. This was an amazing find. As one would expect the three men danced around making all kinds of whoopee.

The following morning the three men staked claims on Rabbit Creek. Canadian mining law normally allows only one claim per man in any one district but the man who makes the discovery is allowed a double claim. Carmack wrote on the upstream side of the nearest tree to the site:

'TO WHOM IT MAY CONCERN
I do, this day, locate and claim, by right of discovery, five hundred feet, running upstream from this notice. Located this 17th day of August 1896.

G. W. Carmack'

Under Canadian mining law all goldfields are made up of a series of claims based on equal sized areas of land, with each man entitled to stake a single claim in any given mining district. The original site is always known as *Discovery Claim* and, as most gold in those days was discovered along creek beds, claims were usually numbered above and below Discovery depending on whether they were upstream or downstream of the original claim. A claim could not exceed 152m in length and if next to a creek had to be limited to one side of it, measuring back a distance of 305m. In the old days this was generally considered to be 500ft by 1,000ft. The law also allows the discoverer of the actual goldfield, in this case George, to stake a second claim for himself (ie: another 1,000ft). Being the only European present George also staked out *One Above* discovery for Skookum Jim and *Two Below* for Tagish Charlie. These were their limits by law. George recorded his find at the police post at Forty-mile Creek and started a stampede that turned Forty-mile into a dead camp. News spread like wildfire around the Yukon. Miners and prospectors came from everywhere. Rabbit Creek was renamed Bonanza Creek and it still carries that name today.

Either by oversight or by spite Henderson was never told of the strike. When he eventually heard he thought he would try his luck at Hunker Creek. Ill health forced him to sell his claim for $3,000 some time later. The claim first netted its new owner $450,000 and he then sold it for another $200,000.

By the winter of 1896–7 about 300 men were working the Bonanza Creek. The rush continued with men arriving by dogteams and on snowshoes. By January 6 1897 500 claims had been staked.

The extreme isolation of the Yukon and Dawson meant that word of the strike did not reach the outside world until the first sternwheelers came upstream after the spring melt of 1897. Some 80 prospectors left Dawson with anything from $25,000 to $500,000 in gold stuffed into metal boxes. At St Michael on the Alaskan coast they transferred to two steamers, the *Portland* and the *Excelsior* bound for Seattle and San Francisco. The *Excelsior* docked first on July 14 1897 and the word was out. Thousands watched as the *Portland* docked and newspapers claimed 'a ton of gold' being unloaded. The resulting 'gold fever' swept across the United States and the rest of the world.

All in all about 100,000 people joined the stampede to the Klondike. About 40,000 made it to Dawson. Most of the claims had been struck by then so most of the new arrivals ended up working for other miners. The Klondike was the most peaceful of the world's gold rushes mainly because of the efforts of the North West Mounted Police who allowed none of the gun related violence that plagued other big strikes.

By 1898 the rush for gold was well and truly over. A new strike near Nome in Alaska prompted a mass exodus from Dawson. Some $50 million worth of gold had been taken out of the ground by then. The Klondike would yield another $50 million over the next five years but by 1899 gold was being mined commercially by technologically sophisticated machinery and the small time amateur prospectors left. The Klondike today still gives up about $65 million annually but at $375–$400 an ounce, that is about 20 times the amount paid during the Stampede.

You may ask whatever happened to Robert Henderson. Well, he was to regret his last comment to George Carmack for the rest of his life. Eventually, the Canadian government recognised his part in discovering gold in the Klondike and gave Henderson a pension of $200 a month. He never changed his racist attitudes and remained embittered towards Carmack and his First Nations relatives to the bitter end. He died in January 1933 from cancer while still prospecting for gold. He never did strike it rich.

What happened to the others concerned with the discovery claim? Well, Carmack eventually deserted Kate for a white woman in 1900. He refused her any part of the fortune he had amassed and also refused her access to their daughter. She lived out the rest of her life on a government pension in Carcross and died penniless in 1920. Tagish Charlie went on to be the first Yukon First Nations person to be granted full Canadian citizenship by an act of parliament because of the wealth and fame he gained from the discovery. He went on to discover gold at Burwash Landing in the Kluane region before selling off his mining properties and buying a hotel in Carcross. On January 26 1908, on a drunken spree, he fell off the railway bridge at Carcross into the freezing river below and drowned. Skookum Jim Mason was desperate to become a white man. He continued the hard life of a prospector despite the wealth from the royalties on his mining properties, reputed at more than $90,000 a year. He died, old and worn out, in 1916.

As for Carmack himself, the white woman he deserted Kate for was one Marguerite Laimee who had been on the fringes of three gold rushes – South Africa, Australia and the Yukon. She was what was sometimes known as a camp follower and ran the 'cigar store' in Dawson City, a euphemism for a bawdyhouse. What she offered must have been good, even if it wasn't cigars, because she would pan the sawdust off the floor each morning and find about $30 in gold dust. She and Carmack lived happily in Vancouver until his death in 1922. He invested well in real estate, built an apartment house and hotel and operated a mine in California. When he died Carmack was a respected member of the Masonic Order and left a very healthy estate. Marguerite inherited it all and died in California in 1949.

Alaska Highway

The Alaska Highway (the AlCan) stretches from Dawson Creek, British Columbia to Fairbanks in Alaska. It is 2,451km long of which 925km lies within the boundaries of the Yukon Territory.

The whole project was an American idea that had its seeds during the 1930s. After the Japanese attacked Pearl Harbour in 1941 the Americans discovered they had plans for an invasion of the Aleutian Islands. The Americans thought that the Japanese might invade North America through Alaska and a land link was needed to maintain the military garrisons established throughout Alaska. (The Japanese subsequently put to task their plans when they invaded Attu and Kiski Islands in August 1942. The Americans reclaimed the islands after a fierce 23-day battle in May 1943 allowing them airfields within striking distance of Japan itself.) Work began in February 1942 and the road is considered one of the most spectacular engineering feats of the 20th century. The reason is the terrain that it had to go through and the speed with which it was built.

The US Army's 97th and 18th Engineers began in Fairbanks and Dawson Creek simultaneously and in just 8 months and 12 days completed a single lane dirt road just about wide enough for a military truck to pass. Some 11,000 US soldiers and 16,000 civilians, including some 3,700 Canadians, were involved. Building the road meant crossing eight mountain ranges, countless streams and endless forests. The workers constructed more than 8,000 culverts and 133 bridges had to be built or put in place. Permafrost often hampered engineering, leading to new construction methods being implemented.

The road cost a massive $US147.8 million. All of which was borne by the US government while Canada provided the right of way. In April 1946 Canada paid the US government $108 million for the 1,954km Canadian section. This price was for ownership of the adjacent buildings, airstrips, telephone systems and other works but not to cover the highway construction costs. The highway was opened for unrestricted civilian traffic in 1947 but maintained by Canadian Army engineers until 1964 when the Department of Public Works took over. About $40 million is spent annually repairing and reconstructing the road. The major problems are still the big holes that tend to appear in the road after the winter thaw. In spring and summer floods can occur with rainstorms. All the work to overcome these difficulties is necessary, as the road is the major link for many communities in the Yukon.

WHITEHORSE

The north has some wonderful place names but none have a more magical ring than Whitehorse. The name originated from the stampeders heading for the Klondike in 1898. In the winter of 1897–8, once over the Chilkoot and White Passes, the stampeders spent their time on the banks of the Lindemann and Bennett Lakes building boats. The only way forward was to negotiate Miles Canyon and the rapids on the Yukon River when the spring thaw came. The rapids reminded the stampeders of the flowing manes of albino horses and, as many of these men had never handled boats before heading for the Klondike, they presented a formidable obstacle. Many of the stampeders drowned before the NWMP stepped in and allowed only expert boat handlers to pilot the rapids. Jack London, the author, earned $3,000 that first summer ferrying stampeders and their goods downstream. This move saved countless lives and supplies – more than 7,000 journeys were made during that summer.

In 1897 two entrepreneurs took advantage of the problems presented by Miles Canyon and the rapids and built two horse-drawn tramways from what was called Canyon City (an old First Nations campsite) to a site below the foaming rapids. As this was the furthest point up river that boats could come and it was an obvious point from where the stampeders could catch a sternwheeler downstream to Dawson City and the digs. Paddle steamers would come upstream from Dawson to Whitehorse and return full of miners back to the digs. A tent city sprang up at the end of the tramway and Whitehorse was born. In 1900 construction of the White Pass and Yukon Route railway from Skagway in Alaska to this tent city past the rapids was completed and Whitehorse grew in size as a railhead for the Klondike.

Whitehorse continued to grow in this role as a transportation hub. In 1920 the first plane landed and in 1942 thousands of US Army troops arrived to build the Alaska Highway. By this time Whitehorse had become an important communications centre for the whole of the Yukon. It was incorporated as a city in 1950 and in 1953 became the capital of the Yukon, taking over from Dawson. Today, with a population of 24,000, it is the largest city in the north.

Getting there and about
By air
There are two flights on most days of the week from Vancouver to Whitehorse. One in the morning and one mid-afternoon. There is also a weekday flight to and from Yellowknife. Whitehorse's airport also has services within the Yukon to Dawson City (daily) and Old Crow in the northwest (daily, ex Sat); to Alaska – Fairbanks (Tue, Thu, Sun) and Juneau (Fri, Sun); to the NWT – Fort Simpson (weekdays), Inuvik, (Mon, Wed, Fri). There are also numerous small charter flights to just about anywhere in the Yukon but these can only be booked locally. The **airport** is situated a couple of kilometres outside the town and is easily reached by taxi. Some of the hotels run shuttle buses to and from the airport and will pick you up if they have your flight details.

On foot
The town itself is fairly small and elongated along the riverfront. If you are not in a hurry to get anywhere then the centre and downtown is easily covered on foot. There is an invaluable **free guide** to Whitehorse that includes a city map and a list of the attractions and services available in town which can be found at the airport and throughout the town in most hotels and tourist information offices.

By road
There are several **car rental** companies in Whitehorse. The best known are Avis (tel: 867.667.2847); Budget (tel: 867.667.6200); Norcan (tel: 867.668.200). All have either a desk or a courtesy phone at the airport, as well as offices in town (see map opposite).

A number of **bus lines** travel in and out of the Yukon. **Alaska Direct** (tel: 867.668.4833) has three trips weekly in summer to Fairbanks and Anchorage and daily trips to Skagway. **Gray Line Yukon** (tel: 867.668.3225; web: www.yukon.net/westours) not only does local city tours and sights of interest but also has scheduled journeys to Skagway, Fairbanks, Haines and

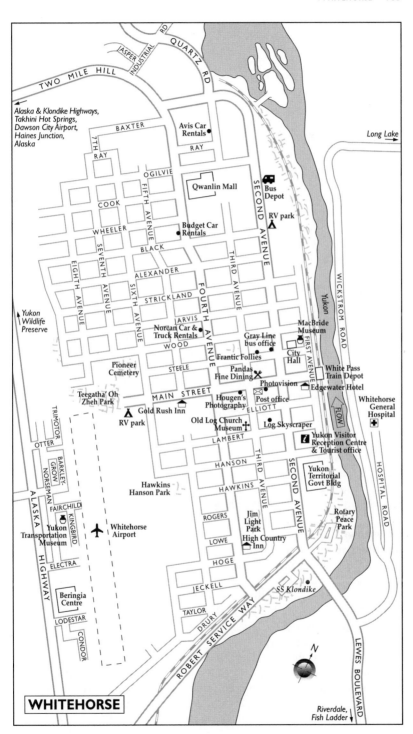

WHITEHORSE

Anchorage in Alaska and other destinations all over the Yukon. Others are **Greyhound Canada** for journeys all over Canada (tel: 867.667.2223), and **Norline Coaches** for the Yukon (tel: 867.668.3355)

The **local bus service** is called Whitehorse Transit with all journeys starting and ending in the bus station opposite the Qwanlin Mall. Timetables are available from the visitor centre or the drivers themselves. A day pass costs about $3.

Where to stay

Whitehorse has a wide choice of accommodation from hotels and motels to B&B establishments, rental cabins and lodges and you will easily find something in a price range to suit your budget. There are also several **campgrounds** and **RV parks**. At the top end of the scale is the **High Country Inn** at 4051 4th Ave (tel: 867.667.4471) and the **Best Western Gold Rush Inn** at 411 Main St (tel: 867.668.4500). Both have all the services a guest would expect with free parking, restaurants, bars, laundry facilities and some rooms with spas and/or jacuzzis.

Where to eat

Whitehorse is not short on places to eat. As well as all the usual **fast food** establishments like KFC and the golden arches, there is an excellent range of budget and mid-range dining places to choose from. Some of the more salubrious establishments are the **Yukon Mining Company** in the High Country Inn (tel: 867.667.4471), the **Cellar Dining Room** at the Edgewater Hotel (tel: 867.667.2572), and **Pandas** (tel: 867.667.2632) at 212 Main St. There are also Mexican, Greek, Chinese, Italian and Thai restaurants. Meals are generally large to suit northern appetites. Breakfasts are usually enormous and fill you up for the day.

What to see

There is plenty of a tourist nature to see in Whitehorse. Sights in the downtown area can easily be covered in one day but for some other attractions you will either need your own transport or to go on an organised tour.

Downtown

The **MacBride Museum** at the corner of 1st Ave and Wood St covers much of the history of the Yukon. Interpretative programs about native culture, the Klondike Gold Stampede, the Mounties and natural history are shown in an old sod-covered log cabin that was once the post office. It is open all year round but the hours are limited in the off season (tel: 867.667.2709).

The **SS *Klondike*** was the last sternwheeler to ply trade on the Yukon River before low road bridges made waterborne traffic impossible. Now beached at the end of 2nd Ave, the *Klondike* was built in 1937 and made as many as 15 trips a season between Whitehorse and Dawson. There is a half-hour guided tour that is great value – the ship has been authentically restored to its former glory. Next door in a tent they show a 20-minute film about the history of riverboats (tel: 867.667.3910). Admission charges apply.

The **Old Log Church Museum** is open from June through to Labour Day and is situated on 3rd Ave and Elliot St. It has some wonderful exhibits of native culture, early exploration, the gold rush, missionary work and church history in the Yukon. The first priest to arrive in Whitehorse in 1900 held services in a tent until this log church and rectory was built in 1901. This was in fact the only wooden cathedral built in the world. The old log church is now fully restored and is the only building remaining in Whitehorse that dates from that period in the town's history. Admission charges apply (tel: 867.668.2555).

Two blocks away on Lambert St is the **Log Skyscraper**. It is still used as an office block.

The **Yukon Visitor Reception Centre** is now located downtown at the corner of 2nd Ave and Hanson St (tel: 867.667.3084) and is operated by Tourism Yukon. There are several audio-visual and interactive displays. The one about the Klondike Gold Stampede is excellent. A great place to get advice on Yukon activities, accommodations and other matters. Open daily.

Outside town

The **Yukon Transportation Museum** is out on the Alaska Highway at the airport. This museum covers the history of transport in the Yukon, including the construction of the Alaska Highway, early flight, dogteams and riverboats. An old aircraft hangs from the ceiling called the *Queen of the Yukon*. She was the first commercial aircraft in the territory. If you are into transport you could easily spend a couple of hours here and keep discovering something new. Open daily mid-May to mid-September (tel: 867.668.4792). The **Yukon Beringia Interpretive Centre** is located next door and offers a presentation on the Yukon during the last Ice Age when woolly mammoths and fearsome scimitar cats roamed the wilderness. Open daily mid-May to mid-September (tel: 867.667.8855).

Takhini Hot Springs is 31km outside town just off the Klondike Highway to Dawson. It is well signposted. This natural mineral-water hot spring bubbles forth at a pleasant 36°C. One can use the proper pool facilities for a fee and there is a small café type dining facility there serving mainly snacks. The area has a nice feel to it and you can see the springs. There are ample picnic facilities and parking. Sadly there is no bus service to Takhini except on any official tour that visits the place.

Whitehorse Fishway is the world's longest wooden fish ladder. Built in 1959 to help the spawning salmon go up the Yukon River and around the Whitehorse Dam, it is 366m in length and 2m wide and deep. It mimics the Whitehorse Rapids that the dam replaced. There are viewing chambers so that you can see the salmon swimming up the ladder. The Fishway is open from June to August and is free, but call for the hours of operation (tel: 867.633.5965).

Miles Canyon is much tamer now than it was when the Stampeders came down the canyon and its subsequent falls in the summers of 1896 and 1897 before the tramway was built. The construction of the Whitehorse Dam in 1959 for hydroelectric power and the body of water it created, now

YUKON QUEST INTERNATIONAL SLED DOG RACE

The Yukon Quest International Sled Dog Race is a 1,000-mile (1,610km) dog-sled race through mostly wilderness between Fairbanks in Alaska and Whitehorse in the Yukon and it begins annually about the first week of February.

This is a true endurance race for both dogs and mushers. Mushers are on their own for much of the race, relying on their dogs and their wits to get them through some thoroughly harsh arctic weather and terrain. They may accept help from other mushers in the race but no one else. There are only seven checkpoints spread unevenly along the 1,000 miles, with a compulsory 36-hour layover in Dawson City. This layover is the only time that the musher gets a rest and his or her handlers can take over the basic care of the dogs. The race itself is weather-dependent with the mushers finishing anywhere between ten and 20 days after starting. The winners complete the course in about 12 days on average. About a third of the competitors do not finish the race for whatever reason, but they always seem to be there at the end to cheer the others on.

The race starts in Whitehorse or Fairbanks in alternate years and there are typically 30 teams competing (the organisers allow a maximum of 50 teams). The sleds must carry all the mushers' and dogs' food; a proper cold weather sleeping bag, a hand axe, snowshoes, veterinary records for all the dogs, eight sets of dog booties for each dog and any promotional materials the race official dictates. Each musher is allowed only one sled and may start the race with a minimum of eight and a maximum of 14 dogs. Dogs are not

called Schwatka Lake, lessened the force of the water passing through the canyon. Only a kilometre upstream is the site of Canyon City although there is not much there now. There is a boat called the MV *Schwatka* at the dam that does two-hour cruises on Schwatka Lake and up to the canyon (tel: 867.668.4716).

White Pass and Yukon Route Rail Road was the rail link from Alaska to the Yukon and some of it is still running today. You can catch a bus in Whitehorse for travel to Fraser in British Columbia then take the train to Skagway in Alaska. The trip from Whitehorse to Skagway costs $US95 one-way at the moment. For tickets and reservations tel: 867.668.7245, or try their website on www.whitepassrailroad.com.

Just along the Alaska Highway about 45 minutes' drive outside Whitehorse is the **Kwaday Dan Kenji** (Long Ago People's Place) run by Harold Johnson and his wife Meta Gage (tel: 867.667.6375). This is a First Nations traditional camp where you can see the way the Southern Tutchone lived for thousands of years. Harold and Meta have built, with the assistance of the tribal elders, lodges, tents, huts, hunting traps and so on, just as their people did for thousands of years as they survived in the Yukon wilderness. A small charge is made for the tour. Camping is allowed for a fee, as is staying in a traditional pole-house.

allowed to be added or replaced in a team once the race starts. There are regular strict veterinary checks and vets can force mushers out of a race without any warning if they have any doubts about their dogs' welfare.

To enter this race you don't have to be mad, but it helps. Most of the mushers I have met are an extremely hardy bunch with a passion for their dogs and mushing. They have to be because the race is so tough. During the course of the event they usually race for six hours then rest for six hours for the duration. Most mushers only get any decent sleep at Dawson City during the layover. I found that nationality makes no difference in the race, they all consider themselves 'northerners', not Canadians or Americans, and have a code of conduct honed by the environment not by the bureaucrats in Ottawa or Washington, DC.

I have only followed the race from Whitehorse to Dawson but I found it non-stop excitement all the way, irrespective of the time of day or night. The followers usually get as little sleep as the mushers do but there is a camaraderie that is shared by everyone present. If you like dogs, and the thought of braving the elements does not phase you, then dog sledging may be the activity for you. As a spectator sport the Yukon Quest is dog sledging at its best. Oh! For those of you who are picky about the finer points of the English language, in North America it is sledding, in the UK it is sledging. A minor matter really but the Yukoners did find my language amusing.

Dates for forthcoming Yukon Quests are 2001 Whitehorse to Fairbanks, 2002 Fairbanks to Whitehorse, 2003 Whitehorse to Fairbanks.

Entertainment
Frantic Follies is a vaudeville style revue of can-can dances with the flavour of a Wild West saloon. Shows are nightly from mid-May to mid-September at the Westmark Whitehorse Hotel, 2nd Ave and Wood St (tel: 867.668 2042; email: ffollies@yknet.yk.ca). There is also a twin **cinema** at the Qwanlin Mall and another at the Yukon Cinema Centre (867.668.6644 for movie info on both theatres).

Shopping
Photographic supplies
There are only two establishments in town to find that forgotten item of kit or a resupply of film. They are **Photovision** in the Qwanlin Mall (tel: 867.677.4525) or at 205A Main St (tel: 867.667.4599) and **Hougen's Photo** on the main floor of the Hougen Centre (tel: 867.668.6808). Both do photo processing and have good supplies of fresh film.

Tour operators
For walking tours of Whitehorse go to **Whitehorse Historical Walking Tours** at 3126, 3rd Ave (tel: 867.667.4704) or the **Yukon Conservation**

Society for free guided nature walks in July and August (tel: 867.668.5678 for details).

For city tours see **Gray Line** (tel: 867.668.3225) or **Jack London Tours** (tel: 867.668.3768).

Outdoor adventure operators

Nature Tours of Yukon (tel: 867.667.2028), offers guided wilderness tours, canoeing, hiking, photography and history.

Rainbow Tours Ltd (tel: 867.668.5598) flies from the airfield at Silver City on Kluane Lake in a tented camp on a glacier in Kluane National Park. Something new and completely different for the Yukon. Skiing, trekking etc available as are day trips. Flight is about 30 minutes over the spectacular ice-fields with views of Mt Logan.

Sky High Wilderness Ranches (tel: 867.667.4321), has wilderness horse adventure treks into the high country around Whitehorse with anything from a few hours to a ten-day pack horse trip.

Tatshenshini Rafting Expeditions at 1602 Alder St, Porter Creek (tel: 867.633.2742), has 1-, 4-, 6- and 11-day rafting trips on the Tatshenshini River – classified as one of the ten best in the world.

Uncommon Journeys Ltd (tel: 867.668.2255; email: uncommon@yukon.net; web: www.uncommonyukon.com) offers daily and weekly guided canoeing, dog-sledging and hiking tours throughout the north. Rod Taylor runs the company. Nice guy and great dogs.

Health and safety

For all emergencies (ambulance, fire, or police/RCMP) dial 911.

To contact these services in a less urgent situation use the following numbers: Police/RCMP 867.667.5555; ambulance service 867.667.8889; fire service 867.668.8699.

The Whitehorse General Hospital is on 867.667.8700. There is an emergency physician on duty 24 hours a day, 7 days a week. The outpatient fee for non-Canadian residents is $178.00.

HAINES JUNCTION

Haines Junction was born during the construction of the Alaska Highway in 1942 when on the site where the Haines Highway joined the Alaska Highway. Supplies were shipped into Haines in Alaska for the Alaska Highway and were then road-transported to the engineers at Haines Junction.

The area's history dates back further than that, though. The nearby Dalton Trail was the only trail over which livestock could be successfully herded into Dawson City during the Klondike Gold Strike. The entrepreneur Jack Dalton slashed a toll trail out of the wilderness and then charged everybody $250 a head to travel along it.

Haines Junction today is a bustling little village of 796 people nestled at the base of the St Elias Mountains. It is the gateway to the Kluane National Park. The village has many services including RV parks, motels, restaurants, gas stations, a general store, the Kluane park headquarters, a bank, an airport and the usual emergency services. Wilderness recreation here includes hiking, horse trekking, river rafting, canoeing, glacier flights, hunting and fishing. There is even an indoor swimming pool.

Where to stay and eat
Haines Junction is a perfect place to stop over if you are heading into or coming from Alaska en route to Whitehorse or south to Haines. There are plenty of places to stay – the choice just depends on what is booked up and which places have beds available. They are all about the same price and have basically the same facilities of TV's, telephones, private bath, and so on. In the village there are the **Cozy Corner Motel & Restaurant** (tel: 867.634.2511), the **Gateway Motel** (867.634.2371), and the **Kluane Park Inn** (tel: 867.634.2261). There is a new place in town, which I have not visited, called the **Raven Hotel** (tel: 867.634.2804) which may be of interest because it has a restaurant that is rated in the top 150 in Canada. The only place to camp is the **Kluane R V Kampground** (tel: 867.634.2709) with all the facilities you could want, need or expect – and it is right in the village. The Cozy Corner and the Gateway motels have restaurants. About 7km outside Haines Junction towards Fairbanks is the **MacKintosh Lodge** with 'homemade' everything. This is a motel, restaurant and RV/camp site and fuel stop (tel: 867.634.2301).

If you have no reason to stop in Haines Junction but think you might need an excuse then go to **Madley's General Store** on the road towards Haines, Alaska. Their motto is 'We've Got It All' and they have – almost. Groceries, fresh fruit, meat and vegetables, hardware, fishing tackle, magazines are all available and the building also houses the post office and bank. Most of the things that make life more comfortable are here. I should think that if they were any more famous they'd be called Harrods.

What to do
I can recommend taking a flight with **Sifton Air** (tel: 867.634.2916) out of Haines Junction airport over the Kluane National Park to see the glaciers. About $90 for a 45-minute flight in a Cessna. Absolutely stunning! They do it in helicopters as well but expect a hefty flight fee.

KLUANE NATIONAL PARK
If you do nothing else in the Yukon come here, if just for the scenery alone. This is a real wilderness park. There are no roads into the interior, although there are a few well-marked walking trails. UNESCO has declared the park alongside its sister parks the Wrangell-St Elias NP in Alaska and the Tatshenshini-Alsek Provincial Park in British Columbia, a World Heritage Site. The area is classified as an outstanding wilderness area of global significance and rightly so. Mountains and icefields dominate 82% of the park.

The St Elias Mountains are Canada's highest and have Canada's tallest and North America's second highest mountain, Mt Logan (5,959m/19,545ft), in their midst. Travellers along the Haines and Alaska Highways will see mountains whose peaks average 2,500m. These guardians of the interior hide from view numerous peaks that soar above 5,000m which, along with numerous glaciers, make up the park's stunning vista.

Kluane National Park and Reserve is the largest non-polar icefield in the world, a legacy from the last Ice Age. Warm, moist Pacific air moves over the St Elias Mountains allowing massive quantities of snow to accumulate and subsequently settle as permanent ice high on the mountain tops. These icefields accumulate and radiate out into the valleys as glaciers. The two most prominent are the Lowell Glacier, which is 65km long, and the Kaskawulsh glacier which feeds both the Yukon River and the Pacific Ocean. The melted ice from these and other glaciers create the Alsek and Tatshenshini Rivers – two of North America's finest whitewater rafting rivers.

There are viewing sites all the way along the two highways but really to appreciate the view you must head into the interior for a day or so and immerse yourself in all its splendour.

Climatically, there is an overlap of the Pacific and Arctic air masses above Kluane. This has resulted in one of the most diverse wildlife and plant domains in northern Canada. A montane forest of white spruce, trembling aspen and balsam poplar trees covers the lower valleys and slopes of the mountains. The treeline varies between 1,050m and 1,200m and is filled with low-growing willow, dwarf birch and alder scrubs. In summer the mountains burst forth with over 200 varieties of alpine flora.

Wildlife here is abundant and varied. This is the prime Canadian habitat of Dall's sheep and most of the year they can be seen foraging on the slopes of Sheep Mountain. Mountain goats, caribou and moose all live here. Grizzly bears live high up in the alpine meadows and black bear are common in the lower forests. There is a transient population of wolves and it is also possible to see wolverine, muskrat, mink, marmot, red fox, lynx, coyote, beaver, snowshoe hares and my favourite, the Arctic ground squirrel or – as he is known further north – the sik-sik. Observant twitchers can expect to see about 150 species of our feathered friends, of which 118 species actually nest in the park. (Full lists of birds for northern Canada and flora and fauna for the Yukon are given in *Appendices 3, 4* and *5*.)

Wildlife viewing is a popular activity. Please help the wildlife, others and yourself by following these guidelines:

• Do not feed the bears or other wildlife as they learn very quickly to depend on humans for food. As a result they often become a hazard to people and are often destroyed.
• Try to view wildlife from a distance with the use of binoculars or a zoom lens rather than getting close and disturbing them.
• Remember that you are visiting these animals' homes. Please be as considerate as if you were visiting friends.

Park practicalities

The park's main reception area is the Kluane National Park Visitor Centre at Haines Junction but there is also another visitor centre at Sheep Mountain, about an hour's drive north along the Alaska Highway. The visitor centres are open during the summer from 09.00–21.00 daily. There is an excellent sight and sound show at Haines Junction, and at Sheep Mountain there are spotting scopes to check out the Dall's sheep if any are about. You can get maps and guidebooks and seek advice from the staff at either centre about where to go and what to see. If you wish to enter the park proper then you must register at these centres. The park staff even lead guided walks for those who are less happy about being in the wilderness alone. Both visitor centres have wheelchair access.

Camping

Camping is available at Kathleen Lake about 20km along the Haines Road. Facilities include firewood, pump water, a kitchen shelter, toilets and a sanitary station for RVs, a boat launch and picnic grounds. Two of the 41 campsites, the toilets and the sheltered kitchen have wheelchair access. Around the lake is a boardwalk called the Kokanee Trail. It begins in the day use area and it is suitable for use by wheelchairs.

THE ROUTE NORTH TO ALASKA

There are lots of interpretive signs and plaques all along the AlCan Highway to Alaska, a great help with the appreciation of the region. All are located with convenient parking and are well signposted so you can't miss them. I'm not going to describe each one. I'll just let you sort them out for yourselves. There are also numerous parking and rest spots along the road, all marked with the traditional blue 'P' sign.

Towns and villages are few and far between but they all have their own very individual characters. If nothing else just have a quick stop to say 'Hi!' The folks there will enjoy a new face and a bit of conversation. Northern people are not nosy, but neither are they shy and retiring. I find their blunt and direct approach to everyone quite refreshing and all northerners will readily strike up a conversation if you are in the mood.

The road is open all year round.

Silver City

Right at the very bottom of Kluane Lake is a turning to the left for Silver City. There's not much there now but the remains of an old trading post and a RNWMP barracks and an airfield. This is where the plane comes for trips to the tented camp on the glacier between Mt Queen Mary and Mt Logan in Kluane National Park. (See Rainbow Tours under *Yukon tour operators*, page 168.)

Destruction Bay

If this village were any quieter it wouldn't exist. Destruction Bay is only 108km from Haines Junction and has a population of about 50 people. The place is named as such because, in 1942, just after they had finished building a new construction camp for the AlCan on the site, it was destroyed by a massive windstorm. The only reason now for coming here is the boat ramp to access the excellent trout fishing on Kluane Lake. There are a small number of services set up for tourists travelling the AlCan Highway.

Where to stay and eat
The Talbot Arm Motel (tel: 867 841.4461) – you can't miss it, it is the only place in the village. Has all the usual facilities with 32 rooms, a filling station, restaurant and cafeteria, a bar, a general store and all the normal services for RVs like gas, dumping stations drinking water, showers, laundromat and so on.

Burwash Landing
Another small village, but with twice the population of Destruction Bay, Burwash Landing came into existence as a result of the gold strike on Fourth of July Creek. On July 4 1904 Dawson Charlie, of the initial Klondike Gold Stampede fame, staked a claim on a creek that was a tributary of the Jarvis River. The creek was named Fourth of July Creek after the event and was the first payable gold discovered in the Kluane region. Two miners, Louis and Eugene Jacquot, knowing there was a more certain profit to be made supplying the miners rather than actually mining, set up a supply centre on the northwestern shore of Kluane Lake. They provided not only goods but a boat service for the miners working the creek. They named their community after their friend Lachlin Taylor Burwash, who was the mining recorder for the short-lived mining town of Silver City. When gold was discovered in Alaska at Chisana River in 1913–15 Burwash Landing continued to serve miners crossing the border. Today, although still a service centre, its customers are more likely to be tourists and truckers than miners but rough'n'ready old prospectors do show up from time to time.

Where to stay and eat
Only one place here – the **Burwash Landing Resort** (tel: 867.841.4441). This small establishment has a hotel, motel, restaurant, RV park, dining room, store and a service station. They can also organise fishing trips, glacier flights and gold panning for those staying locally for a couple of days. This really is a nice quiet spot to take a rest from the road and to enjoy the spectacular scenery.

About 25 miles up the highway towards Alaska is the **Kluane Wilderness Village** (tel: 867.841.4141). Situated on the Kluane River it provides services for the Yukon traveller. Open 24-hours all year with all the usual facilities it is only 320km to Whitehorse if you are heading that way. Alongside a full restaurant service there are 52 log cabins and 6 deluxe motel rooms and 52 full-service RV sites. You can also find fuel and a mechanic, plus there is a towing service, camping, showers and a laundry.

What to see and do
Kluane Museum of Natural History (tel: 867.841.5561) is not only home to the world's largest gold pan (at about 8m across) but it houses an excellent collection of First Nations artefacts, wildlife, minerals and natural history of the Kluane region. It is well worth a visit even if you are only just passing through.

Also worth a look is **Our Lady of the Holy Rosary** (tel: 867.841.5411). This was the first Catholic mission and school built north of Whitehorse along the AlCan Highway. Established by the Oblates in 1944 the living quarters and school have now been restored as a museum of life in the area. There is a short video presentation of life here in the 1950s, which provides a glimpse of another world.

Beaver Creek
This is the westernmost town in the Yukon. It is about five hours from Haines Junction and the last hotel and fuel stop before you enter Alaska. Fill up here, it will be your last chance for a while. The nearby Canada/USA border crossing is open 24 hours all year round but, unless you are in a hurry to get somewhere, stop here and refresh yourself overnight before crossing into Alaska. There is a **Visitor Reception Centre** that is open daily 08.00–20.00 from mid-May until mid-September (tel: 867.862.7321).

Where to stay and eat
Being just before or just over the border depending on which direction you are coming from Beaver Creek is fairly well catered for as far as hotels and restaurants go. There are the **Beaver Creek Motor Inn** (tel: 867.862.7601), **Westmark Inn Beaver Creek** (tel: 867.862.7501), and **Ida's Motel & Restaurant** (tel: 867.862.7902). The Beaver Creek and Westmark are both multi-service hotels with all the facilities you would expect from their kind. All three have restaurants, but I can recommend Ida's for breakfast – the pancake stack is something else. There is RV parking at the Westmark and Ida's, and as the main street, the AlCan itself, is only a couple of hundred metres long from end to end it is no big deal to check out the whole town in one night.

SOUTH OF WHITEHORSE
There are two routes from the south into Whitehorse. The first is along Highway 1, the AlCan Highway, which runs from Dawson Creek in British Columbia, passes through Whitehorse and continues on to Fairbanks in Alaska. The second route is along Highway 2, the Klondike Highway, from Skagway in Alaska, passing through Whitehorse and heading on north to Dawson City, roughly along the line followed by the stampeders in 1898. Both roads are asphalt covered and are open all year round.

Watson Lake
Watson Lake is the third most populous town in the Yukon. Situated just over the provincial border from British Columbia it must truly be considered the

'Gateway to the Yukon'. The town rose to prominence during the construction of the AlCan Highway. Before road construction began an airfield had to be built at Watson Lake. Everything came there the long way round and the journey would make a book in itself. Firstly construction supplies travelled by boat from Vancouver to Wrangell in Alaska. Then they went by barge up the Stikine River to Telegraph Creek from where everything was trucked 122 difficult kilometres overland to Dease Lake before, once again being loaded onto barges. It all then journeyed down the Dease River to its junction with the Liard River at Lower Post. Finally it was all loaded onto trucks once again for the 42km to Watson Lake.

The town's name is derived from a Yorkshireman named Frank Watson who wandered into the region on his way from Edmonton to the Klondike in the spring of 1898. Tired and worn out, he was sure he would not make it to the goldfields and decided to stay where he was and mine and trap there. He built a cabin on the lake's edge and took a First Nations wife from Lower Post. The site became known as Watson Lake rather than its proper name of Fish Lake.

He was still alive when the airport and the highway construction crews arrived. He thought that they were too many people and that they were too noisy so he moved his family to a cabin on the Windid Lake and lived out the rest of his days there.

In 1942 an American soldier called Carl L Lindley painted the name of his hometown of Denville, Illinois, and its distance away on a board and nailed it to a post so that the arrow pointed in the general direction of home. Fifty years and 30,000 signposts later the Signpost Forest is Watson Lake's most famous attraction.

Where to stay and eat

A town the size of Watson Lake has a wide choice of hotels and eateries. The **Belvedere Motor Hotel** (tel: 867.536.7712), **the Big Horn Hotel & Tavern** (tel: 867.536.2020), the **Gateway Motor Inn** (tel: 867.536.7744), and the **Watson Lake Hotel** (tel: 867.536.7782) have all the usual services, although the Watson Lake Hotel is next to the signpost forest. All the hotels have restaurants and there are a couple of fast food establishments.

What to see and do

Besides adding your own sign in the Signpost Forest, there is the **Northern Lights Centre** (tel: 867.536.7522) – the only planetarium in North America dedicated to this atmospheric phenomenon. Take a glimpse at their website: www.yukon.net/northern lights.

Teslin

This small community (population 478) was originally the summer home of the nomadic Tlingit First Nation. A permanent settlement was established here in 1903 with the founding of a trading post. Today there are service stations, restaurants, a general store and accommodation.

Where to stay and eat
Halstead's Teslin Lake Resort (tel: 867.390.2608 summer only; in winter call 813.694.6646), the **Northlake Motel & Café** (tel: 867.390.2571), the **Yukon Motel** (tel: 867.390.2575) and the **Dawson Peaks Resort and RV Park** (tel: 867.390.2244) all have restaurants, rooms and/or cabins and parking for RVs.

What to see and do
George Johnston Museum (tel: 867.390.2550) houses the largest collection of Tlingit artifacts in the Yukon. Old and rare photographs, dioramas, and many post-European and early Yukon collections are all here. There is wheelchair access. Open daily 09.00–19.00 from May long weekend to Labour Day. Admission charges apply.

Carcross
Carcross is about an hour's drive due south of Whitehorse. This picturesque little village (population 400) got its original name, Caribou Crossing, from its significance as a hunting area because large herds of caribou would cross the shallow Nares Lake twice a year. As the town developed to serve the stampeders so it became an important stopping point for the White Pass & Yukon Rail Road in 1898. The Caribou Hotel opened in the same year and is now the oldest continually operating business in the Yukon. When the railroad was completed the final spike was hammered in the track here on July 29 1900.

In 1901 the local priest, a Bishop Bompas, established a school for First Nations kiddies but in 1902 he was forced to lobby to have the town's name changed. It seems that there were two other Caribou Crossings, one in British Columbia and the other in Alaska, and the school's mail was being misdirected too often. The post office adopted the name change but the railroad held out until forced to switch in 1916. The community remained an important rail depot until the station closed in 1982. Today the old station is the visitor centre. Incidentally, the hotel, station and, in fact, most of the town today are not original. A fire swept through the place in 1910 destroying almost the entire place. The hotel, station and store were all rebuilt within the year.

Skookum Jim Mason and Dawson Charlie are buried in Carcross cemetery as is George Carmack's First Nations wife Kate.

Where to stay and eat
Caribou Hotel and Restaurant (tel: 867.821.4501) is probably worth a stay just to say you have visited the oldest hotel in the Yukon. I have not personally tried either the hotel or restaurant – much to my chagrin.

What to see and do
The **Visitor Reception Centre** (tel: 867.821.4431) is located in the old railway depot of the historic White Pass & Yukon Rail Road. It has a full visitor service for advice on activities, attractions, accommodation, etc. The centre is open 08.00–20.00 daily, mid-May to mid-September.

Carcross Barracks (tel: 867.821.4372) is the historic RCMP log barracks and jail filled with antiques, arts and crafts. **Frontierland Heritage Park/ Wildlife Gallery** (tel: 867.667.1055) is 3km north of Carcross. There are live Dall's sheep, lynx and the world's largest bear in the three-hectare heritage theme park. Admission charges apply. The **Matthew Watson General Store and Trading Post** (tel: 867.821.3501) is the oldest store in the Yukon. It is like stepping back through history. Turn-of-the-century stuff plus fresh muffins, ice-cream and more.

NORTH OF WHITEHORSE
Along the Klondike Highway
The northern route from Whitehorse to Dawson City. Travelling time is about 10 hours between the two towns and there are several places to stop off, refuel or rest en route. The highway is open all year round.

Carmacks
Carmacks (population 500) is the first major community you come across after leaving Whitehorse and heading north and probably the most popular stop for travellers along the highway. Named after the discoverer of the Klondike gold strike, George Washington Carmack, and located on the shores of the Yukon River, it was a major refuelling stop for the sternwheelers travelling between Whitehorse and Dawson. The town also seems to be sited on the defining line between the Southern and Northern Tutchone First Nations whose rich history goes back more than 10,000 years. There is everything here from a post office and bank, motels, hotels, a general store, campground, several service stations, a boat launch and an outdoor swimming pool for those brave enough.

Where to stay and eat
Carmacks Hotel (tel: 867.863.5221) has rooms, cabins, a bar and restaurant and all the facilities any traveller on the Klondike Highway needs. They say they cater to all your needs from souvenirs and showers to groceries and cocktails. What more can I say. There are a few cafés along the road through the town before and after the bridge. Ask in any service station for their recommendations.

There is a limited summer-only **campsite and RV park** at Minto, 25km to the north, before Pelly Crossing.

Pelly Crossing
Pelly Crossing is the home of the Selkirk First Nation and has a population of about 300. The Selkirk First Nation runs all facilities in the town including the heritage centre. Services include a free **campsite** with shelters, picnic tables and firewood pits but little else; an **RCMP post** and a **service station** *cum* general store.

Stewart Crossing
Stewart Crossing is located at the junction of the Klondike Highway and the Silver Trail on the south side of the Stewart river. Facilities include a **lodge,**

TINTINA TRENCH

The Tintina Trench provides visible proof of the geological concept of plate tectonics. The trench is part of one of the world's longest topographically distinct features and extends more than 2,500km from Alaska to British Columbia. Dating back about 85 million years, the birth of the trench happened when the Farallon Plate under the western Pacific Ocean floor converged with the westward moving mass of ancient North America. At this time the Yukon had not yet been created. The convergence caused the Farallon Plate to break into two sections. One section headed southwards towards South America and the other, known as the Kula Plate, drifted north towards what we now call the Aleutian Islands off Alaska. These two plates moved past one another, rather than one rising over the top of the other, creating what geologists call a transcurrent fault.

Easily recognised, one geologist has described the Tintina Trench as 'a gun-barrel-straight valley with steep sides and a flat floor some 200m deep.' As all this happened many thousands of years ago there is not that much to see for much of its route and unless one has an interest in geology you would miss it altogether. Fortunately for the rest of us there is an interpretive site at a scenic viewpoint overlooking the Klondike River valley and the Tintina Trench on the Klondike Highway about 120km from Stewart Crossing towards Dawson City. Even the untrained eye can see the feature here.

campground and a **service station** (not 24 hours). Stewart Crossing is situated on the Tintina Trench.

Dawson City

Dawson City has the feel of a real Wild West town. Except for the main road in and out of town the streets are not paved and the pedestrians walk along raised boardwalks. All new buildings in town have to be built in the style of the 1890s. Sadly, today the town lacks the hustle and bustle of its heady days when gold was discovered nearby in Bonanza Creek and, with its current small population, has a distinct feel of isolation. Yet Dawson will never die. As summer approaches the tourists flock to the town to reflect and see what is left of the greatest gold rush the world has ever known – the Klondike Gold Stampede.

Robert Henderson, who led the discoverers to the gold, was showing some small samples of dust to Joseph Ladue, another prospector on Sixtymile River. He said that there was a mother load somewhere near the Klondike but he was not sure where. Ladue figured that, when the rush eventually came, and come it would, there was more money to be made supplying the miners than digging for gold. Barely five days after gold was discovered Ladue arrived at the junction of the Yukon and Klondike Rivers and was staking out the town on

THE DANCE HALL GIRLS

Diamond Tooth Gertie's in Dawson City is Canada's first and only legal gambling hall. The original Klondike dance halls never stooped so low as to employ the popularised Parisian dance hall style of high kicks, petticoats and stockings. They preferred waltzes, reels and polkas with nothing more daring than an exposed ankle. At the peak of the gold strike dance hall girls could command $5 a waltz and would get it. Most of them were known as percentage girls, receiving 25¢ for every dollar the miners paid for a dance, and they often used nicknames to disguise their true identity. They were there to provide some light relief and entertainment for the miners in the style of vaudeville and should not be confused with the variety girls who were usually actresses and singers and rarely mixed with the miners.

The real Diamond Tooth Gertie was Gertie Lovejoy, a dance hall queen during the early days of the Klondike. She wore a small diamond between her two front teeth that gave her the name. On the subject of miners and gold she once said, 'The poor ginks have just gotta spend it, they're that scared they'll die before they have it out of the ground.' Eventually she went on to marry a prominent Dawson lawyer, CWC Taber, but she never managed to live down her dance hall girl's image in Dawson's prudish post-goldrush society.

Another dance hall girl whose name is synonymous with Dawson was Klondike Kate. Her novelty was wearing very expensive Parisian gowns, a belt of $20 gold pieces and a headdress of lighted candles. In 1900, when she was only a teenager, Kitty Rockwell became smitten with the theatre magnate Alex Pagnates. At that time Pagnates owned the Orpheum Theatre, the most successful in Dawson. In 1905 Kitty hit headline news when she sued Pagnates for breach of promise. She claimed in court that she had bought him 75¢ cigars and $15 silk shirts and that when they left Dawson together in 1901 she paid all the travelling expenses. In court she originally asked for $25,000 but later accepted an out of court settlement of $5,000. Kitty eventually took the name 'Klondike Kate' and became a popular subject for newspaper feature writers up to the time of her death in 1957. Pagnates, who arrived in Dawson speaking little English and began work as a waiter, went on to build his theatre chain into a $15 million empire but died poor in 1936 after two very lengthy court cases. In the first he was convicted of rape and in the second his wife was convicted of second degree murder (the result of a car accident). Both verdicts were eventually overturned but they ruined Pagnates.

Today from mid-May to mid-September tourists and gamblers alike fill the hall at Diamond Tooth Gertie's to play roulette, blackjack or Texas hold 'em poker. Slot machines line the walls and there are several daily shows by a number of can-can girls overseen by a Diamond Tooth Gertie impersonator.

the swampy ground fronting the lowland that overlooks the Klondike's mouth. As the Canadian government did not recognise First Nations land claims at that time, Ladue was able to stake out the entire site for himself. Ladue constructed a warehouse and a small cabin for himself that also served as the saloon and went into business. He named the new town Dawson after the famous director of the Geological Survey of Canada, George Mercer Dawson.

In January 1897 there were five houses and a small tent city as miners arrived to try their luck. In the spring the town had a population of 1,400, including at least two women and one Jesuit priest. News of the gold strike still had not reached the outside world by this time but it wouldn't be long.

Ladue and other entrepreneurs made a killing as the town grew. A night in Ladue's saloon would cost $50 and an egg $1. A five-minute bath cost $1.50. The town often struggled against starvation, as resources were sometimes difficult to come by at all and always in short supply, but survive it did. In June Harry Ash opened the Northern Saloon, taking a reputed $30,000 the first night and averaging $3,000 every night thereafter. He left after three months with $100,000 in his pocket. By the end of summer there were 10 saloons in town and dance hall girls were taking $100 a night. Ladue started to sell off the town lots at $200 a square foot and by the end of the summer Dawson's population numbered 3,500 souls.

The departure in June of the first sternwheelers was the start of the real rush when 80 of the first prospectors left for Seattle and San Francisco and the news of their finds spread to the rest of the world. The Klondike Gold Stampede was on. Of the 100,000 people trying to get to Dawson in 1898 only about 40,000 managed the trip. The price of building lots shot up and some sold for $40,000. By July 1 1898 Dawson had become the largest town west of Winnipeg and north of San Francisco.

No sooner was Dawson being called the 'Paris of the North' than its fortunes began to decline. All the best claims were gone and the majority of the 40,000 or so people in Dawson had little chance of striking it rich. The claims going for sale were far too expensive to buy up. A couple of fires swept through the town at the end of 1898 and the beginning of 1899, destroying much of the valuable real estate. By the time it was all rebuilt about 8,000 people had departed Dawson for the new strike near Nome in Alaska.

In 1902 Dawson received the status of city but the population was already in decline. New heavy duty mining methods required fewer men and

WATCH YOUR STEP

A word of warning here! Mining sites are private property and miners are an unfriendly lot at times. The law still allows them to shoot claim jumpers on sight. Do not wander on to the site of a working mine without the express permission of the owner. Curiosity could be your demise!

THE LOST PATROL

Maintaining links between remote Canadian towns and forts was the responsibility of the North West Mounted Police patrols. Leading one such patrol was Inspector Francis Joseph 'Frank' Fitzgerald, a veteran of 14 years service in the NWMP. He was 41 years old.

The 800km route used by the mid winter patrols was a most arduous one, following a complicated series of rivers and creeks, flat treeless valleys and mountainous terrain.

On December 21 1910 Fitzgerald and three other NWMP officers set off south from Fort McPherson on the Peel River in NWT, en route for Dawson City 765km away, in the middle of a particularly harsh winter. The temperature when they left the fort was -29°C. Accompanying Fitzgerald were former-RNWMP Constable Sam Carter (41) who acted as guide, and Constables George Francis Kinney (27) and Richard O'Hara Taylor (26). They had three dog teams and the three sledges had a total of 590kg of provisions including 40kg of food per man (enough for an estimated 30 days), plus mail, despatches and other equipment, bringing the total weight in each sledge pulled by five dogs to 272kg. They also carried only one .30-30 calibre rifle. Usual practice would have been to take an extra .22 calibre rifle or a shotgun.

Both Fitzgerald and Carter had done the route from Dawson to Fort McPherson before, but they had some First Nations guides with them at that time. Now they were travelling in the opposite direction on an unmarked trail which neither really had the know-how to do unguided. Carter felt he could retrace his steps from three years before. From the start it was likely that their food supplies would prove to be inadequate. This was only the seventh patrol over the route and the longest previous patrol had gone from Dawson to McPherson in 56 days, delayed by heavy snow and extreme cold.

Their difficulties began almost immediately. Heavy snow meant they had to break trail from departure and the extreme cold did not help matters. Although they managed 240km in the first 12 days this meant that they would take 9 days more than intended. Fitzgerald felt that the worst mushing was over and the pace would speed up. He did not count on a cold snap that persisted for seven days taking daytime temperatures to -46°C. Deep snow, open water and driftwood on the river ice slowed progress even further until they were down to only 16km a day.

managed higher yields and with the slump in the price of gold about the outbreak of WWI. Dawson never recovered its boom town prosperity. Although there is still mining in Dawson, the serious mass dredging finished in 1952. In 1953 Whitehorse took over as Yukon's capital.

When the patrol reached the junction of the Wind and Little Wind rivers the weather improved and Fitzgerald mushed on but the party now got lost when Carter failed to find the next part of the trail, Forrest Creek, and they wandered for 158km back and forth trying to find it with no success.

Their only choice now was to return to Fort McPherson but they had only 4.5kg of flour, 3.6kg of bacon and some dried fish remaining. Fitzgerald knew that they would have to eat some of the dogs on the way back and would probably fail if they could not find some First Nations people to give them some food. On January 20 they began killing the dogs. Even so, starvation, scurvy and frostbite were soon taking its toll on the men's health and endurance. By February 5 they had only five dogs left and still had some 112km to go to reach Fort McPherson.

A rescue team led by Corporal WJD Dempster set out from Dawson on February 28 and on March 21 discovered the bodies of Kinney and Taylor. Kinney appeared to have died from hypothermia and Taylor had committed suicide with the .30-30. They were 56km from McPherson.

About 16km further along the trail they found Carter's and Fitzgerald's bodies beside a small fire. Carter was neatly laid out with a handkerchief over his face and his hands folded across his chest. Fitzgerald lay next to the fire. A note was found nearby on which Fitzgerald had scrawled a will with a bit of charcoal. It read, 'All money in despatch bag and bank, clothes, etc., I leave to my dearly beloved mother, Mrs. John Fitzgerald, Halifax.' It ended with 'God bless all. FJ Fitzgerald, RNWMP.'

The Mounted Police became a target of public criticism when the news reached the outside world. The explorer Vilhjalmur Stefansson said that if the patrol had followed his method of travelling light and living off the land the episode would not have ended so tragically. In reality Fitzgerald and his companions had succumbed to back luck and persistent poor judgement throughout the entire patrol, a fatal combination in the remote north.

Dempster's official report on the tragedy blamed the patrol's demise on the small stock of supplies Fitzgerald took, the lack of a First Nations guide and the lost time spent trying to regain the route instead of immediately returning to Fort McPherson.

Dawson's fortunes changed and tourism became the major economic earner in town. Today Dawson has a permanent population of around 2,000 people but it receives about 60,000 tourists annually.

Dawson is heaving in summer. The population expands soon after the river

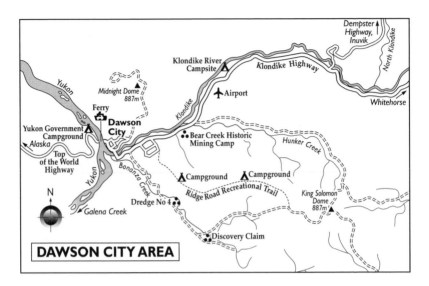

DAWSON CITY AREA

thaws. The locals run a sweepstake on the day, hour and minute that the Yukon River's ice breaks up signalling the end of winter – it has nothing to do with dates and seasons. A bell on the ice tells them the time, and when it is due to happen someone is always watching to see it fall through. During the summer solstice everyone in town goes up to a nearby hilltop, known locally as the Dome, to watch the midnight sun. By the end of September everything is boarded up for the winter. Klondike Kate's Restaurant has a blackboard counting the days to closure and as a laugh it starts on the first day that the summer season begins.

Dawson hibernates during the winter. Temperatures well below zero for months on end are great for dog sledging but little else. Several establishments open for the several days the Yukon Quest is in town. Diamond Tooth Gertie's holds the annual Centennial Ball and Dawson comes alive as the whole town shakes off the winter blues for a few days.

Incidentally, Dawson's real name is the Town of Dawson City. It lost its city status years ago but kept the name. Its new name reflects the town's actual population size and position.

Where to stay and eat

Being a tourist town, Dawson has plenty of places to stay in. Most are only open for the summer from about May until the end of September. I have stayed in the three hotels listed. They all have standard and deluxe rooms and the usual round of facilities. They are the **Triple J** (tel: 867.993.5323) on 5th Ave and Queen St, the **Downtown Hotel** (tel: 867.993.5346) on 2nd Ave and Queen St and the **Eldorado Hotel** (tel: 867.993.5256) on 3rd Ave and Princess St. The last two are open all year round.

When I visit a town and find a good place to eat I tend to go there a lot and try out the full menu. Here's a few I can heartily recommend. The **Jack London Grill** (tel: 867.993.5346) in the Downtown Hotel, the **Bonanza**

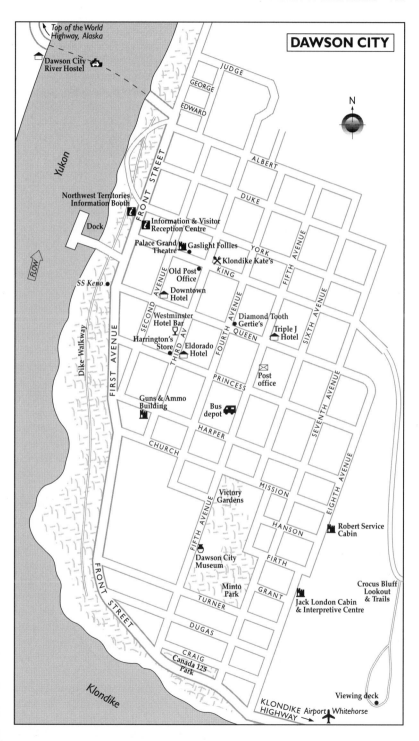

DAWSON CITY

Top of the World
Highway, Alaska

Dawson City
River Hostel

Yukon

Northwest Territories
Information Booth

Dock

Information & Visitor
Reception Centre

Palace Grand
Theatre

Gaslight Follies

Klondike Kate's

Old Post
Office

SS Keno

Downtown
Hotel

Westminster
Hotel Bar

Diamond Tooth
Gertie's

Triple J
Hotel

Harrington's
Store

Eldorado
Hotel

Guns & Ammo
Building

Post
office

Bus
depot

Victory
Gardens

Robert Service
Cabin

Dawson City
Museum

Crocus Bluff
Lookout
& Trails

Minto
Park

Jack London Cabin
& Interpretive Centre

Canada 125
Park

Klondike

Viewing deck

KLONDIKE
HIGHWAY Airport ↟ Whitehorse

FRONT STREET

JUDGE
GEORGE
EDWARD
ALBERT
DUKE
YORK
KING
QUEEN
PRINCESS
HARPER
CHURCH
MISSION
HANSON
FIRTH
GRANT
TURNER
DUGAS
CRAIG

FIRST AVENUE
SECOND AVENUE
THIRD AV
FOURTH AVENUE
FIFTH AVENUE
SIXTH AVENUE
SEVENTH AVENUE
EIGHTH AVENUE
FIFTH AVENUE

Dike Walkway

FLOW

N

Dining Room (tel: 867.993.5451) in the Eldorado Hotel, and **TJ's** in the Triple J Hotel (tel: 867.993.5323) all have a wide variety on the menu, cater for veggies and are very reasonably priced. They even have wine lists.

For the best breakfast on this planet go to **Klondike Kate's Restaurant** (tel: 867.993.6527) on 3rd Ave and King St. This is a busy place in the morning and you may have to wait for a table. Wait! It's worth it. Eggs, home fries, massive sausages and all the trimmings. The pancake stacks have to be seen to be believed. All of this is flushed down with bottomless mugs of serious coffee. Sadly for those visiting Dawson during the Yukon Quest, Kate's is only open from mid-May until mid-September.

What to see and do

The **Visitor Reception Centre** (tel: 867.993.5566) is on Front St facing the river. The visitor centre offers free conducted **walking tours** of the town. They depart four times daily and operate from June 1 until mid-September. There is a handy little **free guide** available in all hotels and tourist offices showing all the attractions and services available in the town. The town is small and everything is within walking distance except the mines. To visit these you will either need a car or to take one of the local tours.

Dawson is full of old buildings most of which have been fully restored by Parks Canada. Many are not open to the public but have displays in their windows of the boom time in Dawson. There is only one original building left from that period, the **Guns and Ammo Building** on the corner of Harper and 3rd Ave, and it has fallen down and is now propped up by scaffolding.

The following is a list of things to see that come under the auspices of the Klondike National Historic Sites (tel: 867.993.7200 for information). These first ones are all out of town – **Bear Creek Gold Dredge Support Camp**, **Dredge #4**, and **Fort Herchmer**, the NWMP post and barracks. The following establishments are in town – **Harrington's Store**, 3rd and Princess St; **Palace Grand Theatre**, 3rd and King St; **1901 Post Office**, 3rd and King St; **Robert Service Cabin**, 8th Ave for daily readings of the famous Yukon bard. On the riverbank on Front St across the road from the visitor centre is the **SS *Keno*** (tel: 867.993.7200), one of the last sternwheelers to ply the Yukon and Stewart Rivers. It is now a National Historic Site and has been restored by Parks Canada.

Other entertainment is the nightly show at **Diamond Tooth Gertie's Gambling Casino** (8tel: 67.993.5575), with gambling, slot machines and a can-can revue. A cover charge applies but it is well worth it. The **Gaslight Follies** at the Palace Grand Revue on King St (tel: 867.993.5575) is two hours of Klondike themed musical comedy. Reservations are recommended. Literary buffs might also be interested in readings of the works of the author Jack London at the **Jack London Cabin and Interpretive Centre** (tel: 867.993.5575) at the far end of town on 8th Ave.

I am not in the habit of recommending bars as such if there is no serious additional entertainment provided other than bands, but one I must include here is the **Westminster Hotel** on 2nd Ave. This looks like an old Western saloon on the outside, something straight out of the movies. You can't miss it as it is painted pink, of all colours. It is where the locals go for a beer and is a wild and woolly establishment indeed, full of some very real characters and not a pub for the faint hearted. If you are looking simply to have a quiet beer this is not the place. The Westminster is open all year round and live and loud country music plays most nights. It is completely the opposite to the special tourist entertainment of Gaslight Follies or Diamond Tooth Gertie's. Enter at your peril or your extreme enjoyment.

Tour operators in Dawson
Gold City Tours (tel: 867.993.5175) is located on Front St opposite the SS *Keno* and operates sightseeing tours of Dawson and the goldfields (recommended). A man called Buffalo who dresses as a 19th century casino croupier runs the company. I have been out with Buffalo a couple of times and he can be quite entertaining. He is also the local fire chief as well as having several other roles in town. Knows absolutely everybody.

Tommy Taylor runs **Fishwheel Charter Services** (tel: 867.993.6857) and, as Dawson's only First Nations guide, offers things a little differently. Summer is for Yukon River trips to see traditional fishwheels in use and have tea and bannock (native bread) served in a First Nations fish camp. In winter he does dog sledging, snowmobiling and winter camping trips into the wilderness.

The **Ancient Voices Wilderness Camp** (tel: 867.993.5605) is one I have not tried personally, as time has not permitted it yet. It is said to offer a glimpse of a traditional First Nations way of life, staying in cabins and/or tents. Nights are filled with story-telling, dances, songs and legends of the northern First Nations. The camp is an hour along the Yukon River and can only be reached by boat or helicopter. Activities vary depending on the time of year.

Eureka Gold Panning Adventures (www.eurekagoldpanning.yk.ca) specialise in adventure holidays.

Further information
Dawson City Museum and Historical Society (www.users.yknet.yk.ca/dcpages/museum.html) can supply information on Dawson's social and mining history.

Klondike Visitors Association (www.dawsoncity.com) is a non-profit society promoting community attractions and visitor services

THE SILVER TRAIL
Think of the Yukon and everyone thinks of gold but the Yukon is also the home of some of the largest deposits of silver to be found in Canada. The Silver Trail lies at the heart of the Na-Cho Nyak Dun First Nations territory and incorporates the communities of Stewart Crossing, Mayo and Keno City and passes through the 'ghost town' of Elsa.

Mayo
Mayo (population 450) is situated on the banks of the Stewart River at the mouth of the Mayo River. Mayo developed at the turn of the century as a river

W J D DEMPSTER RCMP

William John Duncan Dempster (1876–1964) was born in Wales and emigrated to Canada as a young man. He joined the NWMP in 1897 and was posted to the Yukon in 1898, where he was to spend the rest of his 37 years in the RCMP. He received national attention for his involvement in the Lost Patrol incident of 1910–11. Dempster had been involved in patrol work in the area since 1907–08.

With two other members of the force and a First Nations guide Corporal Dempster, as he then was, set out on February 28 1911 in extremely cold weather to find the missing patrol. The wind chill had brought the effective temperature down to -65°C. When Dempster set out he believed that nothing serious could have happened to a man of Fitzgerald's experience in northern work but he soon discovered things that changed his mind – old campsites indicating that the patrol had been lost, an abandoned dog harness and other gear, the paws of a dog cut off at the knees, and a dog's shoulder blade that had obviously been cooked and eaten. On March 21 and 22 Dempster and his men found the bodies.

After this disaster Dempster was ordered to make the route safe by establishing supply caches, building shelters, and blazing the trail with lobsticks – something that might have saved Fitzgerald's and his companions' lives.

Dempster subsequently set a record for the fastest patrol over the route of 19 days only to beat it in 1920 with a time of 14 days over the same ground. Dempster, though, did not take unnecessary chances, nor was he too proud to use native guides and was never afraid to admit he was lost on those rare occasions when this happened. For many years he was regularly sent out on patrol by the government to find and establish new routes and evaluate their suitability. Although best known to the outside world as the man who found the Lost Patrol, his work as a trailblazer and pathfinder earned him the title of the best trail man in the Yukon.

Dempster married Catherine Smith of Sydney, Nova Scotia in 1926 and they had a son and daughter. When he retired in 1934 with the rank of Inspector he was the most respected RCMP officer in the north. Before he died on October 25 1964 he had the pleasure of knowing that the new road north from Dawson to Aklavik was to be called the Dempster Highway in his honour.

settlement and port. It was the furthest up the Stewart River that steamboats could go to bring supplies and take away the silver-lead ore from the mines at Keno City. The town is named after Captain Alfred S Mayo, the owner of a steamboat called the *New Racket*, the name probably reflecting his career change from circus acrobat to steamboat owner, who went on to become a founding member of the Yukon Order of Pioneers. There is an **interpretive centre** in Binet House providing extensive information on the area.

Where to stay and eat
The **Bedrock Motel** (tel: 867.996.2290) and the **North Star Motel** (tel: 867.996.2231) are both located downtown and have most of the services you would expect, but accommodation is limited so book ahead.

Elsa
Elsa lies 45km beyond Mayo on the Silver Trail. It was the site of the Yukon's oldest operating mine, but there has been little to see here since the price of silver was depressed and the mine closed in 1989. There is a small team of security people here looking after the site.

Keno City
Keno City was once the thriving centre of a great silver mining operation but now there is little left but a cluster of small log cabins and a small hotel with a bar and café. It is said to be one of the best and prettiest places to watch the midnight sun. The prospector Louis Beauvette discovered silver here on July 10 1919 but, through lack of finance, had to bring in the Yukon Gold Company to establish the mining claim. News of the discovery leaked and within days a minor silver rush began. By 1920 there were more than 600 claims staked and filed all over Keno Hill. From the beginning the ore had to be transported to Mayo for shipment and only the volume of ore and high prices then available made silver mining in this isolated spot financially viable.

Where to stay and eat
Try **Nash Creek Ent. Rental Cabins** (tel: 867.995.2892) for that small town Yukon experience in cosy, self-contained cabins, or stay at the **Keno City Hotel** (tel: 867.995.2312). **Keno City Campground** (tel: 867.995.2792) has seven sites with firewood, wood stoves, water and shelter and is open from June 1 to the end of August. The **Keno City Snack Bar** (tel: 867.995.2409) across the street from the museum is open 08.00–20.00 daily from June 1 until the end of September. Snacks, soups, sandwiches, pizzas, hot dogs and beverages available.

What to see and do
The **Keno City Mining Museum** (tel: 867.995.2792) is full of memorabilia of the town's past. Open 10.00–18.00 daily, June 1 until the end of September.

Top of the World Highway
This smallish highway runs west from Dawson into Alaska. To leave Dawson you cross over the Yukon River on a government ferry (free) in summer. You can cross the river in winter by driving over an ice bridge but the Top of the World Highway is normally closed once the heavy snows begin. Check in Dawson to see if the road is open before you go. The drive through the

mountains into Alaska is stunning. Once into the USA the road becomes the Taylor Highway and carries on to Tetlin Junction where it meets the Alaska Highway.

It is a delightful trip to go from Whitehorse up the Klondike Highway to Dawson and stay a couple of days, then go along the Top of the World Highway into Alaska and down to Tetlin Junction before turning left onto the Alaska Highway and heading back into the Yukon at Beaver Creek for the return journey to Whitehorse. The road is not paved all the way but it is a properly constructed gravel road. Keep your speed down and enjoy the scenery. Watch out for big trucks and speedy locals. Recommended if you have the time.

When you cross into the United States the Canada and US customs post at Little Gold Creek is open 09.00–21.00 daily (Yukon time). You cannot cross the border if the post is closed. There is an hour's time difference between the Yukon and Alaska.

The Dempster Highway

This highway is named after Corporal WJD Dempster of the RCMP who searched for and discovered the men of the Lost Patrol frozen to death near Fort McPherson in 1911. The highway was completed in 1979 and links southern Yukon with Inuvik, the MacKenzie Delta and other northern communities of the Northwest Territories. It starts 40km south of Dawson and runs through some of the most beautiful and spectacular mountain and tundra scenery in all of Canada. The 741km journey from Dawson to Inuvik will take at least 12 hours but anticipate doing it in two days and really enjoy the scenery.

Travelling the Dempster is driving through unparalleled wilderness terrain and you are advised to be well prepared for the journey. There are only three fuel stops en route and any assistance if you break down will be long in coming. The road is not paved so carry two spare tyres and be aware not only of how to change a wheel but also how to replace a tyre and tube. This is not a journey for inexperienced city drivers. The road is open all year round. There is usually a road closure for about two or three weeks when the ferry services described below cannot operate because of the forming ice and again just after the ice has begun to melt when the moving pack ice is too great an obstacle.

At the start of the highway are eight interpretive panels describing the road and the features, flora and fauna you should see long the way. At 72km you will come across the **Tombstone Mountain Campground** with places for 22 RVs or tents. There is not much else but superb views of the Tombstone Mountain. Just up the road is the Dempster Highway Interpretive Centre with a whole lot of information about the region. It is only open from mid-June until September.

A little further on is another place to see Tombstone Mountain. Originally called Campbell Mountain by William Ogilvie, an early explorer and surveyor, it derived its more common name from its distinctive shape. There is an **interpretive sign** describing the NWMP patrols that passed through this region in 1899 followed by another small government **campground** at 194km.

Eagle Plains comes up at 371km and has the only **hotel** along the whole highway. It is expensive but as there is nothing else you have little choice if you want to have a night's rest. There is an RV **campground** besides the hotel and all the usual facilities like a restaurant and café, a full service station, a mechanic, towing and a store. They even have aviation fuel for those with a plane. At 402km you cross the Arctic Circle and eventually into the Northwest Territories at 447km through the Wright Pass.

There is a ferry service across the Peel River that operates on demand 09.00–01.00 daily from spring to the late autumn. In winter there is an ice bridge (approximately November until April). Once you are into the NWT you will pass through the First Nation villages of Fort McPherson with its RCMP post and Arctic Red River where there is another ferry in summer and an ice bridge in winter. The highway finally ends in Inuvik 726km after you began.

There is a **Northwest Territories Information Centre** in Dawson just across the road from the town's visitor centre on Front St. It has details of road conditions and ferry timings. Information is also available at the Eagle Plains Hotel en route.

Lynx

NORTHWEST TERRITORIES

0 —————— 250km
0 —————— 250 miles

N

Queen Elizabeth Islands

Prince Gustaf Adolf Sea

Ellef Rignes I

Prince Patrick Island

MacKenzie King I

Devon I

Bathurst Island

Cornwallis Island

Melville Island

(North Magnetic Pole)

Resolute Bay

Banks I Bird Sanct No 2

Aulavik National Park

Viscount Melville Sound

Parry Channel

Beaufort Sea

Prince of Wales Island

MacKenzie Bay

Banks Island Bird Sanct No 1

Banks Island

Prince Albert Peninsula

M'Clintock Channel

Franklin Strait

Ivvavik Nat Pk

Sachs Harbour

C Dalhousie

C Bathurst

Anderson River Delta Bird Sanct

Amundsen Gulf

Cape Parry Bird Sanctuary

Holman

Victoria Island

King William Island

Aklavik

Inuvik

Fort McPherson

Paulatuk

TREE LINE (APPROX)

Reindeer Grazing Reserve

Tuktut Nogait Nat Pk Res

Anderson

Cambridge Bay

Queen Maud Gulf

Peel River Preserve

MacKenzie

Arctic Circle

Kugluktuk

Coronation Gulf

Omingmaktok

Bay Chimo

Queen Maud Bird Sanctuary

Fort Good Hope

Coppermine

Kingaok

Bathurst Inlet

NUNAVUT

YUKON

Norman Wells

Great Bear Lake

Fort Franklin

NORTHWEST

Back River

Canol Heritage Trail

MacKenzie Mtns

Wrigley

TERRITORIES

Thelon Game Reserve

Mt Sir James MacBrien 2758m

Ross River

Virginia Falls

Edzo

Yellowknife

Reliance

Approx northern limit of trees

Thelon

Logan Mtns

Nahanni Nat Pk

Nahanni

Fort Simpson

MacKenzie Bison Sanctuary

Great Slave Lake

Alaska

Watson Lake

Nahanni Butte

Fort Providence

Slave River

Highway

Lloyd

Fort Liard

Enterprise

Hay River

Deese

Fort Smith

Fond-du-Lac

Toad River

Meander River

Wood Buffalo National Park

Fort Chipewyan

Dease Lake

Fort Nelson

Peace River

Lake Athabasca

Wollaston Lake

BRITISH COLUMBIA

High Level

Reindeer Lake

The Northwest Territories

The Northwest Territories is the stuff of wilderness Hollywood. It is all about wide tracts of wilderness a person could get lost in, or disappear into if they did not want to be found. The people you meet here mostly seem to come from somewhere else and appear to be constantly on the move. There are only a few pockets of settled population.

The Northwest Territories is one of the last great wildlife refuges on this planet. Large game animals still roam the forests and grasslands and polar bears can be spotted along the Arctic coastline. Sea mammals such as bearded seal and beluga whales are also in abundance along the Arctic coast. The numbers are staggering, with over a million barren-ground caribou, 50,000 muskoxen, 26,000 moose, 15,000 wolves, 5,000 polar bears, 10,000 woodland caribou, 6,000 Dall's sheep, 5,000 grizzlies and the same number of black bears and some 2,500 wood bison. There are, unfortunately for the comfort of animals and humans alike, an unjustifiably large number of insects present in the summer.

About half of Canada's bird species have been recorded in the NWT. It is a birdwatcher's paradise, with more than 200 species either breeding or staging here en route to or from six continents. The Great Slave Lake and the Great Bear Lake are two of the largest in the world and resemble vast inland seas. These lakes, along with a vast array of rivers, are the domain of huge trout, feisty Arctic grayling, king-size northern pike and Arctic char. The MacKenzie River, or Deh Cho as it is known to the Dene people, runs 1,800km from the Great Slave Lake to the Beaufort Sea. Along the way it flows through boreal forests, gathering the waters of many tributary rivers and streams fed by the MacKenzie Mountains, until it fans out into one of the largest untouched river deltas in the world, the MacKenzie Delta.

There are naturalist opportunities in just about every corner of the NWT. You can see bald eagles fishing on the Great Slave Lake, join a First Nations guide for a trip down one of Canada's Heritage Rivers or travel onto the barrens to see caribou and muskoxen in their natural environment. There are four national parks in NWT, Wood Buffalo and Nahanni in the south and Tuktut Nogait and Aulavik in the north. There are eight official languages in NWT but everyone under the age of 40 speaks English and

NORTHWEST TERRITORIES FACTS

Area 1,171,918km², includes 4,480km² of freshwater and 429,706km² of forested land. Water covers 11.81% of the land. 100% is deemed wilderness.

Boundaries To the south the boundary is 60° North latitude, bordering with British Columbia, Alberta and Saskatchewan. In the west the boundary with the Yukon Territory follows a line from a point on the coast roughly 136° 30' West longitude to the southern border at 124° N/60° W. In the Arctic Ocean the boundary basically follows the lines of longitude 110° W and 135° W extending across the Beaufort Sea, in principle as far as the true North Pole, though in reality only as far north as the 80th Parallel. In the east NWT shares a boundary with Nunavut which basically follows the treeline across mainland Canada and divides the Arctic islands of Victoria and Melville in half.

Geographical features The MacKenzie River is the tenth longest in the world and the Virginia Falls in Nahanni National Park is twice the height of Niagara. Officially the highest mountain is a named peak called Mt Sir James MacBrien at 2,762m/9,062ft, but there is an unnamed summit next to it near the head of the South Nahanni River that is higher by 12m/35ft. The lowest point is the coast of the Beaufort Sea.

Time Mountain Standard Time (GMT –7hr). There is Daylight Saving Time from April to October (GMT –6hr).

Population 40,309 with a little over 17,000 living in Yellowknife.

Capital Yellowknife.

Territorial status Northwest Territories became a separate territory of Canada in 1870 when it included 'all the land west of Ontario'. In 1895 Canada established the districts of Ungava, MacKenzie, Franklin and Yukon within the 'Northwest Territories'. Yukon became a separate territory in 1898. On April 1 1999 Northwest Territories was divided into NWT (sometimes known as the Western Arctic) and Nunavut.

although the Dene, Metis and Inuvialuit populations are bridging the gap with the modern world none of these aboriginal groups has abandoned its traditional ways.

Road travel is expanding. There is a fully sealed road from Yellowknife all the way to Edmonton in Alberta and a road is forging its way along the MacKenzie River towards Inuvik, NWT's northernmost town. Most of the other roads are unpaved but are wide hard-packed highways. Some roads are winter access only but the network is expanding.

Almost all wilderness activities are possible in NWT. Whitewater rafting, canoeing, hiking, snowmobiling, skiing and dog sledging are all popular. Most tourists begin arriving in NWT as the days lengthen in late March and early April well before the snows melt to take advantage of the winter-type activities. Outdoor activities then continue into the autumn and end when the snow begins to fall again, the days shorten and winter sets in.

The Northwest Territories has been on the unfortunate end of recent political developments. Over half of its territory has been taken away and established as a new territory in its own right – Nunavut. The publicity surrounding this creation of a new state has naturally given more prominence to the new territory and NWT has been left behind a little. It is not because NWT is any less worthy of the publicity, it is just that most of the available government funding has been directed at promoting the new territory, leaving little in the kitty for re-establishing the old one.

For some reason that I have not, at this stage, been able to fathom out, comparatively little information is available on the NWT. The Yukon's government machine produces an excellent array of information geared towards tourism but there seems a dearth of the same for NWT. Nunavut is trying hard to get on the planet and seems to have the funding to do it but tourism seems to be relatively new to NWT and they are well behind in sorting themselves out. I hope it is only the lack of government funding and not the want of trying that is the problem. So, if the system appears a little slow in NWT, bear with it, they should get you there in the end. Northwest Territories has a lot to offer the traveller; it is just taking a little more time to establish itself in the tourism marketplace.

Tour operators
Nahanni Wilderness Adventures Ltd www.nahanniwild.com. Canoe outfitting for the south Nahanni, route guides etc
Enodah Wilderness Travel/Trout Rock Lodge www.enodah.com. Boat trips up the Yellowknife River, bird-watching tours
Raven Eye Outfitters www.wilds.mc.ca/raven-eye. Guided canoe expeditions on the Kazan and Thlewiaza Rivers
Arctic Nature Tours www.arcticnaturetour.com. Rafting and wildlife viewing trips
Whitewolf Adventure Expeditions www.nahanni.com. Canoeing and rafting remote rivers

HISTORY
Originally the entire Northwest Territories was owned by the Hudson Bay Company when it and all the land to the north was called Rupert's Land after Charles II's son, Prince Rupert, a founding financier in the Company of Adventures – the precursor to the Hudson Bay Company. After Canada seceded from the British throne NWT was known as British North America and as such it set about expanding its land base and establishing its sovereignty over much of the land beyond its established borders.

In 1869, with a loan underwritten by the British Government, Canada acquired Rupert's Land from the Hudson Bay Company for £300,000. The company retained 162km^2 of land surrounding each its trading posts plus

THE NORTHERN LIGHTS

At the time of writing I have only seen this phenomenon once. That was at 9,500m flying home after watching the Yukon Quest International Sled Dog Race in 1998.

The northern lights or *Aurora borealis*, to give it its proper name, is believed to be a direct result of solar winds entering the Earth's ionosphere some 160km above the surface of the planet. These solar winds are streams of charged ions emanating from the sun which collide with the gases in the Earth's upper atmosphere. The sun's particles and the earth's gases pair off, releasing energy that appears as visible light seeming to dance about the heavens. Named after the Roman goddess of dawn, the aurora borealis and other celestial lights have intrigued travellers for centuries and have been the focus for many beliefs and superstitions.

Certain Inuit groups attach particular significance to the phenomenon, believing that they are the spirits of ancestors come to light the long polar night sky; some consider them to be malevolent forces; others believe them to be a storehouse of events past and future. Old time prospectors thought they were vapours given off by ore deposits, and the Japanese believe that a marriage will be particularly successful if consummated beneath them. Whatever your beliefs, the aurora borealis is a stunning display that brings delight to all who watch.

further land to be selected later. This acquisition ended the Hudson Bay Company's trading monopoly over much of Canada and, although the terms for that time were quite tough, the powerful company still pocketed one-twentieth of the land in a most fertile belt including some very rich mineral deposits.

The bulk of the Northwest Territories thus became Crown property in 1869. The entire western Canadian population at that time stood at an estimated 7,000 people, most of them hunters and trappers, or people working in ancillary jobs for the HBC. Lines of communication were long and decidedly slow and the territory under Canadian control was absolutely vast. The whole of the NWT was a vast backwater. There was no Klondike Gold Rush to put the territory on the map; the economy was based on the fur trade which by its very nature needed the territory to remain unpopulated; much of the land was poor in relation to agricultural prospects. Therefore, it was obvious that there would be little expansion within the territory until any of the above situations changed.

There have been a few mineral finds during the last century and oil has been found but extraction and transportation costs have prevented it making a huge change economically to the territory. Any future wealth lies in NWT's tourism potential and this is only just beginning to be developed.

YELLOWKNIFE

Yellowknife is named after the Yellowknife Dene people who moved into this area in the early 1800s. Samuel Hearne called them this because of the knives made of copper which they used. Prospectors en route to the Yukon found gold here in 1896 but the region was considered too remote to mine it successfully. It was not until 1938, after bush pilots had begun opening up the area, that commercial gold mining was possible on the shores of the Great Slave Lake. By 1940 the 'Old Town' of Yellowknife was booming with a population of 1,000 centred on 'the Rock' and Latham Island.

By 1945 the Old Town had outgrown its location and a new site, that of the present day downtown, was surveyed. From 1947 onwards Yellowknife expanded to what it is today and, with a population of 18,000, the city is the business and commercial centre of the Northwest Territories. It has earned itself the title of 'Canada's biggest little town' and is Canada's northernmost city and the only city in the territory. Edmonton is over 1,500km south by road and Yellowknife is situated only 442km below the Arctic Circle.

Isolation has been a byword for Yellowknife since it developed as a mining town. There was no road link between the city and anywhere south before the early 1960s. All goods were transported by barge between June and October when the Great Slave Lake was ice-free. The arrival of the first supply barge was a major event in the town's lifestyle. Even today the town is isolated for a few weeks in spring when the ice bridge across the MacKenzie River just south of Fort Providence begins to thaw. The same applies when the river begins to freeze over in the autumn before the ice is thick enough to support the weight of vehicles.

Today, modern jets link Yellowknife with cities to the south and the northern communities. Satellite communications connect Yellowknife with radio and television networks across North America so isolation is more a state of mind now than a real fact of life, as it was a few decades ago. Having said that, the state of mind still exists and helps maintain a spirit of independence and friendliness that you find throughout the north.

Getting there/about

Yellowknife's airport is five kilometres west of the town's centre. There are several scheduled daily flights from Edmonton to Yellowknife with both Canadian (Canadian North) and Air Canada (NWT Air). Canadian flies three times a week from Ottawa to Yellowknife (Mon, Wed, Fri). First Air has daily flights to Whitehorse (weekdays).

Within the north there are also flights from Yellowknife to Cambridge Bay, Deline, Fort Simpson, Fort Smith, Gjoa Haven, Hay River, Holman, Inuvik, Iqaluit, Kuglutuk, Lutselke, Norman Wells, Pelly Bay, Rae Lakes, Rankin Inlet, Resolute, Snare Lake, Taloyak, Tulita and Wha Ti. The Rankin Inlet service connects to Winnipeg.

There is a thrice-weekly bus service with Frontier Coachlines (tel: 867.873.4892) to Enterprise and Hay River to connect with Greyhound buses to the rest of Canada and beyond. There is also a local bus service in

Yellowknife. There are only two routes; Route #1 is from the airport to Latham Island and back and route #2 is from downtown to Frame Lake and back. Fares are only $2.00 for adults, seniors and under-18s $1.50, and under-5s free.

Avis (tel: 867.873.5648), Budget (tel: 867.873.3366) and National Tilden (tel: 867.920.2970) have booths at the airport as well as offices downtown.

Where to stay

There is lots of accommodation in Yellowknife, as you would expect. Top of the list, literally, is the **Explorer Hotel** (tel: 867.873.3531), situated on a rocky pinnacle overlooking the new town. Also try the **Discovery Inn** (tel: 867.873.4151). Both have restaurants and bars plus all the usual services you would expect from a quality hotel. Both offer an airport shuttle service for booked guests. For something different try the **Prospector Bed and Breakfast** (tel: 867.920.7620) in the Old Town just across the road from the Wildcat Café and right on the edge of the lake.

Where to eat

This is a must-try. The **Wildcat Café** (tel: 867.873 8850) was Yellowknife's first restaurant way back in 1937. It is a small log cabin perched on the edge of the hill below the Bush Pilot's Monument. It serves country fayre like muskox, caribou, Arctic char and delicious soups. You can usually get all you can eat for about $12. There are just a few tables plus some seating outside in summer if the weather is nice. The place is really popular with the locals and the food is all home-cooked and excellent. Open mid-May to September, 07.00–22.30 Mon-Sat, 09.00–22.30 Sun. Be warned, they don't take reservations. Also try the Bar & Grill in the **Prospector** opposite, and if you want to spoil yourself try the restaurants in the **Explorer Hotel** or the **Discovery Inn**. All the usual **fast food** places like McDonalds and KFC are here and there are several other small cafés and restaurants downtown. Most of the bars do food as well. Recommended is the **Black Knight** on 49th Street (tel: 867.920.4041). Bars are all open 'til late.

What to see

The **Visitor Reception Centre** (tel: 867.873.4262) is always a good place to begin. Situated in the Prince of Wales Heritage Centre opposite the Explorer Hotel on 49th St it has some excellent displays of local culture and provides plenty of information. They can do all the usual accommodation booking if you like and it is a good place to get advice on what to see and do both in Yellowknife and throughout NWT.

Almost all of the best sights are on Latham Island and in the Old Town. Take a bus or cab and then do the Old Town on foot. The **Bush Pilot's Monument** is on top of a hill in the middle of the Old Town known as 'the rock' and has excellent views over both towns and the Great Slave Lake. Just down below is the Wildcat Café and, even if you do not eat in there, it is worth remembering that it is the most photographed building in

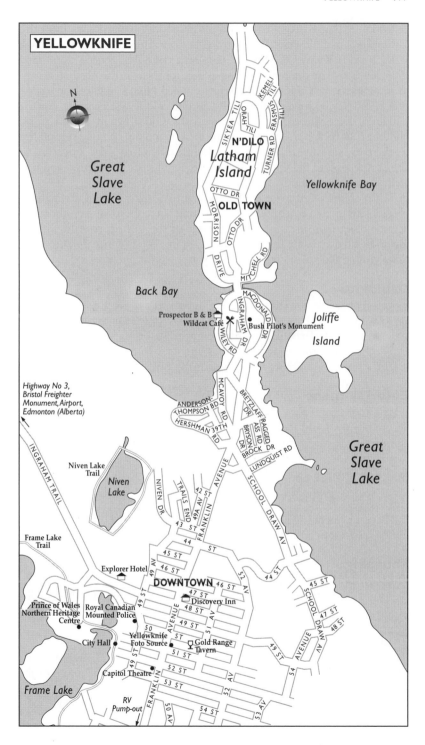

Yellowknife. Ragged Ass Road is full of old shanty town houses from the earliest days of Yellowknife. Back towards town from the Wildcat Café on Wiley Road is **Weaver & Devore**, the north's one-stop general store since 1936. They say you can buy anything in here for travel in the north. It is easy to recognise as it is one of those semi-rounded Nissen huts of corrugated iron sheets made popular during the Second World War as easily erected buildings. Everywhere you look around the Old Town is an old rustic building. On Back Bay is the floatplane base and on the opposite side of 'the Rock' between the mainland and Jolliffe Island are the houseboats. Wandering around the Old Town is a little indulgence in nostalgia and it is well worth soaking up.

To the southeast of town is **Dettah**, a small Dogrib Dene First Nations village. This used to be a seasonal fishing camp but as the town grew the camp became more permanent to take advantage of the services provided by the town yet still maintaining a traditional way of life. The old men don't seem to mind visitors and will quite happily tell you about the old ways and old days.

Outside town
As you approach Yellowknife from the airport you will see a strange sight on top of a small hill above the Welcome to Yellowknife sign. Sitting on a large pedestal is a blue **Bristol Freighter** cargo plane belonging to Wardair. Its significance is that this plane was the first aircraft to land at the North Pole and it is therefore very much a part of modern-day NWT history.

Entertainment
I don't know if this place should be considered sightseeing or entertainment. Technically the **Gold Range Tavern** (tel: 867.873.4441) on 50th St is entertainment yet it has so much local colour that it fits right into the sightseeing mould. It is known locally as 'Strange Range' or 'Bad Sams'. This is a real frontier bar of mayhem, heavy drinking and loud country music but don't let that put you off entering the place. This is the place to hobnob with some real local characters.

There is a cinema on 52nd St called the **Capitol Theatre** (tel: 867.873.2302 for the movie info hotline).

Shopping
Photographic supplies
Best source is **Yellowknife Foto Source** (tel: 867.873.2196) at 5005 Franklin St which has a good supply of Fuji and Kodak film properly kept in the fridge.

Tour operators
Raven Tours has a desk at the Explorer Hotel (tel: 867.873.4776). The company does city tours and offers numerous other programs throughout Yellowknife and the local area. A three-hour city tour costs $25 per person.
Cygnus Ecotours (tel: 867.873.4782) is led by ecologist and author Jamie Baste and does nature tours in the Yellowknife area.

Outdoor adventure operators

Arctic Safaris (tel: 867.873.3212) offers wildlife photographic trips to the barren lands including the migrating caribou.

Bluefish Services (tel: 867.873.4818) does boat tours of the Great Slave Lake plus fishing and birdwatching.

Great Canadian Ecoventures (tel: 867.920.7110) provides wildlife viewing programs and photographic tours to the Arctic. On site aircraft and mobile camps allow you to follow the migrating herds. Also whitewater rafting and canoeing on the Thelon and Clarke Rivers.

Inukshuk Ventures (tel: 867.873.4226) has canoeing and camping programmes aimed at the slightly less adventurous. No whitewater thrills but plenty of outdoor experiences.

Great Slave Sledging Company (tel: 867.873.6070) offers dog sledge and skiing tours from either Yellowknife or Hay River in the winter and spring time. Tent or lodge accommodation. Also snowmobiling, ice fishing, wildlife viewing (wood bison) and aurora watching from wilderness sites.

Health and safety

RCMP tel: 867.669.1111
Stanton Regional Hospital tel: 867.669.4110

Stanton Regional Hospital has a 24-hour emergency service. The hospital is located at 550 Byrne Road in Yellowknife. Switchboard (tel: 867.669.4111)

SOUTH OF YELLOWKNIFE

Most places south of Yellowknife are accessible by road, either from Yellowknife itself or by a long haul up from the south. Some of the roadway is tar sealed, but most of it has a properly formed gravel surface. The two main communities in the south are Hay River on the shores of the Great Slave Lake and Fort Smith, considered the gateway to Wood Buffalo National Park.

Enterprise

Coming across the 60th Parallel from Edmonton the first community you come to is Enterprise. There is not much here but a service station, a restaurant and a couple of rooms at **Ed's Place Motel** (tel: 867.984.3181) at the MacKenzie Highway junction. There is a **campground** 14km north of Enterprise by the road to Hay River called Paradise Gardens (tel: 867.874.6414).

Hay River

Hay River has a population of over 3,600 making it quite a decent size town by northern standards. Like Yellowknife there are two parts to the town – the old town and the new, where most of the hotels, restaurants and government offices are located. For some reason the people of Hay River are very keen on their speedway, golf and serious watersports in the summer.

Where to stay and eat

There is a reasonable range of accommodation in Hay River. Top of the line is the **Ptarmigan Inn Hotel** (tel: 867.874.6781) with 42 rooms, bar, dining lounge and restaurant. The **Hay River Hotel** (tel: 867.874.6022) accommodates 64 in 32 rooms with a mix of shared and private facilities. Other suggestions are the **Cedar Rest Motel** (tel: 867.874.3732), the **Caribou Motor Inn** (tel: 867.874.6706) and the **Migrator Inn** (tel: 867.874.6792), which offers rooms, kitchenettes and deluxe suites with the usual facilities but no restaurant. The Caribou has a restaurant and lounge located in the building next door and some of the rooms have a whirlpool or steambath.

For eating there is the **Skyway Family Dining Restaurant** (tel: 867.874.2783) on the MacKenzie Highway. The **Keys Restaurant** in the Ptarmigan Inn is popular with the locals. Another popular choice is the **Back Eddy Lounge** (tel: 867.874.6680) upstairs at 6 Courtoreille St in the New Town. We mustn't forget the fast food places: there is a **KFC** here.

Entertainment

There are two **cinemas** in Hay River at the Riverview Cineplex in the B&R Rowe Building (tel: 867.874.FLIC).

Information

The **visitor centre** (tel: 867.874.3180) is on your right as you come into town. Open 09.00-21.00 hours daily, mid-May to mid-September.

Health and safety

Local contact numbers are:

RCMP	tel: (867) 874.6555
Ambulance	tel: (867) 874.9333
Fire	tel: (867) 874.2222
Hospital	tel: (867) 874.6512

Fort Smith

Fort Smith is 270km from Hay River and sits right on the 60th Parallel. The road is paved for the first 60km from the Hay River end before it returns to a formed gravel surface. There are a little over 2,500 people in this small town and it was the territorial capital until 1967. Fort Smith is no longer the transport hub it was many years ago so it has remodelled itself as the gateway to Wood Buffalo National Park.

Where to stay and eat

The **Pelican Rapids Inn** (tel: 867.872.2789) is the most modern with 31 rooms, bar, restaurant and cable TV. The **Pinecrest Hotel** (tel: 867.872.2320) has 48 beds in 24 rooms, and the **Portage Inn** (tel: 867.872.2276) has two double rooms, 12 singles and one three-bedroom suite.

Information
Fort Smith **visitor centre** (tel: 867.872 2515) is on Portage Road. It is open
10.00–22.00 daily, mid-May to mid-September.

Wood Buffalo National Park
Wood Buffalo National Park is Canada's largest and the second largest in the
world at 45,000 km². It is not easy to get around as there is limited road access.
The **park headquarters** is located in the federal building in Fort Smith at 126
McDougal Road (tel: 867.872.7900). The only developed facilities are at **Pine
Lake** about 60km south of Fort Smith. There is a campground here with
toilets, kitchen shelters and firewood.

The importance of the park is its large free-roaming herd of bison, about
2,700 animals, and the fact that it is the last natural nesting habitat of the
whooping crane. The 320km² **Salt Plains** are a prominent feature of the park.
These salt plains are all that is left of an ancient ocean and the area is probably
the best place easily to see much of the park's wildlife.

Most of the bison here are hybrids – a mixture of wood bison and plains
bison. The plains bison were introduced from Buffalo National Park near
Wainwright in Alberta in the late 20s and 30s to supplement the wood bison
numbers. Unfortunately they brought with them tuberculosis and brucellosis which killed off large swathes of the native population. Today the population is reasonably healthy through culls of diseased animals and
vaccination programs but there are few if any pure-bred wood bison left in
the park.

Fort Providence
Fort Providence lies about a third of the way between Hay River and
Yellowknife on the northern side of the MacKenzie River. A ferry takes you
across the river in summer and there is an ice bridge for winter traffic. A
Roman Catholic mission was established here in 1861 and, subsequently, a
small community grew up around the mission. The mission promoted the use
of agriculture and operated a school for the Slavey Dene First Nations of the
area. Although Fort Providence is a very nice, quiet, place there is not much to
the town. The church is still there, and there is one hotel, the **Snowshoe Inn**
(tel: 867.699.3511), with excellent accommodation. It has a restaurant situated
on the opposite side of the road and there is the usual gas station and general
store. **Tours** can be organised to explore both the MacKenzie River and the
nearby MacKenzie Bison Sanctuary. On the main road to Yellowknife is the
Big River Motel (867.699.4301). It is located at the fuel station next to the
Fort Providence turnoff. The restaurant is open all hours and there is
accommodation for 22 persons in 12 rooms.

Tour operator
For tours to MacKenzie Bison Sanctuary and around Fort Providence there's
Big John's Tourism. The contact for information is Edward Landry, Box 96,
Fort Providence, NT X0E 0L0, tel: 867-699-4711.

MacKenzie Bison Sanctuary

If you want to easily see wood bison this is the place to come. There are about 2,000 animals in the 10,000km² sanctuary and they are pure wood bison. The MacKenzie River and the Great Slave Lake prevent the herds migrating and mixing with the animals in Wood Buffalo National Park. Anthrax affected the herd some years ago but it has substantially recovered now. Bison can regularly be seen grazing along the verges of Highway 3 towards Yellowknife as the road offers the animals a breezy respite from troublesome insects in summer.

Some local tour operators in Fort Providence have guides who will take you to see the bison inside the sanctuary. They will also fly you into fishing camps well within the sanctuary towards the Great Slave Lake where you can get a chance to observe true wilderness herds and, possibly, their natural predators, the wolves. Time has never permitted me the opportunity to explore the sanctuary further than within a couple of kilometres of Highway 3 and Fort Providence but I have also seen bison in largish numbers every time I have travelled the road. My friend Cooper Langford, who lives in Yellowknife and regularly travels the route, says the same thing.

I would suggest, if you are viewing herds from the road, that you be careful around the bulls. They are not very patient animals and are quick to defend their cows and calves. Do not leave your vehicle when any are in close proximity. Do not follow the animals too closely – remember that all animals have a sense of personal space which it may be unwise to infringe. A bull can weigh up to 1,000kg and would not be averse to charging and ramming your car if it felt threatened. If you see a herd and wish to watch it, stop your car, wait, and let the animals come to you. They then set the rules of interaction and, as I have found, they will walk right past the car without giving you an extra thought.

THE DEH CHO REGION

Deh Cho is a Slavey Dene word meaning 'big river' and basically encompasses the entire MacKenzie River basin. It is a wild uninhabited region of huge mountains, thundering rivers, waterfalls and an abundance of wildlife. I read somewhere that the lakes are so full of fish that you have to bait your hooks behind a tree. It is best known for the UNESCO World Heritage Site of Nahanni National Park which rests astride the Nahanni River. Virginia Falls, at twice the size and height of Niagara, lie at its heart and the Nahanni River is deemed to be Canada's finest wilderness river.

Fort Liard

Fort Liard is 784km south of Yellowknife along the MacKenzie Highway and the Liard Trail. You can also reach Fort Liard by travelling up from Dawson Creek in British Columbia and turning north on to the Liard Highway just after Fort Nelson. This road is unpaved. Situated 6km off the Liard Highway, the town itself is a bit of an oddball here in the north. Locally they call it the 'Tropics of the Northwest' because it is situated amongst a lush forest of poplar and birch and its warm climate and good soil permit a good growth of vegetables. Fort Liard is one of the oldest settlements in the north. The North West Company set up a trading post here in 1805 and it was here that Europeans first came into contact with the Dene First Nations of the area. This small community of 500 has limited accommodation facilities in the **Liard Valley General Store and Motel** (tel: 867.770.4441) and the **Riverside Inn** (tel: 867.770.3607), which also has a restaurant. There is also the **Hay Lake Campground** with toilets, firewood, and drinking water.

Nahanni National Park

Nahanni, in 1979, was the first national park in the world to be designated a World Heritage Site by UNESCO. This designation means that the park is a natural site of universal importance. The South Nahanni River, which thunders along for 322km in the park, divides this spectacular wilderness area. Slicing through four great canyons up to 1,200m deep, the river has created one of North America's finest wild streams. There are **hot springs** at Rabbitkettle and **Virginia Falls** is twice the height of Niagara and completely undeveloped. Also visually stunning are the **Sand Blowouts**, 1.6 hectares of soft sandstone on an exposed hillside which have been weathered by the swirling air currents into natural sculptures over 6m tall. There is a complicated area of what's called karst topography where a labyrinth of underground rivers, closed canyons and sinkholes abound and an extensive cave system in Grotte Valerie that includes more than 2km of linked natural passageways.

As far as wildlife goes there are 13 species of fish, 120 species of birds and 40 animal species, including grizzly and black bears, woodland caribou, beaver and wolf. Alongside 750 other plant species, numerous rare orchids grow around the area of Virginia Falls.

This area is also the stuff of legends. The lure of gold brought prospectors to this beautiful river valley and several of them disappeared supposedly into a cloud of mist. Headless bodies were apparently found at various times, leading to particular parts being called Deadman Valley and Headless Creek.

Access to the park is only by boat or float plane.

The most popular activity in Nahanni is **river touring** by inflatable raft, canoe or kayak. The choice is great. A 3-day 119-km paddle from Rabbitkettle Lake to Virginia Falls is for those who wish to take in the sights and scenery at a leisurely pace. For whitewater enthusiasts there is the 3–4 day trip of 136km from Virginia Falls down through the canyons to the Splits area. Four sets of whitewater punctuate this section, followed by calmer periods to relax and catch your breath. Lastly there is a 70km meandering section from the Splits to Nahanni Butte across a flood plain criss-crossed by numerous secondary channels. This last trip would take the average canoeist two or three days depending on your pace.

There are no developed **hiking** trails as such but the river does provide access to much of the park and several rather primitive routes have been created to points of interest such as the 8km hike to Sunblood Mountain, the 4km hike from Virginia Falls to Marengo Falls plus a couple of short hikes

THE CANOL HERITAGE TRAIL

This is Canada's greatest wilderness walk. It follows the road beside the old pipeline from Norman Wells (mile zero) to the Yukon border 372km away. To hike the entire trail will take you three to four weeks and there are no facilities whatsoever to stock up along the way. Following the road is not in itself difficult, but the logistics of food drops and crossing rivers make this all quite an adventure. There are a few huts along the route which were used and left by the pipeline construction crews and some are still habitable, with bunk beds and cooking stoves. Once you reach the Yukon there is a road that connects the trail to Ross River but you will need to organise a pick-up there otherwise you will have another 330km to walk.

through the karst area near Lafferty Creek and the short walk to see Rabbitkettle Hotsprings.

There are **campsites** at Rabbitkettle Lake, Virginia Falls and at Klaus Hotsprings.

Information and permits

If you want to travel through Nahanni National Park independently then you need to contact the Superintendent at Nahanni National Park, PO Box 300, Fort Simpson, NWT X0E 0N0 (tel: 867.695.2310).

MACKENZIE RIVER VALLEY
Fort Simpson

Fort Simpson is located at the confluence of the MacKenzie and Liard Rivers. It is the most developed community in the area and therefore has the regional headquarters for many government organisations. There is a hospital, RCMP detachment, general store, convenience store, an elementary and a high school, a post office and a library. Fort Simpson is the gateway to the Nahanni National Park and float planes pop in and out throughout the summer taking rafters and canoeists into the park or fishing parties to the numerous lakes for serious fishing.

History

Nothing existed at Fort Simpson before the time of Alexander MacKenzie's travel apart from a small fur-trading post belonging to the North West Company. MacKenzie realised its strategic importance and a settlement developed here from 1821 and was named Fort Simpson. It was to become an important staging post for the river traffic along the MacKenzie. Missions were establish in 1858 and there was some farming here until the road linking Fort Simpson to the rest of Canada made importing food more practical. In the 1960s the town became a base for oil exploration along the MacKenzie Valley and, subsequently, the region's administrative centre.

Where to stay and eat

The **Maroda Motel** (tel: 867.695.2602) and the **Nahanni Inn** (tel: 867.695.2201) are the only two hotels in town and are well positioned in the centre. They offer comfortable but limited facilities, although the Nahanni Inn has the greater number of rooms and a licensed dining room. There is also the pleasant **Bannockland Inn** (tel: 867.695.3337), about 4km outside town overlooking the Liard and MacKenzie River, which offers B&B. The **Northern** store has Pizza Hut and KFC take-aways.

Information

The **visitor centre** (tel: 867.695.3182) is at the south end of town. Inside there is a re-creation of the old Hudson Bay Company post and a few historical displays. Open 08.00–20.00 daily, mid-May to mid-September.

Wrigley

Wrigley is still a traditional community of Dene First Nations about a 2½ hour drive from Fort Simpson on an established gravel road. This is the furthest the all weather road has reached on its journey to Inuvik in the far north. About 200 people live here, mainly in log cabin style accommodation, and many of them still living off the land. There has been a community here since the North West Company opened a post in 1817, though the site of the settlement has moved several times. Today's site of the village is called Roche-qui-trempe-a-l'eau ('rock which plunges into the water'). There is only one place to stay, the **Petanea Co-op Hotel**, (tel: 867.581.3121), with 10 beds in five rooms. Room charges include meals.

Norman Wells

Norman Wells is 330km north of Wrigley on the MacKenzie Highway. This road is open only in winter, usually from mid-December until late March, so most visitors either fly in on daily scheduled flights or, once the river thaws out in June, come by boat from Yellowknife, Fort Simpson or Fort Providence.

As the name implies, Norman Wells was all about oil, that is until 1996 when it all closed down. It all came about during the World War II when there was a large US military presence in Alaska to curb a perceived threat from the Japanese. The troops needed fuel for their aircraft and ships and Norman Wells was the nearest place to get it from. They built a pipeline through the MacKenzie Mountains which became known as the Canol Project. Between 1942 and 1945 30,000 people laid 2,650km of pipeline, plus a communications system and a road beside it all. Within a year of it opening cheaper, more accessible oil was found elsewhere, and in 1947 the pipeline was dismantled.

Because of the oil industry Norman Wells is endowed with more hotels than most of the towns up north. The **MacKenzie Valley Hotel** (tel: 867.587.2511) sleeps 30 in 20 rooms. The **Rayuka Inn** (tel: 867.587.2354) is slightly smaller but has a restaurant in addition to the dining room. The **Yamouri Inn** (tel: 867.587.2744) also has a restaurant and coffee bar. There are no campgrounds in town but people have been known to pitch their tents on the banks of the MacKenzie River without too much bother.

Fort McPherson

Fort McPherson is on the Dempster Highway heading north out of Dawson City in the Yukon (see page 188 for a description of the Yukon section of this route). There has been a trading post here since 1840 when the Hudson Bay Company set up shop. Fort McPherson is most famous for the NWMP and later RCMP patrols that truly opened up the north. On one such patrol four men perished in terrible weather conditions (see *The Lost Patrol*, page 180). They are buried beside the Peel River and a monument stands to their memory. The **visitor centre** is open from mid-May until mid-September 09.00–21.00 daily. There is one hotel, the **Tetlit** (tel: 867.952.2602) whose eight rooms include all meals in the price. It is open all year round.

Inuvik

In 1953 the town at the top of the world was called Aklavik. In spring it usually flooded when the ice broke up and the Canadian government decided to move it 50km away to the site where Inuvik now stands. It is a matter of fact that Inuvik is probably the most planned town in the north. It was the first town above the Arctic Circle to be built to provide all the facilities you would expect of a town. There are banks, schools, a 55-bed hospital, an RCMP detachment and a CBC radio station. The town council even has plans for a nine-hole golf course. Inuvik is the major transportation hub of the north with daily flights to and from Yellowknife and all points north, supporting gas and oil exploration as well as the everyday needs of the town.

Getting around

The town has a **taxi** service if walking is too much (tel: 867.777.2525). There are no meters, just set fares at $4.50 anywhere in town. Fares to the airport are about $30. The visitor centre can also provide road and ferry information for those heading south along the Dempster Highway.

Where to stay and eat

Inuvik's three hotels all have restaurants, coffee shops and basic rooms with private facilities. They are the **MacKenzie Hotel** (tel: 867.777.2861), the **Eskimo Inn** (tel: 867.777.2801), and the **Finto Motor Inn** (tel: 867.777.2647). There are also a couple of B&Bs and guesthouses throughout town. For eating try the **Green Briar Dining Room** (in the MacKenzie Hotel). There is also a place called **To Go's**, the only snack bar in town, on MacKenzie Road.

What to see and do

Walking around the town could easily take you a day. Inuvik's most famous landmark must be **Our Lady of Victory Church,** more commonly known as the 'Igloo Church' because of its shape. The church may not always be open but it is worth visiting since the interior is decorated with a series of paintings

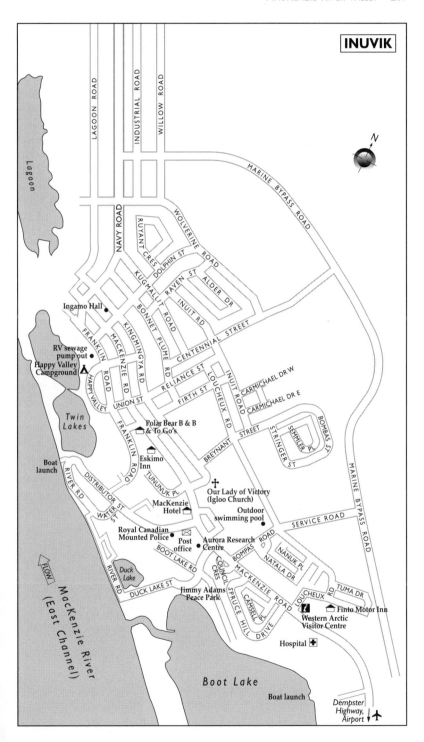

of the Stations of the Cross by the Inuvialuit artist Mona Thrasher. Ask at the rectory for a key if the church is closed or call at the Western Arctic Visitor Centre to arrange a time to visit. Nearby is the **Aurora Research Centre** (tel: 867.777.3838), one of the three support facilities in the NWT for Arctic scientific projects in the physical, social and life sciences (the others are at Iqaluit and Igloolik in the Eastern Arctic). You are welcome to stop by and check out what is happening at the centre. It has an extensive Arctic library.

The **Ingamo Hall**, Inuvik's Native Friendship Centre, is built of white spruce logs and is three storeys tall. What makes it really unusual is the fact that there are no trees this far north. More than 1,000 logs were cut down in southern NWT and rafted down the MacKenzie to build the hall. The hall is used for dances, bingo, workshops and public receptions. There is a **gift shop** attached called the Trading Post that sells native arts and crafts.

Tours can be organised to go birdwatching, see the outlying areas, visit **Herschel Island** in the Beaufort Sea or visit **Ivvavik National Park** to see muskoxen, caribou and barren-ground grizzly bears. Expect to pay about $250 per person per day for any outlying tours because there is usually a flight involved. A three-hour boat cruise with tea and bannock is usually about $40 and evening tours along the river with dinner will cost about $70 per person.

Further afield is **Paulatuk** and the **Cape Parry Bird Sanctuary**. Further still is the **Tuktut Nogait National Park**, a major staging area for the bluenose caribou herd. In spring many outfitters in Inuvik will take clients out to seek polar bears coming in off the melting sea ice around Amundsen Gulf.

Arctic Nature Tours (tel: 867.777.3400) can sort any trips you may desire this far north.

Information
The **Western Arctic Visitor Centre** (tel: 867.777.4727) has all the tour information you could want and is situated at the edge of town – about ten minutes' walk from the centre of things.

Health and safety
RCMP   867.777.2935
Hospital   867.777.2955

THE FAR NORTHERN COMMUNITIES
Various islands in the Arctic Ocean are also part of the Northwest Territories. Of these, two, one of them shared with Nunavut, are possibilities for tourist visits. They are Banks Island and Victoria island. There is only one NWT community on each island and, of the two islands, Banks is deemed to have the best wildlife viewing in all of the Western Arctic.

Banks Island
This island is wholly within the territory of NWT. It is the westernmost island of the Arctic Archipelago and sits north across Admundsen Gulf from Paulatuk. It is an island of barren, rolling hills with several rivers. The largest

river is the Thomsen River, the northernmost navigable river in Canada, which flows northward through **Aulavik National Park** and the Banks Island Bird Sanctuary. The park can only be reached by charter plane from Inuvik. The island has the world's largest population of muskoxen.

Sachs Harbour

This is Banks Island's only settlement. There are only about 140 people living here, mainly Inuvialuit. The settlement was established in the late 1920s and is thought to be one of the finest trapping areas in the Canadian Arctic. There is only one place to stay and that is **Kuptana's Guest House** (tel: 867.690.4151). There are ten beds in five rooms with satellite TV and home cooked meals. This establishment is typical of northern guesthouses with meals as part of the price and taken in a communal atmosphere at fixed times – nothing flashy here at all but very homely and comfortable. The owners can do tundra tours in summer and winter/spring to see muskoxen. There are three **flights** per week (Mon, Thu, Sat) to Sachs Harbour from Inuvik with Aklak Air (tel: 867.777.3777) of Inuvik. There are no restaurants and only a small grocery store. Check with the hamlet office before camping for permission and to organise the right place.

Victoria Island

This island was split between NWT and Nunavut when the dividing line was drawn on the map. There are two communities on the island but only one in each territory. NWT's community is called Holman and is situated on the western side of the island above Prince Albert Sound on the Diamond Jenness Peninsula.

Holman

This community of 325 people lies in an area traditionally hunted by the Copper Inuit in summer. The Hudson Bay Company set up a post at what is now Holman in 1939 and the Inuit settled around it. A missionary called the Reverend Henri Tardi taught the Inuit the art of printmaking and it is now one of the three income earners for the residents of Holman. The other two are hunting and trapping. This is a great area for fishing, with Arctic char and trout abundant. Holman has a **golf course**, the furthest north in the world (in case you are interested the latitude for this course is 70° 44' North). The golf course has an open tournament in mid-July called the Billy Joss Open which attracts many celebrity golfers from around the world.

There is only one hotel, the **Arctic Char Inn** (tel: 867.396.3501). It sleeps 16 in eight rooms. Non-residents can also eat at the inn. There is no campground as such but the locals camp on the shores of Okpilik Lake just outside town. The hamlet office is once again the place to ask about where to camp. Groceries are available at the **Northern** store. The only scheduled **flights** to Holman are from Yellowknife. First Air flies three times a week (Mon, Wed, Fri). Arctic Nature Tours in Inuvik (tel: 867.777.3400) can organise **nature tours** around Holman but trips will cost at least $500 per person per day.

Narwhal

Nunavut

Nunavut. Our Land. It has a nice ring to it. Most of us have a sense of national pride, whether we are Australian, British or American, but we seldom speak of 'our land', it is almost always 'our country'. The Inuit call their place 'Our Land' but their country is Canada to which they have an equal attachment. 'Our land' conjures up thoughts of belonging there in a very special sense. I have often heard farmers refer to their farms as our land, they not only own the land, it is part of them and they would not be whole without it. They also seem to think of themselves as holding their land in trust for their children and grandchildren. Some African tribes even believe that the land they live on is on loan from their children and that they must treat it well, otherwise there will be nothing left for those children.

The Inuit certainly have feelings that run as deep, though they do not express them this way. The Inuit are a woven part of their land. They feel it and it is a part of them. Everything they do effects it; everything in that land gives and takes in some big overall sharing process that would escape the thinking and attitudes of most modern Europeans today.

At first look, Nunavut is dull and barren, a seemingly lifeless frozen waste that is not fit for man or beast. But, as you come to know it, you become surprised by its beauty and it sort of sneaks up on you when you are not looking. You get used to looking where there was nothing and, suddenly, there's something.

Nunavut is a harsh and unforgiving land, yet it has some of the most tender moments – like when the flowers bloom suddenly in spring, all for a very few short weeks, carpeting all round you with the colours of the rainbow. It is a savage land. The weather at times is completely menacing, even life-threatening. There are the wild animals; the predators as big and as savage as they get but there is a gentleness when they are with their young. Nunavut is a land of juxtapositions and it takes time to get under the surface and see what the land is all about. You may love it or hate it but you will not come away without being moved by it.

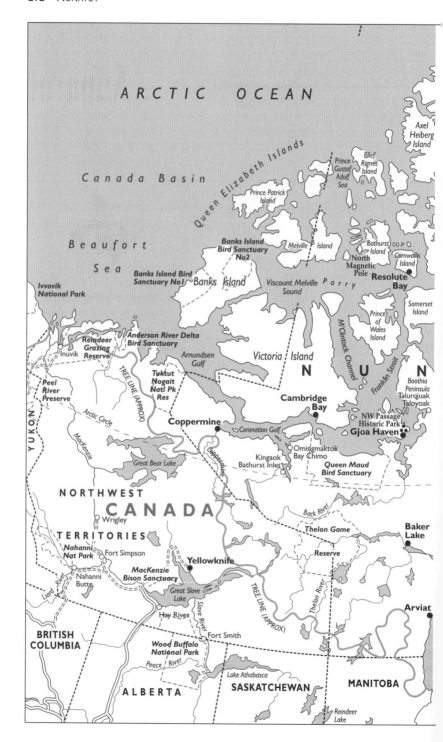

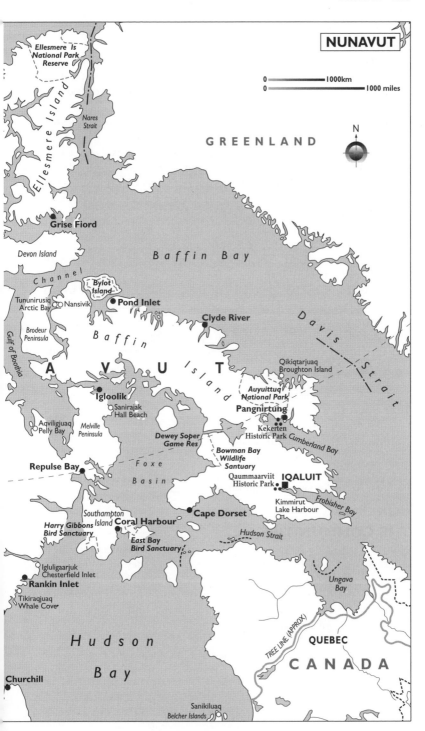

NUNAVUT FACTS

Area At 1,982,182km² Nunavut is more than one fifth of Canada's landmass. It includes 149,853km² of fresh water, and forested land covers 44,797km² or 2.26%. 100% of Nunavut is considered wilderness.

Boundaries To the south the line of 60°N latitude bordering with Manitoba; the western boundary is with Northwest Territories. It includes all of Canada east of Northwest Territories that is not a part of Québec or Newfoundland and extending to a line along the 60°W longitude that is not within the territory of Greenland. It includes the islands of Hudson Bay, James Bay and Ungava Bay that are not within the provinces of Manitoba, Ontario or Québec. In the north the boundary is the limit of Canadian territory between the lines of longitude 110°W and 60°W towards the North Pole.

Time Central (GMT −6hr). There is Daylight Saving Time from April to October (GMT −7hr).

Population 27,219. Some 85% of the population are Inuit spread throughout the territory's 28 communities. Population density of Nunavut is 0.013 persons per km².

Capital Iqaluit (est. population on April 1 1999 4,556).

Territorial status Nunavut became a separate territory of Canada on April 1 1999.

Tour operators

Frontiers North info@frontiersnorth.com

Northwinds Arctic Adventures www.northwinds-arctic.com; email plandry@nunanet.com. Specialising in Northern outdoor equipment rental throughout Nunavut. Tours, dogsledging, north pole, expedition outfitting etc

Bathurst Arctic Services www.virtualnorth.com/bathurst. Canoe rentals throughout Nunavut

THE COMMUNITIES

Nunavut is made up of communities. None of them is connected to any of the others by road, only by air and sometimes by sea. They are spread out right across the Arctic Archipelago with usually only one community on each island. There are 28 of them all told. Some are known by their Inuit names and others by the name they were given by Europeans. In the listings that follow both names are given in the headings with the Inuit name in Roman type and the European one in Italic (though this will normally be obvious). Names in brackets are the old names that have now dropped out of use forever. In general I will use the community's common usage name throughout the ordinary text.

I have covered most of the communities below, though I have left out some which are very small because tourists and travellers venture there only under extremely rare circumstances. There are generally no facilities at all for travellers and the communities themselves offer no programmes or sights to visit and just feeding an extra mouth can weigh down the whole system. Transport to and from these communities is also extremely infrequent with perhaps a single flight per week. I hope the communities themselves will forgive me for omitting them; as they grow and develop they can be added to future editions.

THE BAFFIN ISLAND COMMUNITIES

Baffin Island is the fifth largest island on earth after Greenland, New Guinea, Borneo and Madagascar. At 507,500 km² it's roughly four times the size of England with a total population of less than 10,000 people. This is an island of rugged beauty and extreme diversity. The island is 1,600km long and the north shore is indented with bays and inlets flanked by soaring cliffs. There are one national park, three bird sanctuaries, four territorial parks, an historical park and a wildlife sanctuary. Just for your interest there are no muskoxen on Baffin Island, something that took me a while to find out.

Iqaluit (Frobisher Bay)

Iqaluit (pronounced Ee-kal-oo-it) is the new capital of Nunavut. The Inuit have been in the area for centuries. The Thule and Dorset explorers came here thousands of years ago as the area was a prime hunting and fishing region. There were berries and other types of edible vegetation in season and these nomadic hunters would stay as long as the game did then move on to other areas where the animals were plentiful.

An English sailor, Martin Frobisher, discovered the bay in 1576 while searching for the Northwest Passage. He came here three times during the rest of that decade trying unsuccessfully to find gold. He had several skirmishes with the Inuit, losing five men on one occasion. They were taken hostage and were never seen again. At another time he took four Inuit back to England to show them off but they all died before coming home to tell the tale. Frobisher marked the bay on his maps and during the 18th and 19th centuries other explorers and whalers took shelter in the bay as and when needed. Still there was little contact between the Inuit and the Europeans.

During World War II the Americans, with Canada's permission, built an airstrip at what became known as Frobisher Bay that was long enough to handle large aircraft transporting war materials from the USA to her European allies. The local Inuit were at this time recruited to help with construction and other work and this was the beginning of the first serious contact between Europeans and the Inuit on a broad scale. It was not long before the airbase and its little village appeared on all the maps as Frobisher Bay. The local Inuit, however, have long known the place as Iqaluit – meaning 'a school of fish'. The Hudson Bay Trading Company arrived in 1950 from their post 50km to the south on the edge of the bay. Things heated up when the first crews and supplies arrived for the construction of the DEW Line. By 1963, though, the Americans had turned over the air base to the Canadians and gone home.

STAYING IN SMALL COMMUNITIES

Except for in Iqaluit, accommodation in the communities in Nunavut is scarce. The bigger communities have numerous establishments that resemble real hotels and motels and many have more than one. All invariably have restaurants and these, in general, are open to members of the public as well as being for the guests. But normally there is only one place to stay and the beds are very limited and, for the most part, meals are included in the bill. None of these establishments is cheap. Everything has to come by the annual barge or by plane, making supplies costly and limited in range.

Food is nothing special except when 'country fayre' is served. Vegetarians and vegans aren't really catered for but most cooks and hotel owners will try if asked. It is possible that you may want to assist in the cooking and I am sure all the cooks will oblige you there. In most places guests' meal times are generally fixed for certain hours and you are expected to notify them if you will be delayed. They waste nothing in the north. Some establishments will prepare you a lunch box if asked and providing that you can notify them in advance they will leave a prepared meal behind so you can warm it up in a microwave oven when you return from your outing if you expect to be late.

I have found meals left for me in some places when I have been out all day and some of the night, but that is not the norm and is usually someone being very kind to me. If this does happen please offer some form of thanks as this is truly appreciated and will allow the same special service to continue. At the Iglu Hotel in Baker Lake I found it most delightful that the

Canada made Iqaluit an administrative centre for Baffin Island and an administrative and communications centre for the whole of the Eastern Arctic. When autonomy arrived on April 1 1999 Iqaluit was well placed to become the territorial capital.

Getting there/about

Iqaluit is serviced directly from Ottawa by Canadian and First Air and from Montréal by First Air. There are also flights from Winnipeg and Yellowknife via Rankin Inlet by First Air, Canadian, Air Canada. Taxis have no meters but cost a flat $4.00 to anywhere in town. Do not expect the direct route – they will stop to drop off or pick up other passengers along the way. Welcome to the north.

Where to stay

Iqaluit is growing – rapidly – and so is its accommodation. There is more choice of accommodation in Iqaluit than anywhere else in Nunavut though nothing accommodation-wise in the north is cheap. Top of the bill is the **Regency Frobisher Inn** (tel: 867.979.2222) with 50 rooms in either single or double occupancy. An expansion programme, due for completion in 2001, will cook Peggy, bless her, would leave me meals whether I asked her to or not. It was really appreciated on the nights where I had had a long photographic session and was desperate for a good meal. In other places the restaurants will shut at a stated closing time and you go hungry if you are late. Often as not the whole area is closed off so you can't even make yourself a snack.

Some forms of accommodation resemble someone's home. It probably was once upon a time and they have turned it over to a burgeoning and growing requirement. Rarely are rooms on a single basis and they are usually shared if the house is full. Some have almost dormitory-style accommodation. You could be sharing with other tourists, or miners, construction workers, businessmen, fishermen or hunters.

Simple courtesies work here. Most of the owners will go out of their way to assist you. It is the personal touch of the north that I like. Please return the goodwill. If you expect nothing and get everything you have done well. If you expect nothing and get something, things are as they should be. Everyone will want to know your business and you should freely offer it. New conversation makes the harsh life up north more interesting.

One other word of warning. The Inuit do not generally recognise privacy in the way that other North Americans or Europeans do. They have never felt the need for it themselves and so just walk into a house looking for someone when they feel like it. It is not rudeness but it does seem odd. Patience and tolerance and an acceptance of someone else's lifestyle are all that is needed.

add another 50 rooms. A full list of services is available with licensed dining room, cocktail bar, restaurant and conference facilities. Two other fine hotels are the **Discovery Lodge Hotel** (tel: 867.979.4433) and the **Navigator Inn** (tel: 867.979.6201), both have plenty of fine rooms and all the usual services. The **campground** is at the Sylvia Grinnell Territorial Park near the airport. It is a bit of a walk into town but there are tent platforms, pit toilets, foul-weather shelters and fire pits.

Something new and quiet and away from the main town is **Accommodations by the Sea** (tel: 867.979.6074) overlooking Frobisher Bay with private and shared facilities. There are five double rooms and meals are by request.

Where to eat
All the above hotels/inns have excellent restaurants offering a wide range of menus but expect them to hit your pocket. Nunavut is not a place to be on a budget. Popular with the locals is the **Kamotiq Inn Restaurant**. It is built to look like an igloo and has two dining rooms. The **Quick Stop** convenience store has the Pizza Hut and KFC and a place called **The Snack** has a large eat-

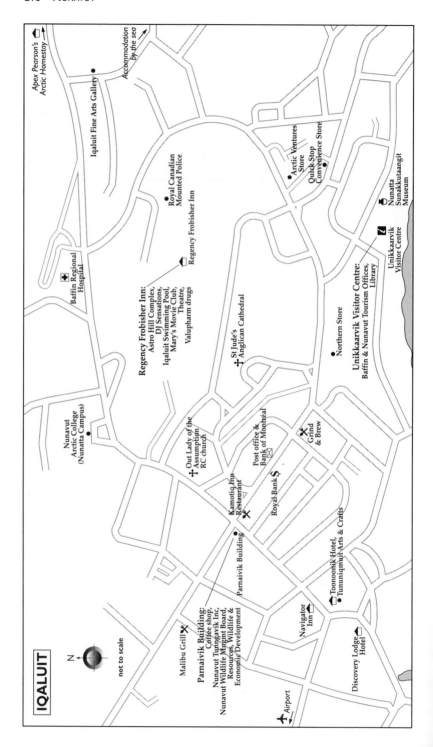

IQALUIT

N

not to scale

Apex Pearson's
Arctic Homestay

Iqaluit Fine Arts Gallery

Accommodation
by the sea

Royal Canadian
Mounted Police

Regency Frobisher Inn

Arctic Ventures
Store

Quick Stop
Convenience Store

Nunatta
Sunakkutaangit
Museum

Unikkaarvik
Visitor Centre

Baffin Regional
Hospital

Regency Frobisher Inn:
Astro Hill Complex,
DJ Sensations,
Iqaluit Swimming Pool,
Mary's Movie Club,
Theatre,
Valupharm drugs

St Jude's
Anglican Cathedral

Northern Store

Unikkaarvik Visitor Centre:
Baffin & Nunavut Tourism Offices,
Library

Nunavut
Arctic College
(Nunatta Campus)

Out Lady of the
Assumption
RC church

Post office &
Bank of Montréal

Grind
& Brew

Kamotiq Inn
Restaurant

Royal Bank

Parnaivik Building

Toonoonik Hotel,
Tununiqmiut Arts & Crafts

Malibu Grill

Parnaivik Building:
Coffee shop,
Nunavut Tunngavik Inc,
Nunavut Wildlife Mngmt Board,
Resources, Wildlife &
Economic Development

Navigator
Inn

Discovery Lodge
Hotel

Airport

in or take-out menu with pizza, burgers, sandwiches and the like. Those who are camping can pick up groceries at the **Northern** or **Arctic Ventures** stores.

What to see and do
Popular for a little stroll or a simple day walk is to go to the **Sylvia Grinnell Territorial Park**. The town itself is a little large for a stroll and there is amazingly little to see. The **visitor centre** (tel: 867.979.4636) and the **Nunatta Sunakkutaangit Museum** (tel: 867.979.5537) next door are well worth a visit. They both have some great displays plus some permanent collections of artefacts that relate to the history of Baffin Island. Remember that Iqaluit is the gateway to Baffin Island and the rest of Nunavut, not a destination in its own right as such.

Entertainment
There is a **cinema** at the Astro Hill Theatre (tel: 867.979.4781) and several stores rent videos if you have a VCR. The town also has a skating arena, a curling rink and a swimming pool, but this is usually closed in the summer.

Shopping
The Inuit are great artists. Much of their work reflects the natural environment. They work in soapstone, stone, metal, ivory (walrus tusk), bone and antler. There is weaving, silkscreen printing and animal hide decoration as well as traditional clothing. The **Arts and Crafts Centre** is located in the Nunavut Arctic College but you might also like to try **Coman Arctic Galleries**, **Iqaluit Fine Arts Gallery**, **Northern Country Arts** and **Tununiqmuit Arts and Crafts**. They all have fine reputations for quality goods.

Tour operators in Iqaluit
NorthWinds Arctic Adventures (tel: 867.979.0551) does dog-sledging and polar trekking on Baffin Island plus trips to Greenland and the North Pole. Paul Landry and his partner Maddy McNair are your hosts here.

Emergencies
RCMP   tel: 867.979.5211
Hospital   tel: 867.979.7300
Ambulance   tel: 867.979.4422

Kinngait/Cape Dorset
Cape Dorset's Inuktitut name means 'high mountains' and it describes the steep rocky hills that overlook the town. The first Europeans arrived in the 17th century but the Inuit and their ancestors, the Thule and Dorset, have been here for 3,500 years. Between 1850 and the early 1900s whalers and missionaries alike visited the area. In 1913 the Hudson Bay Company set up a trading post where the town now stands. By 1953 there were two churches, a school and a few houses. The town is only 1.2km from one end to the other and walking it you will see a nice blend of modern and traditional Inuit culture

with snowmobiles and all-terrain vehicles parked outside the homes, beside fish drying on racks and polar bear and seal skin hides hanging on railings. The two hotels in town are the **Kinngait Inn** (tel: 867.897.8863) with 17 rooms and the **Polar Lodge** (tel: 867.897.8335) with eight double rooms. Rates are available with or without meals. **Huit Huit Tours** (tel: 867.897.8806) does everything from community tours to ice fishing, floe edge tours, camping and traditional cultural evenings of story-telling and throat singing.

Pannirtuuq/Pangnirtung

Pangnirtung means 'place of the bull caribou'. The community is normally just called Pang. It is quite heavily populated with about 1,200 people. Pang is located on a narrow coastal plain on the edge of a fjord that runs into Cumberland Sound. Inuit have lived here for thousands of years hunting seals, walrus and beluga whales and taking the odd bowhead that entered the local waters.

In 1839 a Scottish whaler called William Penny took an Inuk named Eenoolooapik to Scotland for the winter. He returned the following spring and guided Penny to Cumberland Sound. What followed was 80 years of whale exploitation. It changed the way the Inuit lived from a nomadic existence to that of settled people in the whaling stations. When whaling declined the Inuit returned to the old ways.

The Hudson Bay Company set up a post here in 1921 and two years later the RCMP arrived. In 1956 the first teacher was appointed and in 1962 an administrative office opened. Distemper killed off most of the Inuit dogs that same year and they were forced to move into town. Pang was a flourishing seal hunting community until prices dropped. The community currently operates a turbot fishery and the local Inuit are renowned for their weaving.

Parks Canada has an interpretive centre with displays and exhibits of the varied nature of nearby Auyuittuq National Park. There is only one hotel in town, the **Auyuittuq Lodge** (tel: 867.473.8955), which accommodates 50 in 25 rooms with shared facilities. It has a dining room and a TV lounge. Campers can stay at the **Pisuktina Tungavik Territorial Campground** for free but there is not much there. The **Northern** store has a Quick-stop for Pizza Hut and KFC but not much else.

Auyuittuq National Park

Auyuittuq National Park was the first park designated north of the Arctic Circle in 1972. It is popular with hikers, climbers and cross-country skiers. The park's entrance is 25km from Pang at a place called Overlord and depending on the season local outfitters will take you there by either snowmobile or boat (the walk in summer takes two days). There are campsites around the warder's cabin at Overlord and limited toilet facilities (outhouse). Fresh water is drawn from a nearby stream. The trails are well marked. This is really a summer destination and not for the inexperienced walker. The glacial landscape is splendid but you are unlikely to see vast numbers of wildlife. As with all of Canadian national parks there is a fee to enter the park. One day is

$15, $40 for three nights and $100 for more than three days. Remember that in Canada's parks you will be charged for any search and rescue. The **park office** is in Pang (tel: 867.473.8828).

Kangiqtugaapik/Clyde River

Clyde River's Inuit name means 'nice little inlet' and the town is in Patricia Bay off Clyde Inlet on the east coast of Baffin Island. This is very much a traditional Inuit community with most families involved in hunting and camping activities. With the decline in the market for sealskins and other furs, most employment is in government jobs and handicrafts, but there is still some subsistence hunting. This is the place to experience the real Inuit way of life with travel by dogteam and local home stays popular. There is only one hotel in the community. The **Qammaq Hotel** (tel: 867.924.6201) has 12 beds in double occupancy rooms. Meals are included in the rates but non-residents can book to eat there. The **visitor centre** (tel: 867.924.6034) can arrange outfitters and homestays and the **Northern** and **Manimiut** stores both sell groceries and other necessities. There are cooking facilities available at the visitor centre. There is a health centre, RCMP and post office in the community as well.

Mittimatalik/Pond Inlet

Pond Inlet is at the northern tip of Baffin Island and is considered to be the most beautiful place in all of Nunavut. Pond Inlet is probably the best place to see wildlife on Baffin – caribou, wolves and more than 30 species of nesting birds are found locally. Most popular are trips to the floe edge in spring to see polar bears. Narwhal, beluga and walrus are also here and there are several outstanding archaeological sites nearby. Local activities include cross-country skiing, dogsledging, snowmobiling, hiking and kayaking. Once again only one hotel, the **Sauniq Hotel** (tel: 867.899.8928), with 17 rooms with double occupancy and private facilities. Prices are available with or without meals and non-residents have to book meals. The **Toonoonik Sahoonik Co-op** (tel: 867.899.8912) operates a restaurant that is open during store hours. There are several outfitters in town and all can be booked through **Tununiq Travel** (tel: 867.899.8994). In the community there is a health centre, RCMP and a post office.

Bylot Island

Perched 700km above the Arctic Circle is Bylot Island, one of the richest wildlife habitats in Nunavut. It can only be reached via Pond Inlet but travellers can go the year round except when the ice is breaking up in July or during freeze-up in October/November. What makes it so important is the large *polynya* in Baffin Bay to the east of Bylot Island. *Polynyas* are areas of unfrozen open water created by warm, upwelling sea currents which prevent the surface from freezing. In the midst of normally frozen pack ice the floe edges created by this *polynya* are vital as feeding areas for a wide variety of marine animals.

Polar bears den on the island's northeast coast and alongside these massive animals are walrus, five species of seal, narwhal, beluga, bowhead and orcas in summer. There are an estimated 300,000 thick-billed murres and 80,000 black-legged kittiwakes nesting on the island's cliffs during the summer. Outfitters can be organised from Pond Inlet.

THE MAINLAND COMMUNITIES
Arviat

Arviat (pronounced Ar-vee-at) is quite a big community on the edge of Hudson Bay with over 1,500 residents. It used to be called Eskimo Point and you may still see this on some older maps. This place has always been the traditional site for various groups of coastal and inland Inuit to get together. Today the community is rich in traditional values and knowledge and hunting traditions are still maintained. The **Arviat Tourism Office** (tel:867.857.2941) can arrange anything you would like to do in the area. Dog sledging and snowmobiling are popular to see polar bears hunting seals. There is good fishing locally for trout, grayling and arctic char. Once again only one hotel, **Padlei Inns North** (tel: 867.857.2919), with ten beds in five rooms and a dining room open to non-residents. **Ralph's B&B** has nine beds in six rooms and can do all meals. Non-residents need to book meals. **Jeannie's Bakery** and **Neevee's Coffee Shop** offer confectionery and fast foods.

Kangiqsliniq/Rankin Inlet

Rankin Inlet is a big community, Nunavut's second largest in fact, and when viewed from the air this is quite obvious. It is an important centre for cross-Nunavut travel with one of the busiest airports in the territory. Rankin Inlet also likes to describe itself as the 'business capital' of Nunavut and for the past 20 years it has also been the administrative centre for the Kivalliq region – one of the many administrative districts that made up the original Northwest Territories and has now been absorbed into the new territory of Nunavut.

The land surrounding Rankin is of rolling hills and open tundra and readily accessible from town. A short walk away from the edge of the hamlet and you are in wilderness. I have found Rankin cold but that is due to its openness and the wind for which it is famous. Rankin is the major jumping off point for the ecotourist facility of **Sila Lodge** (contact Frontiers North Inc in Winnipeg, Manitoba, tel: 204.949.2050) on Wager Bay. This is a prime area to watch polar bears and caribou in their natural habitat and at close range. There are two hotels in Rankin; the **Siniktarvik** (tel: 867.645.2949) is the business facility in town with 94 rooms, gift shops and a restaurant. The other is the **Nanuq Inn** (tel: 867.645.2513) which although smaller and less luxurious is quite comfortable. It, too, has a restaurant. The **Nunavut Tourism** office (tel: 867.645.3838) is located at the airport and there are several outfitters in town which can provide dogteams and sea kayaking as well as journeys onto the tundra by all-terrain vehicles. For dog sledging try **Tumi Tours** (tel: 867.645.2650).

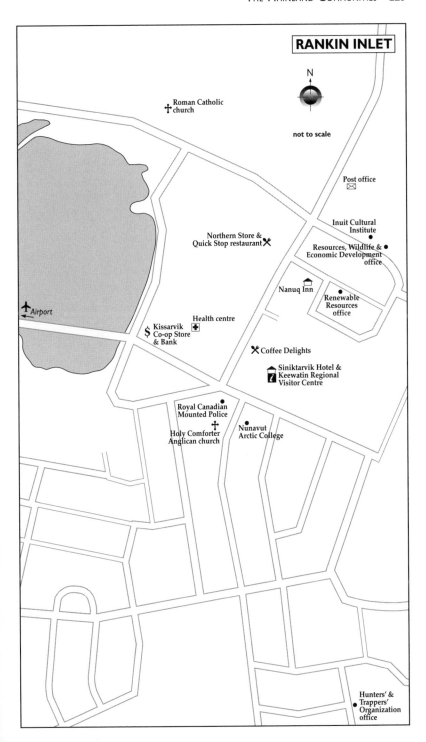

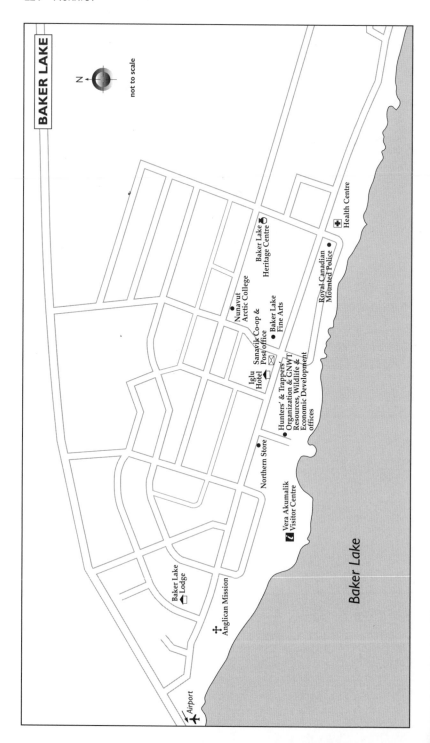

BAKER LAKE

not to scale

Health Centre

Baker Lake
Heritage Centre

Nunavut
Arctic College

Baker Lake
Fine Arts

Royal Canadian
Mounted Police

Sanavik Co-op &
Post office

Iglu
Hotel

Hunters' & Trappers'
Organization & GNWT
Resources, Wildlife &
Economic Development
offices

Northern Store

Vera Akumalik
Visitor Centre

Baker Lake
Lodge

Anglican Mission

Baker Lake

Airport

Qamani'tuaq/Baker Lake

Baker Lake is the geographical centre of Canada and home to the only inland group of Inuit. This is a small community but one that has a warm and friendly feel to it. Unfortunately when I was here most of the town's population was out for the annual caribou hunt at the southern end of the lake. Tourist information is available from the **Vera Akumalik Visitor Centre** (tel: 867.793.2874) in the old Hudson Bay post. There are two hotels in the community, the **Iglu Hotel** (tel: 867.793.2801) and the **Baker Lake Lodge** (tel: 867.793.2905). The Iglu is the bigger and meals are included. Its dining room is open to non-residents as well. It is a really friendly place with everyone quite chatty. There is a **campground** on the lakeshore between the community and the airport, with tent pads, bathroom and shelter. The **Northern** store has a quick stop fast food place with, you guessed it, Pizza Hut and KFC. **Edwin Evo** can provide tours of the local area (tel: 867.793.2293), and a must-see is the **Baker Lake Heritage Centre**. It has a stunning display of Inland Inuit life and it is a good place to meet some of the elders and listen to a few stories.

Naujaat/Repulse Bay

The only community actually on the Arctic Circle, its most recent claim to fame is the bowhead whale hunt in 1996 (see *Whalers and sealers*, page 12). This is a very traditional community of hunting, fishing and trapping. Belugas, narwhals, seals, caribou, walrus and lots of fish are all here in abundance. **Inns North** (tel: 867.462.9943) is the only hotel and has 11 rooms accommodating 23 people. There is a TV lounge and meals are provided. Non-guests can also eat here. Contact the **Arviq Hunters' and Trappers' Organisation** if you want to go out with the Inuit (tel: 867.462.4334). The hotel should also be able to help.

Kugluktuk/Coppermine

Kugluktuk or 'place of moving water' is set between the Coppermine River and the shores of Coronation Gulf on the Arctic Ocean. It is the traditional home of the Copper Inuit (their weapons and tools were made from copper). Unfortunately I have never stayed here and have only passed through with a 20-minute stop-over at the airport. There are two hotels in town, the **Coppermine Inn** (tel: 867.982.3333) and The **Enokhok Inn** (tel: 867.982.31297). They offer the usual services for hotels up here including meals. I am told the **heritage centre** is well worth a visit (tel: 867.982.3232).

Victoria Island
Kaluktutiak/Cambridge Bay

I came here to see muskoxen. They are just outside the town all year round and you rarely have to travel far to see at least one. Cambridge Bay is the regional centre and was Canada's most westerly station in the DEW (Defence Early Warning) line of strategic warning radar stations set up by

BIRDS OF CAMBRIDGE BAY AREA
Kevin Smart, Department of Sustainable Development

Snowy owl	Nesting in large numbers when lemming population is high
Short-eared owl	Very few
Rough-legged hawk	Common: Mt Pelly, West Arm, Dew Line Road
Peregrine falcon	Common: Mt Pelly, West Arm, Long Point, Augustus Hills
Common raven	Common all year
Long-tailed jaeger	Common, nesting on the tundra
Pomarine jaeger	Common in years when there are plenty of lemmings
Parasitic jaeger	Common during years of high lemming population
Rock ptarmigan	Nest in the area but at times difficult to spot
Willow ptarmigan	Nest in the area but at times difficult to spot
Glaucous gull	Common
Thayer's gull	Not as plentiful
Sabine's gull	Common
Arctic tern	Common
Tundra swans	Common
Sandhill crane	Sometimes hard to find
Canada goose	Common
Greater white-fronted goose	'Speckle Belly' Common
Snow goose	Not as plentiful
Red-throated loon	Common
Pacific loon	Common
Yellow-billed loon	Can be seen in the larger lakes
Red-breasted merganser	Few
King eider	Common, males leave nesting area late June/early July
Common eider	Some
Red phalarope	Common
Red-necked phalarope	Common
Oldsquaw	Common
Northern pintail	Common, sometimes hard to locate
Buff-breasted sandpiper	Difficult to locate

the USA and Canada during the Cold War. A large communications facility is still here. For information on the town and its surrounding go to the **Arctic Coast Visitor Centre** (tel: 867.983.2224). Very helpful staff and a good place for a sit and read. They may even offer you coffee. There are a couple of hotels in town but highly recommended is the **Arctic Islands**

Stilt sandpiper	Common
Baird's sandpiper	Common
Pectoral sandpiper	Common
Black-bellied plover	Common
Semipalmated sandpiper	Common
Ruddy turnstone	Common
Semipalmated plover	Common
Snow bunting	Common
Lapland longspur	Common
Horned lark	Common
American pipit	Mt Pelly
Red knot	Top of Mt Pelly
Savannah sparrow	Some
White-rumped sandpiper	Scarce (hard to find)
Brant	Common
Sanderling	migrating in August
Dunlin	Rare
Whimbrel	Uncommon
Merlin	Uncommon
Gyrfalcon	Rare (migrating?)
Yellow-rumped warbler	Occasionally
Mountain bluebird	Nested and raised 3 young in 1995
Barn swallow	Rare (1999)
Varied thrush	A couple observed 1997/98/99
Hermit thrush	Rare
American robin	Rare 1998
Dark-eyed junco	Rare 1997 (Fall)
Harris' sparrow	Rare
Thick-billed murre	Rare
Northern shoveler	Rare (1998)
Ross' goose	Rare
Hoary redpoll	Few
Common redpoll	Few

Additional sightings

Cliff swallow	Observed 1997 (dead)
Common goldeneye	Observed 1997

Lodge (tel: 867.983.2345). It is the most comfortable place I have ever stayed in up north. The other establishment is the **Ikaluktutiak Co-op/Inns North** (tel: 867.983.2215). Both offer all the facilities you could want and more. They can organise local tours to see the surrounding area and the wildlife.

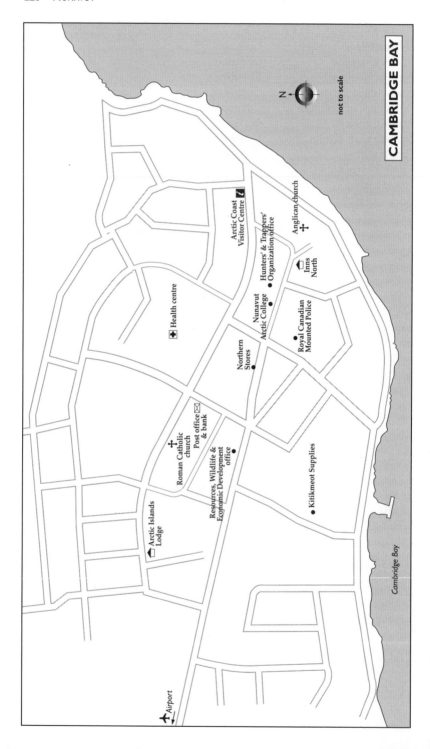

CAMBRIDGE BAY

King William Island
Oqsuqtooq/Gjoa Haven
The Norwegian explorer Amundsen called Gjoa Haven the finest little harbour in the world. To the locals its name means 'place of plenty of blubber', something to do with the large herds of seals that once flourished here. Today Gjoa Haven is better known as the home of the **North West Passage Historic Park**. There are two hotels in town; the **Amundsen** (tel: 867.360.6176) is newer, and longer-established is **Mary's Inn** (tel: 867.360.6032). Both do meals and offer food to non-residents.

Southampton Island
Salliq/Coral Harbour
Coral Harbour is situated at the southern end of Southampton Island and at the northern end of Hudson Bay. It is a big community of about 730 people. There are walrus, beluga whales, several species of seal and polar bears here. The best place to see walrus is on Coats Island about 7 hours south by boat or on Walrus Island, a small rocky outcrop somewhere in the middle of the two. Polar bears are plenty and they do like walrus calf. Coral Harbour gets its name from the coral that's found in the bay's icy waters indicating that at some point this region must have been tropical. Only two places to stay, **Leonie's Place** (tel: 867.925.9751) and the **Co-op Esungarq Motel** (tel: 867.925.9926). **Kajjaarnaq Arctic Tours** (tel: 867.925.8366) does tours to see walrus and other wildlife and can organise dog teams and snowmobiles for trips further inland. Walrus viewing is purely a summer and autumn activity as the sea ice is not safe to travel across over the vast distances needed to get to where the animals are.

Cornwallis Island
Qausuittuq/Resolute Bay
People come here to head for the North Pole and it strikes me that this is the only reason for the place existing. There are only a couple of hundred people living here. Yet it has excellent air transport to other parts of Canada and Greenland and really is the stepping-off point for anyone wishing to travel to either the magnetic or geographic poles. There are just a couple of places to stay here. The **Narwhal Inn** (tel: 867.252.3968) and the **Tudjaat Inns North** (tel: 867.252.3900) both have single and double occupancy, cafeteria style and home-cooked meals. The cost will be frightening for the average traveller but for those heading for the poles it will not be of a consequence in the overall budget. No one comes for an off-chance spot of touring here but it does get busy during the trekking season in summer.

Ellesmere Island
Ausuittuq/Grise Fiord
This is another little community that was established to confirm Canadian sovereignty over the Arctic Archipelago. It is Canada's most northerly community. This is the place of icebergs, glaciers and stunning mountain

vistas. The Inuktitut name means 'place that never melts or thaws out'. The only hotel in the community is the **Grise Fiord Lodge** (tel: 867.980.9913), which has nine rooms and rates include meals. There is a TV lounge. There are no restaurants in Grise Fiord bar the hotel. There are walrus, beluga whales, seals, polar bears, guillemots and murres in the local area. People come here mainly to photograph icebergs and the seascape. The town is a stepping off point for other activities on Ellesmere Island such as trekking and sea kayaking. For Ellesmere activities in Iqaluit try **North Winds Arctic Adventures** (867.979.0551 or www.northwinds-arctic.com) or in the UK try either **Arcturus** (tel: 01389 830204 or arcturus@btinternet.com) or **Windows on the Wild** (tel: 020 8742 1556 or www.windows- on-the-wild.com).

Iglulik/Igloolik

Igloolik is an off-the-beaten-track destination for travellers to the Arctic. The geographic centre of Nunavut, it is blessed with an abundance of wildlife and the Inuit culture that thrives on it. Walruses, seals, polar bears, caribou and whales are all to be seen here at various times of the year. There are numerous archaeological sites from the Thule and Dorset cultures dotted throughout the island, but these need to be visited when the island is snow free from mid-June to mid-September. Igloolik Island is relatively flat, making it perfect terrain for dog-sledging, and late April to September is the best time when there is almost permanent daylight and the temperatures rise to an acceptable level. Until mid-July travel is mainly by dog-team but once the sea ice breaks up boats are used to see walrus resting on floating pack ice and bowhead whales as they migrate north toward their summer feeding grounds near Foxe Basin.

There is only one hotel in town, the **Tujormivik Hotel** (tel: 867.934.8814) with eight rooms, seven of which can accommodate up to three people. The restaurant serves non-resident guests. The only other restaurant (tel: 867.934.8595) is operated by the **Igloolik Co-op** which also has a coffee shop (tel: 867.934.8948) that offers light snacks.

Tour operators

The **Hunters and Trappers Organisation** (tel: 867.934.8807) organises tours, as does Igloolik Outdoor Adventures (tel: 867.934.8759).

Tours can also be organised through **Frontiers North** in Winnipeg (tel: 204.949.2050 or e-mail: info@frontiersnorth.com).

The Fringes

ALASKA

This, of course, is not primarily a guidebook about Alaska – after all it is certainly not a part of northern Canada – but it is oh so close. Certain parts of the state certainly reflect that spirit of the north where the very nature of the people extends beyond national boundaries. Thinking about the Yukon without Alaska would be like cutting off your hand; you could function quite adequately but things would seem a whole lot easier if you were complete. The terrain is similar; the people are very much alike; and the wildlife regularly moves between states blissfully unaware of the imaginary line that humans have drawn on their maps.

I did not discover this properly until I went to the Yukon Quest International Sled Dog Race a couple of years ago. The Yukoners and the Alaskans seem to come from the same mould. They have a similar outlook on life; speak in the same terms; tolerate the same weather conditions for the most part; and have similar attitudes and expectations of a people living in a relatively harsh environment with only themselves for help and assistance. It is this northern spirit that leads me to incorporate some of the eastern parts of Alaska into this book because it is as much a part of the region as the Yukon is itself.

Many visitors to the Yukon choose to touch on part of Alaska by travelling in the circular route between Whitehorse and Dawson City along the AlCan Highway and returning along the Klondike Highway. By following the AlCan out of Whitehorse until you reach Tetlin Junction inside Alaska you then turn north along the Taylor Highway towards Chicken and Boundary before crossing back into Canada and taking the Top of the World Highway to Dawson City. From Dawson it is downhill all the way along the Klondike Highway back to Whitehorse. This gives all those travelling through the Yukon a circular route to travel rather than travelling to and from Dawson along the same road. The AlCan is tar sealed all the way now but once you reach Tetlin Junction it turns into a well-made gravel pitch road all the way to Dawson. From Beaver Creek, where you leave the Yukon on this route, to Dawson City via the AlCan, Taylor and Top of the World Highways should take you about 10 hours and unless you are self-sufficient and self-contained you should anticipate doing this section of the journey in a single day.

It is important to remember that distances in the USA are always given in miles in all official information, making life confusing when coming from Canada where the distances are in kilometres.

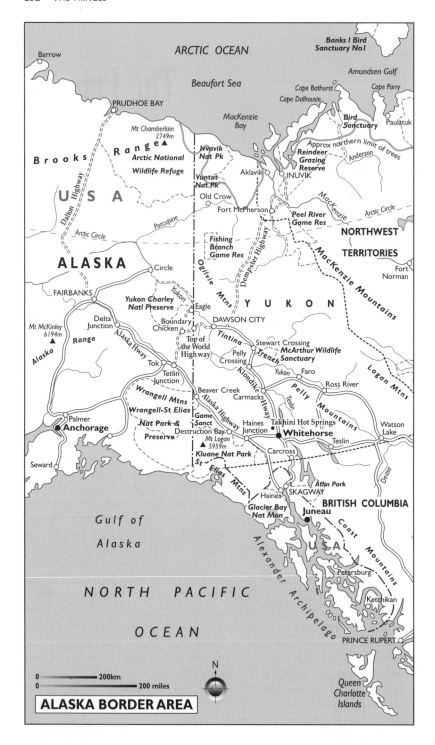

Barrow

ARCTIC OCEAN

Banks I Bird
Sanctuary No1

Amundsen Gulf

Beaufort Sea

Cape Parry

PRUDHOE BAY

Cape Bathurst

Cape Dalhousie

Paulatuk

Mt Chamberlain
2749m

MacKenzie
Bay

Bird
Sanctuary

Range

Brooks

Arctic National

Wildlife Refuge

Ivvavik
Nat Pk

Approx northern limit of trees

Reindeer
Grazing
Reserve

Anderson

U S A

Vuntut
Nat Pk

Aklavik

INUVIK

MacKenzie

Arctic Circle

Dalton Highway

Old Crow

Fort McPherson

Peel River
Game Res

NORTHWEST

Porcupine

Arctic Circle

Dempster Highway

TERRITORIES

ALASKA

Fishing
Branch
Game Res

Circle

Ogilvie Mtns

Y U K O N

Fort
Norman

FAIRBANKS

Yukon

MacKenzie Mountains

Mt McKinley
6194m

Range

Yukon Charley
Natl Preserve

Eagle

DAWSON CITY

Delta
Junction

Boundary
Chicken

Alaska Hwy

Alaska

Top of
the World
Highway

Tintina

Stewart Crossing

Logan Mtns

McArthur Wildlife
Sanctuary

Tok

Pelly
Crossing

Trench

Yukon

Faro

Tetlin
Junction

Klondike Hwy

Ross River

Wrangell Mtns

Beaver Creek

Carmacks

Pelly
Mountains

Wrangell-St Elias

Game
Sanct

Alaska Highway

Haines
Junction

Takhini Hot Springs

Palmer

Nat Park &
Preserve

Destruction Bay

Whitehorse

Watson
Lake

Anchorage

Mt Logan
5959m

Teslin

Teslin

Seward

Kluane Nat Park

Carcross

Dease

St

Elias Mtns

Atlin Park

Gulf of

Haines

SKAGWAY

BRITISH COLUMBIA

Alaska

Glacier Bay
Nat Mon

Juneau

Coast

U S A

N O R T H   P A C I F I C

Alexander Archipelago

Mountains

Petersburg

O C E A N

Ketchikan

0 ——— 200km
0 ——— 200 miles

N

PRINCE RUPERT

Queen
Charlotte
Islands

ALASKA BORDER AREA

ALASKA FACTS

Area 1,518,750km². Alaska is one fifth of the landmass of all the lower 48 states of the US put together. Alaska is considered 100% wilderness. There are 10,686km of coastline. If you count the islands there are 54,561km of shoreline – more than the whole of the rest of the entire United States.

Boundaries Although it is almost completely surrounded by water, Alaska does share a border with its northerly Canadian neighbour, the Yukon, at 141° West longitude plus a small Pacific coastal strip which borders Canada's British Columbia province. The Bering Strait separates it from Russia. Alaska is the most northerly part of the United States and, because it straddles the International Dateline, in a sense it also has the country's easternmost and westernmost points.

Geographical features Highest mountain is Mt McKinley (6,194mm/20,306ft) in the Alaska Mountain Range which is the highest point in North America. The lowest point is anywhere along the coast. Alaska is surrounded by four major bodies of water; the Beaufort, Chukchi and Bering Seas and the Pacific Ocean. The Aleutian Island chain and St Lawrence Island are included within Alaskan territory. The Yukon River is the longest river of 3,000 found in the state. There are also 3 million lakes. Alaska has more active glaciers and ice fields than the rest of the inhabited world. There are 70 potentially active volcanoes in Alaska and Alaska had the strongest recorded earthquake in North America, on March 27 1964 (8.6 on the Richter Scale – this figure has since been revised to 9.2 to meet the new criteria for measuring earthquake magnitude).

Time Pacific Standard Time (GMT −8hr). There is Daylight Saving Time April to October (GMT −7hr).

Population 621,400, with 15.6% being Native American. Biggest city is Anchorage with 257,820 people.

Capital Juneau (30,684).

Territorial status The American flag was raised over Alaska on October 18 1867 after the land was purchased from Russia on March 30 that year by Secretary of State William H Seward. The price paid was $US7,200,000 or just two cents an acre. The Alaska Territory became the 49th State of the USA on January 3 1959.

Road border procedures

The Canadian Customs post is 3km outside Beaver Creek and is a drive-through post with just a cursory check of your passport if you are heading west into Alaska. Eastwards you must go through the full immigration form filling procedures for entry into Canada. Once you reach the American post a further 19km up the road you must enter the United States properly if you are not a citizen of Canada or the USA. The form filling here takes only a few minutes and the border police are always interested in where you are going and coming from. I should think they do not see too many travellers and I imagine the conversation brightens up their day as they go through all the formalities. The posts here are open year round.

On the northern end of the Taylor and the Top of the World highways the frontier posts are fairly rudimentary establishments. Passing out of the US is a simple affair of just flashing your passport and the normal visa checks. The US post is called Poker Creek. A little further on the Canadians will then go through the full immigration bit again with a stamp that calls the post Little Gold, Yukon Territory. These border posts are open 09.00–21.00 daily from mid-May until mid-September.

I have found that both posts are friendly, courteous and helpful to foreign travellers but the AlCan posts are the busiest. Patience in queues is expected and with the northern posts do not arrive late as you will be made to wait until the following day. Full vehicle searches have been known for drugs and guns (the Canadians frown on the import of firearms) but I have only found these just a passing glance. It must be the way I smile or the fact that they don't see Australians that far north too often.

North from Beaver Creek
Once through the border facilities at Beaver Creek it's 135km (84 miles) along the Alaska Highway to the junction of the Taylor Highway. The intersection is known as Tetlin Junction. Here you turn right following signs for Chicken, Jack Wade, Eagle and Boundary. The road becomes a wide, fast, gravel pitch surface. The scenery is stunning and there are plenty of places to stop along the way to take in the views. Remember that most of the traffic along this road travels fast, so beware of loose gravel and flying stones.

Chicken
Chicken is the first place you come to. Population is about a dozen. The early miners called this place Ptarmigan but had trouble with the spelling so they renamed it. The original Chicken is now an abandoned mining camp but there is a new site just above or below the main road (depending on your outlook) where there is a gas station and a gift shop. Just down the road toward the airfield is the 'downtown' area and **Chicken Mercantile**. You can get burgers, coffee and booze here as well as T-shirts, gold and other Chicken souvenirs. A café and bar are attached to the building. Check and make sure you have plenty of fuel and water on board here. There is not a lot else before Dawson City.

Jack Wade
Jack Wade is another old mining camp that has been generally abandoned, but there are still some mines operating so tread carefully here and do not trespass. They shoot claim jumpers here and it is legal! Just up the hill on the left heading north is the **gas station** which also has a quick snack facility but not much else. There is a mining dredge just down the road of a similar design to

the one at Bonanza Creek near Dawson but this one is much smaller and in nowhere near as good a condition.

Eagle

Eagle isn't actually on the road to Dawson; it's at the end of a road that branches off at Jack Wade and heads north for 105 km (65 miles). The road is slow, narrow and winding with steep gradients, lots of hairpin bends and not a lot of traffic. You'd have to want to go there to bother and most people don't. Having said that, it's a delightfully photogenic little town with plenty of museums and a place where every resident seems to be a bit of a historian. Today's population is about 150 souls. Although originally a small trading post situated on the banks of the Yukon River, Eagle developed as a supply town in response to the heavy-handed laws and taxes that the Canadians enforced on stampeders coming to the Klondike. The town is now headquarters of the Yukon-Charley Rivers National Preserve. Sights in the town include the restored courthouse, customs house and five buildings that were once part of the US Army's Fort Egbert. They now house numerous museum exhibits. For info on the town contact the **Visitors Information Center** (tel: 907.547.2233). The Historical Society has a full register of everyone who has lived in the town since 1897 and helps in researching relatives involved in the Klondike Gold Stampede. Their address is Box 23, Eagle, AK 99738.

Boundary

I have been in some unusual places throughout the world in my time and Boundary is up there with the best of them. Situated on top of a hill, Boundary consists of a bunch of log cabins, various vehicle and machinery wrecks, a few trailers or caravans, an airstrip and the **Boundary Lodge** with its drop-pit outhouse. The Boundary Lodge is also the fuel station and souvenir store. They have a microwave oven for quick snacks like burgers and hot-dogs and a pot of coffee is always ready for self-serve. If you don't ask the bearded fellow behind the bar you won't get served – you are expected to help yourself and pay before you go. The outhouse is something else and is free to use by anyone passing. Comfort is not part of the plan.

Just outside the lodge is a log cabin that is full of antiquities from the past and a whole lot of other junk and makes a great picture. This is the last place for fuel before Dawson City and a good spot to take time out from the long drive up from Beaver Creek.

Top of the World Highway

It's 111km to Dawson from here along the upper taiga and alpine tundra of the White Mountains. The Top of the World is an amazing road. About 5km or 6km before you reach Dawson there is a splendid view over the town from the side of the road. Beware of oncoming traffic. In the valley below you may have to wait a while for the free ferry to take you across the Yukon River to Dawson. In winter there is an ice bridge across here but you are unlikely to need it since much of the road is closed for the winter months. The snowploughs do not work this side of Dawson in the winter and the border posts are shut as well. Having said that it is great to head out of Dawson on a snowmobile and see the Top of the World in all its glory under the veil of a crisp winter snow.

Further afield in Alaska
Venturing further into Alaska is beyond the scope of this guidebook but I will offer some brief suggestions.

Tok
Tok is a pretty little town 19km after Tetlin Junction on the AlCan and en route to Fairbanks. It has a visitor centre, several RV parks, motels, a campground and several restaurants and cafés. It caters to the truckers travelling the AlCan and sprang up during the construction of the highway in the 40s. It's 525km (326 miles – we are in the USA now remember!) to Anchorage in the south and a further 330km (206 miles) to Fairbanks. Tok is a major junction for the **Alaskon Express buses** rolling along the highways of the north. Here you can get a bus to and from Skagway, Fairbanks, Beaver Creek, and Anchorage a few times a week. The visitor centre has details and timetables.

I have read that Tok is a hitchhiker's version of hell with people waiting for days for a lift. Legend has it that men grow beards and women reach menopause before their ride arrives, but it is not at all like that. Traffic is just few and far between and you may have to wait a day or so for a lift. The visitor centre has plenty on to while away the hours and can help suggest the best place to stick that thumb out. Tok is a small town so everyone knows everyone else's business. It will not be long before everybody knows that you want a lift and to where and a ride will just magically appear as if from nowhere.

Fairbanks
Fairbanks rates a mention here if only because of the Yukon Quest. The race starts or finishes here depending on the year and although I am a bit biased I should think it is the biggest event on the city's annual calendar.

Fairbanks is a real frontier town and the second largest in the state. Anchorage is nearly four times bigger, but Fairbanks has that real compact and comfortable homeliness that shines through with all frontier towns. Sadly, there is nothing visually attractive about the place. The streets are laid out haphazardly; there are a couple of military bases, numerous churches, hotels, restaurants and cafés. The bars are full of hard-drinking, colourful, brash pioneering sorts of the type you would expect to see. The type that looks like they have just come in from months of prospecting and are letting off a little steam before melting back into the wilds once again.

There is a **Dog Mushers Museum** here full of all the artefacts that you would expect from the dog-mushing capital of the world. The museum seems to keep moving and the **visitor centre** (tel: 907.456.5774) on First Ave should be able to help as to its current place of residence. The **Yukon Quest** has a store here at the corner of Cushman and Second St (tel:

907.451.8985). There is also an **Ice Museum** here that is called 'The Coolest Show in Town' (tel: 907.451.8222) with numerous ice sculptures on show in a 743m² walk-in freezer.

Accommodation-wise there are hotels, motels, rooming houses, B&Bs, hostels, campgrounds and RV parks. As for food a big town like Fairbanks caters for it all, from snack bars and cafés to multi-national restaurants like Chinese, Thai, Italian or Mexican. The Westmark Fairbanks has the most exclusive restaurant in town – the **Bear and Seal**. The **Howling Dog Saloon** at 11 Mile, Old Steese Highway in Fox, just outside the city limits on the road to Circle, has the 'Farthest Northern Rock'n'Roll Bar in the World'. I am told that it has all the hottest bands around and really jives.

One other thing: near Fairbanks is a town called North Pole. It is really a suburb of Fairbanks but it will legitimately allow you to say you have been to the North Pole without all that cold weather stuff.

From Fairbanks you can access the rest of Alaska including all the true wilderness regions. **Denali National Park and Reserve** is just down the road. Great for bear viewing.

Coming to the Yukon north from Alaska on the Trail of '98

There is a coastal strip to Alaska bordering with Canada's province of British Columbia. It is known, commonly, as the Inside Passage. In bygone days boats from Seattle and San Francisco travelled north up the west coast to the towns of Haines or Skagway, opening up that region to trade – mainly furs – for most of the 19th century. For most people coming from the United States for the Klondike Gold Stampede in 1898 it was the simplest and cheapest way to reach the north. Even today there are few roads so for those travelling through the area, for the most part, the ferries still provide the main methods of travel along the inside passage.

Whether you wish to begin your journey in the north by flying direct into Juneau, Alaska's capital, and catching a ferry north or whether you fancy exploring the Trail of '98 more fully by travelling the 560km (350 miles) Whitehorse/Skagway/Haines/Whitehorse loop you get to travel through a historically packed region that has plenty to see for the wildlife orientated.

Skagway

Skagway is one of those frontier towns of the movies: small and quintessentially 19th century with many of the buildings restored to that period in time when Skagway was the gateway to the Chilkoot and White Pass trails, a time when so many thousands of fortune seekers passed en route to the goldfields. Today Skagway thrives on the visitors who come each summer to explore the trail that led to gold so many years ago. Cruise ships sailing the Inside Passage regularly visit Skagway, making it the most popular cruise port in Alaska. The docks can handle up to five cruise ships at a time, making it a very busy place at the height of summer. Sadly, too many tourists take something away from a town and it loses much of the atmosphere that independent travellers seek. Please don't be dismayed by this, as one glance at the mountains surrounding the town as the sun is going down and the majority of tourists have left will leave you with the feeling that you are indeed standing at the foot of something historic.

History

In 1896 Skagway was but a single log cabin built by part-time resident Captain William Moore. News of the Klondike gold strike reached Seattle in July 1897 and all hell broke loose. By early August Moore's lonely cabin was surrounded by over 4,000 people huddled in a booming tent city. Frank Reid, a surveyor, set to work and the town sprung up. Almost immediately Skagway became 'the most outrageously lawless quarter' on the globe. Into this breach stepped a con-artist called Soapy Smith (Jefferson Randall Smith). He oversaw an extensive system of theft, cons, and even murder to get his gains. Every thug in the north worked for Soapy in a force that resembled a private army. Eventually people had had enough of Soapy and his men and, as one would expect in a frontier town in 19th century America where greed ruled, a gunfight ensued. Soapy was shot in the chest by Frank and died immediately. Frank caught a bullet in the groin and died a week later. Funnily enough, Frank's tombstone reads, 'He gave his life for the honor of Skagway'.

Skagway calmed down a little after this.

Two routes to the goldfields began in Skagway. Firstly there was the White Pass over the Coastal Range to Bennett Lake and the headwaters of the Yukon River. This route attracted the more financially better-off prospectors who could afford to hire mules and packhorses to carry the 'ton of goods' each man required when entering the Klondike. But it all proved something of a disaster. The trail was narrow and precipitous and the weather unpredictable. Most of the mules and horses died during that first year by, as some men put it, 'leaping off the cliffs to commit suicide'.

The second route and the more famous was for the poorer people – the Chilkoot Trail which started 15 miles/24km from Skagway at Dyea (pronounced die-ee) which is now a ghost town. The supplies were manhandled 33 miles/53km to Lindeman Lake including as many as 40 trips up and down the 'Golden Stairs' of the 3,550ft/1,083m pass. A well-used and popular old photograph of the line of men struggling up the Chilkoot Pass is one of the most dramatic images taken of the Klondike Stampede. Anyway, somewhere during this mass movement of men and supplies an Irish-Canadian engineer called Michael J Heney came into the fold and built the 110-mile (177km) White Pass and Yukon Route Railway from Skagway to Whitehorse. The line took almost two years to build in temperatures well below –30°C. When it was completed in 1900 it flourished until gold and metal prices fell in 1982 when the line was shut down. It was re-opened in 1988 to carry lead-zinc ore from Yukon's Anvil Range to Japan via Skagway and the WP&YR now continues to flourish as a tourist railway carrying upwards of 110,000 passengers each summer. It is Skagway's best attraction and North America's only operating narrow gauge railway. (See the section under Whitehorse for travelling times and costs for the WP&YR on page 166.)

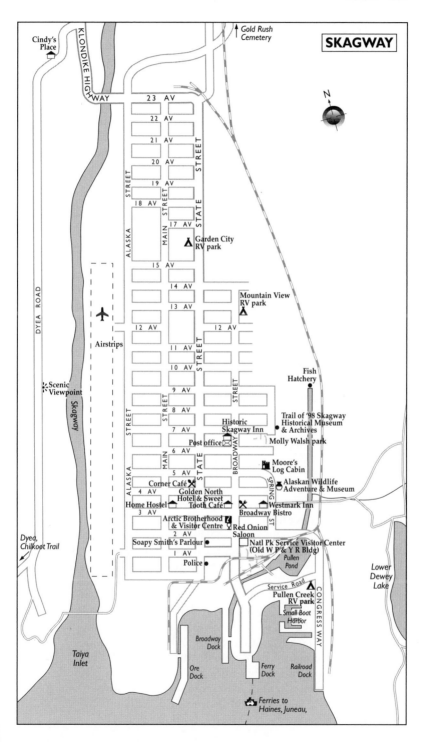

SKAGWAY

Gold Rush Cemetery

Cindy's Place

KLONDIKE HIGHWAY

23 AV
22 AV
21 AV
20 AV
19 AV
18 AV
17 AV

Garden City RV park

15 AV
14 AV
13 AV

Mountain View RV park

12 AV
12 AV
11 AV
10 AV

Fish Hatchery

9 AV
8 AV
7 AV

Trail of '98 Skagway Historical Museum & Archives

Historic Skagway Inn

Post office

Molly Walsh park

6 AV

Moore's Log Cabin

5 AV

Corner Café

4 AV

Alaskan Wildlife Adventure & Museum

Golden North Hotel & Sweet Tooth Café

Home Hostel

3 AV

Westmark Inn

Broadway Bistro

Arctic Brotherhood & Visitor Centre

Red Onion Saloon

2 AV

Soapy Smith's Parlour

Natl Pk Service Visitor Center (Old W P & Y R Bldg)

Pullen Pond

1 AV

Police

Lower Dewey Lake

ALASKA STREET
MAIN STREET
STATE STREET
BROADWAY
SPRING ST
CONGRESS WAY

DYEA ROAD

Scenic Viewpoint

Skagway

Dyea, Chilkoot Trail

Airstrips

Service Road

Pullen Creek RV park

Small Boat Harbor

Taiya Inlet

Broadway Dock

Ore Dock

Ferry Dock

Railroad Dock

Ferries to Haines, Juneau,

N

Where to stay

Many places are only open during the summer and their prices reflect it being the high season but there is something in the few establishments in town to suit all pockets. The cheapest in town is the **Skagway Home Hostel** (tel: 907.983.2131) on Third and Main offering youth-hostel type accommodation ($15–20). **Cindy's Place** out on the Dyea Road is open only during the summer. This log cabin establishment has only four units and is quite popular (tel: 907.983.2674) ($45–95). The **Golden North Hotel** (tel: 907.983.2451) is the oldest operating hotel in Alaska and right in the centre of town ($115). **Historic Skagway Inn B&B** (tel: 907.983.2289; web: www.skagwayinn.com), at the same price, is non-smoking, has its own restaurant and is located in the most historic part of town. The most expensive and luxurious is the **Westmark Inn Skagway** (tel: 907.983.2291) with 209 rooms and two restaurants but it is only open in the summer ($79–136).

Where to eat

Plenty here with numerous small diners and cafés as well as all the bigger hotels and inns having their own restaurants. Try the **Corner Café** at Fourth and State St for breakfast and great salmon burgers. Good breakfasts are also to be had at the **Sweet Tooth Café** on Broadway. Try pizza and nachos at the **Red Onion Saloon** also on Broadway or at the **Broadway Bistro**.

If you are self-catering then there's the **Fairway Market** at Fourth Ave and State St, and fresh fish is available from the **Skagway Fish Co** at the small boat harbour near the ferry terminal.

What to see and do in Skagway

Many of Skagway's old buildings are maintained by the US National Parks Service as the Klondike Gold Rush National Historic Park. These restored buildings are then subsequently leased to private businesses. The town itself is quite small and can be seen comfortably in a couple of hours; hence its popularity with cruise ships. Most of the more interesting buildings are along Broadway which runs off the end of the Alaska Ferry Terminal.

First on the right is the old White Pass & Yukon Route Railway administration building. It now houses the **National Park Service Visitor Center** (tel: 907.983.2921). In the summer it is open daily 08.00–18.00; the rest of the year 09.00–17.30 Mon–Fri. Here there are films, talk and a place where you can pick up guided tours of the town and the counter staff have all the latest timetables, weather information etc – all you would expect of a visitor centre. What's left of **Soapy Smith's Parlour** is across the road on Second Avenue. The building was closed to the public last time I was there.

Next down Broadway is the **Arctic Brotherhood Hall**. This odd-looking building is made entirely of driftwood and some say it is the most photographed building in all of Alaska. the Trail of '98 Museum, which has a good replication of pioneer life in the late 1800s, can be found on 7th and Spring Streets. It is open daily 09.00–17.00 (tel: 907.983.2420).

There are numerous other historic buildings on Broadway that are worth investigating. The **Golden North Hotel**, Alaska's oldest; the **Mascot Saloon** exhibiting saloon life in the days of '98; **Corrington's Museum of Alaskan History** (tel: 907.983.2580) is worth a visit just to see the scrimshaw done on walrus ivory (tusks); and finally the **Alaskan Wildlife Adventure & Museum** (tel: 907.983.3600) at the corner of Fourth Avenue for a collection of about 70 or so mounted animals from Alaska and the Yukon.

Moore's log cabin still exists at Fifth Avenue and Spring Streets. The National Parks Service has refurbished the building and lined the walls with newspapers from the 1800s.

Two other places to visit here are the two **cemeteries**, at Skagway and Dyea. Skagway has the graves of both Frank Reid and Soapy Smith, and the cemetery at Dyea has the graves of the hundred or so people who died in an avalanche in 1898. All the headstones have the same date: April 3 1898.

The White Pass & Yukon Route Railway is covered in the Whitehorse section of the guide. Suffice it to say, this is the end of the line – or the start – depending on how you look at it.

Additional information on Skagway can be found at the **Skagway Convention and Visitors Center** on the west side of Broadway between Second and Third Streets (tel: 907.983.2855).

The Chilkoot Trail

One of the main reasons travellers come to Skagway is to walk the Chilkoot Trail in the footsteps of the stampeders. The trail begins at the bridge over the Taiya River at Dyea, some nine miles to the west of Skagway. Skagway White Pass Tours will drop you off at the trail start for about $10. As you must register with National Parks your intention to walk the trail and pay the necessary fee for the privilege, I suggest you ask at their visitor centre for advice about anyone heading out that way.

The trail is 53km (33 miles) and, depending on your speed, fitness levels and how much scenery ooh-arh-ing you do, it will take you anything from three to five days to complete the journey. There are designated areas for camping. These have outhouses for your convenience. You must be prepared for bears along the trail with proper food caches etc (see *Bears: General Safety*, page 124). Although there are several shelters along the way, these are only for protection if the weather turns nasty. There is no accommodation available so camping is the only option – and then just in designated sites. However, with lots of people walking the trail in the summer you won't be short of conversation, companionship or security of numbers in campsites along the way.

Everyone heading north must clear Canadian customs, just as the stampeders did in 1898, at either Fraser, Carcross or Whitehorse. Some other practicalities are that you can only light campfires at Sheep Camp and Canyon City; you must not remove anything from the trail but your own rubbish as anything else may date from the stampede and is protected by law with severe penalties for their removal if caught.

As a last word, may I suggest that for keen walkers the Chilkoot Trail is unsurpassed by anything in Alaska or western Canada for scenery and historical value. If you were well prepared and experienced in tramping in adverse weather conditions, hiking the Chilkoot Trail in winter would be one of the best all-time experiences to be had. You would have a real taste of what the stampeders went through as they struggled to seek fame and fortune on the Klondike Stampede of 1898.

Haines

Haines is but a short one-hour ferry journey from Skagway. The service is run by the Alaska Marine Highway Service. They have a website for the latest information at www.akmhs.com. The ferry terminal at Skagway (tel: 907.983.2941) will give you times and sell tickets for passengers and vehicles. There are usually two ferries per day in the summer. In Haines the ferry terminal (tel: 907.766.2111) is four miles outside of the town to the north. If you're on foot there are usually taxis meeting all the ferries.

Haines is a bigger town than Skagway with about twice the population and, whereas Skagway is famous for the Chilkoot Trail and the Klondike Gold Stampede, Haines is all about outdoor adventure and wildlife activities.

To the southwest of Haines is the Glacier Bay National Park and Reserve; the Chilkat Range overlooks the town and the Chilkat Bald Eagle Preserve comes into its own during the late autumn and early winter when the salmon migrate upstream and hundreds of birds of prey gather for the feast.

Seventy kilometres north of Haines along Alaska Route 7 you cross the border into Canada, first passing through British Columbia for a further 80km before reaching the Yukon on the road south of Haines Junction near the Southern Tutschone First Nations summer community of Klukshu. The US border is situated at a place known as Dalton Cache where Jack Dalton of the Dalton Trail fame once stored his provisions and charged a toll for all travellers along the trail. The Canadian side is just around the corner at Pleasant Camp. Both posts are open 07.00–23.00 daily (US time – for Canadian time add one hour). I am told that Canadian customs used to hassle backpackers because they were travelling on the cheap, so be prepared for some questions.

Haines sees few tourists with only one large cruise ship a week during the summer. Most of the people visiting the town are usually travellers heading into Canada or coming south from Whitehorse. Having said that there are plenty of activities to keep visitors busy.

History

Haines' early history was as a trading centre for the Chilkat and Chilcoot tribes of Tlingit native Americans and, although there had been a proper village here since missionaries established themselves in the 1880s, it never came into prominence until the Klondike Gold Stampede. The town is incidentally named after Mrs F E H Haines who was part of the Presbyterian Home Missions Board. She never visited the town named after her.

During the gold stampede an adventurer and businessman, Jack Dalton, developed a 305-mile trail which followed an old native trade route into the Yukon to service the miners in Dawson with supplies and fresh meat. Travellers along his trail were charged a fee for its use. Armed men never failed to collect the $250 toll. The trail still exists and, although much of it is returning to natural forest, people do walk or horse-trek along its route for its historical value. It passes through some great country along the St Elias Mountains and Kluane National Park.

Although the Klondike stampede opened up the area, not much happened until the World War II when, because of fear of a Japanese invasion of Alaska, a road was built between Haines and Haines Junction in the Yukon as an emergency evacuation and supply route for the AlCan Highway. Haines is now a regional centre with a diversified economy based on fishing, tourism and government.

Where to stay
There are plenty of hotels and motels to choose from. There is a youth hostel in Haines called **Bear Creek Camp** about 3–4km outside the town with dorm beds for about $15 per person. In town most of the places operate year round with high and low season tariffs. Some suggestions are **Captain's Choice Motel** (tel: 907.766.3111) with a restaurant and all the usual services. Rates vary from $76 to $145 per night. The **Hotel Halsingland** (tel: 907.766.2000) offers similar services from $75 to $95 per night. Something slightly cheaper but on the edge of town near Fort Seward is the **Mountain View Motel** (tel: 907.766.2900). Rates vary between $50 and $85 again depending on the season.

Where to eat
Haines is typical of Alaskan towns; though the food might not be cheap by mainland American standards it is reasonable by Alaskan ones. For big breakfasts try the **Bamboo Room** on Second Avenue. The **Lighthouse Restaurant** on Main Street does buttermilk pies which I am told are delicious and **Porcupine Pete's** just down the way does fabulous sourdough pizzas. There is a nightly all-you-can-eat salmon bake in the tribal house at Fort Seward if you are a lover of salmon. (The west coast of North America has five species of salmon, all tasting slightly different, and coming at different times of the year. In the UK we have only one species – the Atlantic salmon – so we are at a natural disadvantage.) There are good restaurants in the **Hotel Halsingland** and the **Captain's Choice Motel**.

What to see and do
There's not much in town to see bar the **Sheldon Museum** (tel: 907.766.2366) which houses a fine collection of native woven blankets and items from the gold stampede. I'd avoid the **American Bald Eagle Foundation Natural History Museum** (tel: 907.766.3094) unless you like looking at stuffed animals and birds when the real things are so close by.

The **Visitor Information Center** (tel: 907.766.2234) is on Second Avenue. It is open 08.00–20.00 Mon–Fri all year round; from mid-May until mid-September it is also open at weekends 10.00–13.00 and 14.00–19.00. During the rest of the year it is open 08.00–17.00 Mon–Fri. They have a website at www.haines.ak.us for those seeking more relevant information at the time of their journey.

There are several **hiking trails** in the vicinity of Haines itself. There are three trails to the top of nearby Mt Riley. The shortest one is 3km and takes about three hours for the round trip. There is a small car park at the beginning of the trails.

The Mt Ripinski trail takes a full day to trek to the top and back but the views are superb. At 3,900ft (1,190m) Mt Ripinski is covered in snow for much of the year so be prepared for adverse weather conditions.

The visitor centre has details of all the surrounding trails including maps.

If you are interested in historical buildings of a more recent era take a look at Fort Seward at the southern end of town. It's a great place to seek out those much-wanted native American arts and crafts.

The **Chilkat Bald Eagle Preserve** is just north of Haines near the Tlingit village of Klukwan along the Tsirku River. This 48,000-acre preserve becomes home to the largest gathering of bald eagles in the world during the salmon run in the autumn. It's a bird photographer's paradise and probably the best chance you will ever get to see bald eagles up close in all of North America. During the peak salmon run (Nov–Jan) there are some 3,500 birds here alongside wolves, ravens, bears, gulls and magpies – all feeding on the migrating salmon and the carcasses left behind by the major predators. During the rest of the year the resident 400 or so eagles are readily seen along the river so it is a great spot any time of the year. Beware of low water levels and avoid disturbing the birds by attempting to get too close. The other photographers will chastise you for this. Get a longer lens or use a two-times converter: a 500mm will get good close-up shots; a 300mm will show a little environment as well. Two points always to remember. First, bald eagles are not only great fishermen but they are avid scavengers, being inherently lazy like all large birds of prey. They won't work for a feed if someone has done all the work for them. Second, do keep a wary eye out for bears. In your haste to get the great bald eagle shot you may find that you have become a bear's supper.

There is a state **campsite** nearby at Mosquito Lake just 8km north of Klukwan and 5km off the highway. It does get full during the main salmon runs.

Useful website
www.haines.ak.us; www.skagway.org

CHURCHILL, MANITOBA
Manitoba does not strictly form part of this guidebook either, but polar bears do, and there is no better place to see the largest land predator in the world than at Churchill. It is known as 'the Polar Bear Capital of the World'. Every autumn the area surrounding Churchill hosts the largest concentration of

Above St Elais Mountains, Yukon, with Dezadeash Lake in foreground (GR)

Left St Paul's Church, Dawson City, Yukon (GR)

Below Baker Lake, Nunavut, from the lakeshore (GR)

Above left Preparing fish for drying, Rankin Inlet, Nunavut (GR)

Above right Fish drying on a rack, Coral Harbour, Nunavut (GR)

Below left Inuit identification tag, no longer used (GR)

Below right Cottongrass used by the Inuit for fire and light wicks (GR)

Above Stained glass window of Anglican church, Cambridge Bay, Nunavut (GR)
Below Float planes outside the visitor centre at Baker Lake, Nunavut (GR)

Above Snowmobile on Yukon River, Dawson City (GR)
Right Dog sledging (GR)
Below Horse trekking, Haines Junction, Yukon (GR)

polar bears in the world. During the winter polar bears can be found anywhere on Hudson Bay hunting their favourite prey, seals. As the pack ice retreats some of the bears find themselves far to the south in too warm a climate and begin to migrate north in search of an early freeze over and the return of the pack ice. This period is a time of fasting for the bears. Polar bears are pure carnivores, unlike their other bear cousins which can live on a diet of berries, sedges and grasses, and at this time of year their favourite prey has the advantage of its natural environment being free of ice. The bears, although strong swimmers, are not as fast as seals so the seals have several months of respite from the ever-hungry bears.

In their search for cooler climes the bears that find themselves at the southern end of Hudson Bay migrate north along the shoreline. Churchill is a favourite resting-place for these bears and most of this resting activity takes place during October and November, although bears can be seen at anytime around Churchill, even during the height of summer.

Churchill is situated on the east bank of the Churchill River. Its estuary is a popular place for beluga whales to have their calves in July. The surrounding area harbours all manner of wildlife – birds like the tundra swan and snowy owls are common during the spring and summer, and animals like caribou, moose, arctic foxes and wolves are to be found quite close to the town. The town's population is about 800 in the winter but it rises to 1,500 in the summer to cater to the large number of visitors to the area.

A little history to orientate you here. The Company of Adventurers established a fur-trading post called Fort Nelson in 1682 at the mouth of the Hayes and Nelson rivers. The French burnt it down in 1684 and a new fort called York Factory, named after the then Duke of York (later King James II), was quickly erected. Within a few years the trade had become brisk and the company advanced further up the coast establishing a string of forts. Churchill, originally a small trading post established in 1685, became a fort in 1717 and grew from there. The town as it is today was built over permafrost and muskeg and is the end of a rail link with Winnipeg constructed in 1929. Mosquitoes and blackflies are a problem in the summer.

What became of the original York Factory? The fort changed hands several times until by the Treaty of Utrecht (1713) it became British. As York Factory it was the chief port, supply depot and headquarters for the fur-trading centres of northern Canada, but its importance declined with the completion in 1885 and 1915 of the transcontinental railroads and in 1931 of the branch line to Churchill on Hudson Bay, 140 miles (225km) northwest. The trading post closed in 1957, ending 275 years of nearly continuous operation; it has been designated a national historic site and is accessible only by air or canoe.

Getting there

The trip by rail takes two-nights/one day to travel the 1,600km in almost grand luxury. The railway line is also used for transporting cargo for onward shipment on the barges that supply the towns and communities of the north in summer once the ice has broken up. To get there by rail call VIA Rail

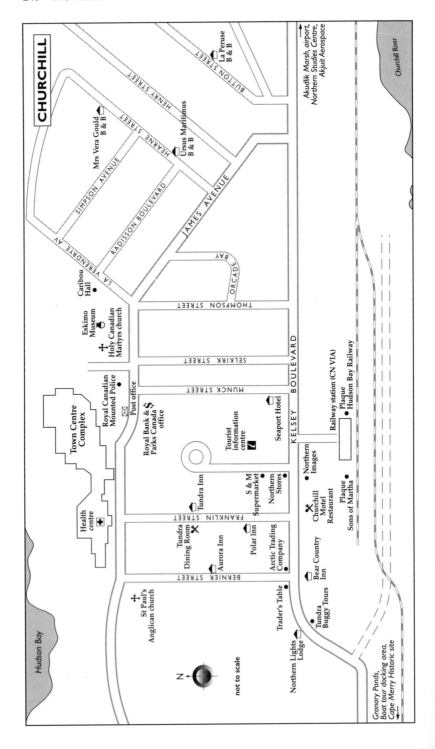

Canada (tel: 1-800-561-8630 in Canada and 1-800-561-3949 in the USA). Trains operate year round departing Winnipeg on Sunday, Tuesday and Thursday evenings arriving in Churchill on Tuesday, Thursday and Saturday mornings. In early 2000 the fare for a ticket from Winnipeg to Churchill, in a lower berth, was $203 one-way and $406 return plus taxes (about $34 on the return fare). You can book at their website, www.viarail.ca/en.index.html.

Calm Air flies daily during the polar bear season and Monday to Friday from Winnipeg all year round.

Where to stay and eat

There are several hotels and motels in Churchill but these quickly fill during the polar bear season so make your reservations well in advance of heading off to see the bears. The **Tundra Inn** (tel: 204.675.8831) is probably the best, but the others are the **Polar Inn** (tel: 204.675.8878), **Churchill Motel (tel**: 204.675.8853), **Seaport Hotel** (tel: 204.675.8807), **Bear Country Inn** (tel: 204.675.8299), the **Aurora Inn** (tel: 204.675.2071) and the **Northern Lights Lodge** (tel: 204.675.2403). All are within the town centre and provide similar features like TVs, private baths, and so on. For B&Bs try **Mrs Vera Gould** (tel: 204.675.2544), **La Peruse House** (tel: 204.675.2254) and the **Ursus Maritimus (Polar Bear) B&B** (tel: 204.675.2819). There are no camp grounds, for obvious reasons. The restaurants are limited and, with few exceptions, what they offer is nothing special. All the hotels, of course, have their own restaurants and there is a snack bar in the Town Centre Complex. The **Traders Table** (tel: 204.675.2141) has the best food but also with prices to match. There is also the **Gipsy Bakery** (tel: 204.675.2322) which serves snacks and light meals.

What to see and do

Besides the polar bears there are over 200 species of birds which nest or pass through Churchill during their yearly migrations. Beluga whales come in close to shore to calve in the safer and warmer waters of the Churchill River and can be readily seen once the ice has broken up. Caribou are all along the coast as they migrate north to their summer calving grounds. Dog sledging and snowmobiling are available in winter and kayaking in the summer. You can even go walking with an armed guide or rent mountain bikes. Lastly, it is easy to get here to view the *Aurora borealis* in those perfect clear night skies from August until April when the long summer days return to the north.

Churchill also has an annual Dip in the Bay race on Canada Day (it was delayed once, in 1997, because the water really was too cold).

There is also an international commercial spaceport complex here. Their first launch, on April 29 1998, was a space physics payload to 400km above the earth to measure the ozone layer. Their plan is to launch small satellite constellations, single satellites and sounding rockets for the Canadian Space Agency and other interested parties. Most of the stuff is sub-orbital but it is all amazing for Canada and Churchill.

The **Parks Canada Visitor Centre** (Bayport Plaza; tel: 204.675.8863) is open throughout the year but times vary with the seasons. Just down the road from here is the **Eskimo Museum** on La Verendrye Avenue. This museum has a reasonable collection of Inuit artefacts from the collection of the missionary Oblate Fathers of Mary Immaculate. The town also has a curling rink, a swimming pool, a bowling alley and a cinema.

Most people come for the bears.

Polar bear viewing

The vehicles are called 'tundra buggies' and stand some 3m off the ground on 2m tyres, keeping you well out of harm's way. A day trip will cost about $100 and includes lunch on the tundra. Tours leave around 08.00 and return about 17.00 and during the peak season you are almost guaranteed seeing bears (really you can't help it since they wander around the town's streets looking for food). Trained guides explain all about the bears and the rest of the tundra with minimal disturbance to the wildlife. I have only used one of the companies which does tundra buggy tours, **Great White Bear Tours** (tel: 204.675.2781), and there are more, such as **Tundra Buggy Tours** (tel: 204.675.2121; email: info@tundra-buggy-tours.com; web: www.tundra-buggy-tours.com). Most people book outside Canada with a reputable tour operator for a complete package which usually includes flights, accommodation and tours to see the bears. Getting on a tour locally is not usually a problem but space can be at a premium during the season.

Parks Canada and the staff at Natural Resources actively search out polar bears for public safety. Known as the polar bear police force their job is to remove those bears that become a nuisance in the town. They are not killed but rather darted, tranquillised and moved to the polar bear prison – a collection of 20 or so cells that houses the bears until Hudson Bay freezes over again. The bears are then transported about 50km north of town by helicopter and released. You cannot visit these bears, as they are kept isolated to avoid them becoming familiar with humans or developing a dependence on us. The town does not want them back accustomed to people and looking to meet more.

Appendix 1

LANGUAGE
Questions

English	Inuinnaqtan	Inuktitut	Sounds like
How are you? (singular)	*Qanuritpin?*	ᖃᓄᐃᑉᐃᑦ	Ka-new-it-pin
How are you? (plural)	*Qanuritpisi?*		Ka-new-it-pee-see
Who are you?	*Kinauvin?*	ᑭᓇᐅᕕᑦ	Key-now-vin
Where are you from?	*Namirmiutauyutin*	ᓇᒥᕐᒥᐅᑕᐅᔪᑎᑦ	Naa-mik-mute-tau-you-tin
Where am I?	*Namiitunga*	ᓇᒥᒃᑐᖓ	Naa-meet-toon-ga
Who is that person?	*Kina taamna*	ᑭᓇᑖᒻᓇ	Kee-na tom-na
Where is the store?	*Nauk niuvirvik*	ᓇᐅᒃ ᓂᐅᕕᕐᕕᒃ	Naouk-new-viq-vik
How much is this?	*Una qaffitaalauyuq*	ᐅᓇ ᖃᕝᕆᑖᓚᐅᔪᖅ	Oona-kaaff-ee-dolla
Do you have a phone?	*Talafuutiqaqtutin*	ᑕᓚᕴᑎᖃᖅᑐᑎᑦ	Tal-la-fone-kaak-too-tin
Do you have a camera?	*Piksaliutiqaqtutin*	ᐱᒃᓴᓕᐅᑎᖃᖅᑐᑎᑦᐱ	Pick-saw-leo-tea-kak-too-tin
Can you cut this?	*Una pilakaalaaqtan*	ᐅᓇᐱᓚᒡᒌᓇᖅᑎᐅ	Oona-pee-lak-aa-lak-tan
Would you like to go for a walk?	*Pihuuyarumayutin*	ᐱᓲᔪᒪᔪᓚᐃᑦ	Pee-hoo-yaag-oo-maah-yoo-tin
May I ask you a question?	*Apirillaglagin*	ᐊᐱᕆᓪᓚᒡᓚᒋᑦ	Aa-pee-gee-lug-la-geen

Phrases

English	Inuinnaqtan	Inuktitut	Sounds like
This is nice	*Una pinnaiqtuq*	ᐅᓇ ᐱᐊᐃᑦᑐᖅ	Oona peen-nik-took
I am going to work	*Havagiaqniaqtunga*	ᐱᖃᓇ ᐊᒃᓂᐊᖅᑐᖓᒪ	Ha-ve-gee-ak-nee-aak-tun-ga
I am going home now	*Angilrauniaqtunga*	ᐊᖏᕐᐅᓂᐊᖅᑐᖓᒪ	Ang-eel-gha-oo-nee-aak-tun-ga
I am hungry	*Kaaliqtunga*	ᑳᓕᒃᑐᖓ	Kaa-leek-tun-ga
I need help (help me!)	*Ikayullannga*	ᐱᑲᔪᓪᓚᖓ	Ee-kaa-you-laan-ga
I like those	*Aliagiyatka taapkua*	ᐱᒃᑕᐊᐱᐅᑎᓪᓯᑦᑲᑦ	Aa-lee-a-gee-yat-kaa-top-kua

I will see you tomorrow	*Aqaguttauq*	ᖃᐅᐸᑕᐅᖅ	Aa-kaa-goot-ta-ouk
My name is…	*Atira*	ᐸᑎᕋ	Aa-tee-gaa
I have a daughter	*Paniqaqtunga*	ᐸᓂᖃᖅᑐᖓ	Bun-nee-kak-tun-ga
I have a son	*Irniqaqtunga*	ᐱᕐᓂᖃᖅᑐᖓ	Eng-ni-kak-tun-ga
Thanks	*Quana*	ᒍᔭᓇᒥᒃ	Ka-na
Thank you	*Quanaqqutin*	ᒍᔭᓇᒥᕋᓗᒃ	Ka-nak-ku-tin
Thank you very much	*Quanaqpiaqqutin*	ᒍᔭᓇᒥᒪᓐ	Ka-nak-pee-aak-ku-tin
I am fine	*Quanuingitunga*	ᕋᓄᐃᖕᒋᑦᑐᖓ	Ka-u-ing-ee-tun-ga

Numbers

1	*atauhiq*	ᐸᑕᐅᓯᖅ	aa-tau-heek
2	*malruuk*	ᓚᕈ	mal-ruut
3	*pingahut*	ᐱᕐᖓᓱᑦ	peen-ga-hoot
4	*hataman*	ᓱᑕᒪᑦ	he-ta-mun
5	*talliman*	ᑕᓕᒪᑦ	tal-li-man

Expressions (often made with facial features)

Yes	*Ee* (made with raised eyebrows)	ᐃ	eee
No	*Ukka* (made with a frown)	ᐸᒃᑲ	oo-kaa
What did you say?	*Uh!* (sound with mouth agape - means 'say again')		same expression in English

Utensils

knife	*havik*	ᓴᕕᒃ	ha-vik
fork	*kapuraut*	ᑲᐳᐃᖅ	ka-pu-rout
spoon	*aluut*	ᐊᓗᑎ	a-loot
plate	*akkiutaq*		a-key-ou-taak
cup	*qallut*	ᐸᓂᑲᖅ	ka-loot

Places

England	*Elizapee Nunanga*		Eliza-pee Na-nun-ga
Canada			

Animals

polar bear	*nanuq*	ᓇᓄᖅ	naa-nuk
seal	*netsik*	ᓇᑦᓯᖅ	net-sik
caribou	*tuktu*		took-tu
grizzly	*aklak*	ᒍᓄ7ᖕᒍᐊᒃᖕ	uk-lak
walrus	*aivik*		aa-vik

ground squirrel	*siksik*		sik-sik
muskoxen	*umingmak*		oo-ming-mak
wolf	*amaruq*	⊲Lᒋˢᵇ	a-mar ruk
wolverine	*qavvik*	ᔅˢᐅᵇ	qua-vik

Other useful words

husky	*kingmik*	king-mik
dogsledge	*komatik*	ko-ma-tik
boat	*umiak*	oo-mi-ak
kayak	*qaqak*	ki-yak
house	*igloo*	ig-lu
tent	*tupik*	too-pik
snowknife	*pana*	paa-na
curved kitchen or woman's knife	*ulu*	oo-lu
boots (usually made of seal skin)	*kamik*	kaa-mik
person	*inuk*	inn-ook
people	*Inuit*	Inn-u-it
language	*Inuktitut*	In-nook-ti-tuk
harpoon	*siatko*	sigh-at-ko
European	*Kabloona*	Kaa-bloo-naa ('the bushy brows')
Eskimo★	*Eskimo*	Es-ki-mo ('eaters of raw meat')
Indian	*Adlit*	Add-lit ('egg of the lice')
Nunavut	*Nunavut*	Noo-na-voot ('our land')

★ French translation of Cree Indian word *Eskimantsik*

Appendix 2

GLOSSARY

A cord of wood A measure of cut wood (usually taken to mean 128ft³ or 3.6m³).

Inukshuk Inuit word meaning 'likeness to man'. A stone cairn that has been used as a guide to the Inuit for centuries leading them to hunting grounds, sheltered inlets and friendship.

Lobsticks Trees stripped bare except for their top branches and two lower horizontal branches. Used as trail markers.

Moiety system From the french word *moitié* – half. Anthropologists use this term in relation to First Nation society as being divided into two halves or clans. Each clan would belong to either a wolf or crow moiety. Membership is matrilineal and if a person was of the wolf clan then that person's opposite moiety was crow and its members were patrilineal. Traditionally a crow was required to marry a wolf and vice versa and intermarriage within a moiety was strictly forbidden. It was important to be able to identify one's moiety to know who was on an individual's mother's side and who was on the father's side. See *Northwest Coast First Nations*, page 64.

Mushers From the French *marche*. The command yelled by French-speaking dog sled operators to set their teams off. Misinterpreted by the English-speaking explorers as 'mush', this has developed into the word 'mushers' being used for those who drive dog-teams. Today most dog-sledders call out 'mush' to set their dogs off. The other terms mushers use are 'haw' and 'gee' to turn the dogs left or right; 'whoa' to stop; 'easy' to slow down; and 'on by' to keep to the same trail.

Paddlesteamer A boat propelled by a paddle-wheel either at the rear or at the sides and driven by steam power. Suitable only for the calmer open waters of rivers and estuaries as the paddle-wheel disengages from the water in rough weather. Usually used on boats with flat bottoms along shallow draft rivers.

Potlatch Simply put a First Nations party. On the northwest coast of Canada a potlatch was usually a gift giving time. Potlatches were big lavish affairs held by a wealthy First Nations person and confirm rank and status, lines of privilege and power. In the Yukon they are more about society and the *moiety* clan system and were often held as a memorial service for someone who died.

Gift giving featured strongly but between one *moiety* clan and another. A big chance to eat, dance and celebrate.

Sternwheeler A boat propelled by a paddle-wheel placed at the rear of the vessel. The most common form of riverboat transport in the north.

Treeline A physically imaginary line normally drawn on maps of Canada that provides a rough idea where the boreal forest ends and the flat, treeless tundra begins. The actual transition takes place over dozens of kilometres and at a variety of latitudes depending on the topography and climate of any particular area.

Caribou

Appendix

BIRDS OF NORTHERN CANADA

This is a complete list of all the birds found in northern Canada. There is as yet no listing for Nunavut so this is still included under NWT. Not included in the lists are those species which have been sighted and identified but have come to the region because they were lost, blown off course during their migration or have basically strayed out of their own home territory due to some unforeseen circumstances. The list does, however, include all rare and endangered species, and those at risk from human intervention within their habitats. An excellent guidebook to the birds of North America is listed under *Further Reading*.

Hard copies of the field check lists are available from most tourist offices in the region and they can also be downloaded from the internet from the following two sites: For NWT, go to www.NWTChecklist.com where files are provided in both MS Word and WordPerfect. For the Yukon go to www.ren-res.gov.yk.ca where they have some really interesting stuff about the wildlife in the Yukon. Both checklists can be returned to the respective organisations so that they can update their files on species, ranges, sightings etc. This will, of course, be of interest to serious 'twichers'.

Species	Scientific name	Yukon	NWT
Loons			
Red-throated loon	*Gavia stellata*	Y	Y
Pacific loon	*Gavia pacifica*	Y	Y
Common loon	*Gavia immer*	Y	Y
Yellow-billed loon	*Gavia adamsii*	Y	Y
Grebes			
Pied-billed grebe	*Podilymbus podiceps*	Y	Y
Horned grebe	*Podiceps auritus*	Y	Y
Red-necked grebe	*Podiceps grisegena*	Y	Y
Eared grebe	*Podiceps nigricollis*		Y
Fulmars, shearwaters			
Northern fulmar	*Fulmaris glacialis*		Y
Great shearwater	*Puffinus gravis*		Y
Bitterns			
American bittern	*Botaurus lentiginosus*		Y

Pelicans, cormorants

American white pelican	*Pelecanus erythrorhynchos*		Y
Double-crested cormorant	*Phalacrocorax auritus*		Y

Herons

Great blue heron	*Ardea herodias*	Y	

Swans, ducks, geese

Tundra swan	*Cygnus columbianus*	Y	Y
Trumpeter swan	*Cygnus buccinator*	Y	Y
Great white-fronted goose	*Anser albifrons*	Y	Y
Snow goose	*Chen caerulescens*	Y	Y
Ross' goose	*Chen rossii*		Y
Brant	*Branta bernicla*	Y	Y
Canada goose	*Branta canadensis*	Y	Y
Green-winged teal	*Anas crecca*	Y	Y
American black duck	*Anas rubripes*		Y
Mallard	*Anas platyrhynchos*	Y	Y
Northern pintail	*Anas acuta*	Y	Y
Blue-winged teal	*Anas discors*	Y	Y
Cinnamon teal	*Anas cyanoptera*	Y	
Northern shoveler	*Anas clypeata*	Y	Y
Gadwell	*Anas strepera*	Y	Y
Eurasian wigeon	*Anas penelope*	Y	
American wigeon	*Anas americana*	Y	Y
Canvasback	*Aythya valisineria*	Y	Y
Redhead	*Aythya americana*	Y	Y
Ring-necked duck	*Aythya collaris*	Y	Y
Greater scaup	*Aythya marila*	Y	Y
Lesser scaup	*Aythya affinis*	Y	Y
Common eider	*Somateria mollissima*	Y	Y
King eider	*Somateria spectabilis*	Y	Y
Harlequin duck	*Histrionicus histrionicus*	Y	Y
Oldsquaw	*Clangula hyemalis*	Y	Y
Black scoter	*Melanitta nigra*	Y	Y
Surf scoter	*Melanitta perspicillata*	Y	Y
White-winged scoter	*Melanitta fusca*	Y	Y
Common goldeneye	*Bucephala clangula*	Y	Y
Barrow's goldeneye	*Bucephala islandica*	Y	Y
Bufflehead	*Bucephala albeola*	Y	Y
Hooded merganser	*Lophodytes cucullatus*	Y	Y
Common merganser	*Mergus merganser*	Y	Y
Red-breasted merganser	*Mergus serrator*	Y	Y
Ruddy duck	*Oxyura jamaicensis*	Y	Y

Hawks, eagles

Black vulture	*Coragyps atratus*	Y	
Osprey	*Pandion haliaetus*	Y	Y

Sharp-shinned hawk	*Accipiter striatus*	Y	Y
Northern goshawk	*Accipiter gentilis*	Y	Y
Swainson's hawk	*Buteo swainsoni*	Y	Y
Cooper's hawk	*Accipiter cooperii*		Y
Red-tailed hawk (Harlan's)	*Buteo jamaicensis*	Y	Y
Rough-legged hawk	*Buteo lagopus*	Y	Y
Golden eagle	*Aquila chrysaetos*	Y	Y
Bald eagle	*Haliaeetus leucocephalus*	Y	Y
Northern harrier	*Circus cyaneus*	Y	Y

Falcons

American kestrel	*Falco sparverius*	Y	Y
Merlin	*Falco columbarius*	Y	Y
Peregrine falcon	*Falco peregrinus*	Y	Y
Gyrfalcon	*Falco rusticolus*	Y	Y

Grouse, ptarmigan

Spruce grouse	*Dendragapus canadensis*	Y	Y
Blue grouse	*Dendragapus obscurus*	Y	Y
Ruffed grouse	*Bonasa umbellus*	Y	Y
Willow ptarmigan	*Lagopus lagopus*	Y	Y
Rock ptarmigan	*Lagopus mutus*	Y	Y
Sharp-tailed grouse	*Tympanuchus phasianellus*	Y	Y
White-tailed ptarmigan	*Lagopus leucurus*	Y	Y

Coots, rails

Yellow rail	*Coturnicops noveboracensis*		Y
Sora	*Porzana carolina*	Y	Y
American coot	*Fulica americana*	Y	Y

Cranes

Sandhill crane	*Grus canadensis*	Y	Y
Whooping crane	*Grus americana*		Y

Plovers

Black-bellied plover	*Pluvialis squatarola*	Y	Y
Pacific or lesser golden plover	*Pluvialis fulva*	Y	
American golden plover	*Pluvialis dominicus*		Y
Common ringed plover	*Charadrius hiaticula*		Y
Semipalmated plover	*Charadrius semipalmatus*	Y	Y
Killdeer	*Charadrius vociferus*	Y	Y

Sandpipers

Marbled godwit	*Limosa fedoa*		Y
Hudsonian godwit	*Limosa haemastica*	Y	Y
Greater yellowlegs	*Tringa melanoleuca*	Y	Y
Lesser yellowlegs	*Tringa flavipes*	Y	Y
Solitary sandpiper	*Tringa solitaria*	Y	Y

Wandering tattler	*Heteroscelus incanus*	Y	Y
Spotted sandpiper	*Actitis macularia*	Y	Y
Eskimo curlew	*Numenius borealis*		Y
Upland sandpiper	*Bartramia longicauda*	Y	Y
Whimbrel	*Numenius phaeopus*	Y	Y
Ruddy turnstone	*Arenaria interpres*	Y	Y
Surfbird	*Aphriza virgata*	Y	
Red knot	*Calidris canutus*	Y	Y
Sanderling	*Calidris alba*	Y	Y
Western sandpiper	*Calidris mauri*	Y	Y
Least sandpiper	*Calidris minutilla*	Y	Y
Semipalmated sandpiper	*Calidris pusilla*	Y	Y
Biard's sandpiper	*Calidris bairdii*	Y	Y
Pectoral sandpiper	*Calidris melanotos*	Y	Y
Dunlin	*Calidris alpina*	Y	Y
Stilt sandpiper	*Calidris himantopus*	Y	Y
Purple sandpiper	*Calidris maritima*		Y
White-rumped sandpiper	*Calidris fuscicollis*		Y
Buff-breasted sandpiper	*Tryngites subruficollis*	Y	Y
Short-billed dowitcher	*Limnodromus griseus*	Y	Y
Long-billed dowitcher	*Limnodromus scolopaceus*	Y	Y
Common snipe	*Gallinago gallinago*	Y	Y
Wilson's phalarope	*Phalaropus tricolor*	Y	Y
Red-necked phalarope	*Phalaropus lobatus*	Y	Y
Red phalarope	*Phalaropus lfulicaria*	Y	Y

Gulls, terns

Pomarine jaeger	*Stercorarius pomarinus*	Y	Y
Parasitic jaeger	*Stercorarius parasiticus*	Y	Y
Long-tailed jaeger	*Stercorarius longicaudus*	Y	Y
Franklin's gull	*Larus pipixcan*		Y
Little gull	*Larus minutus*		Y
Bonapart's gull	*Larus philadelphia*	Y	Y
Mew gull	*Larus canis*	Y	Y
Ring-billed gull	*Larus delawarensis*	Y	Y
California gull	*Larus californicus*	Y	Y
Herring gull	*Larus argentatus*	Y	Y
Thayer's gull	*Larus thayeri*	Y	Y
Iceland gull	*Larus glaucoides*		Y
Glaucous-winged gull	*Larus glaucescens*	Y	
Glaucous gull	*Larus hyperboreus*	Y	Y
Ivory gull	*Pagophila eburnea*		Y
Ross' gull	*Rhodostethia rosea*		Y
Black-legged kittiwake	*Rissa tridactyla*	Y	Y
Sabine's gull	*Xema sabini*	Y	Y
Caspian tern	*Sterna caspia*		Y

Common tern	*Sterna hirundo*		Y
Black tern	*Chlidonias niger*		Y
Arctic tern	*Sterna paradisaea*	Y	Y
Dovekie	*Alle alle*		Y
Thick-billed murre	*Uria lomvia*		Y
Razorbill	*Alca torda*		Y
Black guillemont	*Cepphus grylle*	Y	Y
Atlantic puffin	*Fratercula arctica*		Y

Pigeons

Rock dove	*Columba livia*	Y	
Mourning dove	*Zenaida macroura*	Y	Y

Owls

Great-horned owl	*Bubo virginianus*	Y	Y
Snowy owl	*Nyctea scandiaca*	Y	Y
Northern Hawk owl	*Surnia ulula*	Y	Y
Barred owl	*Strix varia*		Y
Great gray owl	*Strix nebulosa*	Y	Y
Long-eared owl	*Asio otus*		Y
Short-eared owl	*Asio flammeus*	Y	Y
Boreal owl	*Aegolius funereus*	Y	Y

Nighthawks

Common nighthawk	*Chordeiles minor*	Y	Y

Hummingbirds

Rufous hummingbird	*Selasphorus rufus*	Y	

Kingfishers

Belted kingfisher	*Ceryle alcyon*	Y	Y

Woodpeckers

Yellow-bellied sapsucker	*Sphyrapicus varius*	Y	Y
Downy woodpecker	*Picoides pubescens*	Y	Y
Hairy woodpecker	*Picoides villosus*	Y	Y
Three-toed woodpecker	*Picoides tridactylus*	Y	Y
Black-backed woodpecker	*Picoides arcticus*	Y	Y
Northern flicker	*Colaptes auratus*	Y	Y
Pileated woodpecker	*Dryocopus pileatus*	Y	Y

Flycatchers

Olive-sided flycatcher	*Contopus borealis*	Y	Y
Western wood-peewee	*Contopus virens*	Y	Y
Alder flycatcher	*Empidonax alnorum*	Y	Y
Least flycatcher	*Empidonax minimax*	Y	Y
Yellow-bellied flycatcher	*Empidonax flaviventris*		
Hammond's flycatcher	*Empidonax hammondii*	Y	Y
Eastern phoebe	*Sayornis phoebe*	Y	Y
Dusky flycatcher	*Empidonax oberholseri*	Y	

Say's phoebe	*Sayornis saya*	Y	Y
Eastern kingbird	*Tyrannus tyrannus*	Y	Y

Larks

Horned lark	*Eremophila alpestris*	Y	Y

Starlings

European starling	*Sturnus vulgaris*	Y	Y

Swallows

Tree swallow	*Tachycineta bicolor*	Y	Y
Violet-green swallow	*Tachycineta thalassina*	Y	Y
Bank swallow	*Riparia riparia*	Y	Y
Cliff swallow	*Hirundo pyrrhonota*	Y	Y
Barn swallow	*Hirundo rustica*	Y	Y

Ravens, jays

Gray jay	*Perisoreus canadensis*	Y	Y
Clarke's nutcracker	*Nucifraga columbiana*	Y	
Steller's jay	*Cyanocitta stelleri*	Y	
Black-billed magpie	*Pica pica*	Y	Y
American crow	*Corvus brachyrhynchos*	Y	Y
Common raven	*Corvus corax*	Y	Y

Chickadees

Black-capped chickadee	*Parus atricapillus*	Y	Y
Siberian tit	*Parus cinctus*	Y	Y
Boreal chickadee	*Parus hudsonicus*	Y	Y
Mountain chickadee	*Parus gambeli*	Y	

Nuthatches

Red-breasted nuthatch	*Sitta canadensis*	Y	Y

Creepers

Brown creeper	*Certhia americana*	Y	

Wrens

Winter wren	*Troglodytes troglodytes*		Y

Dippers

American dipper	*Cinclus mexicanus*	Y	Y

Kinglets, thrushes

Bluethroat	*Luscinia svecica*	Y	
Golden-crowned kinglet	*Regulus satrapa*	Y	Y
Ruby-crowned kinglet	*Regulus calendula*	Y	Y
Northern wheatear	*Oenanthe oenanthe*	Y	Y
Mountain bluebird	*Sialia currucoides*	Y	Y
Townsend's solitaire	*Myadestes townsendi*	Y	Y
Gray-cheeked thrush	*Catharus minimus*	Y	Y
Swainson's thrush	*Catharus ustulatus*	Y	Y

Hermit thrush	*Catharus guttatus*	Y	Y
American robin	*Turdus migratoris*	Y	Y
Varied thrush	*Ixoreus naevius*	Y	Y

Pipits
Yellow wagtail	*Motacilla flava*	Y	Y
Water pipit	*Anthus rubescens*	Y	Y

Waxwings
Bohemian waxwing	*Bombycilla garrulus*	Y	Y
Cedar waxwing	*Bombycilla cedrorum*		Y

Shrikes
Northern shrike	*Lanius excubitor*	Y	Y

Warblers, Sparrows
Solitary vireo	*Vireo solitarius*		Y
Warbling vireo	*Vireo gilvus*	Y	Y
Philadelphia vireo	*Vireo philadelphicus*		Y
Red-eyed vireo	*Vireo olivaceus*		Y
Tennessee warbler	*Vermivora peregrina*	Y	Y
Orange-crowned warbler	*Vermivora celata*	Y	Y
Yellow warbler	*Dendroica petechia*	Y	Y
Magnolia warbler	*Dendroica magnolia*		Y
Cape May warbler	*Dendroica tigrina*	Y	Y
Yellow-rumped warbler	*Dendroica coronata*	Y	Y
Townend's warbler	*Dendroica townsendi*	Y	
Palm warbler	*Dendroica palmarum*	Y	Y
Bay-breasted warbler	*Dendroica castanea*		Y
Blackpoll warbler	*Dendroica striata*	Y	Y
Black-and-white warbler	*Mniotilta varia*		Y
Northern waterthrush	*Seiurus noveboracensis*	Y	Y
Ovenbird	*Seiurus aurocapillus*		Y
American redstart	*Setophaga ruticilla*	Y	Y
MacGillivray's warbler	*Oporornis tolmiei*	Y	
Mourning warbler	*Oporornis agilis*		Y
Common yellowthroat	*Geothlypis trichas*	Y	Y
Wilson's warbler	*Wilsonia pusilla*	Y	Y
Western tanager	*Piranga ludoviciana*		Y
American tree sparrow	*Spizella arborea*	Y	Y
Chipping sparrow	*Spizella passerina*	Y	Y
Brewer's sparrow	*Spizella breweri*	Y	
Clay-colored sparrow	*Spizella pallida*		Y
Vesper sparrow	*Pooecetes gramineus*		Y
Savannah sparrow	*Passerculus sandwichensis*	Y	Y
Le Conte's sparrow	*Ammodramus leconteii*	Y	Y
Nelson's sharp-tailed sparrow	*Ammodramus nelsoni*		Y

Fox sparrow	*Passerella iliaca*	Y	Y
Song sparrow	*Melospiza melodia*	Y	Y
Lincoln's sparrow	*Melospiza lincolnii*	Y	Y
Swamp sparrow	*Melospiza georgiana*	Y	Y
White-throated sparrow	*Zonotrichia albicollis*	Y	Y
Golden-crowned sparrow	*Zonotrichia atricapilla*	Y	Y
White-crowned sparrow	*Zonotrichia leucophrys*	Y	Y
Harris' sparrow	*Zonotrichia querula*	Y	Y
Dark-eyed junco	*Junco hyemalis*	Y	Y
Lapland longspur	*Calcarius lapponicus*	Y	Y
Smith's longspur	*Calcarius pictus*	Y	Y
Snow bunting	*Plectrophenax nivalis*	Y	Y
Yellow-headed blackbird	*Xanthocephalus xanthocephus*		Y
Red-winged blackbird	*Agelaius phoeniceus*	Y	Y
Rusty blackbird	*Euphagus carolinus*	Y	Y
Brewer's blackbird	*Euphagus cyanocephalus*	Y	Y
Common grackle	*Quiscalus quiscula*		Y
Brown-headed cowbird	*Molothrus ater*	Y	Y
Evening grosbeck	*Coccothraustes vespertinus*		Y
House sparrow	*Passer domesticus*		Y

Finches

Gray-crowned rosy	*Finch Leucosticte tephrocotis*	Y	Y
Rose-breasted grosbeak	*Pheucticus ludovicianus*		Y
Pine grosbeak	*Pinicola enucleator*	Y	Y
Purple finch	*Carpodacus purpureus*	Y	Y
Red crossbill	*Loxia curvirostra*	Y	Y
White-winged crossbill	*Loxia leucoptera*	Y	Y
Common redpoll	*Carduelis flammea*	Y	Y
Hoary redpoll	*Carduelis hornemanni*	Y	Y
Pine siskin	*Carduelis pinus*	Y	Y

Appendix 4

MAMMALS OF THE YUKON

Species	Scientific name	
Shrews		
Masked shrew	*Sorex cinereus*	P
Vagrant shrew	*Sorex vagrans*	?
Dusky shrew	*Sorex obscurus*	P
Water shrew	*Sorex palustris*	E
Pygmy shrew	*Microsorex hoyi*	E
Bats		
Little brown bat	*Myotis lucifugus*	C
Pikas, hares		
Pika	*Ochotona princeps*	C
Snowshoe hare	*Lepus americanus*	C
Rodents		
Least chipmunk	*Eutamias minimus*	C
Woodchuck	*Marmota monax*	R
Hoary marmot	*Marmota caligata*	C
Arctic ground squirrel	*Spermophilus parryii*	C
Red squirrel	*Tamiasciurus hudsonicus*	C
Northern flying squirrel	*Glaucomys sabrinus*	R
Beaver	*Castor canadensis*	C
Deer mouse	*Peromyscus maniculatus*	C
Bushy-tailed wood rat	*Neotoma cinerea*	E
Red-backed vole	*Clethrionomys rutilus*	P
Heather vole	*Phenacomys intermedius*	R
Meadow vole	*Microtus pennsylvanicus*	C
Northern vole	*Microtus oeconomus*	C
Long-tailed vole	*Microtus longicaudus*	C
Singing vole	*Microtus miurus*	P
Muskrat	*Ondatra zibethicus*	E
Siberian lemming	*Lemmus sibiricus*	?
Meadow jumping mouse	*Zapus hudsonius*	P
Porcupine	*Erethizon dorsatum*	C
Northern bog lemming	*Synaptomys borealis*	P

Carnivores

Coyote	*Canis latrans*	C
Wolf	*Canis lupus*	C
Red fox	*Vulpes vulpes*	C
Black bear	*Ursus americanus*	P
Grizzly bear	*Ursus arctos*	C
Marten	*Martes americana*	P
Ermine	*Mustela erminea*	P
Least weasel	*Mustela nivalis*	P
Mink	*Mustela vison*	P
Wolverine	*Gulo gulo*	C
River otter	*Lontra canadensis*	P
Cougar	*Felis concolor*	V
Lynx	*Lynx lynx*	C

Ungulates

Mule deer	*Odocoileus hemionus*	R
Moose	*Alces alces*	C
Woodland caribou	*Rangifer tarandus*	U
Dall's sheep	*Ovis dalli dalli*	C
Mountain goat	*Oreamnos americanus*	C

KEY

C	Common	Easily found in proper habitat.
E	Expected	Not confirmed in park, but is found in surrounding area.
P	Present	Present but abundance unknown.
R	Rare	Occurrence unpredictable. Not always seen every year.
U	Uncommon	Usually found in small numbers in the proper habitat.
V	Very rare	May not be seen at all some years.
?	Unknown	Uncertain presence.

Appendix 5

PLANTS OF THE YUKON

Species	Scientific name
Alaska moss heath	*Cassiope stelleriana*
Alaska willow	*Salix alaxensis*
Alkali bluegrass	*Poa juncifolia*
Alkali grass	*Puccinellia interior*
Alpine bluegrass	*Poa alpina*
Alpine fescue	*Festuca ovina*
Alpine milk-vetch	*Astragalus alpinus*
Alpine speedwell	*Veronica alpina*
American hedysarum	*Hedysarum alpinum*
Arctic aster	*Aster sibiricus*
Arctic bluegrass	*Poa arctica*
Arctic raspberry	*Rubus arcticus*
Arrowleaf	*Senecio triangularis*
Balsam poplar	*Populus balsamifera*
Baltic rush	*Juncus balticus*
Baneberry	*Acteae rubra*
Barclay's willow	*Salix barclayi*
Barratt willow	*Salix barrattiana*
Barren ground willow	*Salix brachycarpa*
Bearberry, kinnikinnick	*Arctostaphylos uva-ursi*
Bellard's kobresia	*Kobresia bellardii*
Blackened sedge	*Carex atrata*
Bluebell	*Mertinsia paniculata*
Bluebell, harebell	*Campanula rotundifolia*
Bluejoint	*Calamagrostis canadensis*
Blueleaved strawberry	*Fragaria virginiana*
Bog blueberrry	*Vaccinium uliginosum*
Bog labrador-tea	*Ledum groenlandica*
Boreal aster	*Aster alpinus*
Boreal wormwood	*Artemisia arctica*
Bristly stickseed	*Lappula myosotis*
Broadglumed wheatgrass	*Agropyron trachycaulum*
Broadleaf lupine	*Lupinus arcticus*
Buffaloberry, soapberry	*Sheperdia canadensis*

Canada butterweed	*Senecio pauperculus*
Chestnut rush	*Juncus castaneus*
Cleft-leaf groundsel	*Senecio streptanthifolius*
Common horsetail	*Equisetum arvense*
Common mountain juniper	*Juniperus communis*
Cow parsnip	*Heracleum lanatum*
Creeping juniper	*Juniperus horizontalis*
Creeping silene	*Silene repens*
Crowberry	*Empetrum nigrum*
Cuski's bluegrass	*Poa cusickii*
Diamond-leaf willow	*Salix planifolia*
Diverse-leaved cinquefoil	*Potentilla diversifolia*
Drummond's rockcress	*Arabis drummondii*
Dune goldenrod	*Solidago spathulata*
Dunhead sedge	*Carex phaeocephala*
Dwarf blueberry	*Vaccinium caespitosum*
Dwarf mountain fleabane	*Erigeron compositus*
False hellebore	*Veratrum viride*
Feather-grass	*Stipa occidentalis*
Fescue	*Festuca altaica*
Few-seeded draba	*Draba oligosperma*
Field crazyweed	*Oxytropis campestris*
Fireweed	*Epilobium angustifolium*
Four-parted gentian	*Gentianella propinqua*
Fringed brome	*Bromus ciliatus*
Glaucous bluegrass	*Poa glauca*
Gorman's penstemon	*Penstemon gormani*
Gray daisy	*Erigeron caespitosus*
Greyleaf willow	*Salix glauca*
Ground cedar, creeping jenny	*Lycopodium complanatum*
Hairy rockcress	*Arabis hirsuta*
Heart-leaf listera	*Listera borealis*
Heartleaf arnica	*Arnica cordifolia*
High bush cranberry	*Viburnum edule*
Holboell's rockcress	*Arabis holboellii*
Horned dandelion	*Taraxacum lacerum*
Kotzebue's grass-of-parnassus	*Parnassia kotzebuei*
Kuchei's lupine ·	*Lupinus kuschei*
Labrador lousewort	*Pedicularis labradorica*
Lance-leaved draba	*Draba lanceolata*
Lanceleaved stonecrop	*Sedum lanceolatum*
Lapland cassiope	*Cassiope tetragona*
Leafless pyrola	*Pyrola asarifolia*
Lingonberry	*Vaccinium vitis-idaee*
Little tree willow	*Salix arbusculoides*
Long-beaked willow	*Salix bebbiana*

Longstock starwort	*Stellaria longipes*
Low blueberry willow	*Salix myrtillifolia*
Low northern sedge	*Carex concinna*
Maritime sedge	*Carex maritima*
Marsh arrow-grass	*Triglochin palustris*
Marsh horsetail	*Equisetum palustre*
Meadow arnica	*Arnica chamissonis*
Menzie's silene	*Silene menziesii*
Milk-vetch	*Astragalus adsurgens*
Monkshood	*Aconitum delphinifolium*
Moonwort	*Botrychium lunaria*
Mountain alder	*Alnus crispa*
Mountain timothy	*Phleum alpinum*
Mountain wormwood	*Artemisia tilesii*
Netleaf willow	*Salix reticulata*
Northern androsace	*Androsace septentrionalis*
Northern bedstraw	*Galium boreale*
Northern daisy	*Erigeron acris*
Northern gentian	*Gentianella amarella*
Northern goldenrod	*Solidago multiradiata*
Northern gooseberry	*Ribes oxyacanthoides*
Northern grass-of-parnassus, bog star	*Parnassia palustris*
Northern green bog-orchid	*Habenaria hyperborea*
Northern halimolobos	*Halimolobus mollis*
Northern hedysarum	*Hedysarum boreale*
Northern red currant	*Ribes triste*
Northern reedgrass	*Calamagrostis inexpansa*
Northern rush	*Juncus alpinus*
Northern starflower	*Trientalis arctica*
Pacific anemone	*Anemone multifida*
Pale larkspur	*Delphinium glaucum*
Parry sedge	*Carex parryana*
Partridge foot	*Luetkea pectinata*
Pasque flower	*Anemone patens*
Pendantpod crazyweed	*Oxytropis deflexa*
Polar grass	*Arctagrostis latifolia*
Polar willow	*Salix polaris*
Prairie cinquefoil	*Potentilla pennsylvanica*
Prairie sagewort	*Artemisia frigida*
Prickly rose	*Rosa acicularis*
Prickly saxifrage	*Saxifraga tricuspidata*
Primrose	*Primula stricta*
Pumpelly brome	*Bromus inermis*
Purple reedgrass	*Calamagrostis purpurascens*
Quaking aspen	*Populus tremuloides*
Red fescue	*Festuca rubra*

Red raspberry	*Rubus idaeus*
Red-mountain heather	*Phyllodoce empertriformis*
Reddish sandwort	*Arenaria rubella*
Richardson's anemone	*Anemone richardsonii*
River beauty	*Epilobium latifolium*
Ross sedge	*Carex rossi*
Rosy pussy-toes	*Antennaria rosea*
Sandberg's bluegrass	*Poa sandbergii*
Scouler's willow	*Salix scouleriana*
Seaside plantain	*Plantago maritima*
Sedgelike horsetail	*Equisetum scirpoides*
Setchell's willow	*Salix setchelliana*
Shady horsetail	*Equisetum pratense*
Shore buttercup	*Ranunculus cymbalaria*
Short-anthered cottongrass	*Eriophorum brachyantherum*
Short-beaked agoseris	*Agoseris glauca*
Showy polemonium	*Polemonium pulcherrimum*
Shrub birch	*Betula glandulosa*
Shrubby cinquefoil	*Potentilla fruticosa*
Sidebells pyrola	*Pyrola secunda*
Silverberry	*Eleaagnus commutata*
Silverweed	*Potentilla anserina*
Single-spike sedge	*Carex scirpoidea*
Sitka alder	*Alnus rugosa*
Slender cinquefoil	*Potentilla gracilis*
Slimstem reedgrass	*Calamagrostis neglecta*
Small northern bog orchid	*Habenaria obtusata*
Small wallflower	*Erysimum inconspicuum*
Small-flowered penstemon	*Penstemon proceras*
Small-flowered anemone	*Anemone parviflora*
Small-flowered woodrush	*Luzula parviflora*
Spike rush	*Eleocharis palustris*
Spike trisetum	*Trisetum spicatum*
Spreadingpod rockcress	*Arabidopsis divaricarpa*
Squirrel-tail grass	*Hordeum jubatum*
Star gentian	*Lomatogonium rotatum*
Star-flowered solomon's seal	*Smilicina stellata*
Stiff clubmoss	*Lycopodium annotinum*
Sweet coltsfoot	*Petasites frigidus*
Tall cinquefoil	*Potentilla arguta*
Tall mountain shooting star	*Dodecatheon jeffreyi*
Thread-leaved sedge	*Carex filifolia*
Timber danthonia	*Danthonia intermedia*
Tufted hairgrass	*Deschampsia caespitosa*
Twinflower	*Linnaea borealis*
Umber pussy-toes	*Antennaria umbrinella*

Vanilla grass	*Hierochloë odorata*
Water sedge	*Carex aquatilis*
Western columbine	*Aquilega formosa*
Western dog violet	*Viola adunca*
Western meadowrue	*Thalictrum occidentale*
White camass	*Zygadenus elegans*
White mountain avens	*Dryas integrifolia*
White spruce	*Picea glauca*
Wild blue flax	*Linum perenne*
Wind river draba	*Draba ventosa*
Yarrow	*Achillea millefolium*
Yellow bog sedge	*Carex gynocrates*
Yellow dryas	*Dryas drummondii*
Yukon aster	*Aster yukonensis*
Yukon indian paintbrush	*Castilleja yukonis*
Yukon wheatgrass	*Agropyron yukonense*

Gyrfalcon

Appendix 6

FURTHER READING
History

Davis, Richard C ed *Lobsticks and Stone Cairns: Human Landmarks in the Arctic.* A background to some of the people who influenced and made Arctic history from the 16th century to the present.

Mowat, Farley *The Farfarers: Before the Norse* Key Porter Books, Toronto. Discovery of Canada before the Vikings arrived in the 12th century.

Newman, Peter C *Company of Adventures* Viking. The History of the Hudson Bay Company Vol 1. ★

Newman, Peter C *Caesars of the Wilderness* Viking. Vol 2 of the Hudson Bay Company story. ★

★Penguin have combined these two volumes into one paperback edition called *Empires of the Bay* [ISBN 014027488-X] It is only published in Canada.

Rasky, Frank *The Polar Voyagers: Explorers of the North* McGraw-Hill. There are supposed to be two volumes of this but I can only find the first volume. Vol 1: Polar exploration from the Vikings to the close of the 18th century. Vol 2: Exploration by American, Scandinavian, British and Canadian north pole adventurers who transformed the 19th century into the Golden Age of Arctic discovery.

Thomson, George Malcolm *The North-West Passage* Secker & Warburg, London, 1975. Historical background about the search for the north-west passage route to China and the far east.

Woodcock, George *The Canadians* The Athlone Press, London, 1980. A light background read to the Canadian people. Contains a very readable chapter on those people who opened up and inhabited the north.

Natural history

Burt, Page *Barrenland Beauties: Showy Plants of the Arctic Coast* Outcrop Publishers, Yellowknife, NWT, 1991.

Collins Pocket Guide to Birds of North America, Collins London, £16.99 ISBN 0-00-220109-7. The complete guide to all the birds of the USA and Canada produced in association with the American Bird Conservancy. Includes distribution maps, line drawings and all relative habitats.

Gotch, A F *Mammals – Their Latin Names Explained: a Guide to Animal Classification*

Gray, David R *The Muskoxen of Polar Bear Pass* Life of the muskoxen in Canada's High Arctic.

Miles, Hugh and Salisbury, Mike *Kingdom of the Ice Bear: A Portrait of the Arctic* BBC Books, London, 1985. The story behind the filming of the *Kingdom of the Ice Bear* series for BBC television. A perception of wildlife filming, the Arctic wildlife and living for extended periods in the region. Some insight into the lives of the people who live there. Covers northern Canada and Greenland.

Pielou, E C *A Naturalist's Guide to the Arctic* University of Chicago Press, London, 1994. A good all round guide to the Arctic flora, fauna, geology and geography.

Stirling, Ian *Polar Bears* Fitzhenry & Whiteside, Ontario, Canada. 1998. Large format book on polar bears with excellent photographs by Dan Guravich. The full insight into the natural history of polar bears from a biologist's point of view. Very readable.

Trelawney, John G *Wildflowers of Yukon, Alaska and Northwest Canada* Sono Nis Press, Victoria, BC, 1988.

General

Morton, Keith *Planning a Wilderness Trip in Canada and Alaska* Rocky Mountain Books, Alberta, Canada. 1997 (Distributed in the UK by Cordee Books). A well- rounded and illustrated guide with sound advice as to planning your wilderness adventure. Specifically related to Canada and Alaska, particularly the north.

Wiseman, John *The SAS Survival Handbook* HarperCollins, London 1986, £14.99; Collins Gem Version 1993, £4.99.

Websites
Tourism
Canadian Tourism Commission www.canadatourism.com/ctc/index.html. Links to Nunavut and NWT home sites as well as companies who specialise in adventure travel for Canada's north

Nunavut www.arctic-travel.com/www.nunatour.nt.ca; email nunatour@nunanet.com

Northwest Territories www.nwttravel.nt.ca; emmail nwtat@nwttravel.nt.ca

Yukon Territory www.touryukon.com; email info@yukontour.com

General Canadian and government sites
Royal Canadian Geographical Society www.rcgs.org; email cgs@cangeo.ca

Canadian Geographic Magazine www.canadiangeographic.ca; on-line version of magazine www.cangeo.ca

Canadian Nature Federation www.cnf.ca. Links to provincial and local nature groups

Canadian Resource Page www.cs.cmu.edu/Unofficial/Canadiana. Lots of useful links to a variety of Canadian sites including history, politics, travel and tourism, on-line newspapers, weather forecasts etc.

The **Canadian Wildlife Service** in Yellowknife has a useful site for those serious about birds. It offers a checklist of all species found in NWT/Nunavut and a file can be downloaded to print your own list before going. A survey is being conducted and all sightings returned go onto a database of birds. Information can be found on www.mb.ec.gc under the pages designated Northern. Checklist can be downloaded from www.NWTChecklist.com

Canadian History Society www.historysociety.ca
US Department of State Background Notes: Canada travel.state.gov/Canada.html
Canadian Museum of Civilization www.civilization.ca
Government of Canada www.Canada.gc.ca. Links to all government departments
Canadian Heritage Rivers site is www.voyageur.carleton.ca/chrs/chrs.html. This site gives the full blurb on the rivers that are part of Canada's natural heritage. Currently there are 28 rivers listed.

Northwest Territories

Northern Frontier Visitors' Association www.northernfrontier.com. Information for visitors to the Yellowknife area
City of Yellowknife www.city.yellowknife.nt.ca. Information on the City of Yellowknife
For field checklists of the region's **birds**, go to www.NWTChecklist.com where files are provided in both MS Word and WordPerfect.

Nunavut

Nunavut Handbook www.arctic-travel.com. On-line version of the *Nunavut Handbook*, includes information on people, culture, history and wildlife
Inns North www.arctic-travel.com/INNSN/innsnorth.html. Offers accommodation at 19 locations across Nunavut
Nunatsiaq News www.nunanet.com/~nunat. The site of Nunavut's leading weekly newspaper, updated every Friday

Yukon

Whitehorse Tourism www.city.whitehorse.yk.ca. Information on attractions, events and entertainment in Whitehorse
White Pass & Yukon Rail Route www.whitepassrailroad.com
For field checklists of the region's **birds**, go to www.renres.gov.yk.ca where they have some really interesting stuff about the wildlife in the Yukon.

Alaska

Alaskan State Tourism www.dced.state.ak.us. Separate pages and sites for students, visitors and travel agents.
Travel Alaska www.travelalaska.com. Issues a guide and travel planner to Alaska

General interest

Foreign & Commonwealth Office Travel Advice www.fco.gov.uk
National Maritime Museum, Greenwich www.nmm.ac.uk

Index

accommodation 96
Alaska 231–44, *232*
 Chilcoot Trail 241
 Fairbanks 236
Alaska Canada Highway 160, 231
 boundary 235
 Chicken 234
 Eagle 235
 facts 233
 Haines 242
 Jack Wade 234
 on the Trail of '98 237
 road border procedures 233
 Skagway 237
 Tok 236
Alba 8
Alberta 18
AlCan Highway *see* Alaska Canada Highway
altitude sickness 111
American Civil War 23
American Revolution 23
Amundsen, Roald 11
Arctic Circle 4
Arctic Ocean 18, 26
Arviat 222
Aurora borealis 194
 best place to see 84
Ausiuttuq 229
Auyuittuq National Park 220

Baffin Island 46
Baffin, Sir William 10, 13
Baffin Island, the Communities 215
Baker Lake *224*, 225
banking 95
Banks Island 28, 208
bears
 behaviour 126
 behaviour in presence of 129
 black 29, 34, 125
 general safety 124
 grizzly 29, 34, 125
  best viewing 85
 Kodiak or coastal brown 34
 polar 29, 34, 130
  behaviour 131
  best viewing 85
  travelling in polar bear country 133
  viewing 247
 shooting a bear 135
 travelling in bear country 127
Beaufort Sea 25

beaver 41
Beaver Creek 173
Belcher, Inspector Robert 23
birds
 Arctic 49
 Arctic tern 57
 best viewing sites 86
 Cambridge Bay 226–7
 common loon 58
 eagle
  bald 53
  golden 29, 53
 falcons
  gyrfalcons 56
  kestrel 56
  merlin 56
  peregrine 56
 harrier, northern 53
 hawks
  goshawk 52
  red-tailed 52
  rough-legged 52
  sharp-shinned 52
  Swainson's 52
  woodland 52
 migratory sanctuaries 50, 54
 Northern Canada 254–61
 osprey 53
 owls 56, 57
 Pacific loon 58
 raptors 50
 red-throated loon 58
 seabirds 57
 spruce grouse 58
 thick-billed murre 57
 tundra swan 58
 white-tailed ptarmigan 58
bison 30
 plains or American 30
 wood 30
  best viewing 85
biting bugs 113
Bluenose Lake 31
boats, skin 8
Bobcat 39
Bonanza Creek 21
British North America 20
British North America Act (1867) 24
British Columbia 24, 26
Burwash Landing 172
Bylot Island 221

Cabot, John 10
Cambridge Bay 28, 225–8, *228*
Canada, Dominion of 23–4
Canadian Wildlife Service 50
Canadian Pacific Railway 22
Canol Heritage Trail 204
Cape Dorset 219
Carcross 175
caribou 31
    and native people 70
    annual activity chart 32
    best viewing 86
    Greants 31
    nutrient sources 71
    Peary 31
    woodland 31
Carmack, George Washington 21, 158, 160
Carmack, Kate 21, 158, 160
Carmacks 176
Cartier, Jacques 10
Charles II, King 16, 19
Chilcoot Pass 23
Chilcoot Trail 241
Chilkat Bald Eagle preserve 244
Chipewyan 17
Churchill, Manitoba 17, 244–7, *246*
    getting there 245
    polar bear viewing 247
    what to see and do 246
    where to eat 246
    where to stay 246
climate 4, 5
    land of the midnight sun 4
clothing 93
clothing sizes 97
Clyde River 221
Coats Island 46, 47
Cold War 25
Columbus, Christopher 9
Company of Adventurers, *see* Hudson Bay
    Company
Cook, Captain James 10
Coppermine 31, 225
Coppermine River 18
Coral Harbour 229
Cornwallis Island 229
cougar 34, 38
coyote 38
currency *see* money
customs regulations 88

Dall's sheep 29
    best viewing 86
Dance Hall Girls 178
Davis, John 10
Dawson 21, 26
Dawson Charlie, *see* Tagish, Charlie
Dawson City 177-85, *182*, *183*
    tour operators 185
    what to see and do 184
    where to eat 182
    where to stay 182

Defence Early Warning 25
Deh Cho region 202
dehydration 111
Dempster Highway 188
Dempster, Cpl W J D (RCMP) 186
Destruction Bay 171
DEW Line *see* Defence Early Warning
diarrhoea 110
dog-sledging 83
Drake, Sir Francis 10
driving 85

Eagle Plains 188
Ebud Islands 8
Edmonton 141–3, *142*
    getting about 141
    what to see and do 143
    where to eat 141
    where to stay 141
El Dorado, of copper 17
electric current 98
elk, American 33
Ellesmere Island 28, 46, 229
Elsa 187
English Muscovy Company 12
enterprise 199
equipment 93–4
Eric the Red 9
Eskimo, word, origins of 17
Europeans, arrival 78
exchange rates 94
Exxon Valdez 12

first aid kit 115
First Nations
    Algonquin groups 69
    arrival 63
    Athabascan groups 66
    Beaver 68
    Chipewyan 66
    Dogrib 67
    Kutchin 68
    moieties 64
    Northwest Coast 64
    potlatches 66, 252
    Slave 67
    Slavey 31
    Tlingit 64
    today 69
    Yellowknife 68
fishing 99
flight specialists 90
food and drink 96
forestry 25
Fort Liard 202
Fort McPherson 206
Fort Providence 30, 201
Fort Simpson 26, 204
Fort Smith 200
foxes 37
    Arctic 37
    red 38

Franklin, Lady Jane 10
Franklin, Sir John 10
Frobisher, Sir Martin 10
further reading 269–70
fur trade 16–19

gateway cities 137–51
geography, general 2–6
geology 6
getting about,
    by air 92
    by road 93
getting there 89–90
Gilbert, Sir Humphrey 10
Gjoa Haven 229
glacial viewing 83, 169
glossary 252–3
gold 10
    mining 84
Great Bear Lake 28
Great Slave Lake 18
Grise Fiord 229

Haines 242–3
    what to see and do 243
    where to eat 243
    where to stay 243
Haines Junction 168
    what to do 169
    where to stay 169
hare, snowshoe 43
Hay River 199
health 109–15, 122–3
Hearne, Samuel 10, 17
Henderson, Robert 158, 160
history 8–26
Holman 209
Hudson, Henry 10
Hudson Bay 46
Hudson Bay Company 16, 18, 19–21, 22, 24
hunting 100

Igloolik 230
Iglulik 230
Industrial Revolution 13
Inuit 71–4, 79
Inuktitut 249–51
Inuvik 26, 206, 207
    getting around 206
    what to see and do 206
    where to stay 206
Iqaluit 215–19, 218
    emergencies 219
    entertainment 219
    getting there 216
    shopping 219
    tour operators 219
    what to see and do 219
    where to eat 217
    where to stay 216

Kaluktutiak 225

Kangiqsliniq 222
Kangiqtugaapik 221
Kelsey, Henry 10
Keno City 187
King William Island 10, 229
Kinnigait 219
Klondike 24
Klondike Gold Stampede 21–2, 157
Kluane National Park 29, 30, 169
Kugluktuk 225
Kwaday Dan Kenji 166

Ladue, Joseph 177
Lake Athabasca 18
language, Inuktitut 249–51
Larsen, Sargent Henry A , RCMP 11
lion, mountain see cougar
Lost Patrol, the 180
lynx 39

MacKenzie Bison Sanctuary 30, 202
MacKenzie Mountains 29, 30, 31
MacKenzie River 18, 29
MacKenzie Valley 31
MacKenzie, Sir Alexander 10, 17, 18, 24
Magellan, Ferdinand 9
mammals, Yukon 262–3
Manitoba 24
marten 42
Matonabbee 17
Mayo 185
McClintock, Captain 10
media and communications 98–9
medical insurance 89
Melville Island 28
Metis 79
Metis, uprising 22
Mexico 27
Miles Canyon 165
mining 25
    Canadian gold mining laws 159
mink 42
Mittimatalik 221
monarch butterfly 27
money 94–5
Montréal 149–51, 151
    getting about 149
    what to see and do 151
    where to eat 151
    where to stay 149
moose 33
    best viewing 87
Mt Logan 157
muskoxen 28
    best viewing 86
muskrat 41

Nahanni National Park 203
Napoleon 10
National Maritime Museum, Greenwich,
    London 10
national holidays 97

National Geographic Society 47
Native American *see* First Nations
natural history 27–62
Naujaat 225
New Brunswick 24
newspapers 98
Nome, Alaska 22, 159
nor'westers 18, 20
Norman Wells 18, 25, 28, 205
northern lights *see Aurora borealis*
North West Company 20
North West Mounted Police 22–3
Northwest Passage 9, 11, 17
Northwest Territories 24, 191–210, *190*
    history 193
    tour operators 193
Nova Scotia 24
Nunavut 24, 75–7, 214–30, *212–13*
    Communities 214
    land claims 76
    mainland communities 222
    staying in small communities 216–17
    territory, 77
    tour operators 214
NWMP 159
    change to RCMP 23
    see also North West Mounted Police

Ontario 24
Oqsuqtooq 229
Ottawa 146–8, *147*
    getting about 146
    what to see and do 148
    where to eat 148
    where to stay 148
otter, river 40

Pangnirtung 220
Pannirtuuq 220
Parry, Sir William 10
Peel River 29
Pelly Crossing 176
permafrost 7, 8
Perry River 29
petroleum 13, 18
photography 100–7
    equipment 101
    film 102
    practical tips 105
    technicalities 103
    wildlife 103
plants, northern 58
    Yukon 264–8
Pond Inlet 221
postal services 99
Prince Albert 17, 20
Prince Edward Island 24
Prince of Wales Island 46
Prince Rupert's Land 19, 24
puma *see* cougar
Pytheas 8

Qamaniítuaq 225
Qausiuttuq 229
Québec 24

Rae, John 11
RAMSAR Convention 50
Rankin Inlet 31, 222–3, *223*
red tape 88
reindeer 31
Repulse Bay 225
Resolute Bay 229
Richardson Mountains 29
right whales 12
RNWMP *see* North West Mounted Police
Rocky Mountains 33
Ross, Sir John 10

Sachs Harbour 209
safety 115
    personal security 115
    water safety 116
Salliq 229
Scoresby, William Snr and Jnr 13
seals 43
    bearded 44
    harp 14, 43, 44, 45
    ringed 44
sealers 12–16
sealskin boats 12
shopping 96–7
sik-sik, see squirrel, Arctic ground
Silver City 171
Silver Trail, The 185
Skagway 237–41, *239*
    history 238
    what to see and do 240
    where to eat 240
    where to stay 240
Skookum Jim Mason 21, 158, 160
Southampton Island 46, 229
spice trade 9
Spitsbergen 12
squirrel, Arctic ground 43
Steele, Superintendent Samuel B 23
Stewart Crossing 176
Stone's sheep 29
sunburn 112
survival 118–23
    accidents 121
    car travel 119
    getting lost 120
    on the trail 119
    survival kit 118

Tagish, Charlie 21, 158, 160
Takhini Hot Springs 165
taxes 94
telephone 98–9
television 98
Teslin 174
Thelon Game Sanctuary 28
time zones 98

Tintina Trench 177
tipping 95
Tombstone Mountain 188
Top of the World Highway 187, 235
tour operators 90–2
tourism 26
tourist information 87–8
travel insurance 109
trees 59–61

US Army, Chilcoot Pass 23

Vancouver 138–40, *139*
    getting about 138
    what to see and do 140
    where to eat 140
    where to stay, hostels 140
    where to stay, hotels 138
Vancouver Island 24
vegetation 7
Victoria Island 28, 209, 225, 228
Vikings 9
visas 88

walrus 45
    best viewing 86
    hunting 14
wapiti see elk
water, resources 25
    sterilisation 109
Watson Lake 173
websites 270
whalers 12–16
    Aleuts 12
    Coastal Native Americans 12
    Inuit 12
    Japanese 12
whales 47
    beluga 47
    bowhead 12, 49
    narwhal 47
    orcas 48
    watching 16, 86
whaling 12, 14
    Repulse Bay 15
what to take *see* equipment
when to go 87
White Pass 23
White Pass & Yukon Route Railroad 166
Whitehorse 26, 161–9, *163*
    emergencies 168
    entertainment 167
    fishway 165
    getting about 162
    getting there 162
    shopping 167
    tour operators 167
    what to see, downtown 164
    what to see, outside town 165
    where to eat 164
    where to stay 164
wilderness survival 117

wildlife viewing 85–7
    birds 86
    caribou 86
    Dall's sheep 86
    grizzly bears 85
    moose 87
    muskoxen 86
    polar bears 85
    ten best viewing sites 85
    walrus 86
    whales 86
    wood bison 85
Winnipeg 143–6, *144*
    getting about 143
    what to see and do 145
    where to eat 145
    where to stay 145
wolverine 29, 40
wolves 28, 29, 30, 32, 34
    Arctic 37
    timber 37
    tundra or caribou 37
Wood Buffalo National Park 201
Wren, Sir Christopher 19
Wrigley 205

Yellowknife 30, 195–9, *197*
    emergencies 199
    entertainment 198
    getting about 195
    getting there 195
    shopping 198
    tour operators 198
    what to see 196
    where to eat 196
    where to stay 196
York Factory 20
Yukon 21, 24, 154, 154–7
    history 156
Yukon Quest International Sled Dog Race 166